Beauvoir and Belle

PHILOSOPHY OF RACE

Series Editors
Linda Martín Alcoff, Hunter College and the Graduate Center CUNY
Chike Jeffers, Dalhousie University

Socially Undocumented: Identity and Immigration Justice
Amy Reed-Sandoval

Reconsidering Reparations
Olúfẹ́mi O. Táíwò

Unruly Women: Race, Neocolonialism, and the Hijab
Falguni A. Sheth

Critical Philosophy of Race: Essays
Robert Bernasconi

Beauvoir and Belle: A Black Feminist Critique of The Second Sex
Kathryn Sophia Belle

Beauvoir and Belle

A Black Feminist Critique of
The Second Sex

KATHRYN SOPHIA BELLE

OXFORD
UNIVERSITY PRESS

Oxford University Press is a department of the University of Oxford. It furthers the University's objective of excellence in research, scholarship, and education by publishing worldwide. Oxford is a registered trade mark of Oxford University Press in the UK and certain other countries.

Published in the United States of America by Oxford University Press
198 Madison Avenue, New York, NY 10016, United States of America.

© Oxford University Press 2024

All rights reserved. No part of this publication may be reproduced, stored in a retrieval system, or transmitted, in any form or by any means, without the prior permission in writing of Oxford University Press, or as expressly permitted by law, by license, or under terms agreed with the appropriate reproduction rights organization. Inquiries concerning reproduction outside the scope of the above should be sent to the Rights Department, Oxford University Press, at the address above.

You must not circulate this work in any other form
and you must impose this same condition on any acquirer.

Library of Congress Cataloging-in-Publication Data
Names: Belle, Kathryn Sophia, author.
Title: Beauvoir and Belle : a Black feminist critique of the Second sex / Kathryn Sophia Belle.
Description: New York, NY : Oxford University Press, [2024] |
Series: Philosophy of race | Includes bibliographical references and index.
Identifiers: LCCN 2023006293 (print) | LCCN 2023006294 (ebook) |
ISBN 9780197660201 (paperback) | ISBN 9780197660195 (hardback) |
ISBN 9780197660225 (epub)
Subjects: LCSH: Beauvoir, Simone de, 1908–1986. Deuxième sexe. | Women, Black. |
Feminism. | Feminist theory. | African American feminists.
Classification: LCC HQ1208.B36 B45 2023 (print) | LCC HQ1208.B36 (ebook) |
DDC 305.42089/96—dc23/eng/20230413
LC record available at https://lccn.loc.gov/2023006293
LC ebook record available at https://lccn.loc.gov/2023006294

DOI: 10.1093/oso/9780197660195.001.0001

Contents

Preface	vii
Acknowledgments	xiii
Introduction: bell hooks: "Female identity is shaped by gender, race, and class, and never solely by sex"	1

PART I. BLACK FEMINIST FRAMEWORKS

1. A Select Genealogy of Black Feminist Frameworks for Identities and Oppressions: "If we are not careful the work we are doing now is going to have to be 'rediscovered' at some point"   39

2. Claudia Jones: "The Negro question in the United States is *prior* to, and not equal to, the woman question"   74

3. Lorraine Hansberry: "*The Second Sex* may well be the most important work of this century"   108

4. Audre Lorde: "Difference is that raw and powerful connection from which our personal power is forged"   137

PART II. WHITE FEMINIST FRAMEWORKS

5. Simone de Beauvoir's Analogical Approach: "There are deep analogies between the situations of women and blacks"   165

6. Slavery and Womanhood: "Assimilating woman to the slave is a mistake"   206

7. Abolition and Suffrage in the United States: "They undertook a campaign in favor of blacks"   232

vi CONTENTS

PART III. FRAMEWORKS BEYOND
THE BLACK/WHITE BINARY

8. The Coloniality of Gender and the Other Others: "The
category of *Other* is as original as consciousness itself"   263

Conclusion: Simone de Beauvoir: "I think *The Second
Sex* will seem like an old, dated book, after a while.
But nonetheless . . . a book which will have made its
contribution"   302

Bibliography   331
Index   345

Preface

In some ways it is shocking to me that I chose to write this book. I was introduced to Black feminist theory as a student at Spelman College (a historically Black liberal arts college for women)—at that time under the leadership of its first Black woman president, Johnnetta B. Cole. I received an undergraduate education in which Black women theorists and activists were intentionally and systematically placed at the center rather than on the margins of course syllabi. Positive exposure to Black feminism began during my freshman year in courses like African Diaspora and the World, and continued throughout my matriculation, up to and including a feminist-theory course my senior year with Beverly Guy-Sheftall in which we read her powerful anthology *Words of Fire: An Anthology of African American Feminist Thought* (1995). Black feminism was even present in my philosophy courses (which is not typical in the discipline of philosophy).

For example, I recall a feminist philosophy course taught by James Winchester (a white male philosophy professor at Spelman College) in which we read Jessica Benjamin's *The Bonds of Love: Psychoanalysis, Feminism, and the Problem of Domination* (1988); *Feminist Contentions: Philosophical Exchange* (1994) edited by Seyla Benhabib, Judith Butler, Drucilla Cornell, and Nancy Fraser; Judith Butler's *Gender Trouble: Feminism and the Subversion of Identity* (1990); Elizabeth Spelman's *Inessential Woman: Problems of Exclusion in Feminist Thought* (1988); and Patricia Hill Collins' *Black Feminist Thought: Knowledge, Consciousness, and the Politics of Empowerment* (1990). As a philosophy major, I wrote an undergraduate thesis on the philosophical underpinnings of "self-definition" in which I examined Hill Collins' analysis of Black women's use of self-definition against prevailing controlling images, Butler's notion of gender performativity, and Elaine Brown's autobiography *A Taste of Power: A Black Woman's Story* (1992) as an example of these two

viii PREFACE

theoretical frameworks (performativity and self-definition) coming together in praxis. Throughout my time at Spelman College I was inspired and transformed by too many Black women scholars and books to name. In addition to those already mentioned, a few others that stand out (and that I return to repeatedly in my own teaching and scholarship) are Anna Julia Cooper's *A Voice from the South by a Black Woman from the South* (1892); Angela Davis' *Women, Race, and Class* (1981); bell hooks' *Ain't I a Woman: Black Women and Feminism* (1981); and Paula Giddings' *When and Where I Enter: The Impact of Black Women on Race* (1984). The theoretical frameworks offered by these sister scholars have continued to influence my scholarship far beyond my college years up to and including this book manuscript.[1]

I did not think of myself as a "feminist" before going to Spelman. However, once I became immersed in Black feminist theory and praxis—I realized that I was raised in a family and community of Black feminists. Even if they did not explicitly identify as "feminists," the Black women in my life were quite feminist in their actions, activism, and commitments. Having read a plethora of white feminist thought without recognizing myself and my lived experience (or the lived experiences of my mother, grandmother, great-grandmother, and countless godmothers, aunties, and sister scholars), I celebrate and appreciate the ways that Black feminism speaks to *us*, not only in theoretically rich, transformative, eye-opening, earth-shattering, life-changing books, but also in our lived experiences and everyday practices (as family members, friends, educators, activists, caretakers, lovers, etc.). Reading these books (and at this point in my life having the distinct privilege of meeting and getting to know many of these authors), it always felt as if their content was created especially for me. These texts speak to me, saying, "Kathryn . . . I see you. I acknowledge you. I believe in you. I affirm you. I celebrate you. You are a part of a long legacy of Black women laborers, activists, intellectuals, writers, teachers, and lovers. You are drawing from and contributing to a well-spring of knowledge, wisdom, and understanding. You will not face any challenges that have not already been faced and overcome. You can do this!"

I often hear white women of generations that came before me talk about the transformative impact of Simone de Beauvoir's *The Second*

PREFACE   ix

Sex (1949), but that was not my experience. My first introduction to *The Second Sex* was through Elizabeth Spelman's critique of the text in *Inessential Woman: Problems of Exclusion in Feminist Thought (1988)*, and I found her arguments compelling. But I did not read *The Second Sex* as a college student or even as a graduate student. When I went to graduate school to continue my studies in philosophy, my work on Beauvoir was filtered through her engagements in debates between Jean-Paul Sartre and Maurice Merleau-Ponty, as well as her memoirs that provided details about Black male interlocutors like Richard Wright and Frantz Fanon. By the time I did finally read *The Second Sex* in its entirety, I found that Beauvoir did not speak to me in the ways that Cooper, Hill Collins, Davis, hooks, and others speak to me. Furthermore, when I really engage and analyze the text, I see that Black women are in some cases altogether absent and in other cases problematically present in it. I see how the race/gender analogy and slave/woman analogy are operating throughout the text. I see the misinformation about things like the abolition and suffrage movements in the United States in the text. More importantly, I see all the ways Black feminist theorists gave me different (in)sights and taught me to see with different eyes. Eventually, I decided to write about it.

My journey with this project began over a decade ago (though I did not know I was embarking on such a journey at the time) with a book chapter titled "Sartre, Beauvoir, and the Race/Gender Analogy: A Case for Black Feminist Philosophy" (published under my former name in a book I co-edited titled *Convergences: Black Feminism and Continental Philosophy*, 2010). Since then, I felt drawn back to Beauvoir by feedback and commentaries from other scholars. For example, Margaret ("Peg") Simons told me in an email correspondence, "No one has read my chapter on R. Wright and Simone de Beauvoir as carefully as you have—or at least no one has ever discussed it as you have . . . It would be good to . . . dig deeper into those questions of influence." And in a commentary on my aforementioned chapter, Stephanie Rivera Berruz asserts, "Works like that of Gines' [now Belle] . . . are of utmost importance in opening a new theoretical terrain that considers the importance of black feminist thought and its utility in thinking through race, gender, and sexuality within different philosophical traditions."[2] There is also Nathalie Nya, who used Beauvoir to offer a feminist

X PREFACE

critique of Sartre and Fanon's often male-centric examinations of colonialism in her dissertation for which I served as director. She went on to publish a book titled *Simone de Beauvoir and the Colonial Experience: Freedom, Violence, and Identity* (2019). Two additional essays I wrote on Beauvoir (also published under my former name) include "Comparative and Competing Frameworks of Oppression in Simone de Beauvoir's *The Second Sex*" (in *Graduate Faculty Philosophy Journal*, 2014) and "Simone de Beauvoir and the Race/Gender Analogy Revisited" (in Nancy Bauer's and Laura Hengehold's *Blackwell Companion to Beauvoir*, 2017).

All that to say, yes, I decided to write a book on Simone de Beauvoir, or rather, a book about Black women's and other Women of Color's critical approaches to Beauvoir's *The Second Sex*. I remained motivated to finish the book by expanding my perspective and intentions. At my core, I am a philosopher—a true lover of wisdom derived from a wide variety of sources. I remind myself to remain intellectually curious about Beauvoir, *The Second Sex*, and her philosophical impact (for better or worse) on feminist philosophies and theories of gender, sex, and sexuality. I am most excited about this project when I expand beyond Beauvoir to focus on the fascinating ways that Black women and other Women of Color have critically approached her classic text and ideas. It has been wonderful to research these important connections to and critiques of this text. Much of this scholarship previously went unnoticed by me—until I started looking for it. It sparks joy for me to take a closer look at passages in the text that have been under-engaged. My experience of the text shifts when I examine those passages more closely with different lenses offered by Black feminists and other Women of Color feminists. With all of this in mind, I present to you: *Beauvoir and Belle: A Black Feminist Critique of The Second Sex.*

Notes

1. For example, see Kathryn Sophia Belle (formerly Kathryn T. Gines), "A Critique of Postracialism: Conserving Race and Complicating Blackness Beyond the Black-white Binary," *Du Bois Review* 11, no. 1 (Spring 2014): 75–86; "Race Women, Race Men and Early Expressions

of Proto-Intersectionality, 1830s–1930s," in *Why Race and Gender Still Matter: An Intersectional Approach*, ed. Namita Goswami, Maeve M. O'Donovan and Lisa Yount (Brookfield, VT: Pickering and Chatto Publishers Limited, 2014), 13–25; "Reflections on the Legacy and Future of Continental Philosophy With Regard to Critical Philosophy of Race," *The Southern Journal of Philosophy* 50, no. 2 (June 2012): 329–344; "Black Feminism and Intersectional Analyses: A Defense of Intersectionality," *Philosophy Today* 55, SPEP Supplement (2011): 275–284; and "Queen Bees and Big Pimps: Sex and Sexuality in Contemporary Hip-Hop," in *Hip Hop and Philosophy: Rhyme 2 Reason—a series in Pop Culture and Philosophy*, vol. 16, ed. Tommie Shelby and Derrick Darby (Chicago: Open Court, 2005), 92–104.

2. Stephanie Rivera Berruz, "Ressenha: GINES, Kathryn T. - Sartre, Beauvoir, and the Race/Gender Analogy: A Case for Black Feminist Philosophy" (in *Sapere Aude*, Belo Horizonte, v. 3, n. 6, p. 504–507—2° semester 2012—ISSN 2177-6342, page 505).

Acknowledgments

I want to acknowledge my four children (J. Elliott, Kyra, Jaden, and Kalia) who understand (more or less) my need for space and time to think and write and speak. They are learning to see me not only as their mother, but also as a whole person with my own projects beyond motherhood. Gratitude also to the multitude of women writers who answered my call when I started an intensive virtual writing group (La Belle Vie Writing Program) with two hours of daily writing during the final push to submit the manuscript to the press. Writing in community is so much more encouraging and inspiring than writing in isolation!

I received critical feedback on earlier iterations of my larger book project from Margaret Simons, Nancy Bauer, Penelope Deutscher, Sabine Broeck, and Joycelyn Moody. Eddie O'Byrn and Kevin Cedeño-Pacheco worked as my research assistants. Shirley Moody Turner is an insightful and inspirational interlocutor, always. It has been my great fortune to have Linda Martín Alcoff in the audience as I have presented parts of this project in multiple contexts. She pushed me on my critiques of analogies. And with her characteristic generosity, she also recommended readings to help strengthen my arguments. Thanks also participants' helpful questions and comments at various conferences where I have presented this research over the years: philoSO-PHIA; People in Support of Women in Philosophy; Diverse Lineages of Existentialism; Black Women Philosophers Conference; American Philosophical Association Conference; Modern Language Association Conference, Society for Phenomenology and Existential Philosophy Conference; and Race and Philosophy Conference. And thanks to the students and faculty offering feedback at invited lectures at colleges and universities including Williams College, Georgetown University, University of North Carolina, Goldsmiths University, Haverford College, Villanova University, Purdue University, Grinnell

xiv ACKNOWLEDGMENTS

College, Emory University, The Pennsylvania State University, and The Graduate School at City University of New York. And I am especially appreciative for the invitation to speak at Spelman College where I studied philosophy as an undergraduate student over two decades ago! Beverly Guy Sheftall (one of my former and now forever favorite professors) noted that for her *The Second Sex* was an influential and inspirational text because it theorized the situation of women in ways (and on a scale) she had not seen before—which was important for me to hear amidst all of my critiques. And, of course, I have deep appreciation to the four (yes four) readers of my manuscript for Oxford University Press, all of whom enthusiastically endorsed its publication.

Some sections of this book were published earlier in the form of articles and chapters including: "Book Review: *Anna Julia Cooper, Visionary Black Feminist: A Critical Introduction* by Vivian M. May (New York: Routledge, 2007); *Black Women's Intellectual Traditions: Speaking Their Minds* edited by Kristin Waters and Carol B. Conaway (Burlington: University of Vermont Press, 2007); *Black Women in the Ivory Tower, 1850–1954: An Intellectual History* by Stephanie Y. Evans (Gainesville: University Press of Florida, 2007); and *Daughter of the Revolution: The Major Nonfiction Works of Pauline E. Hopkins* edited by Ira Dworkin (New Brunswick: Rutgers University Press, 2007)" in *SIGNS 34*, no. 2 (Winter 2009). "Sartre, Beauvoir, and the Race/Gender Analogy: A Case for Black Feminist Philosophy" in *Convergences: Black Feminism and Continental Philosophy*, edited by Maria Davidson, Kathryn T. Gines [now Kathryn Belle], and Donna Dale Marcano (New York: State University of New York Press, 2010). "Race Women, Race Men and Early Expressions of Proto-Intersectionality, 1830s–1930s" in *Why Race and Gender Still Matter: An Intersectional Approach*, edited Namita Goswami, Maeve M. O'Donovan and Lisa Yount (London: Pickering and Chatto Publishers Limited, 2014). "Ruminations on Twenty-Five Years of Patricia Hill Collins' *Black Feminist Thought: Knowledge, Consciousness and the Politics of Empowerment*" in *Ethnic and Racial Studies 38*, no. 13 (2015). "'Comparative and Competing Frameworks of Oppression in Simone de Beauvoir's *The Second Sex*': A Reply to Critical Commentaries" in *Symposia on Gender Race and Philosophy 12*, no. 1 (Spring 2016). "Simone de Beauvoir and the Race/Gender

ACKNOWLEDGMENTS XV

Analogy Revisited" in *Blackwell Companion to Beauvoir*, edited by Nancy Bauer and Laura Hengehold (Hoboken, NJ: Wiley-Blackwell, 2017). "At the Intersections: Existentialism, Critical Philosophies of Race, and Feminism" in *The Routledge Companion to the Philosophy of Race*, edited by Paul C. Taylor, Linda Martín Alcoff, and Luvell Anderson (New York: Routledge, 2017). Review of: *"On ne naît pas femme: on le devient . . ." The Life of a Sentence*, edited by Bonnie Mann and Martina Ferrari (New York: Oxford University Press, 2017) in *Notre Dame Philosophical Review* (June 28, 2018). "Interlocking, Intersecting, and Intermeshing: Critical Engagements with Black and Latina Feminist Paradigms of Identity and Oppression" in *Critical Philosophy of Race 8*, nos. 1–2 (2020). And a slightly revised and translated version of the suffrage chapter from this manuscript will appear in an edited volume in Sweden.

A sabbatical semester and several research fellowships over the years provided protected time for me to write: Center for Humanities and Information Faculty Fellowship; Institute for the Arts and Humanities Fellowship; and Rock Ethics Institute Faculty Fellowship. Finally, I reviewed the index and finished writing these acknowledgments for the manuscript while on fellowship at The New Institute in Hamburg, Germany.

Introduction

bell hooks: "Female identity is shaped by gender, race, and class, and never solely by sex"

This book's title, *Beauvoir and Belle: A Black Feminist Critique of The Second Sex*, is inspired by bell hooks' essay "True Philosophers: Beauvoir and bell."[1] I delight in the boldness with which bell hooks unapologetically names herself a "true philosopher" alongside Simone de Beauvoir. The discipline of philosophy (specifically the Western philosophical tradition) has historically been and continues to be excluding and unkind to women in general, and to Black people, Indigenous People, People of Color, and women at these intersections in particular. For many decades Beauvoir herself was not readily included in the Western philosophical canon despite her formal educational training in philosophy. Looking more specifically at Black women, Joyce Mitchell Cook was the first Black American woman to earn a doctorate in philosophy in the United States (Yale, 1965). Even now, two decades into the twenty-first century, there are still only about fifty Black women in the United States with doctorates of philosophy in philosophy. In the case of bell hooks, she audaciously and accurately self-identifies as a philosopher, though her doctorate is in literature.[2] In a world in which Black women are historically misnamed (see Hortense Spillers' "Mamas Baby, Papa's Maybe: An American Grammar Book") or not named at all (consider the activist calls to #SayHerName), the past and present significance of Black women's self-naming cannot be overstated.

Of course, even the moniker "bell hooks" is a chosen name for Gloria Jean Watkins, who took on the name of her maternal great-grandmother Bell Blair Hooks and chose to use all lowercase letters rather than following the custom of capitalizing the first letter of proper names. There is a decisive disruption of norms and deliberate breaking of grammatical rules that is necessitated by this request. For example,

Beauvoir and Belle. Kathryn Sophia Belle, Oxford University Press. © Oxford University Press 2024.
DOI: 10.1093/oso/9780197660195.003.0001

2 BEAUVOIR AND BELLE

a writer must override the "autocorrect" function in an electronic document that defaults to capitalizing bell or hooks at the beginning of a sentence. hooks' self-naming in all lowercase letters causes a disruption each time her name is written, typed, cited. Like hooks, and like my own maternal grandmother, I also renamed myself. My maternal grandmother changed her name from Kathryn Smallwood to Kathryn Bell by the time she was in high school. Her chosen name is used in her high school yearbook. She was a model who appeared on the cover of *Jet* and other magazines several times using her chosen name. In 2017 I changed my name to Kathryn Sophia Belle to honor the legacy of my maternal grandmother Kathryn Bell, as well as bell hooks, and other Black women like Sojourner Truth, Pauli Murray, Maya Angelou, and Toni Morrison who have also practiced self-naming. I added the extra "e" (from Bell to Belle) for self-differentiation and for the meaning (beautiful, good). Often our names are patrilineal. Women frequently (not always) carry the names of fathers and then husbands. It is powerful to me that my maternal grandmother named herself, and it is an honor to connect to that power and legacy by choosing my version of a matrilineal name. I am also connecting to bell hooks' boldness by naming myself alongside Simone de Beauvoir in the title of my book.

In her essay "True Philosophers: Beauvoir and bell," hooks asserts, "Simone de Beauvoir, as intellectual, philosopher, culture critic, and as a politically radical leftist woman charted a path that was vital to me throughout the process of my intellectual growth."[3] But hooks also notes, "Influenced by the life and writing of Beauvoir, it was essential for me to move beyond her focus on woman as 'other' to bring together critical perspectives for understanding female identity that began from the standpoint that *female identity is shaped by gender, race, and class, and never solely by sex*."[4] Although hooks describes Beauvoir as an inspiring woman thinker and writer, she also describes the need to transcend Beauvoir's limited conceptualization of woman that neglects interlocking identities and oppressions, or what hooks names as *imperialist white supremacist capitalist patriarchy*. She elaborates, "Our perspectives on gender fundamentally differ . . . While Beauvoir separates issues of class, race, and gender—a perspective that distorts the true reality of human being—I continually insist that we cannot understand what it means to be female or male without critically

INTRODUCTION   3

examining interlocking systems of domination."[5] Likewise, *Beauvoir and Belle: A Black Feminist Critique of The Second Sex* centers Black feminist frameworks of identity and oppression, contextualizing the discourses and vocabularies we have created to articulate our existence and experience at the intersections of race, class, gender, and other identities for over two centuries. Focusing on the rich and diverse historical and philosophical developments of Black women as thinkers, speakers, writers, and political actors is valuable in itself, and it also anchors my Black feminist critique of Simone de Beauvoir's *The Second Sex*.

Simone de Beauvoir's *Le deuxième sexe* (1949) translated *The Second Sex* (first by H. M. Parshley in 1952 and then by Constance Borde and Sheila Malovany-Chevallier in 2009) is a foundational white feminist text offering important existential insights on freedom, choice, responsibility, identity, oppression, and a plethora of other key philosophical concepts.[6] One of the significant contributions Beauvoir makes in this text is her identification of various interconnected forms of objectification, othering, and oppression on the basis of various social and political differences. Unfortunately, she undermines her own insights and contributions when she approaches these systems of oppression and differences analogically—drawing analogies among sex oppression, gender oppression, and other forms of oppression (e.g., by repeatedly evoking the race/gender analogy and the slave/woman analogy throughout the two volumes). Furthermore, she frequently presents sexism, racism, classism, antisemitism, and colonialism as comparative and competing frameworks of oppression rather than as systems of oppression that could be better delineated in contemporary terms as interlocking, intersecting, and/or intermeshed.

Looking closely at *The Second Sex*—alongside select divergent secondary literature on that text—I have observed that Beauvoir's critics are keenly aware of the arguments in support of Beauvoir. However, some of her supporters maintain an epistemological standpoint of ignorance concerning certain limitations of her feminist philosophy. This observation has also been made while attending philosophy conferences where Beauvoir is prominently featured. For example, when exclusions of Black women in *The Second Sex* are pointed out, some scholars attempt to defend Beauvoir by asserting that she did not

4 BEAUVOIR AND BELLE

have access to resources on Black women in the 1940s. Others have responded by claiming that *The Second Sex* has had more impact on women's lives around the world than any other text because it resonates with so many women—suggesting that if the text was so exclusionary it could not resonate with other women. These defensive responses and ongoing efforts to protect Beauvoir's legacy undermine her supporters' ability to really hear and acknowledge the shortcomings of Beauvoir's philosophy, especially from the perspective of many Black women and other Women of Color who have our own rich philosophical resources to draw from—resources that exceed the limits of white feminism in general and of *The Second Sex* in particular.

With all of this in mind, my intention is to center some of the feminist frameworks, discourses, and vocabularies of Black women and other Women of Color that existed prior to and have continued after *The Second Sex*. This approach also functions as a corrective to some of the exclusionary tendencies in *The Second Sex* itself. Having said that, I also want to take seriously the ways that Black women and other Women of Color have productively engaged this text. By presenting how Black women and other Women of Color have critically engaged with this text, I am also exposing the ways that existing Beauvoir scholarship has mostly ignored these engagements, thereby replicating Beauvoir's exclusions in the text. I make the following main arguments about *The Second Sex*: despite its noteworthy contributions and insights, some of the limitations of the text include the analogical approach to identity and oppression, the deployment of comparative and competing frameworks of oppression, as well as the ways in which Black women and other Women of Color are either not engaged at all in some cases or problematically engaged in other cases in the text. Additionally, focusing on select secondary literature, I argue that while seeking to enshrine Beauvoir in the gilded halls of philosophy, much of the white feminist secondary literature on *The Second Sex* duplicates her exclusions of Black women and other Women of Color (e.g., by not citing Black feminists and other Women of Color feminists who explicitly take up this text or by citing but not substantively engaging the arguments offered by Black women and other Women of Color), thereby perpetuating the very silencing of women's voices that they often decry in the discipline of philosophy. For the most part, my scope

INTRODUCTION 5

is limited to this text and to specific recurring exclusions therein. I do not claim to attend to all of the exclusions in *The Second Sex*, in the secondary literature on that text, in the rest of Beauvoir's corpus, and/or in white feminist philosophy more broadly.

I would like to make explicit my citational practices: I am committed to prioritizing citations of and engagements with Black women and other Women of Color as relevant to my project. Nonetheless, there are citations of Black men, as well as citations of white women and even some white men when pertinent to the intentions and aims of my project. Concerning my engagements with and citations of *The Second Sex*, I am not providing an overview of this text as a whole, nor am I offering a response to white women's responses to this text. Those books have already been written, and if you are interested in those topics, you should read that extant literature. Rather, I am focusing on those aspects of the text that best show Beauvoir's use of analogies (e.g., the race/gender analogy and the slave/woman analogy), her comparative and competing frameworks of oppressions (e.g., racism, sexism, classism, colonialism), as well as her lack of and/or problematic engagements with Black women and other Women of Color. Concerning my engagements with and citations of white feminist secondary literature on *The Second Sex*, I have intentionally focused primarily on white feminists who have taken seriously racial critiques of this text as well as critiques of the use of analogies in this text. So if you think I should center white feminist analyses of the Other in Beauvoir, or you think I should center how Beauvoir talks about white women across class difference, or you think I should consider how if we read Beauvoir in a certain way she actually is very intersectional, or you want to question how Beauvoir could have possibly been expected to know anything at all about Black women—then you are deflecting to defend Beauvoir, you are recentering whiteness (specifically white woman-ness), and you are missing the point.

It is also worth noting that while I take a critical Black feminist approach to *The Second Sex*, I do not think that we should stop reading, teaching, and/or writing about it. Like any philosophical text, it makes significant contributions that can be taken up and responsibly repurposed. But we can only do this when we also re-examine its shortcomings and limitations. My hope is that in acknowledging and

6 BEAUVOIR AND BELLE

analyzing rather than ignoring, apologizing for, or whitesplaining such shortcomings and limitations in the text, we are able to consider the serious implications they have for the important insights offered, while also exploring potential paths forward. I have lost patience with condescending white women who assume that I and/or other Black women and Women of Color critique the text because we did not read it in its entirety and/or because we somehow did not understand it. We read it. We understand it. And on that basis, we have critiques of it. I name the issues that come up for me as a Black woman philosopher, professor, coach, and happily unmarried mother of four children who is also reading, teaching, and writing about *The Second Sex*. I am sharing the ways that I follow my intellectual curiosities, analyzing and critiquing the problematics of text, and attending to my interests and inquiries. All of this is an effort to continue to cultivate my own love of wisdom as a "true philosopher" in the spirit of bell hooks. I am filled with gratitude every time a student or community member tells me that they use my work to help them articulate their own critiques and/or to push back on professors and other interlocutors who insist on pretending that such shortcomings in these philosophical texts do not exist. If my commitment to my reading and writing processes continues to offer some methodologies and theoretical resources for others who see similar issues and have similar concerns, then that is an added bonus for which I also have gratitude.

Recovering Simone de Beauvoir as a Philosopher

There has been a concerted effort to recover Simone de Beauvoir as a legitimate philosophical figure despite her protestations to the label of philosopher and her preference for self-identifying as an author or writer. Secondary white feminist literature on Beauvoir in the United States often begins from a defensive position, building a case that she was in fact a philosopher, and offering justifications for her philosophical significance. Some earlier attempts to recover Beauvoir as an original philosophical thinker emphasize that she is not merely a follower of Jean-Paul Sartre, and furthermore, that it is Sartre who took up Beauvoir's innovative philosophical insights for his own intellectual

INTRODUCTION 7

development. Although it is frequently suggested (at times by Beauvoir herself) that she followed Sartre's philosophical lead, some scholars have sought to prove that the opposite was the case. For example, in *Simone de Beauvoir and Jean-Paul Sartre: The Remaking of a Twentieth-Century Legend* (1994) Kate and Edward Fullbrook analyze Sartre's *War Diaries*[7] and Beauvoir's *Letters to Sartre*[8] to make the case that:

> It is now utterly clear to us that Beauvoir was always the driving intellectual power in the joint development of the couple's most influential ideas. The story of their partnership has been told backwards. Our detailed work on the genesis of *She Came to Stay* shows, incontrovertibly we believe, that the major ideas behind *Being and Nothingness* were fully worked out by Beauvoir and adopted by Sartre before he even began his famous study.[9]

Margaret Simons has also debunked the commonly held view of Beauvoir as a follower (and mere companion) of Sartre in *Beauvoir and The Second Sex: Feminism, Race, and the Origins of Existentialism* (1999).[10] Citing sexism in many representations of their relationship, Simons argues: "From the standpoint of feminist theory, a most serious aspect of this sexist view of Beauvoir's relationship to Sartre is the discounting of Beauvoir as an original thinker and the refusal to acknowledge, analyze, and critically study her work as social theory and social philosophy."[11] Highlighting the backward telling of the story of influence between Sartre and Beauvoir, she continues, "This view fails to recognize the originality of Beauvoir's insights and is thus unable to appreciate her considerable influence on Sartre's development of a social philosophy of existentialism, and on contemporary feminist theorists as well."[12] Simons points out that Beauvoir's 1927 diary gives an account of her "struggle against despair and the temptation of self-deception, which anticipates her later concept of 'Bad Faith'" along with "the opposition of the self and the other," both major themes in *The Second Sex* and *Being and Nothingness*.[13] Claims that Beauvoir not only was a philosopher in her own right, but also influenced Sartre's philosophical development, are significant, especially within the male-centric discipline of philosophy. While Sartre is readily embraced within existentialism and continental philosophy, Beauvoir has been

8 BEAUVOIR AND BELLE

relatively marginalized—often relegated to feminist philosophy anthologies and readers.[14]

Simons revisits this issue in her introduction to *Simone de Beauvoir: Philosophical Writings* (2004), where she names Sartre's overshadowing of Beauvoir as a persistent problem. Simons reminds readers that "from the beginning, she was assumed to be Sartre's philosophical follower and her work merely an application of his philosophy."[15] Additional reasons given for why Beauvoir's philosophy is under-analyzed and misunderstood have to do with her highly original philosophical methodology, her rejection of systems-building, and her position that philosophy should reflect the ambiguities of life, while focusing on concrete problems. Some of Simons' earlier recovery work of Beauvoir includes numerous edited volumes such as *Feminist Interpretations of Simone de Beauvoir* (1995) and *The Philosophy of Simone de Beauvoir: Critical Essays* (2006), and perhaps even more significant, a Simone de Beauvoir book series with University of Illinois Press featuring collected translations of Beauvoir's previously untranslated writings.[16]

There have been other more recent efforts to recover Beauvoir by insisting not only that she is heavily influenced by white male philosophers in the Western philosophical canon, but also that she originated her own significant philosophical insights, and on this basis, she too has earned her place in the canon. For example, Nancy Bauer has underscored various influences on Beauvoir's work (from Descartes and Husserl to Hegel, Heidegger, and, of course, Sartre), while also insisting, "Beauvoir's aspirations to write about being a woman are inextricably intertwined with her discovery of what I argue is both her own philosophical voice and a model for doing philosophical work that lies waiting to be appropriated by both feminists and philosophers."[17] Bauer problematizes the ways in which Beauvoir has been neglected as a philosophical figure and states:

> I can't imagine anyone doubting that part of the reason for this neglect is the simple fact of her having been a woman. (Can we name a woman philosopher whose work has been sufficiently acknowledged? Can we specify the significance of being a woman philosopher?—which is to ask, Do we know what it means to be a

INTRODUCTION   9

woman philosophizing? That we find resources in *The Second Sex* to begin thinking about these issues is, to my mind, only one of its great—neglected—achievements.)"[18]

For Bauer, we must acknowledge that "Beauvoir has repeatedly been a victim of flat-out sexism."[19] Connected to the issues of sexism are condescension and patriarchy. Bauer identifies five gestures of condescension toward Beauvoir:

1. a conception of Beauvoir as the mother of modern feminism . . . [whose] inaugural text . . .consists mostly of insights that have been surpassed by others' later acts of writing; 2. a view of *The Second Sex* as a book that is eye-opening but not radical . . .; 3. an identification of the philosophical dimension of *The Second Sex* as consisting in nothing other than warmed-over Sartrean existentialism; 4. a linking of what are taken to be shortcomings of *The Second Sex* with biographical facts about Beauvoir, particularly her relationship with Sartre; and 5. an understanding of numerous features of Beauvoir's book, sometimes her shortcomings and quite often her achievements, as products of the writing of which she is *unconscious*.[20]

Following Toril Moi, Bauer offers a compelling analysis of patriarchal ideology to explain the condescension toward Beauvoir, even by her supporters. She explains, "On Moi's view, condescension to Beauvoir is a product of 'patriarchal ideology,' which she sees as fundamentally hostile to the idea of the intellectual woman (and, a fortiori, the idea of a woman *philosopher*)."[21]

Bauer is building on Moi's analysis in *Simone de Beauvoir: The Making of an Intellectual Woman* (1994, 2008). Focusing on the French reception of Beauvoir, Moi asserts, "Here I shall simply indicate how her [Beauvoir's] specific position as an intellectual woman can account for much of the hostile reception of her work and—more importantly—how it may help us understand why her place in the current cannon of modern French literature is decidedly precarious."[22] Exploring philosophy in particular, Moi notes that although overwhelmingly male (in terms of its practitioners), "the discipline

10 BEAUVOIR AND BELLE

of philosophy was represented as female, a subject to be handled with respect, violence or dominance by the elite males who were equal to it."[23] Rather than engage Beauvoir's arguments, both men and women interlocutors (from the 1950s to the 1990s) present surface critiques and personal attacks. Moi explains, "their aim is clearly to discredit her as a speaker, not to enter into debate with her."[24] And adds, "These critics are out to cast doubts on Beauvoir's right to produce any kind of public discourse."[25]

Looking even more specifically at the French feminist reception of Beauvoir, Moi notes that many either dismiss her as outdated and irrelevant or ignore her altogether. Engagements with Beauvoir by French feminists fall into one of two main camps. On the one hand, there are those who take Beauvoir to be calling for social equality of the sexes, failing to value women's difference, and/or seeking to abolish sexual difference.[26] On the other hand, there are those who reject the so-called cult of difference and instead make a case for material feminism, which Moi describes as being "very much in the spirit of Simone de Beauvoir herself."[27] In defense of Beauvoir, Moi asserts that her critics "utterly fail to grasp that Beauvoir's political project is radically different from their own."[28] She elaborates, "For Beauvoir, the opposite of freedom is oppression: her problematics is one of *power*, not one of identity and/or difference."[29] I find it fascinating (even ironic) that power is juxtaposed with identity and difference here, and furthermore that the "cult of difference" invoked emphasizes sexual difference without any mention of the myriad ways that sexual difference is simultaneously informed by other types of difference (e.g., race, class, nationality, religion), as well as by power. When Moi states that for Beauvoir, "the scandal of human history is the fact that one group of free subjects have been coerced into defining themselves as objects, as *other* in relation to another group of free subjects," she is bracketing the other forms of objectification, othering, and difference that Beauvoir actually acknowledges (e.g., racism, classism, antisemitism, and colonialism).[30] For Beauvoir it is not only one group of subjects that have been made *other*, but multiple (e.g., women, Black people, Jewish people, the colonized, the proletariat). Again, this is a place of both interesting insight and oblivious oversight for Beauvoir.

INTRODUCTION   11

To be fair, Moi does not altogether ignore these connections insofar as she offers some reflections on racism, the colonial question, and the woman question in France. For example, Moi asserts that Beauvoir is one of few scholars in France to take up and critique colonialism during her time. Describing *Les Temps Modernes* as "the only periodical [in France] consistently to publish critical reports on colonial conflicts," Moi notes this is significant in part because "the French media paid little or no attention to colonial questions before the Algerian War of Independence (1954–1962) finally forced the issue to the top of the French political agenda."[31] Following Beauvoir's model of comparative and competing frameworks of oppression, she goes on to claim that the woman question was even more marginal than questions concerning colonialism and racism.[32] Thus, Moi asserts, "It is not a coincidence that throughout her essay [*The Second Sex*] Beauvoir makes frequent comparisons between the situation of women and that of Jews and blacks."[33]

A more recent book written in defense of Beauvoir is Meryl Altman's *Beauvoir in Time* (2020).[34] She notes, "the reception of *The Second Sex* has been caught between two paradoxes. First, how could a mass movement have been started by a book which barely sketches the possibility of collective action? And then, what are we to do with a book that does not speak of differences between women in the ways identity politics came to demand, but that nonetheless appears to have spoken to women of color around the world, from Lorraine Hansberry to Sara Ahmed, in a powerful way?"[35] Altman is one of the few white women defenders of Beauvoir who cites and engages some of the secondary literature on *The Second Sex* by Black women and other Women of Color. Unfortunately, the rhetorical strategies and tone in the text are often offensive and condescending. For example, when citing a passage from Anna Julia Cooper's "Woman Versus Indian," Altman states, "Now, if I wanted to be a jerk, I could point out that the second sentence of that magnificent paragraph follows the same 'all of the women were white, all of the Negros were men' structure that has been so fully criticized in the theorizing of white women, including Beauvoir."[36] Altman seems to be gesturing at, but is misquoting, the book title *All of the Women Are White, All of the Blacks Are Men, But Some of Us Are Brave: Black*

12   BEAUVOIR AND BELLE

Women's Studies, and the critiques of white feminism that the book (re) presents.

This is one demonstration of the epistemic violence that Black women face if and when our scholarship gets engaged in the secondary literature on Beauvoir by white women.[37] For Altman to infer that Anna Julia Cooper is in any way erasing Black women is a non-starter. To suggest that Cooper's work—work that intentionally and explicitly centers Black women, including her own "voice from the South"—is in any way comparable to how white women have ignored and/or marginalized Black women in their scholarship is unscrupulous.[38] Furthermore, Altman appropriates the language of "identity politics" as well as "intersectionality" (both concepts introduced by Black feminist activist scholars) in ways that ultimately displace Black women to recenter white women. Such recoveries of Beauvoir celebrate her foundational contributions to feminism, as well as her insights about other forms of oppression such as anti-Black racism, antisemitism, and colonialism. Or, in the case of Altman, attempt to use favorable readings of *The Second Sex* by some Black women (e.g., Hansberry and Holland) to neutralize critiques by other Black women (e.g., Glass and Gines [now Belle]). But these works stand in stark contrast to sharp criticism of Beauvoir for her exclusions of Black women and other Women of Color, as well as for her appropriations of the suffering of others as a rhetorical strategy to advance her arguments about the oppression of white women.[39] These issues will be taken up in greater detail in this book.

Background and Context for *The Second Sex*: France in the 1940s

Simone de Beauvoir wrote *The Second Sex* between 1946 and 1949, during which time she also published *All Men Are Mortal* (1946), *Ethics of Ambiguity* (1947), *L'existentialisme et la sages des nations* (1948), and *America Day By Day* (1948). Volume 1 of *The Second Sex* would be published on its own (along with excerpts of it appearing in *Les Temps Modernes*) as she turned her attention to finishing Volume 2. One way to situate *The Second Sex* is to consider some of the major issues and

INTRODUCTION 13

events in France at the time it was written and published. Moi offers some context for gender, class, and colonial politics in France in the 1940s. Concerning gender politics, she describes the Vichy regime as "brutally misogynistic" insofar as "women were refused the right to work, except in traditionally female occupations, abortion became a crime against the state, and contraception remained illegal."[40] And even after the Vichy regime, there remained rigid limitations of women's parental rights, financial rights, professional rights, and access to contraception and abortion. But Moi notes, "In 1944 French women are given the right to vote, as a reward for their participation in the resistance."[41] Concerning class politics, she asserts, "By 1948, the French socialists and communists were also irredeemably divided."[42] And, of course, there was the issue of French colonialism and anticolonial resistance. Here Moi highlights three massacres in particular—one in Algeria and two in Madagascar—"As early as May 1945, after a nationalist riot in the Algerian town in Sétif in which 29 Europeans died, French troops massacred between 6,000 and 8,000 Algerian Muslims. In 1947 an uprising in Madagascar left 550 Europeans and 1,900 natives dead. In April 1948 a French expeditionary force proceeded to ruthless retaliation: according to official figures 89,000 Madagascans were killed."[43] Naming not only the violent events themselves, but also the numbers of persons killed—particularly the disproportionate number of Europeans killed in contrast to the number of Algerians and Madagascans killed—is especially significant here. It speaks to the violent system of colonialism and the violence used to maintain that system.[44]

Against this backdrop of historical and political events, Moi describes *The Second Sex* as "startlingly unique" and adds, "the fact remains that in France in 1949, women's issues were not central to the political agenda of any major party or faction, nor was there an independent women's movement outside the established parties; in this historical situation, *The Second Sex* is nothing short of unique."[45] But I would like to offer additional context to this broad and brief historical overview by examining the Black Feminist writing and scholarship circulating before and during this time period (1920s–1940s) in France and in Martinique (a former colony and current overseas territory of France).

14 BEAUVOIR AND BELLE

By the late 1940s Black women in France and in French colonies like Martinique had been writing and publishing about race, culture, language, gender, sex, class, and colonialism for at least two decades (1920s–1940s). This is most evident in Negritude and precursors to that major movement. In *Negritude Women* (2002), T. Denean Sharpley-Whiting identifies Suzanne Lacasade, author of the novel *Claire-Solange, âme africaine* (1924), as a "proto-Negritude" writer.[46] Putting this literary work in context, she notes, "Rarely would an Antillean in 1924 have proudly called herself or himself African instead of French. More rarely still would an educated West Indian have published her or his first novel as an act of cultural preservation by adding an appendix and a vocal recording of Antillean songs in Creole."[47] Supporting her claim that Lacasade was a proto-Negritude writer, she asserts that racial essentialism is a "defining and importantly critiqued characteristic of Negritude" and argues, "It is this use of racial essentialism, specifically with respect to the 'essence' of *black femaleness*—novel for the era yet pervasive in later Franco-Caribbean and African poetry, fiction, and non-fiction—that situates Lacasade, like her contemporary René Maran, as a Negritude literary forerunner and forebear."[48] In addition to Lacasade's proto-Negritude writing, special attention is given to Suzanne Césaire and the Nardal sisters (Paulette, Jane, and Andrée) as often erased co-founders of Negritude.[49]

Most accounts of the Negritude movement center three men (*les trois péres* Léon Damas, Léopold Senghor, and Aimé Césaire) who are typically identified as its founders. They started *L'estudiant noir* (1934), a literary review previously called *L'estudiant martiniquais* that was influenced by the earlier journal *Légitime défense* (1932).[50] But before *L'estudiant noir* and *Légitime défense* there was *La Revue du monde noir* (1931–1932), conceptualized at the Clamart salon, launched in October 1931 and running until April 1932.[51] *La Revue du monde noir* was collaboratively edited by the Nardal sisters (from Martinique) along with Léo Sajous (from Haiti), Clara Shepard (from the United States), and Louis-Jean Finot.[52] Located in the Paris apartment of Jane and Paulette Nardal, the Clamart salon offered an important social and intellectual space where African, West Indian, and American Black intellectuals gathered to exchange ideas.[53] It has been identified as "the first multiracial, gender-inclusive salon in Paris set up by black

INTRODUCTION   15

Francophone women."[54] And even before *La revue du monde noir*, there was *La Dépêche africaine* (1928–1932), a newspaper for which Paulette and Jane Nardal were also collaborators and contributors.[55] About a decade after the launch of *La revue du monde noir*, Aimé and Suzanne Césaire, along with René Ménil co-founded the review *Tropiques* (1941–1945).[56] Suzanne Césaire, herself a philosophy student in Paris before marrying Aimé Césaire, published several pieces in *Tropiques*, though her brilliance and significant contributions to Surrealism and Negritude have been largely marginalized.[57] It is also worth noting that S. Césaire took up issues like the sexual exploitation of Black women by white men in the historical contexts of slavery and colonialism.[58] There is also Mayotte Capécia's *Je suis Martiniquaise* (1948), a book that was famously and bitterly critiqued by Frantz Fanon that "garner[ed] her a metropolitan readership and a literary prize while immediately estranging her from the Negritude crowd."[59] These Black women of the Negritude era not only articulate a heightened race consciousness, but also write with special attention to the nuances at the intersections of gender, race, culture, language, class, colonialism, internationalism, and humanism.[60] Sharpley-Whiting explains, "The Antillean woman in Paris, learned in ways of occidental culture yet rejected by that culture on the basis of her ethnicity, gender, and color, experiences a profound social isolation . . . She is not a Frenchwoman like other Frenchwomen; she is a racialized Franco-Antillean woman."[61]

The Negritude movement and issues of colonialism would become more popularized for a larger (white) audience when Jean-Paul Sartre wrote prefaces for Senghor ("Black Orpheus" was published in 1948 as the preface to Leopold Senghor's classic *Anthology of New Negro Poetry*) as well as for Fanon (preface to *The Wretched of the Earth*).[62] As Sharpley-Whiting observes, "By 1948, Sartre had picked up the word *Negritude* and heralded its emergence as a new literary and philosophical movement in a highly masculinized language on the French intellectual landscape, even though its philosophical praxis had been ongoing and its theoretical precepts woman-generated."[63] With this in mind, we should not forget the Negritude women and the fact that they generated and circulated their philosophies through novels, journals, newspapers, and the Clamart salon years before *les trois péres* and

16 BEAUVOIR AND BELLE

decades before Beauvoir's *The Second Sex*. We know that Beauvoir is aware of Negritude and familiar with the poetry of Senghor, which she cites in *The Second Sex* when talking about reciprocity, women's bodies, and the feminine ideal (TSS 176 n 14). But there is no evidence of intellectual engagement with and/or citations of Negritude women in her classic text.[64] The same is true for her lack of engagement with and/or citations of Black American women in that text.

Black Feminist Thought in the United States in the 1940s

Some may argue that Beauvoir should not be expected to have known and/or engaged Black women intellectuals in the US context at the time she was writing *The Second Sex*. This is debatable given her engagements with Black American male intellectual Richard Wright, her multiple citations of his work in *The Second Sex*, and the serial publications of some of his major writings that appeared in *Les Temps Modernes*. Also *America Day By Day*, Beauvoir's memoir about her extended visit to the United States dedicated to Richard and Ellen Wright, was written and published while she was still working on *The Second Sex*. It is worth noting that she makes no mention of meeting and/or interacting with Black American women in any substantive ways in the memoir. That is to say, there are no mentions of significant conversations with Black women or of her reading scholarship by Black women. Nonetheless, there are passing descriptions of Black women in the memoir—including voyeuristic gazing upon Black women's fashion and dancing, anecdotes about racial discrimination (from Black women in clubs being denied service, to observations that there are clubs in which Black people were allowed to perform but were not allowed to sit in the audience).[65]

Beauvoir mentions seeing "a large cardboard Negress, a kerchief tied around her head, who smiles while pointing avidly to the creole specialty" in front of a pastry and praline shop during a visit to New Orleans, Louisiana.[66] At another club she describes, "A young

INTRODUCTION 17

black woman, half drunk, is at the piano, and she plays some old jazz very movingly."[67] Later, after gesturing at the problems of what is now described as the prison industrial complex in the United States, Beauvoir raises the issue of miscegenation and the sexual exploitation of Black women.[68] On this point she notes, "With even more flagrant bad faith, whites see all black women as loose and corrupt."[69] Rejecting this bad-faith misrepresentation of Black women, she explains, "But in the South it's impossible for these women to defend themselves against the sexual advances of white men, and it's impossible for black men to defend their families; the women are simple prey."[70] Beauvoir goes on to put this in the context of false claims of white "purity" against the reality of the "mixed blood" of children fathered by white men— asserting, "White men are not embarrassed to mix their blood with that of black women, but it is true that their children then belong to the black caste and the white race is not altered."[71] On this point she explores the myth of the "inferiority of mulattoes in relation to pure Negros," noting that this myth "is meaningless because 80 percent of black citizens are mulattos," and then adding, "Moreover, this myth has never prevented white men from sleeping with Negro women."[72] Beauvoir includes references to John Dollard's Caste and Class (1937), Gunnar Myrdal's An American Dilemma (1944), and Richard Wright's Black Boy (1945) in this section of America Day By Day—but no citations of Black women.

Of course, by the 1940s, Black women in the United States already had over a century of feminist speeches, writings, and activism focused on identifying, analyzing, and critiquing race, class, and gender oppression—including adept analyses of sexual exploitation and miscegenation. Beverly Guy Sheftall's Words of Fire: An Anthology of African American Feminist Thought (1995) offers a treasure trove of essays and speeches going back to Maria Stewart's 1831 speech "Religion and the Pure Principles of Morality, the Sure Foundation on Which We Must Stand" and going forward to Alice Walker's "In the Closet of the Soul" from 1988.[73] Additional nineteenth-century Black women featured in this anthology include: Sojourner Truth, Frances Ellen Watkins Harper, Anna Julia Cooper, Julia Foote, Gertrude Bustill Mossell, Mary Church Terrell, and Ida B. Wells. Black women

18   BEAUVOIR AND BELLE

featured in a section titled "Triumph and Tribulation: Defining Black Womanhood, 1920–1957" include: Elise Johnson McDougald, Alice Dunbar Nelson, Amy Jacques Garvey, Ula Taylor, Sadie Tanner Mossell Alexander, Florynce "Flo" Kennedy, Claudia Jones, and Lorraine Hansberry. And Angela Davis appears in a section titled "Civil Rights and Women's Liberation: Racial/Sexual Politics in the Angry Decades" along with Frances Beale, Mary Ann Weathers, Linda La Rue, Patricia Haden, Donna Middleton, Patricia Robinson, Pauli Murray, and Michele Wallace. All that to say, Black women in the United States (and globally) have a centuries-long history of writing and theorizing. And all of this against the odds of slavery, laws prohibiting teaching Black people to read and write, an ongoing lack of access to education and/or limited access to education post-emancipation, among other forms of systematic oppression and repression.

Black women have been doing feminist intellectual and emotional labor alongside physical labor on and off of slave and sharecropping plantations, within and outside of the home, long before the publication of Simone de Beauvoir's *America Day By Day* and *The Second Sex*. Scholarship and activism by Black women has continued long after these two texts were published. Black feminist philosophy, history, and literature has been and continues to be produced, documented, and disseminated in anthologies, syllabi, and on other platforms.[74] Nonetheless, Black feminism has been and continues to be under-engaged or altogether unacknowledged in much of the white feminist philosophy canon where there is in some cases persistent neglect or in other cases blatant misrepresentation of Black feminist speeches, writings, and activism—before and after Beauvoir. I want to under-score three main points here: (1) Black women's theorizing has been and still is happening, (2) Beauvoir misses an opportunity for substantive engagement with Black women in *The Second Sex*, and (3) there is a persistent historical and contemporary neglect of Black women and other Women of Color, not only by Beauvoir, but also in much of the scholarship on Beauvoir. I offer a broad overview of Black feminist frameworks of identity and oppression as well as an examination specific Black women's relationships to Beauvoir and *The Second Sex* in more detail in this book.

INTRODUCTION 19

Over Sixty Years of Women of Color Feminist
Engagements with *The Second Sex*

Black women and other Women of Color feminists who explicitly engage Beauvoir's *The Second Sex* have remained largely unacknowledged in the philosophical secondary literature. As a corrective to this erasure, I call attention to several examples of these scholarly contributions, written over six decades (1957–2019). Here I offer a few highlights of this important scholarship that will be engaged in more detail throughout this book. Looking at the second half of the nineteenth century, Claudia Jones prevented a negative review of *The Second Sex* from running in the Communist Party's cultural journal *Masses and Mainstream*, and she also assisted in getting Elizabeth Lawson's more favorable review, "Woman: Second Sex," published in the *Worker* (1954).[75] Lorraine Hansberry (1957) offers a positive reading of *The Second Sex*, affirming Beauvoir's analysis of the woman question, and critiquing the gender politics that prevented adequate attention to the theories advanced in the text.[76] Angela Davis (1971) cites Beauvoir's accounts of the sexual relations of animals in *The Second Sex* as a way of critiquing the sexual assaults endured by enslaved Black women by white male masters.[77] Audre Lorde notes in her famous essay "The Masters Tools Will Never Dismantle the Master's House" (1979), "Simone de Beauvoir once said: 'It is in the knowledge of the genuine conditions of our lives that we must draw our strength to live and our reasons for acting.'"[78] This quote is from *Ethics of Ambiguity*, but Lorde's remarks were initially presented at the 1979 conference in New York commemorating the thirtieth anniversary of the publication of *The Second Sex*.[79] Chikwenye Ogunyemi (1985) presents Beauvoir as one example of the differences in the projects of Black and white feminism and writing.[80] Deborah King (1988) critiques Beauvoir's (and other white feminists') use of the race/gender analogy in their analyses of patriarchy.[81] Jamaica Kincaid (1990) makes a passing reference to *The Second Sex*, noting that its famous line could not really explain the life of the Black woman protagonist in her novel *Lucy*. And Norma Alarcón (1994) contrasts Beauvoir's singular and individualist approach to subjectivity in *The Second Sex* with the multiple-voiced

20 BEAUVOIR AND BELLE

approach to subjectivity by Women of Color in *This Bridge Called My Back.*

Moving into the twenty-first century, Oyèrónké Oyĕwùmí (2000) argues that a problem with Beauvoir (and white feminists more generally) is that they too often try to universalize from their own experience in which woman often equals wife—the subordinated half of a couple in a nuclear family.[82] Judith Wilson (2003) notes the impact of Beauvoir on her in 1973 and states, "I seized the 'f-word' gladly—not only because de Beauvoir's insights illuminated so many of my own experiences as daughter, sister, student, worker, and lover. The breathtaking depth and range of her thinking was as important to me as ideological content."[83] Mariana Ortega (2006) details Latin American and US Latina feminist engagements with existentialism and phenomenology through Beauvoir.[84] Kathy Glass (2010) examines how the continental philosophical tradition, including Simone de Beauvoir, duplicates "patriarchal patterns of racial exclusion"—while looking to Audre Lorde, bell hooks, and Cornel West to theorize sisterhood across race, class, and sexuality.[85] In earlier publications (2010, 2014, and 2017) I have critiqued Beauvoir's use of the race/gender analogy as well as comparative and competing frameworks of oppression in *The Second Sex.*[86] Again, bell hooks (2012) favorably presents Beauvoir as a powerful example of a woman thinker-writer, but also differentiates Beauvoir's tendency to think about female identity as shaped by sex, from her own inclination to analyze female identity as also shaped by gender, race, and class.[87] Sharon Patricia Holland (2012) takes up Beauvoir's existentialism and concept of the erotic as a site of revolutionary potential in her analysis of the interconnections between our erotic lives and racist practices.[88] Kyoo Lee (2012, 2017) analyzes how Beauvoir's "pivotal formulation of femme remains oddly un/re/translatable" in both the Parshley and the Borde and Malovany-Chevallier English translations (while also taking into account Chinese and Korean translations of the famous sentence "*On ne naît pas femme: on le devient*").[89] Lee (2013) also engages Beauvoir alongside Du Bois as she contemplates the "auto-ethnographical textuality of thinking" as "a source of intersubjective imperatives as well as inspirations."[90] Stephanie Rivera Berruz (2012, 2016) asserts that "the woman of color suffers from a certain epistemic exclusion in *The Second Sex*"

INTRODUCTION 21

and later argues that Latinas are rendered imperceptible in that text.[91] For Berruz, "At stake in this discussion is whose oppression and lived experiences can be named and identified as meaningful."[92] Like Lee, Céline Leboef (2015) considers Beauvoir's famous sentence and its implications for the sex-gender distinction.[93] Patricia Hill Collins (2017) examines "Beauvoir's approach to women's oppression as a form of non-freedom, paying special attention to the way she develops arguments about oppression and freedom using analogical thinking about race and gender."[94] Alia Al-Saji (2018) critiques Beauvoir's representations of Muslim and Arab women (in *The Second Sex* and *Ethics of Ambiguity*).[95] And more recently, Nathalie Nya centers the issue of colonialism in Beauvoir's writings in *Simone de Beauvoir and the Colonial Experience: Freedom, Violence, and Identity* (2019). The chapters that follow take up most of these scholars' critical approaches to Simone de Beauvoir's *The Second Sex*.

Overview of the Chapters

This book is written at the intersections of multiple tensions. On the one hand, I am centering and amplifying the voices of Black women and other Women of Color. On the other hand, I am bringing attention to their connections to Simone de Beauvoir's *The Second Sex* and demonstrating the myriad ways that their feminist frameworks exceed the limits of that figure and text—providing viable alternatives and correctives. To be sure, these Black feminist and Women of Color feminist frameworks are significant in their own right. My goal is not to ground the significance of their work in the shortcomings of Beauvoir and white feminism, or for that matter to recenter white feminism even as I critique it. Rather, my intention is to highlight Black women and other Women of Color feminisms, which entails taking seriously their responses to *The Second Sex* (including my own). These tensions inform the organizational structure of the book.

In Part I, "Black Feminist Frameworks," the first four chapters intentionally foreground Black feminist philosophy and praxis while also exploring direct and indirect connections with *The Second Sex*. Chapter 1, "A Select Genealogy of Black Feminist Frameworks for

22 BEAUVOIR AND BELLE

Identities and Oppressions: 'If we are not careful the work we are doing now is going to have to be "rediscovered" at some point,' " offers a selective genealogy of Black feminist frameworks for identity and oppression that underscores the creation of discourses and vocabularies that express our existence and experience. I argue that Black women have a matrilineal legacy of creating discourses and vocabularies to express our existence and experience going back to Lucy Terry and Phillis Wheatley (in the context of eighteenth-century colonial America), and furthermore, that Black women have been offering what I would now characterize as feminist frameworks for identity and oppression going back to Maria Stewart in the early nineteenth century (1831) that continue until today.

Chapter 2, "Claudia Jones: 'The Negro question in the United States is *prior* to, and not equal to, the woman question,' " examines Jones' Black left internationalist feminist analyses and activism related to the issues of fascism, imperialism, capitalism, poverty, sexism, slavery and rape, abolition and suffrage, Jim Crow and segregation, lynching, and police brutality as represented in her essay: "An End to the Neglect of the Problems of the Negro Woman!" (1949). I argue that Jones' triple-oppression analysis takes seriously the simultaneity of racial oppression, gender oppression, and class oppression in ways that explicitly center and make visible Black women's lived experience as well as their militant agency. I also argue that although Jones and Beauvoir take quite different approaches to the issues of their times (both publishing their most popular text in 1949), Jones must be credited for facilitating one of the earliest recoveries of *The Second Sex* in the US context.

Chapter 3, "Lorraine Hansberry: '*The Second Sex* may well be the most important work of this century,' " offers a close reading of Lorraine Hansberry's critical commentary on *The Second Sex*, highlighting several key themes in the commentary, including her critique of the biographical imperative approach to Beauvoir and *The Second Sex*, as well as the positive and negative reception of the text (by Hansberry and others) when it was first published and translated into English. I also underscore some important differences between Hansberry and Beauvoir in their approaches to the woman question, the Negro question, and Marxism, as well as existentialism and complicity. I argue that unlike Beauvoir, who emphasizes woman's complicity and

INTRODUCTION   23

compares woman's oppression to other systems of oppressions (but ultimately privileges the former over the latter), Hansberry emphasizes the non-complicity and agitation of the oppressed and notes how class, colonial, and gender oppressions are interconnected systems of oppression. Furthermore, Hansberry prefers historical materialism to existentialism.

Chapter 4, "Audre Lorde: 'Difference is that raw and powerful connection from which our personal power is forged,'" takes up Lorde's iconic essay "The Master's Tools Will Never Dismantle the Master's House" (presented at a 1979 conference commemorating the thirtieth anniversary of the publication of *The Second Sex*). I argue that Lorde's 1979 remarks and Jessica Benjamin's reflections on Lorde over two decades later (2000) offer a case study for problematic white feminist engagement with Black feminist thought and thinkers. When Black feminists and other Women of Color feminists request serious attentiveness to race, sexuality, class, and age within feminist discourse, white feminists often accuse us of being angry, divisive, and/or playing "identity politics." This chapter also takes up the coining of the phrase "identity politics" in "The Combahee River Collective: A Black Feminist Statement" by Barbara Smith, Beverly Smith, and Demita Frazier, and the ways that it has been misappropriated and strategically deployed against Black women and other Women of Color.

In Part II, "White Feminist Frameworks," the next three chapters focus on Beauvoir's analogical approach to identity and oppressions (e.g., her use of the race/gender analogy and the slave/woman analogy) as well as her brief but significant account of abolition and suffrage in the United States. Chapter 5, "Simone de Beauvoir's Analogical Approach: 'There are deep analogies between the situations of women and blacks,'" gives a close textual analysis of the use of the race/gender analogy and other comparative and competing frameworks of oppression in *The Second Sex*. I make the following arguments: (1) Beauvoir's comparative and competing frameworks of oppression pose at least two problems—on the one hand, at times she collapses diverse systems of oppression as the same. On the other hand, at times she also attempts to distinguish among these systems of oppression by privileging gender difference and oppression above other forms of identity and oppression; (2) Beauvoir's utilization of the race/gender analogy omits

24 BEAUVOIR AND BELLE

the experiences and oppressions of Black women and other Women of Color who experience racial and gender oppression simultaneously; and furthermore, (3) even when white feminists critique Beauvoir's use of analogies and/or other comparative and competing frameworks of oppression, often they do not cite and engage Black and Latina feminists who have taken up these issues in Beauvoir.

Chapter 6, "Slavery and Womanhood: 'Assimilating woman to the slave is a mistake,'" distinguishes the aforementioned race/gender analogy from the slave/woman analogy (e.g., when Beauvoir portrays woman as enslaved by man, enslaved by domestic duties, and enslaved by the body's reproductive functions for the species, as well as her use of Hegel's master-slave dialectic as a theoretical framework for the subjugation of woman). I argue that Beauvoir's historical and metaphorical accounts of slavery do not adequately address racialized slavery. As a corrective, I examine critiques of her use of the slave/woman analogy while also taking seriously the lived experiences of enslaved Black women in the United States. Chapter 7, "Abolition and Suffrage Movements in the United States: 'They undertook a campaign in favor of blacks,'" takes up claims made by Alva Myrdal in "A Parallel to the Negro Problem" and by Beauvoir in *The Second Sex* about the abolition and suffrage movements in the United States. Both situate (white) women's early political engagements within the abolitionist movement and assert that white women fought for abolition only to be betrayed by Black men on the issue of suffrage. I argue that a more nuanced understanding of the abolition and suffrage movements in the United States is made possible when we shift from Myrdal's and Beauvoir's narratives (which center white women) to the counternarratives offered by Ida B. Wells, Angela Davis, bell hooks, and Paula Giddings (all of whom recover the leadership roles of Black women and men in the abolition and suffrage movements). These issues have been examined for decades but have reemerged with renewed interest and insight since the two-hundredth anniversary of woman's suffrage in the United States.

In Part III, "Frameworks Beyond the Black/white Binary," the final chapter takes up *The Second Sex* beyond the Black/white binary and US focus. Chapter 8, "The Coloniality of Gender and the Other Others: 'The category of *Other* is as original as consciousness itself," examines Beauvoir's analysis of the situation and oppression of "woman"—including the limits of biology, psychoanalysis, and historical materialism; her preference for an existential analysis; as well as history, facts, and myths that have contributed to woman's situation as Other. I examine Beauvoir's grand historical narratives about the oppression of the white Western woman juxtaposed with her problematic claims about Indians, Asians, Arabs, and Muslims. I argue that when Beauvoir explicitly takes up non-white, non-Western women in the text, this uptake is often presented through a colonial gaze and imaginary that seeks to lock these other Others into a perpetual primitive past, even in her present moment. I turn to insightful analyses of Beauvoir presented by Sally Markowitz (who critiques her orientalism) and Alia Al-Saji (who critiques her colonial tourist gaze and colonial dissonance). I also explore Kyoo Lee's more generous readings. And I take seriously Stephanie Rivera Berruz's critiques. Finally, I turn to the counter-narratives offered by María Lugones' analysis of the coloniality of gender and the importance of decolonial feminisms, as well as Oyèrónké Oyewùmí's critical analysis of colonialism and gender impositions from the West.

The conclusion, "Simone de Beauvoir: 'I think *The Second Sex* will seem like an old, dated book, after a while. But nonetheless . . . a book which will have made its contribution,'" takes up interviews with Beauvoir about *The Second Sex* and how her relationship to the text evolved over time (between 1974 and 1979). In a 1976 interview with John Gerassi ("Simone de Beauvoir: *The Second Sex* Twenty-Five Years Later") she acknowledges the limits of the text and says that if a project like that were to be done again it should be a collaborative effort with different women speaking from their own lived experiences and situations. Unfortunately, she goes on to undermine this important insight when she also asserts that Black women in America should be listening to white women instead of supporting Black men: "It is the same in America, where black women refused to listen to the women's liberation movement proselytizers because they were white. Such black women remained supportive of their black husbands despite the exploitation, simply because the person trying to make them aware of the exploitation were white."[96] Thus, in one of the few instances in which Beauvoir takes up Black women in the United States, she assumes we

26 BEAUVOIR AND BELLE

are ignorant of our own oppression and should be enlightened by white women liberators to raise our consciousness about our situation. I revisit Audre Lorde, specifically her "Open Letter to Mary Daly" and its implications for Beauvoir and *The Second Sex*. I also revisit identity politics and intersectionality as coalitional practices, return to Maria Lugones on decolonial feminisms and coalition, and conclude with Mariana Ortega's call for coalitional politics and a praxis of intersectional philosophy.

Notes

1. bell hooks, "True Philosophers: Beauvoir and bell," in *Simone de Beauvoir in Western Thought: Plato to Butler*, ed. Shannon M. Mussett and William S. Wilkerson (Albany, NY: SUNY Press, 2012). (Hereafter hooks 2012.)
2. bell hooks earned her doctorate in literature from University of California–Santa Cruz writing a dissertation on Toni Morrison.
3. hooks 2012, 233.
4. hooks 2012, 233. (Emphasis added.)
5. hooks 2012, 235.
6. *Le deuxième sexe* (1949) was initially published in France by Éditions in two volumes, *Le deuxième sexe: Les faits et les mythes* (Volume 1) and *Le deuxième sexe: L'experience vécue* (Volume 2). The text was translated to English as *The Second Sex* first in an abridged version by H. M. Parshley in 1952, followed by an unabridged version translated almost sixty years later by Constance Borde and Sheila Malovany-Chevallier in 2010. (Hereafter LDS and TSS.) Both translations have been critiqued. For more on these translations, see *"On ne naît pas femme: on le devient . . ." The Life of a Sentence* (2017), edited by Bonnie Mann and Martina Ferrari. The book is organized into four sections—Section I: "Intellectual History"; Section II: "History of Scandal"; Section III: "The Philosophers' Debate"; and Section IV: "The Labor of Translation." This robust collection of essays offers an invaluable contribution to scholarship on Beauvoir's most famous text. The contributors examine the philosophical and feminist implications of Beauvoir's most famous sentence in that text (*"On ne naît pas femme: on le devient . . ."*)—including the perceived consequences of translating the sentence with the indefinite article ("One is not born, but rather becomes, a woman") as Parshley does versus translating the sentence without the indefinite article ("One is not born, but rather becomes,

woman") as Borde and Malovany-Chevallier do. For a review of this text, see Kathryn Sophia Belle, review of *"On ne naît pas femme: on le devient . . ." The Life of a Sentence*, ed. Bonnie Mann and Martina Ferrari (Oxford: Oxford University Press, 2017), *Notre Dame Philosophical Review*, June 28, 2018, https://ndpr.nd.edu/news/on-ne-nait-pas-femme-on-le-deviant-the-life-of-a-sentence/.

7. Jean-Paul Sartre, *Carnets de la drôle de guerre* (Paris: Gallimard, 1983); *War Diaries: Notebooks from a Phony War 1939–40*, trans. Quintin Hoare (London: Verso, 1984).

8. Simone de Beauvoir, *Lettres à Sartre*, ed. Sylvie Le Bon de Beauvoir (Paris: Gallimard, 1990); *Letters to Sartre*, trans. Quintin Hoare (New York: Vintage Books, 1991).

9. Kate Fullbrook and Edward Fullbrook, *Simone de Beauvoir and Jean-Paul Sartre: The Remaking of a Twentieth Century Legend* (New York: Basic Books A Division of Harper Collins Publishers, 1994), 3.

10. It is important to note that Simons is a Beauvoir scholar who has taken seriously issues of race and influences by Black scholars like Richard Wright and W. E. B. Dubois. See also Simons, "Beauvoir and the Problem of Racism," in *Philosophers on Race: Critical Essays*, ed. Julie K. Ward and Tommy L. Lott (Malden, MA: Blackwell Publishers Ltd., 2001).

11. Margaret Simons, *Beauvoir and The Second Sex: Feminism, Race, and the Origins of Existentialism* (Lanham, MD: Rowman and Littlefield, 1999), 1–2. (Hereafter Simons 1999.)

12. Simons 1999, 2.

13. Simons 1999, xiv.

14. This is slowly beginning to change due in large part to the impact of scholars like Fullbrook, Simons, Bauer, Moi, Deutscher, and others over decades.

15. Margaret Simons, "Introduction" to *Simone de Beauvoir: Philosophical Writings*, ed. Margaret Simons and Marybeth Timmerman (Chicago: University of Illinois Press, 2004), 2. Simons also notes these influences: Bernard, Hegel, Fouillée, Husserl, Heidegger, 9. (Hereafter Simons and Timmerman 2004.)

16. *Simone de Beauvoir: Philosophical Writings*, ed. Margaret Simons and Marybeth Timmerman (2004); *Simone de Beauvoir: Diary of a Philosophy Student*, volume 1, *1926–1927*, ed. Barbara Klaw, Sylvie Le Bon Beauvoir, Margaret Simons and Marybeth Timmerman (2006); *Simone de Beauvoir: Wartime Diary*, ed. Margaret Simons (2008); *Simone de Beauvoir: Political Writings*, ed. Margaret Simons and Marybeth Timmerman (2012); *Simone de Beauvoir: "The Useless Mother" and Other*

28 BEAUVOIR AND BELLE

Literary Writings, ed. Margaret Simons and Marybeth Timmerman (2013); *Simone de Beauvoir: Feminist Writings*, ed. Margaret Simons and Marybeth Timmerman (2015); *Simone de Beauvoir: Diary of a Philosophy Student*, volume 2, *1928–1929*, ed. Barbara Klaw, Sylvie Le Bon Beauvoir, Margaret Simons, and Marybeth Timmerman (2019).

17. Nancy Bauer, *Simone de Beauvoir, Philosophy, and Feminism* (New York: Columbia University Press, 2001), 10. (Hereafter Bauer 2001.)

18. Bauer 2001,11.

19. Bauer 2001, 11.

20. Bauer 2001, 13.

21. Bauer 2001, 12.

22. Toril Moi, *Simone de Beauvoir: The Making of an Intellectual Woman* (Oxford: Oxford University Press, 2008), 89. (Hereafter Moi 2008.)

23. Moi 2008, 79.

24. Moi 2008, 95.

25. Moi 2008, 95.

26. Moi 2008, 202. (Moi places Luce Irigaray in this camp.)

27. Moi 2008, 202.

28. Moi 2008, 203.

29. Moi 2008, 203.

30. Moi 2008, 203.

31. Moi 2008, 207. *Les Temps Modernes* was founded in 1945. Contra Moi's claim, there were newspapers and journals in France and French colonies taking up issues of colonialism before and after *Les Temps Modernes* was founded: *La Dépêche africaine* (1928–1932); *L'estudiant noir* (1934), a literary review previously called *L'estudiant martiniquais*; *Légitime défense* (1932); *La Revue du monde noir* (1931–1932); *Tropiques (1941–1945)*. *Présence africaine* would come later (1947).

32. "Neglected by dominant political discourses, the subject of woman's oppression was, if anything, even more marginal in France than questions of colonialism and racism" (Moi 2008, 209).

33. Moi 2008, 209.

34. Meryl Altman, *Beauvoir in Time* (Leiden: Brill Rodopi, 2020). Many thanks to one of the anonymous readers of my book manuscript for bringing this text to my attention. (Hereafter Altman 2020.)

35. Altman 2020, 4.

36. Altman 2020, 158.

INTRODUCTION 29

37. Concerning epistemic violence, see Kristie Dotson, "Tracking Epistemic Violence, Tracking Practices of Silencing," *Hypatia* 26, no. 2 (Spring 2011), 236–257.

38. She attempts to pit Women of Color readers of *The Second Sex* against one another, praising Hansberry's positive reading while being dismissive of other Women of Color critiques. "In short, the question is whether *The Second Sex* speaks to women of color cannot have a single answer. That women of color have more standing than I do to answer is undisputable. But when those who have greater understanding speak and say opposite things, I must think for myself, white though I be" (Altman 2020, 157). And while Altman painstakingly offers block quotes and translations of *The Second Sex* throughout the book, when it comes to Lorraine Hansberry's reading of the text, rather than offering a close textual analysis of Hansberry, she simply advises readers to read the review for themselves. She states, "Frankly, I am finding it difficult not to quote the whole thing, not just because it supports my views about Beauvoir, but because it makes so painfully clear what a loss was for feminist theory ... But since you already own *Words of Fire* (don't you?) you can go and look for yourself" (Altman 2000, 157). It is also worth noting, contra Altman, that I highlight places where Hansberry offers different perspectives from Beauvoir on women's complicity. See Chapter 3 in this text.

39. See Sabine Broeck, "Re-reading de Beauvoir 'after Race': Woman-as-Slave Revisited," *International Journal of Francophone Studies* 14, nos. 1–2 (2011): 167–184. (Hereafter Broeck 2011.)

40. Moi 2008, 205–206.

41. Moi 2008, 205.

42. Moi 2008, 206.

43. Moi 2008, 207.

44. This is examined more closely by Frantz Fanon in *The Wretched of the Earth* and Jean-Paul Sartre in *Critique of Dialectical Reason*. See also Alistair Horne, *A Savage War of Peace: 1954–1962*.

45. Moi 2008, 208.

46. T. Denean Sharpley-Whiting, *Negritude Women* (Minneapolis: University of Minnesota Press, 2002), 14. (Hereafter Sharpley-Whiting 2002.)

47. Sharpley-Whiting 2002, 16.

48. Sharpley-Whiting 2002, 16. (Emphasis added.)

49. According to Sharpley-Whiting, "The masculinist genealogy constructed by the founding poets and shored up by literary historians, critics, and Africanist philosophers continues to elide and minimize the presence and

30 BEAUVOIR AND BELLE

contributions of French speaking black women to Negritude's evolution" (Sharpley-Whiting 2002, 14.) She later elaborates, "Nardal asserts clearly that Antillean women were the vanguard of the radicalized culture revolution that would later be called Negritude and identified as male-inspired and -forged. It was the women who recognized a need for racial solidarity, who had first experienced a veritable race consciousness" (Sharpley-Whiting 2002, 75).

50. Sharpley-Whiting notes, "Formerly known as *L'Estudiant martiniquais*, the Antillean organ of expression was rebaptized *L'Estudiant noir* in late 1934" (Sharpley-Whiting 2002, 1). She also notes that Paulette Nardal is "the only woman featured in its pages" (Sharpley-Whiting 2002, 4).

51. *La Revue du monde noir* was also circulated among and read by Black Americans in the United States including, for example, Anna Julia Cooper, whose archived papers at Howard University's Moorland-Springarn Center includes an original issue priced at 7 francs 50, or 30 cents US. The issue contains contributions including: "Race Equality" by Louis-Jean Finot, "The Creole Race" by Maître Jean-Louis, a poem by Claude McKay, and "A Negro Woman speaks at Cambridge and Geneva" by Paulette Nardal. This is just one example of the international connections and collaborations among Black women intellectuals throughout the African diaspora. Of course, these connection and collaborations were already evident insofar as Clara Shepard, a Black American woman fluent in English and French, served as one of the editors of the *Revue*.

52. Sharpley-Whiting 2002, 55. Finot was a novelist. His essay "Egalité des races" appears in the first issue of *La revue du monde noir*. I have not been able to find Finot's nationality. See also Gobineau's "L'Inegalité des races humaines" (1853–1855).

53. Social and intellectual interactions at salons (in the United States, France, and elsewhere) contributed to the development of race consciousness not only in the 1920s and 1930s through literary movements like the Harlem Renaissance, but also well into the 1940s and 1950s through the Negritude movement and historic meetings like the First International Congress of Black Writers and Artists in 1956 in Paris, France, and the Second International Congress of Black Writers and Artists in 1959 in Rome, Italy. These latter meetings were also significant insofar as they heightened awareness of the colonial condition and anticolonial resistance—not only among the colonized, but also among white European intellectuals.

54. Sharpley-Whiting 2002, 22.

INTRODUCTION 31

55. Sharpley-Whiting notes, "The sections of the newspaper titled 'La Dépêche politique,' 'La Dépêche économique et sociale,' and 'La Dépêche littéraire' owed their cultural and literary pan-*noirisme* to the global literacy of Mlles Jane and Paulette Nardal" (Sharpley-Whiting 2002, 37).

56. Surrealism has been emphasized in the writings of both Aimé and Suzanne Césaire. See Mickaella Perina's "Encountering the Other: Aesthetics, Race and Relationality," *Contemporary Aesthetics* 2 (2009): 1. See also T. Denean Sharpley-Whiting, "Tropiques and Suzanne Césaire: The Expanse of Negritude and Surrealism," in *Race and Racism in Continental Philosophy*, ed. Robert Bernasconi and Sybol Cook (Bloomington: Indiana University Press, 2003).

57. See Suzanne Césaire, "Léo Frobenius et le problém des civilisations," *Topiques* 1 (April 1941): 27–36; "Alain et esthétique," *Tropiques* 2 (July 1941): 53–61; "André Breton, poét" *Tropiques* 4 (January 1942): 31–37; "Misére d'une poésie: John Antoine-Nau," *Tropiques* 4 (January 1942): 48–50; "Malaise d'une civilisation," *Tropiques* 5 (April 1942): 43–49; "1943: Le Surréalisme et nous," *Tropiques* 8–9 (October 1943):14–18; "Le Grand camouflage," *Tropiques* 13–14 (September 1945):, 267–273. See also Anny Dominqiue Curtis' *Suzanne Césaire: Archéologie littéraire et artistique d'une mémoire empêchée* (Paris: Karthala, 2020). (Thanks to Jennifer Boiton for that last reference.)

58. See S. Césaire, "Le Grand camouflage," *Tropiques* 13–14 (September 1945): 271.

59. Sharpley-Whiting 2002, 15. Capécia won the Grandprix littéraire des Antilles in 1949. See also Frantz Fanon's *Peau noire, masques blancs* (Paris: Éditions du Seuil, 1952); *Black Skin, White Masks*, trans. Charles Lam Markmann (New York: Grove Press, 1967). See also Keja L. Valens, "Lost Idyll: Mayotte Capécia's Je suis martiniquaise," in *Desire Between Women in Caribbean Literature* (New York: Palgrave Macmillan, 2013).

60. Sharpley-Whiting notes, "Trying to ascertain whether these women were feminists in the American sense of the word is necessarily fraught with cultural complications, for féministe in the France and Martinique of 1920–1950, and even today, does not readily translate with the same 'engaged' nuances" (Sharpley-Whiting 2002, 22).

61. Sharpley-Whiting 2002, 76. Here she is exploring Paulette Nardal's reading of Robertre Horth's "Historie sans imporance" (published in *La revue du monde noir* 2, December 1931, 48–50), in P. Nardal's "L'Éveil de la conscience de race chez les étudiants noirs," *La Revue du monde noir* 6, April 1932, 30, which she also connects with Mayotte Capécia's *Je sues*

32 BEAUVOIR AND BELLE

Martiniquaise. Sharpley-Whiting notes, "Nardal again elaborated on the black feminine dimension of this newly found and celebrated race consciousness among French-speaking black intellectuals in the 1930s four years later, in the June 1936 interview-essay 'Black Paris,' with Eslanda Goode Robeson. In her chronicling of the evolution of race consciousness among women, Nardal describes the curious situation of black male privilege and black female circumspection in matters of race, sex, and class" (Sharpley-Whiting 2002, 77).

62. Jean-Paul Sartre, "Orphée Noir," in *Anthologie de la nouvelle poésie nègre et malgache de langue française* (Paris: Presses Universitaires de France, 1948), trans. John MacCombie in *The Massachusetts Review* (1965), reprinted with minor revisions as "Black Orpheus," in *Race*, ed. Robert Bernasconi (Boston: Blackwell Publishers, 2001). Frantz Fanon responded to "Orphée Noir," with "L'éxperience vécue du Noir," *Esprit* 19, no.179 (May 1951): 659–679, trans. Valentine Moulard, "The Lived Experience of the Black," in *Race*, ed. Robert Bernasconi (Boston: Blackwell Publishers, 2001). For more about the Negritude debate between Sartre and Fanon, see Kathryn Sophia Belle (formerly Kathryn T. Gines), "Sartre and Fanon Fifty Years Later: To Retain or Reject the Concept of Race" *Sartre Studies International* 9, no. 2 (2003): 55–67. See also Fanon's *The Wretched of the Earth* (New York: Grove Press, 1963).

63. Sharpley-Whiting 2002, 20. She adds, "Negritude may have been new to Sartre, but not to the *soeurs* Nardal and Suzanne Césaire" (NW, 20).

64. In *Beyond Negritude: Essays from Women in the City*, T. Denean Sharpley-Whiting notes, "Simone de Beauvoir and Paulette Nardal would have certainly found themselves circling about and through various cafes and seminars at the Sorbonne in the late 1920s. But unfortunately, the encounter seems not to have taken place" (Sharply-Whiting 2009, 17). She goes on to elaborate on their differences (Nardal's "social conservatism" and Catholicism contrasted with "Beauvoir's bohemian lifestyle and professed atheism") and well as some similarities ("both women recognized womanhood as a process of acculturation, adaptation, and in Nardal's case, assimilation") (Sharpley-Whiting 2009, 18). She adds, "Nardal and Beauvoir concur that women indeed become women, though Nardal embraces the idea of a 'feminine essence' as long as it does not impinge upon women's rights or enact gendered hierarchies" (Sharpley-Whiting 2009, 18).

65. Simone de Beauvoir, *L'Amérique au jour le jour* (Paris: Editions Gallimard, 1954), trans. Carole Cosman, *America Day By Day* (Berkeley: University of California Press, 1999). 38, 71. (Hereafter ADD.)

INTRODUCTION   33

66. ADD, 219. She would have been familiar with similar stereotypical representations of Black people in France and French colonies. Fanon critiques the French colonial "sho' good eatin'" ads in *Black Skin, White Masks*.

67. ADD, 224.

68. ADD, 240–241.

69. ADD, 240.

70. ADD, 240.

71. ADD, 242.

72. ADD, 242–243. To this she also notes, "Indeed, quite to the contrary among blacks themselves there's a prejudice in favor of individuals with light skin, which offers them opportunity for greater success" (ADD, 243). And also adds, "Almost all important black men are mulattos" (ADD, 243).

73. Beverly Guy Sheftall, ed., *Words of Fire: An Anthology of African American Feminist Thought* (New York: The New Press, 1995).

74. A few sample anthologies: Toni Cade Bambara, ed., *The Black Woman: An Anthology* (New York: Washington Square Press, 1970); Roseann P. Bell, Bettye J. Parker, and Beverly Guy Sheftall, eds., *Sturdy Black Bridges: Visions of Black Women in Literature* (New York: Anchor Books, 1979); Gloria T. Hull, Patricia Bell Scott, and Barbara Smith, eds., *All of the Women are White, All of the Blacks Are Men, But Some of Us Are Brave: Black Women's Studies* (New York: The Feminist Press, 1982). Also worth mentioning is the important primary source text by Gerda Lerner, *Black Women in White America: A Documentary History* (New York: New York Vintage Books, 1973). One example of Black feminist resources presented on other platforms includes Stephanie Evans', "The Black Women's Studies Booklist" (https://bwstbooklist.net).

75. Shirley Chen, "'To work, write, sing, and fight for woman's liberation': Proto-Feminist Currents in the American Left, 1946–1961" (BS Honors Thesis, University of Michigan, 2011), 78n21.

76. Lorraine Hansberry, "Simone de Beauvoir and *The Second Sex*: An American Commentary," in *Words of Fire: An Anthology of African American Feminist Thought*, ed. Beverly Guy Sheftall (New York: The New Press, 1995).

77. Angela Davis, "Reflections on the Black Woman's Role in the Community of Slaves," *The Black Scholar* 3, no. 2 (December 1971): 2–15.

78. Audre Lorde, "The Masters Tools Will Never Dismantle the Master's House," in *Sister Outsider: Essays and Speeches by Audre Lorde* (Freedom: The Crossing Press, 1984), 113.

34 BEAUVOIR AND BELLE

79. Simone de Beauvoir, *The Ethics of Ambiguity* (New York: Kensington Publishing Group, 1948), 9.

80. Chikwenye Ogunyemi, "Womanism: The Dynamics of the Contemporary Black Female Novel in English," *Signs: Journal of Women in Culture and Society* 11, no. 1 (Autumn 1985): 63–80.

81. Deborah King, "Multiple Jeopardy, Multiple Consciousness: The Context of a Black Feminist Ideology," *Signs: Journal of Women in Culture and Society* 14, no. 1 (Autumn 1988): 42–72.

82. Oyèrónké Oyewùmí, "Family Bonds/Conceptual Binds: African Notes on Feminist Epistemologies," *Signs: Journal of Women in Culture and Society* 25, no. 4 (Summer 2000): 1093–1098, 1094.

83. Judith Wilson, "One Way or Another: Black Feminist Visual Theory," in *The Feminism and Visual Culture Reader*, ed. Amelia Jones (New York: Routledge, 2003), 20. Wilson considers parallels between Frantz Fanon's *Black Skin, White Masks* and Beauvoir's *The Second Sex*, noting, "Both were 'Others" who'd stolen white patriarchal fire to blaze liberatory trails" (ibid, 20). Wilson adds, "While each has been usefully critiqued in recent years, their radical impact remains my benchmark for the critical potential for 'theory'" (ibid, 20). I would like to acknowledge and thank Black visual culture scholar Jasmine Cobb for bringing this article by Judith Wilson to my attention.

84. Mariana Ortega, "Phenomenological Encuentros: Existential Phenomenology and Latin American & U.S. Latina Feminism," *Radical Philosophy Review* 9, no. 1 (2006): 45–64. (Hereafter Ortega 2006.)

85. Kathy Glass, "Calling All Sisters: Continental Philosophy and Black Feminist Thinkers," in *Convergences: Black Feminism and Continental Philosophy*, ed. Maria del Guadalupe Davidson, Kathryn Sophia Belle (formerly Kathryn T. Gines) and Donna Dale Marcano (New York: SUNY Press, 2010).

86. Kathryn Sophia Belle (formerly Kathryn T. Gines), "Sartre, Beauvoir, and the Race/Gender Analogy: A Case for Black Feminist Philosophy," in *Convergences: Black Feminism and Continental Philosophy*, ed. Maria Davidson, Kathryn Sophia Belle (formerly Kathryn T. Gines), and Donna Dale Marcano (New York: SUNY, 2010), 35–51; "Comparative and Competing Frameworks of Oppression in Simone de Beauvoir's *The Second Sex*," in *Graduate Faculty Philosophy Journal* 35, nos. 1–2 (2014): 251–273; and "Simone de Beauvoir and the Race/Gender Analogy Revisited," in *Blackwell Companion to Beauvoir*, ed. Nancy Bauer and Laura Hengehold (Hoboken: Wiley-Blackwell, 2017).

INTRODUCTION 35

87. bell hooks, "True Philosophers: Beauvoir and bell," in *Simone de Beauvoir in Western Thought: Plato to Butler*, ed. Shannon M. Mussett and William S. Wilkerson (Albany: SUNY Press, 2012).

88. Sharon Patricia Holland, *The Erotic Life of Racism* (Durham: Duke University Press, 2012).

89. Kyoo Lee, "Should My Bum Look Bigger in This?—Re-Dressing the Beauvoirian Femme," *Women's Studies Quarterly* 41, no. 1/2 (Spring/Summer 2012): 184–193. See also Lee, "Second Languaging *The Second Sex*, Its Conceptual Genius: A Translingual Contemporazation of '*On ne naît pas femme: on le devient*," in *Blackwell Companion to Beauvoir*, ed. Nancy Bauer and Laura Hengehold (Hoboken: Wiley-Blackwell, 2017).

90. Kyoo Lee, "Why Asian Female Stereotypes Matter to All: Beyond Black and White, East and West," *Critical Philosophy of Race* 1, no. 1 (2013): 86–103, here 88.

91. Stephanie Rivera Berruz, "Ressenha: GINES, Kathryn T.—Sartre, Beauvoir, and the Race/Gender Analogy: A Case for Black Feminist Philosophy," in *Sapere Aude*, Belo Horizonte, v. 3, n. 6, p. 504–507—2° semester 2012—ISSN 2177-6342), page 506.

92. Stephanie Rivera Berruz, "At the Crossroads: Latina Identity and Simone de Beauvoir's *The Second Sex*," *Hypatia* 31, no. 2 (2016): 319–333.

93. Céline Leboef, "'One is not born, but rather becomes, a woman': The Sex-Gender Distinction and Simone de Beauvoir's Account of Woman: *The Second Sex*," in *Feminist Movements: Reading Feminist Texts*, ed. Katherine Smits and Susan Bruce (London: Bloomsbury Academic, 2016).

94. Patricia Hill Collins, "Simone de Beauvoir, Woman's Oppression and Existential Freedom," in *Blackwell Companion to Beauvoir*, ed. Nancy Bauer and Laura Hengehold (Hoboken, NJ: Wiley-Blackwell, 2017).

95. Alia Al-Saji, "Material Life: Bergsonian Tendencies in Simone de Beauvoir's Philosophy," in *Differences: Rereading Beauvoir and Irigary*, ed. Emily Anne Parker and Anne can Leeuwen (New York: Oxford University Press, 2018).

96. John Gerassi, "Simone de Beauvoir: *The Second Sex* Twenty-Five Years Later," *Society* 13, no. 2 (January–February 1976): 79–85, 84.

PART I
BLACK FEMINIST FRAMEWORKS

1

A Select Genealogy of Black Feminist Frameworks for Identities and Oppressions

"If we are not careful the work we are doing now is going to have to be 'rediscovered' at some point"

"Let's face it. I am a marked woman, but not everybody knows my name."[1] Thus begins Hortense Spillers' groundbreaking article "Mama's Baby, Papa's Maybe: An American Grammar Book" (1987), in which she describes "the African-American female's misnaming," "gender 'undecidability,'" and "the lack of integrity of the male/female gender."[2] Almost two decades later (in 2006) Spillers has a conversation with Saidiya Hartman, Farah Jasmine Griffin, Shelly Eversley, and Jennifer L. Morgan about the impact of her article, as well as some of her motivations and intentions for writing it. Spillers explains, "What I was trying to do when I wrote that essay many years ago was to find a vocabulary that would make it possible, and not all by myself, to make a contribution to a larger project."[3] One of the projects that she has in mind is feminism or taking seriously what it means for Black women to enter into—or, perhaps better stated, to be recognized as interlocutors in—conversations about feminism. Spillers elaborates, "And so my idea was to try to generate a discourse, or a vocabulary that would not just make it desirable, but would necessitate that black women be in the conversation."[4] She is clear about the necessity of creating such discourses and vocabularies, as well as the challenges of trying to preserve them. Spillers warns, "if we are not careful the work we are doing now is going to have to be 'rediscovered' at some point . . . people are going to have to keep doing it again, or rediscover it again, or reassert it because the forces of opposition are so forceful and so powerful

Beauvoir and Belle. Kathryn Sophia Belle, Oxford University Press. © Oxford University Press 2024.
DOI: 10.1093/oso/9780197660195.003.0002

40 BEAUVOIR AND BELLE

and they are always pushing against us, they always want to enforce forgetfulness."[5]

Returning to the import of creating vocabularies that articulate our experiences, Morgan responds, "There are people across the academy who are looking for that vocabulary, and that's why the essay speaks so powerfully across so many fields and to such a wide variety of those of us who are working to confront the violence of the past and in our fields."[6] Notice that Morgan uses the present tense "are looking" and not the past tense "were looking" to describe those in search of that vocabulary. To this, Griffin adds, "In many ways I think that the project of 'Mama's Baby, Papa's Maybe' is successful because it did become a work that we did not have to do again. 'Mama's Baby, Papa's Maybe' gave us a vocabulary."[7] This discussion provides an important reference point for the imperative to examine the historical and philosophical contexts of Black feminist frameworks for identities and oppressions, thereby laying claim to our lineage of creating discourses and vocabularies to express our existence and experience. As my daughter once wrote on the wall of my sister's apartment at the age of four or five: KYRA HAS BEEN HERE. It was Kyra's own written record of her presence in that space and time, a declaration of the significance of that fact, and her desire to share that with a Black woman she loved and admired—her amazing aunt Tiffani Jenae Johnson.

In this chapter, I offer a selective (not exhaustive) genealogy of Black feminist frameworks for identity and oppression that underscores the creation of Black matrilineal discourses and vocabularies that express our existence and experience.[8] My attentiveness to these critical discourses and vocabularies lays the groundwork for the chapters that follow by offering an account of the historical and philosophical developments of Black women as thinkers, speakers, writers, and political actors with dynamic legacies, traditions, and innovations that have persisted despite the aforementioned forces of opposition that want to enforce forgetfulness. Black women continually bring new energy and new ideas that create necessary change and facilitate growth. We are living participants in and witnesses to Octavia Butler's declaration, "All that you touch you change. All that you change changes you. The only lasting truth is change. God is Change." We must also remember Ntozake Shange's declaration, "i found god in myself and i

SELECT GENEALOGY OF BLACK FEMINIST FRAMEWORKS 41

loved her. i loved her fiercely." May we continue to touch truth and embrace change as we repeatedly return to ourselves, constantly finding God there, and always fiercely loving Her.

The chapter is organized temporally into broad sections focusing on "The Eighteenth Century" (Lucy Terry and Phillis Wheatley), "The Nineteenth Century" (Maria Stewart, Sojourner Truth, Anna Julia Cooper, and Ida B. Wells), "The First Half of the Twentieth Century" (Fannie Barrier Williams, Mary Church Terrell, "The Colored Woman's Statement to the Women's Missionary Council, American Missionary Association," Sadie Tanner Mossell Alexander, Ella Baker and Marvel Cooke, Louise Thompson, Esther Cooper, and Claudia Jones), and then "The Second Half of the Twentieth Century" (Pauli Murray, Francis Beale, Barbara Smith, Beverly Smith, Demita Frazier, and Kimberlé Crenshaw). I argue that Black women have a matrilineal legacy of creating discourses and vocabularies that express our existence and experience going back to Lucy Terry and Phillis Wheatley (in the context of eighteenth-century colonial America), and furthermore, that Black women have been offering what I would now characterize as feminist frameworks for identity and oppression going back to Maria Stewart in the early nineteenth century (1831) continuing until today. My evidence is a broad overview of the aforementioned figures from Lucy Terry's 1746 poem "Bars Fight" to Kimberlé Crenshaw's "Demarginalizing the Intersection of Race and Sex: A Black Feminist Critique of Antidiscrimination Doctrine, Feminist Theory and Antiracist Politics" (1989) and "Mapping the Margins: Intersectionality, Identity Politics, and Violence Against Women of Color" (1991).

The Eighteenth Century

Before the United States became the United States (i.e., before the Declaration of Independence of thirteen colonies from the British empire on July 4, 1776), young girls kidnapped from Africa and enslaved in colonial America had already been thinking, writing, and publishing in a land that was not their motherland and a language that was not their mother tongue. It has been argued that the birth of a

42 BEAUVOIR AND BELLE

Black literary tradition during the colonial period is to be traced back to Lucy Terry (Prince) (1730?–1821) and Phillis Wheatley (Peters) (1753?–1784)—an infant and a young child stolen from Africa and sold into slavery in North America. Ann Allen Shockley puts into perspective the historical context out of which these young Black teenage girls created poems in a new tongue and against insurmountable odds when she posits, "No doubt, there were among the terrified African women, estranged forever from their home, many muses whose words would never be heard, silenced forever by enforced illiteracy, the lash, and death."[9] Despite these treacherous circumstances facing Black girls and women in colonial America, Shockley notes, "Fortunately two of these early stolen females, Lucy Terry and Phillis Wheatley, managed to speak and write, becoming the first black female poets and inaugurating Afro-American literature," and I would add, African-American philosophy.[10]

Thought to be born in 1730 (she was kidnapped from Africa as an infant and sold into slavery in Rhode Island), Lucy Terry was only about sixteen years old when she composed her 1746 poem "Bars Fight" about an ambush that took place in Deerfield, MA.[11] It was preserved orally for over a century before appearing in print posthumously for the first time in 1854.[12] In addition to making history with this poem, Nafissa Thompson-Spires notes that "Lucy litigated before the Vermont supreme court, making her the first woman—and Black woman—to argue before the court and to win her case at that."[13] Furthermore, Lucy would plead a case on behalf of her son, who was denied admission to Williams College on the basis of his color, though she would not be as successful in that case before the trustees as she had been with the state supreme court. Thompson-Spires observes, "each of Terry Prince's seeming transgressions against the expectations of her gender and her race . . . might equally resituate her within them . . . Terry Prince demonstrates the performative dexterity often required of African American women across history to survive, to avoid singing the backlash blues."[14]

Thought to be born in 1753 (her age estimated by the Wheatley family at the time they purchased her in Boston, MA, in 1761), Phillis Wheatly would have been about fourteen years old when her first published

SELECT GENEALOGY OF BLACK FEMINIST FRAMEWORKS 43

poem, "On Messrs. Hussey and Coffin," appeared in the *Newport* [Rhode Island] *Mercury* in 1767.[15] Alexis Pauline Gumbs explains that Wheatley appended a note to the poem for the printer indicating that it was "composed by a Negro Girl."[16] And Gumbs goes on to assert, "we could read this first published poem, about almost dying at sea, and the note that contextualizes it as the first act of Black speculative writing in English in the Americas."[17] Of course, Wheatley was the first Black person of any gender and the second woman (though it bears repeating that Wheatley was still a teenage girl at the time) to publish a book of poems when her collection, *Poems on Various Subjects, Religious and Moral*, was published in London in 1773.[18]

Henry Louis Gates, Jr., provides some background that helps to situate the publication of this poetry collection. In 1772, Wheatley was orally examined by "eighteen of Boston's most notable citizens" who assembled "to question closely the African adolescent on the slender sheaf of poems that she claimed to have 'written by herself.'"[19] After being subjected to this oral examination and successfully replying to their queries, the group would go on to attest that Wheatley was, in fact, the author of her poems. Published as a preface to the collection, Gates notes that their "Attestation" describes "Phillis" as "a young Negro Girl, who but a few years since, brought an uncultivated Barbarian from *Africa*, and has ever since been, and now is, under the Disadvantage of serving as a Slave in a Family in this town."[20] And therein lay some of the complexities of being a Black girl philosopher who thinks and writes and speaks, despite her enslaved status. In Wheatley's case these complexities included: learning to speak, read, and write in new languages for her (e.g., English, Latin, and Greek) while still performing forced domestic labor, initially being denied publication (publishers in the colonies did not want to publish the writings of an African girl), then having her credibility and legibility (for the publishers in London and for her future international reading audience) to hinge on an oral qualifying examination—the success of which results in her examiners attesting to her ability to write this collection of poems *despite* her assumed uncultivated, barbarian, African origins, and even in the face of the ongoing disadvantages (to be sure an understatement) of her being enslaved!

44 BEAUVOIR AND BELLE

The Nineteenth Century

There is a long Black feminist philosophical tradition of articulating analyses of multifaceted identity and oppression on the basis of race, class, and gender. Going into the nineteenth century, from pre-emancipation to post-emancipation and reconstruction/post-reconstruction, we begin to see several guiding threads in Black women's speeches and writings about these issues, including: (1) an emphasis on the racial and gendered aspects of Black women's identities, (2) a distinction of Black women's situations from Black men's as well as from white women's and men's, and (3) an emphasis on intersecting identities *and* intersecting oppressions (especially related to racism, sexism, and class oppression, but also at times with attentiveness to heterosexism connected to sexual identity), as well as an emphasis on agency and action. Following Beverly Guy-Sheftall's approach in *Words of Fire: An Anthology of African-American Feminist Thought* (1995), I frequently begin with Maria W. Stewart to explore Black feminist frameworks of identities and oppressions that would lay the groundwork for the creation of vocabularies like "triple oppression," "interlocking oppressions," and "intersectionality" in the twentieth century.[21]

Maria W. Stewart (1803–1879) has been identified as the first woman in the United States to speak to an audience of both men and women in public, and furthermore as America's first Black woman political writer.[22] In her published speech "Religion and the Pure Principles of Morality, The Sure Foundation on Which We Must Build" (1831), Stewart critiques *racism* (namely, the systematic subjugation and assumed inferiority of Blacks) and *sexism* (the unequal treatment of women, paternalism of men, and inconsistent constructions of femininity).[23] Recognizing these dual oppressions faced by Black women, Stewart encourages "the fair daughters of Africa" to awake, arise, distinguish themselves, and unite in support of one another. In addition to race and gender oppression, Stewart is also critical of class oppression, underscoring the exploitation of Black women's labor and encouraging the practice of cooperative economics to gain financial independence.[24] In this way she is naming what would later be called the triple oppressions of racism, sexism, and classism. But she also

SELECT GENEALOGY OF BLACK FEMINIST FRAMEWORKS   45

takes seriously agency and corresponding action. Stewart calls for the intellectual development and economic empowerment of Black girls and women to build churches and schools in the community. She advises: "Possess the spirit of men, bold and enterprising, fearless and undaunted. Sue for your rights and privileges. Know the reason you cannot attain them."[25] In another lecture delivered at Franklin Hall in 1832, Stewart again points to the negative forces of race, gender, and class prejudice—specifically the ways that these forms of discrimination limit young Black girls and women to servile labor, despite the other qualities and characteristics they possess. Noting the different experiences of womanhood, she asserts that while Black women have had to labor and toil, many white women's hands have been "unsoiled" and their muscles are "unstrained."[26] These published speeches are central to Stewart's activism and campaigning against multiple systems of oppression. Marilyn Richardson asserts that we find in Stewart's writings "indeed a triple consciousness, as she demonstrates the creative struggle of a woman attempting to establish both a literary voice and an historical mirror for her experience as 'an American, a Negro,' and a woman."[27]

Sojourner Truth (1797–1883) was born in New York, where she was enslaved until 1827. Unlike Stewart, Truth did not leave behind published letters, essays, and speeches of her own writing.[28] She is perhaps best known through her famous slave narrative (*Narrative of Sojourner Truth; a bondswoman of the olden time, emancipated by the New York Legislature in the early part of the present century; with a history of her labors and correposndance drawn from her "Book of Life"*), Harriett Beecher Stowe's "Libyan Sibyl," and more recently Nell Irvin Painter's biography.[29] There is controversy surrounding the words that have been attributed to Truth, from the use of the refrain "Ar'n't I am Woman?" to the famous "Frederick, is God dead?" line, but multiple accounts have made it clear that Truth was an amazing orator who leveraged her lived experiences to impact her audience. She made frequent appearances on the lecture circuit for both race and gender organizations fighting for the abolition of slavery and for women's suffrage. She argued for universal suffrage (for women and the enslaved), making space to advocate for voting rights for Black women who occupied both categories.[30] Described by Beverly Guy-Sheftall as "the

46 BEAUVOIR AND BELLE

person most responsible for linking abolition and women's rights, and demonstrating the reality of Black women's gender and race identities,"[31] Truth interrupted representations of "woman" as exclusively white and of "Black" as only male. Painter identifies triple identities and oppressions when she presents Truth as "the embodiment of the need to reconstruct an American history that is sensitive simultaneously to race, class, and gender."[32]

Moving from the early (1830s) and mid- (1850s) to the late (1890s) nineteenth century, we have the publication of Anna Julia Cooper's (1858/9–1964) *A Voice from the South* (1892).[33] An educator, scholar, and clubwoman, Cooper was active in fighting against racism and sexism—for example co-founding the Colored Women's League in 1894 in Washington, DC, and participating in the Pan African Congress in London in 1900. Like Stewart, Cooper examines not only the roles of women as mothers and educators, but also their responsibilities outside of the home as contributors to debates about economic and political issues. One of her more frequently cited quotes comes from "The Status of Woman in America," where Cooper declares, "The colored woman of to-day occupies, one may say, a unique position in this country . . . She is confronted by both a woman question and a race problem, and is as yet an unknown or an unacknowledged factor in both."[34] In "My Racial Philosophy" Cooper underscores the interconnectedness of race and gender prejudices, particularly for Black women. Analyzing the roles of both race and gender in constructing identities and oppressive systems, Cooper asserts, "the whips and stings of prejudice, whether of color or sex, find me neither too calloused to suffer, nor too ignorant to know what is due me."[35] On the one hand, Cooper contends, "When I encounter brutality I need not always charge it to my race," while on the other, she is clear that it is wrong to imagine "that oppression goes only with color."[36] Thus, brutality and oppression manifest neither always nor only as racism, but also as sexism.

In "What Are We Worth?" Cooper takes up race, gender, and class, offering statistics on Black schools (including early childhood development centers, colleges, and universities) as well as teachers, ministers, and other professionals (e.g., doctors and lawyers) to make the case for the "unassisted effort of the colored people for self-development."[37]

SELECT GENEALOGY OF BLACK FEMINIST FRAMEWORKS 47

She also provides statistics on the high mortality rates, the economic disempowerment of share-cropping systems, and the limited housing opportunities among Black Americans. Cooper describes the white labor unions of the North as tyrannical while also noting that their working conditions are far more preferable to those of Black men working for fifty cents per day in the fields. She also pays special attention to the exploitation of Black women as domestic laborers, "the pinched and down-trodden colored women bending over wash-tubs and ironing boards—with children to feed and house rent to pay, wood to buy, soap and starch to furnish—lugging home weekly great baskets of clothes for families who pay them for a month's laundrying barely enough to purchase a substantial pair of shoes."[38] Cooper would continue to teach and write well into the twentieth century.

Ida B. Wells (Barnett) (1862–1931) is another scholar, educator, race woman, and clubwoman who confronted gender and racial oppression. Wells fought against racial segregation in transportation (she successfully sued the railroad in Tennessee, though the case was overturned by the Supreme Court) and in education (as an educator and journalist, she wrote articles condemning the deplorable conditions of segregated schools). Furthermore, she was among the founding members of the National Association for the Advancement of Colored People.[39] Wells' anti-lynching activism brought global awareness to the horrors of lynching in the United States.[40] Articles in *Memphis Free Speech* (the paper she edited and co-owned) along with publications like *Southern Horrors: Lynch Law in All Its Phases* (1892), *A Red Record* (1895), and *Mob Rule in New Orleans* (1900) demonstrates Wells' insights into lynching in America as a political issue with race, class, and gender implications. She documented the fact that the victims of lynching included Black women and children, not exclusively Black men. By meticulously researching and recording the numerous cases of lynching in the United States, Wells argued that many lynch victims were attacked for their economic status, political activism, and/or resistance to white supremacy—debunking the prevailing myth that the only victims of lynching were Black men being accused of raping white women. Taking up the race, class, and gendered dynamics of segregation of train cars, she notes: "White men pass through these 'colored cars' and ride in them whenever they feel inclined to do so, but no colored woman however refined, well educated or well dressed may ride in the ladies, or first class coach, in any of these states unless she is a nurse-maid traveling with a white child." In addition to her anti-lynching and anti-segregation activism, Wells was at the forefront of controversy surrounding the 1893 World's Columbian Exposition.[41] Like Cooper, Wells would continue to write and organize well into the twentieth century.

First Half of the Twentieth Century

In the early twentieth century in the United States, there was an increase of anti-Black violence in the form of lynching, continuing sexual and economic exploitation of Black girls and women (especially but not exclusively domestic workers), as well as an ongoing push for voting rights for Black people (men and women) and white women. Fannie Barrier Williams (1855–1944) was born in New York and educated in the arts. She achieved many "firsts" in her lifetime as a Black woman and, like Wells, was active in suffrage activism and the Black Women's Club Movement. Williams also helped with the founding of the National Association for the Advancement of Colored People and is credited with successfully advocating for Black representation at the aforementioned World's Columbian Exposition in Chicago, where she presented two addresses ("The Intellectual Progress of the Colored Women in the United States" and "What Can Religion Do to Advance the Condition of the American Negro?"). In her 1904 essay "A Northern Negro's Autobiography," Williams is attentive to the intersections of race, gender, and class in her analysis of the ongoing impact of the brutalities of slavery. More specifically, she describes how Black girls and women were unprotected targets of sexual exploitation that persisted long after emancipation, especially among Black domestic workers in white homes.[42] Noting Black mothers' inability to protect their daughters, and suggesting that white women are complicit with their husbands' actions, Williams states, "Their own mothers cannot protect them and white women will not, or do not."[43]

SELECT GENEALOGY OF BLACK FEMINIST FRAMEWORKS   49

She concludes on a somber note, "I dare not cease to hope and aspire and believe in human love and justice, but progress is painful and my faith is often strained to the breaking point."[44]

Mary Church Terrell (1863–1954), also a leading race woman, club woman, suffragist, and anti-lynching activist, helped found the National Association of Colored Women with the famous motto, "Lifting as we climb." And like Williams, Terrell was also a founding member of the National Association for the Advancement of Colored People. As late as 1950, in her late eighties, she was still fighting to challenge discrimination by protesting racial segregation in restaurants in Washington, DC. But decades earlier, Terrell wrote an article titled, "Lynching from a Negro's Point of View" (1904). The essay was written in part as a requested response to Thomas Nelson Page's problematic article, "The Lynching of Negroes—Its Cause and Its Prevention" (1904), in which he resorts to negative stereotypes and propaganda about Black men, what Angela Davis would later describe as "The Myth of the Black Male Rapist."[45] Expressing sentiments about Black life and Black death that are just as pertinent today as when the article was first published, Terrell notes, "Hanging, shooting and burning black men, women and children in the United State have become so common that such occurrences create but little sensation and evoke but slight comment now."[46] She implicitly disrupts the myth of the Black male rapist as the motivation for lynching by identifying women and children as fellow victims of the heinousness of lynching. And she goes on to explicitly identify several false assumptions among white people about lynching:

> In the first place, it is a great mistake to suppose that rape is the real cause of lynching in the South"; "In the second place, it is a mistake to suppose that the negro's desire for social equality sustains any relation whatsoever to the crime of rape"; "The third error on the subject of lynching consists of the widely circulated statement that the moral sensibilities of the best negroes in the United States are so stunted and dull, and the standard of morality among even the leaders of the race is so low, that they do not appreciate the enormity and heinousness of rape.[47]

50 BEAUVOIR AND BELLE

Terrell reminds readers that the KKK has been terrorizing Black people with violence since emancipation; that even in cases in which a Black man may have actually raped a white woman, he had never heard of or experienced social equality—and furthermore if "social equality" is a euphemism for rape, then it "was originated by white masters of slave women"; and finally, that "only those who are densely ignorant . . . would accuse thousands of reputable men and women of sympathizing with rapists, either black or white, or of condoning their crime."[48] And if white people are genuinely troubled by sexual assault, then where is the outrage about the violations against Black girls and women by white men? Bringing visibility to the Black girls and women whose experiences are concealed by the myth of Black men raping white women, Terrell notes, "Throughout their entire period of bondage colored women were debauched by their masters. From the day they were liberated to the present time, prepossessing young colored girls have been protected neither by public sentiment nor by law . . . White men are neither punished [for invading the Negro's home], nor lynched for violating colored women and girls."[49] According to Terrell, there are two key causes of lynching: race hatred and lawlessness in the aftermath of slavery. And like Williams, Terrell underscores the complicity and collaboration of white women in the institution of slavery and the practice of lynching, which is a byproduct of slavery.[50] She issues a call to action for white women to choose differently this time, "what a mighty foe to mob violence Southern white women might be, if they would arise in the purity and power of their womanhood to implore their fathers, husbands and sons no longer to stain their hands with the black man's blood."[51]

We also find similar articulations of multiple oppressions and an explicit call to solution-oriented action later in the co-authored document "The Colored Women's Statement to the Women's Missionary Council, American Missionary Association" (1919).[52] The statement opens with an overview of broader issues for context, namely, "the many unjust and humiliating practices of which colored women of the South have been the victims."[53] From there the statement calls for coalitional action from white women. The co-authors state, we "call to the attention of white women certain conditions which affect colored women in their relations with white people, and which,

SELECT GENEALOGY OF BLACK FEMINIST FRAMEWORKS   51

if corrected, will go far toward decreasing friction, removing distrust and suspicion, and creating a better atmosphere in which to adjust the difficulties which always accompany human contacts."[54] They go on to identify concrete problems in several core areas: domestic service, child welfare, conditions of travel, education, lynching, suffrage, and press. They also offer viable recommendations for corrective measures including regulation of domestic labor, childcare facilities, equal travel accommodations, vocal protests from white women against lynching, support from white women for suffrage for all citizens, and for white women to correct false reporting about Black people in the white press of the South.

(Gertrude) Elise Johnson McDougald (Ayer) (1885–1971) worked as an educator and journalist. In "The Double Task: The Struggle of Negro Women for Sex and Race Emancipation" (written for Alain Locke's *Survey Graphic* in 1925), McDougald argues that Black women are not a monolithic group and identifies various forms of race, gender, and class oppressions operating together and with which Black women have to contend simultaneously. She points to a plethora of problems confronting Black women, from what Patricia Hill Collins would later call controlling images and stereotypes (e.g., "the grotesque Aunt Jemimas" or the mammy), to dominant standards of beauty, to economic hardships and poor working conditions. McDougald enumerates several groups of Black women working outside of the home,

> First, comes a very small leisure group—the wives and daughters of men who are in business, in the professions and a few well-paid personal service occupations. Second, a most active and progressive group, the women in business and the professions. Third, the many women in the trades and industry. Fourth, a group weighty in numbers struggling on in domestic service, with an even less fortunate fringe of casual workers, fluctuating with the economic temper of the times.[55]

Naming the interconnections among multiple oppressions, she asserts, "Like women in general, but more particularly like those of other oppressed minorities, the Negro woman has been forced to submit to

52   BEAUVOIR AND BELLE

over-powering conditions. Pressure has been exerted upon her, both from without and within her group."[56] Thus, McDougald clarifies differences between the situation of women in general and the situation of oppressed minorities in particular, while highlighting the intergroup and intra-group pressures placed upon Black women along the lines of race, class, and gender.

Economist and lawyer Sadie Tanner Mossell Alexander (1898–1989) was a graduate of M Street High School (1915) in Washington, DC, and then went on to study at the University of Pennsylvania, where she graduated from the College of Education in 1918 and then earned an MA in 1919 before becoming the first Black American woman to earn a PhD in economics in the United States. Like McDougald, Alexander is writing during the New Negro movement, but Alexander nuances frameworks of novelty of that time, noting, "In my opinion there is no more a new woman among us than there is a new Negro."[57] For Alexander, it is not woman who is changing, but rather her status in a new social order marked by the mechanical age, or the Industrial Revolution. She analyzes the triple oppressions of race, gender, and class by examining Black women's wages in "Negro Women in Our Economic Life" (1930). Supporting her arguments with statistical data, Alexander explains, "The wages of all women in industry have been found to be below that of men. It is not surprising, therefore, to find that the wages of Negro women, who are the marginal workers, should not only be lower than that of men employed in like pursuits, but also lower than that of white women."[58] Considering both wages and types of employment, she notes, "Not only are the wages of Negro women lower than those of white women, but Negro women as a whole are confined to the simpler types of work, and are not engaged in highly skilled labor, although many of the occupations in which Negro women are found require care and a number require some skill."[59] She asserts that improving the condition of Black women workers improves the conditions of all workers.

Each of these early Black feminists (Stewart, Truth, Cooper, Wells, Williams, Terrell, McDougald, and Alexander, along with many others)—identifies and combats racism and sexism not as separate categories of identity and oppression, but as interconnected systems that present different problems for Black women insofar as we

SELECT GENEALOGY OF BLACK FEMINIST FRAMEWORKS   53

experience them simultaneously and differently than do white women and/or Black men—all this while also being attentive to the nuances of class oppression across race and gender categories. This Black feminist tradition of articulating multiple identities and oppressions continues into the 1930s, when the triple-oppression thesis is explicitly articulated.

Ella Baker (1903–1986) and Marvel Cooke (1903–2000) published an article on "The Bronx Slave Market" in *The Crisis: A Record of the Darker Races* in November 1935. They argued that the street corners of The Bronx functioned as slave auction blocks where Black women were assessed and selected to perform domestic labor for white and Jewish middle-class housewives. The co-authors assert, "the Simpson avenue block exudes the stench of the slave market at its worst. Not only is human labor bartered and sold for a slave wage, but human love is also a marketable commodity."[60] Here they are referring to domestic work and sex work. Baker and Cooke explain the circumstances that gave rise to these exploitative conditions quite succinctly, "Paradoxically, the crash of 1929 brought to the domestic labor market a new employer class. The lower middle-class housewife, who, having dreamed of the luxury of a maid, found opportunity staring her in the face in the form of Negro women pressed to the wall by poverty, starvation and discrimination."[61]

They talk to some of the women being exploited who are well aware of the institutional structures working against them. Baker and Cooke make the case that the women need to be organized to be in a position to demand higher wages. They cite the head of an employment agency contrasting the slave-like conditions of these domestic laborers with chattel slavery, "The well-meaning employment agencies endeavoring to obtain respectable salaries and suitable working conditions for deserving domestics are finding it increasingly difficult due to the menace and obstacles presented by the slavish performances of the lower types of domestics themselves who, unlike the original slaves who recoiled from meeting their masters, rush to meet their mistresses."[62] Baker and Cooke identify the following core issues:

> The roots, then of The Bronx Slave Market spring from: (1) the general ignorance and apathy towards organized labor action; (2) the

54 BEAUVOIR AND BELLE

artificial barriers that separate the interest of the relief administrators and investigators from that of their 'caseloads,' the white collar and professional worker from the laborer and the domestic; and (3) organized labor's limited concept of exploitation, which permits it to fight vigorously to secure itself against evil, yet passively or actively aids and abets the ruthless destruction of Negros.[63]

Cooke goes on to revisit the issue of the Bronx slave market in a series of articles published in *The Daily Compass* in 1950.

The year after Baker and Cooke's "The Bronx Slave Market," Louise Thompson (Patterson) (1901–1999) published "Towards a Brighter Dawn" (1936) in the Communist Party USA journal *Woman Today*. She uses the metaphor of the dawn to describe the ways in which Black women's labor is exploited in the South from domestic work ("There are Negro women trudging to the Big House to cook, to wash, to clean, to nurse children—all for two, three, dollars for the whole week."), to sharecropping work ("The sharecropper's wife—field worker by day, mother and housewife by night."), to the aforementioned Bronx slave market in the North ("The Bronx 'slave market' is a graphic monument to the bitter exploitation of this most exploited section of the American working population—the Negro women."). From here Thompson explicitly names triple exploitation, "Over the whole land, Negro women meet this triple exploitation—as workers, as women, and as Negroes." Naming this troubling triple exploitation provides context for the establishment of the National Negro Congress in Chicago in 1936 as well as the emphasis on organization and unity in the resolution passed by the Congress. Thompson explains, "The resolution embodied a three-point program: (1) Organization of women domestic workers into trade unions of the American Federation of Labor; (2) organization of housewives into housewives' leagues to combat the high cost of living, and educational facilities for their families; and (3) organization of professional women." Here we see planning and programming that takes seriously the differential class, social, and professional statuses of Black women rather than treating them as a monolithic group.

A few years after Baker and Cooke's "The Bronx Slave Market" and Thompson's "Towards a Brighter Dawn," Esther Cooper (Jackson) (1917–2022) wrote a master's thesis at Fisk University titled, "The

SELECT GENEALOGY OF BLACK FEMINIST FRAMEWORKS   55

Negro Woman Domestic Worker in Relation to Trade Unionism" (1940). She was offered the opportunity to earn her PhD in Chicago but turned it down to organize in the South. In "The Negro Woman Domestic Worker in Relation to Trade Unionism" Cooper offers a historical, sociological, and economic overview of the issues of Black women domestic laborers, unionization efforts, and the "triple handicap" against Black women.[64] She notes differences in the marital status of white and Black domestic workers: "In the case of white women, domestic work is done characteristically by single, widowed and divorced women. Among Negro domestic workers, however, the married woman is the rule."[65] And she argues that the poor working conditions of Black women domestic workers is not only a micro issue for the workers themselves, but also a macro issue for society at large.[66] Like Baker, Cooke, and Thompson before her, Cooper also took up the infamous Bronx slave markets as one example of the dire circumstances of Black domestic workers as well as a catalyst for union organizing.[67] She argues that Black women domestic workers can and should unionize, "While the future of unionization among domestic workers in the United States cannot be predicted, nevertheless, it can be concluded that the problems faced by Negro women domestic workers are responsive to amelioration through trade union organizations even when we recognize the many difficulties which are involved in unionizing this occupation."[68]

The article "For New Approaches to Our Work Among Women" (1948) by Claudia Jones (1915–1964) lays the groundwork for her later, better-known article "An End to the Neglect of the Problems of the Negro Woman!" (1949).[69] In this earlier article, Jones frequently speaks of "American" women in general as well as of working-class and Black women in particular. For example, she states, "The importance of winning American women, especially in working-class and Negro communities, to militant resistance to Wall Street's program of fascism and war, can be fully understood only if we correctly assess the decisive role American women can play in the political life of the nation."[70] After giving statistics on women workers, housewives, and working mothers, she examines the situations of women in general and Black women in particular with regard to the wage gap. Jones notes that while women generally receive lower wages, "There are growing trends

56 BEAUVOIR AND BELLE

which show that these postwar employment difficulties are falling most heavily on Negro women, who were the first to be fired in the layoffs especially in the heavy industries."[71] Like her predecessors, Jones is attentive to the woman question and how different issues and concerns emerge when race and class are also factored into the gender equation. Her general tone communicates very clearly that the Communist Party needs women, especially militant Black women, more than Black women need the Party.

Jones does not shy away from identifying the problems, weaknesses, and failures of the Party. But she also offers concrete solutions, for example, more attention to the woman question in the Party's publications and promoting women into more leadership positions. Jones also argues that the Party can be strengthened, and its racial tensions ameliorated, by paying attention to the triple oppression of Black women. She asserts, "Greater attention to the triple handicaps of Negro women can help to strengthen our Party life and the building of Negro and white unity."[72] I want to underscore Jones' emphasis here on Black women as agents of militant resistance, not merely victims of triple oppression. Looking specifically at the effectiveness of Black women as organizers, she states, "Of special interest is the need to tap deeply the tremendous potential and organizational abilities of our Negro women comrades."[73]

Second Half of the Twentieth Century

Beverly Guy-Sheftall notes that 1970 marked a reemergence of (manuscript length) Black feminist writings with the publication of Toni Cade Bambara's *The Black Woman: An Anthology*, Shirley Chisholm's *Unbought and Unbossed*, and Toni Morrison's *The Bluest Eye*.[74] Of course, Black feminists also continued to write essays and political statements. For example, Pauli Murray (1910–1985) was an activist, attorney, and priest—the first Black person to earn a JD from Yale Law School and first Black American woman ordained an Episcopal priest. It is worth noting that the Pauli Murry Center for History and Social Justice (Durham, NC) uses s/he and they/them/their pronouns for Murray, whom they remind readers was a "self-described 'he/she

SELECT GENEALOGY OF BLACK FEMINIST FRAMEWORKS   57

personality.' "[75] I follow their lead on pronoun use here. In "The Liberation of Black Women" (1970) Murray asserts, "Black women, historically have been doubly victimized by the twin immoralities of Jim Crow and Jane Crow. Jane Crow refers to the entire range of assumptions, attitudes, stereotypes, customs, and arrangements from participating fully in society as equals with men."[76] Like others, Murray not only examines the history of slavery and its impact on Black men and women, but also names the impact of Black women as abolitionists and later their roles in the civil rights movement. S/he critiques patriarchal attitudes in media representations of the Black Power movement (especially the emphasis on Black men as militant and Black women as secondary). Murray identifies dual victimization, barriers, and burdens faced by Black women. But s/he also expands beyond this duality as s/he states, "Confronted with the multiple barriers of poverty, race, and sex, the quandary of black women is how to best distribute their energies among these issues and what strategies to pursue that will minimize conflicting interests and objectives."[77] Murray also confronts the Black matriarchy thesis, identifies concerns about the Black family, and discusses Black access to education based on gender. Additionally, s/he looks at statistics contrasting Black women and white women concerning their access to marriage, their representation in the workforce, and what kinds of jobs they can access. Again, the economic exploitation of Black women as domestic workers, here referred to as "private household workers," is emphasized.[78] According to Murray, "The lesson of history is that all human rights are indivisible and that the failure to adhere to this principle jeopardizes the rights of all is particularly applicable here."[79]

Francis Beal (1940–) identifies the multiple systems of oppression facing Black women along the lines of race, class, and gender—from racism to capitalism to sexism to imperialism—in "Double Jeopardy: To Be Black and Female" (1970). She debunks constructed gender roles and stereotypes of "manhood" and "femininity" while also holding space for the oppressions experienced by Black women (including economic and sexual exploitation) and Black men (including lynching and other brutalities). Beal also rejects the Black matriarchy thesis and the accompanying narrative that Black women are co-conspirators in the castration and emasculation of Black men. She asserts, "it is a gross distortion of fact to state that black women have oppressed black men."[80] Regarding Black men Beal asserts, "It is fallacious reasoning that in order for the black man to be strong, the black woman has to be weak. Those who are asserting their 'manhood' by telling black women to step back into a domestic, submissive role are assuming a counterrevolutionary position."[81] Concerning the white women's liberation movement, Beal is clear, "Any white group that does not have an anti-imperialist and antiracist ideology has absolutely nothing in common with the black woman's struggle."[82] Thus, we see her challenging not only male supremacy and white supremacy, but also imperialism. Beal brings attention to international issues in her analysis of the International Ladies Garment Workers Union, as well as critiques of racist apartheid in South Africa. Furthermore, she characterizes the United States as a colonialist exploiter that has sponsored sterilization campaigns and medical experimentation in India and Puerto Rico, as well as in the United States, where Black women were subjected to sterilization to receive welfare benefits and were also victims of experimentation that would later benefit middle-class white women. Nonetheless, Beal imagines a new world in which all forms of oppression are eliminated and better interpersonal relationships are possible.

Frequently cited as an important and impactful expression of (and response to) interlocking systems of oppression including race, class, gender oppression, and heterosexism, is "The Combahee River Collective: A Black Feminist Statement" (1977).[83] The CRC statement was revisited in earnest in 2017, the year marking the fortieth anniversary of the statement's initial writing. For example, Keeanga-Yamahtta Taylor's *How We Get Free: Black Feminism and the Combahee River Collective* (2017) includes the original statement alongside interviews with each of the co-authors, an interview with Black Lives Matter co-founder Alicia Garza, and a commentary by Barbara Ransby.[84] In the CRC statement, co-authors Smith, Smith, and Frazier assert, "The most general statement of our politics at the present time would be that we are actively committed to struggling against racial, sexual, heterosexual, and class oppression, and see as our particular task the development of integrated analysis and practice based upon the fact that the major systems of oppression are *interlocking*."[85] For Smith, Smith, and

SELECT GENEALOGY OF BLACK FEMINIST FRAMEWORKS   59

Frazier, articulating the interlocking aspects of multiple oppressions is not merely a theoretical exercise. It is primarily a political commitment for how they examine and resist real, concrete oppressions in the world. They take an antiracist and antisexist position that also addresses heterosexism and capitalism.[86] Smith, Smith, and Frazier explain, "The major source of difficulty in our political work is that we are not just trying to fight oppression on one front or even two, but instead to address a whole range of oppressions."[87] It is also important to note that these authors resist the idea of oppressions as separate or separable. They assert, "We also often find it difficult to separate race from class from sex oppression because in our lives they are most often experienced simultaneously."[88] Smith, Smith, and Frazier developed an integrated analysis of interlocking systems of oppression and articulated their active commitment to identifying, analyzing, and fighting against racial, sexual, heterosexual, and class oppressions. They characterize Black feminism as a political movement seeking to confront and overcome the interlocking systems of oppression against all Women of Color.[89]

Moving into the 1980s and 1990s, some of the seminal single-authored Black feminist texts of this period include bell hooks' *Ain't I a Woman: Black Women and Feminism* (1981) and *Feminist Theory from Margin to Center* (1984), Angela Davis' *Woman, Race, and Class* (1981), Alice Walker's *The Color Purple* (1982) and *In Search of Our Mother's Gardens* (1983), Audre Lorde's *Sister Outsider: Essays and Speeches by Audre Lorde* (1984), Paula Giddings' *When and Where I Enter: The Impact of Black Women on Race and Sex in America* (1984), Hazel Carby's *Reconstruction Womanhood: The Emergence of the Afro-American Woman Novelist* (1987), and Patricia Hill-Collins' *Black Feminist Thought: Knowledge, Consciousness, and the Politics of Empowerment* (1990). We could also look at powerful anthologies and edited collections by Black women and other Women of Color during this period—for example, *Sturdy Black Bridges: Visions of Black Women in Literature* (1979) edited by Roseann P. Bell, Bettye J. Parker, and Beverly Guy Sheftall; *This Bridge Called My Back: Writings by Radical Women of Color* (1981) edited by Cherríe Moraga and Gloria Anzaldúa; *All of the Women Are White, All of the Blacks Are Men, But Some of Us Are Brave* (1982) edited by Gloria T. Hull, Patricia Bell-Scott,

60 BEAUVOIR AND BELLE

and Barbara Smith; *Black Women Writers (1950–1980): A Critical Evaluation* (1983) edited by Mari Evans; *Conjuring: Black Women, Fiction, and Literary Tradition* (1985) edited by Marjorie Pyrse and Hortense Spillers; Gayatri Chakravorty Spivak's essay "Can the Subaltern Speak?" (1988); *Third World Women and the Politics of Feminism* (1991) edited by Chandra Talpade Mohanty, Ann Russo, and Lourdes Torres; and Aída Hurtado's *The Color of Privilege: Three Blasphemies on Race and Gender* (1996).

Up to this point we have considered various Black feminist frameworks of identities and oppressions, including the creation of vocabularies such as "the race question and the woman problem" (Anna Julia Cooper), the "triple oppression" thesis (Louise Thompson, Esther Cooper, Claudia Jones), and "interlocking" systems of oppression (Barbara Smith, Beverly Smith, and Demita Frazier). Each of these frameworks and vocabularies provided a foundation for the now widely known and used (not to mention misused and abused) term "intersectionality" coined by lawyer, legal scholar, and civil rights advocate Kimberlé Crenshaw (1959—).[90] Crenshaw introduced and explained this term in "Demarginalizing the Intersection of Race and Sex: A Black Feminist Critique of Antidiscrimination Doctrine, Feminist Theory and Antiracist Politics" (1989), a talk published in *The University of Chicago Legal Forum*.[91] Her objectives and aims are already named in the title. She explains, "I have chosen this title as a point of departure in my efforts to develop a black feminist criticism because it sets forth a problematic consequence of the tendency to treat race and gender as mutually exclusive categories of experience and analysis."[92] Thus, Crenshaw explicitly expresses her development of a Black feminist critique problematizing the treatment of race and gender as separate categories that are outside of each other.

Crenshaw centers Black women's experience, "in order to contrast the *multidimensionality* of Black women's experience with the single-axis analysis that distorts these experiences."[93] The limitations of the single-axis analysis that she seeks to expose are most readily found in antidiscrimination law as well and in the theoretical and political projects of (white) feminism and (male) antiracist projects. Crenshaw argues, "this single-axis framework erases Black women in the conceptualization, identification, and remediation of race and sex

SELECT GENEALOGY OF BLACK FEMINIST FRAMEWORKS   61

discrimination by limiting inquiry to the experiences of otherwise-privileged members of the group."[94] Intersectionality underscores multidimensionality (in contrast with the single-axis approach). Crenshaw identifies the multidimensionality of Black women's experience and specifies the limitations of single-axis analyses that not only distort this multidimensionality but also erase the racial privilege of white women and the gender privilege of Black men. She states, "This focus on the most privileged group members marginalizes those who are multiply-burdened and obscures claims that cannot be understood as resulting from discrete sources of discrimination."[95] Her argument is clearly stated, "I argue that Black women are sometimes excluded from feminist theory and antiracist policy discourse because both are predicated on a discrete set of experiences that often does not reflect the interaction of race and gender."[96]

To be sure, Crenshaw is not presenting an additive analysis of identity and oppression. That is, she is not merely suggesting that we add Black women within the race framework on the one hand and within the gender framework on the other, both of which have heretofore marginalized or erased us. Crenshaw rejects this additive approach because "the intersectional experience is greater than the sum of racism and sexism, [therefore] any analysis that does not take intersectionality into account cannot sufficiently address the particular manner in which Black women are subordinated."[97] The limiting boundaries of the single-axis framework do not encompass Black women's experiences. Crenshaw explains that this is a both/and analysis not an either/or analysis. It is *both* the case that "Black women sometimes experience discrimination in ways similar to white women's experience; sometimes they share very similar experiences with Black men," *and* it is also the case that this is not simply racism plus sexism, but "double-discrimination—the combined effects of practices which discriminate on the basis of race and on the basis of sex . . . not the sum of race and sex discrimination, but as Black women."[98] The very meanings of racism and sexism needs to be expanded, in part because "the continued insistence that Black women's demands and needs be filtered through categorical analyses that completely obscure their experiences guarantees that their needs will seldom be addressed."[99]

62   BEAUVOIR AND BELLE

While Crenshaw emphasizes Black women in her conceptualization of intersectionality in "Demarginalizing the Intersection of Race and Sex: A Black Feminist Critique of Antidiscrimination Doctrine, Feminist Theory and Antiracist Politics," she later expands the concept to include other Women of Color in "Mapping the Margins: Intersectionality, Identity Politics, and Violence Against Women of Color" (1991).[100] Here Crenshaw reiterates the import of intersectionality, stating, "My focus on the intersections of race and gender only highlights the need to account for *multiple* grounds of identity when considering how the social world is constructed."[101] She describes "structural intersectionality" (including the differential experiences of violence by Women of Color and white women[102]), "political intersectionality" (highlighting "the fact that women of color are situated within at least two subordinate groups that frequently pursue conflicting political agendas"[103]), and "representational intersectionality" (namely, the "cultural construction of women of color"[104]). Again, noting the limits of other frameworks and looking specifically at political intersectionality, she asserts, "Because women of color experience racism in ways not always the same as those experienced by men of color and sexism in ways that are not always parallel to experiences of white women, antiracism and feminism are limited, even on their own terms."[105] Crenshaw further explains, "The failure of feminism to interrogate race means that resistance strategies of feminism will often replicate and reinforce the subordination of people of color, and the failure of antiracism to interrogate patriarchy means that antiracism will frequently reproduce the subordination of women. These mutual elisions present a particularly difficult political dilemma for women of color."[106] Going beyond the Black-white binary, Crenshaw's framework of intersectionality here recognizes and empowers Women of Color (not only Black women) rather than ignoring and subordinating us within other dominant discourses. She acknowledges that identity has multiple dimensions while also accounting for the social construction of identities, the unique situatedness of Women of Color in the face of single-axis approaches, and the limitations of conflicting agendas that often seek to erase or ignore us.[107]

Conclusion

In this chapter I have provided a broad overview of Black feminist frameworks of identity and oppression that have been articulated over more than two centuries, along with corresponding matrilineal discourses and vocabularies that have been created to express our existence and experience. Toward that end, I presented figures and texts ranging from Lucy Terry in the early eighteenth century to Kimberlé Crenshaw in the late twentieth century. This is certainly not an exhaustive account, which would be impossible to provide in one chapter, but it is intended to disrupt what Spillers described as those forces that want to enforce forgetfulness about the discourses and vocabularies that have been created by Black women. Feminism is not new to Black women. We did not suddenly discover our identities and oppressions along the lines of race, class, gender, and sexual orientation (nor our agency to confront those oppressions) through white feminist texts that focused on gender without taking seriously its intersections with race and other aspects of our identities and oppressions. Another objective of this chapter has been to lay the groundwork for the chapters that follow by first taking seriously these rich and diverse historical and philosophical developments of Black women as thinkers, speakers, writers, and political actors. The next three chapters build on this foundation with a more in-depth focus on three major Black feminist philosophers: Claudia Jones, Lorraine Hansberry, and Audre Lorde—each of whom belongs to, has been shaped by, and has helped to shape Black feminist traditions. Each of these figures also has an interesting connection to Simone de Beauvoir's *The Second Sex*. This chapter also serves the purpose of providing a reference point for Black feminist frameworks of identities and oppressions as interlocking and intersecting, in contrast with white feminist approaches to identities and oppressions as analogical. More specifically, I am interested in the white feminist analogical approach and its inattentiveness to Black feminist frameworks of identities and oppressions as represented in Beauvoir's *The Second Sex*, which will be taken up in more detail in Part II, "White Feminist Frameworks," Chapters 5–7.

Notes

1. Hortense Spillers, "Mama's Bay, Papa's Maybe: An American Grammar Book," *Diacritics* 17, no. 2, *Culture and Countermemory: The "American" Connection* (Summer 1987): 64–81), here 65. (Hereafter Spillers 1987.)
2. Spillers 1987, 66.
3. Hortense Spillers, Saidiya Hartman, Farah Jasmine Griffin, Shelly Eversley, and Jennifer L. Morgan, "Whatcha Gonna Do?—Revisiting 'Mama's Bay, Papa's Maybe: An American Grammar Book,'" *Women's Studies Quarterly* 35, no. 1/2 (Spring 2007, Social Science Premium Collection): 299–309, here 300. (Hereafter Spillers et al. 2007.)
4. Spillers et al. 2007, 300.
5. Spillers et al. 2007, 301.
6. Spillers et al. 2007, 302. A quick note about fields of study: Spillars has a PhD in English from Brandeis University, Saidiya Hartman has a PhD from Yale University, Farah Jasmine Griffin has a PhD in American studies from Yale University, Shelly Eversley has a PhD in American literature from Johns Hopkins University, and Jennifer Morgan has a PhD in history from Duke University. Of course, all of their scholarship has import in the field of philosophy.
7. Spillers et al. 2007, 302.
8. We might also think about this in terms of what Brittney Cooper would later call *listing*: "this intentional calling of names created an intellectual genealogy for race women's work and was a practice against intellectual erasure" practiced by Black women thinkers. See Brittney Cooper, *Beyond Respectability: The Intellectual Thought of Race Women* (Urbana: University of Illinois Press, 2017), 26.
9. Ann Allen Shockley, *Afro-American Women Writers 1746–1933: An Anthology and Critical Guide* (Boston: G.K. Hall & Co, 1988), 3–4. (Hereafter Shockley 1988.)
10. Shockley 1988, 4–5.
11. Shockley 1988, xix.
12. See Nafissa Thompson-Spires, "1744–1749: Lucy Terry Prince," in *Four Hundred Souls: A Community History of African America, 1619—2019*, ed. Ibram X. Kendi and Keisha N. Blain (New York: One World, 2021), 115. (Hereafter Thompson-Spires 2021.)
13. Thompson-Spires 2021, 116. The case involved a dispute over inherited land that a white man tried to claim.
14. Thompson-Spires 2021, 118.

SELECT GENEALOGY OF BLACK FEMINIST FRAMEWORKS   65

15. Shockley identifies Wheatley's first poem as "To the University of Cambridge" (1767), a poem "giving advice to college boys" and her first published poem as "On the Death of the Rev. Mr. George Whitfield" (1770) (Shockley 1988, 18). This 1770 poem has also been referenced as "An Elegiac Poem, on the Death of that Celebrated Divine, and Eminent Servant of Jesus Christ, the Reverend and Learned George Whitfield." But in 1969 Carl Bridenbaugh identified Wheatley's first published poem as "On Messrs. Hussey and Coffin" (1767) published in Newport, Rhode Island's *Mercury*. See Carl Bridenbaugh, "The Earliest Published Poem of Phillis Wheatley," *New England Quarterly* 42 (1969): 583–584. There is also a more recently discovered poem by Wheatley from 1773 titled "Ocean," and the original manuscript sold at auction in 1998 for a total of $68,500.00. See Julian Mason, "'Ocean': A New Poem by Phillis Wheatly," *Early American Literature* 34, no. 1 (1999): 78–83.

16. Alexis Pauline Gumbs, "1764–1769: Phillis Wheatley," in *Four Hundred Souls: A Community History of African America, 1619–2019*, ed. Ibram X. Kendi and Keisha N. Blain (New York: One World, 2021), 131. (Hereafter Gumbs 2021.)

17. Gumbs 2021, 131.

18. The first woman of any race to publish a book of poems from colonial America is Anne Bradstreet, a white woman born Anne Dudley in England in 1612. Wealthy and well educated, her brother facilitated the publication of her book of poems, *The Tenth Muse Lately Sprung Up in America*, in England in 1650.

19. Henry Louis Gates, Jr., "Foreword to the Schomburg Supplement," in *The Pen Is Ours: A Listing of Writings by and about African American Women before 1910 With Secondary Bibliography to the Present*, compiled by Jean Fagan Yellin and Cynthia D. Bond (New York: Oxford University Press, 1991), xiv. (Hereafter Gates 1991.)

20. Gates 1991, xiv–xv. (Emphasis original.)

21. I also follow Guy-Sheftall in identifying these figures and texts as Black "feminist." Elsewhere I have used the term "proto-intersectionality" to describe these early explorations and examinations of intersecting identities and oppressions in the nineteenth century and early twentieth centuries. See Kathryn Sophia Belle (formerly Kathryn T. Gines), "Race Women, Race Men and Early Expressions of Proto-Intersectionality, 1830s–1930s," in *Why Race and Gender Still Matter: An Intersectional Approach*, ed. Namita Goswami, Maeve M. O'Donovan, and Lisa Yount (Brookfield, VT: Pickering and Chatto Publishers Limited, 2014), 13–25.

66   BEAUVOIR AND BELLE

22. See Marilyn Richardson, *Maria W. Stewart, America's First Black Political Writer: Essays and Speeches* (Bloomington: Indiana University Press, 1987). (Hereafter Richardson 1987.) Richardson asserts: "In September of 1832, in Boston, Massachusetts, Maria W. Stewart, a black woman, did what no American-born woman, black or white, before her is recorded having done. She mounted a lecture platform and raised a political argument before a 'promiscuous' audience, that is, one composed of both men and women" (Richardson 1987, xiii). See also Carol B. Conaway and Kristin Waters, *Black Women's Intellectual Traditions: Speaking Their Minds* (Burlington: University of Vermont Press, 2007); Kathryn Sophia Belle, "1829–1834: Maria Stewart," in *Four Hundred Souls: A Community History of African America, 1619–2019*, ed. Ibram X. Kendi and Keisha Blain (New York: One World, 2021); and Kristin Waters, *Maria Stewart and the Roots of Black Political Thought* (Jackson: University of Mississippi Press, 2022).

23. Published by William Lloyd Garrison's *The Liberator*, 8 October 1931. See "Religion And The Pure Principles Of Morality, The Sure Foundation On Which We Must Build" in Richardson 1987. Also available in Beverly Guy-Sheftall's *Words of Fire: An Anthology of African-American Feminist Thought* (New York: The New Press, 1995). (Here after Guy-Sheftall 1995.)

24. Stewart asks, "How long shall a mean set of men flatter us with their smiles, and enrich themselves with our hard earnings, their wives' fingers sparkling with rings, and they themselves laugh at our folly?" She replies, "Until we begin to promote and patronize each other" (Richardson 1987, 38).

25. Richardson 1987, 38. We find even more diverse roles and expectations for women, especially Black women, outlined in her 1833 farewell address to her friends in Boston. Offering examples of women in the Bible as well as women from various cultures (Greek, Roman, Jewish, Ethiopian, and even "barbarous nations")—Stewart makes the case for Black women to be able to make a public demand for their rights (Richardson 1987, 68–69). Richardson has identified the full source of Stewart's citations as John Adams' *Woman, Sketches of the History, Genius, Disposition, Accomplishments, Employments, Customs and Importance of the Fair Sex in All Parts of the World Interspersed with Many Singular And Entertaining Anecdotes by a Friend of the Sex* published in London in 1790 (Richardson 1987, 24).

26. Richardson 1987, 48.

27. Richardson 1987, 82. Here Richardson is playing on Du Bois' notion of double consciousness but adds "woman" to "American" and "Negro." But

SELECT GENEALOGY OF BLACK FEMINIST FRAMEWORKS 67

I am playing on triple consciousness to highlight Stewart's insights on the triple oppressions of racism, sexism, and classism.

28. Nell Irvin Painter has framed and theorized much of the controversy surrounding the problematic images and representations of Truth by figures such as Olive Gilbert and Frances Titus (publishing editions of her narrative) as well as Harriet Beecher Stowe and Frances Dana Gage, who published essays appropriating Truth for their own purposes. See Painter's "Sojourner Truth in Life and Memory: Writing the Biography of and American Exotic," *Gender and History* 2 (1990): 3–19; *Sojourner Truth: A Life, A Symbol* (W. W. Norton and Company, 1997); and her "introduction" to *Narrative of Sojourner Truth* (New York: Penguin Classics, 1998), vii–xx.

29. *Narrative of Sojourner Truth* (New York: Penguin Classics, 1998); Library of Congress full title: *Narrative of Sojourner Truth; a bondswoman of the olden time, emancipated by the New York Legislature in the early part of the present century; with a history of her labors and correposndance drawn from her "Book of Life"* (edited by Olive Gilbert, Battle Creek, MI, 1878); Harriett Beecher Stowe, "Libyan Sibyl," *Atlantic Monthly* 11, no. 66 (April 1863), 473–481); and more recently Nell Irvin Painter, "Sojourner Truth in Life and Memory: Writing the Biography of and American Exotic," *Gender and History* 2 (1990): 3–19 and *Sojourner Truth: A Life, A Symbol* (W. W. Norton and Company, 1997).

30. She also explicitly criticized Black male patriarchy toward Black women, arguing that Black men's rights should not be prioritized over Black women's rights and asserting "if colored men get their rights, but not colored women get theirs, there will be a bad time about it" (Sojourner Truth, "When Woman Gets Her Rights Man Will Be Right," Guy-Sheftall 1995, 37). Kimberlé Crenshaw references Truth in her article "Demarginalizing the Intersection of Race and Sex: A Black Feminist Critique of Antidiscrimination Doctrine, Feminist Theory and Antiracist Politics" *University of Chicago Legal Forum* 139, no. 1 (1989): article 1, 153–154. (Hereafter Crenshaw 1989.)

31. Guy-Sheftall 1995, 35.

32. Nell Irvin Painter, "Truth in Life and Memory," *Gender and History* 2, no. 1 (Spring 1990): 3–16, here 13.

33. For more on Cooper, see Vivian May, *Anna Julia Cooper: Visionary Black Feminist, A Critical Introduction* (New York: Routledge, 2007). See also "Anna Julia Cooper," ed. Kathryn Sophia Belle (formerly Kathryn T. Gines) and Ronald R. Sundstrom, special issue, *Philosophia Africana: Analysis of*

68 BEAUVOIR AND BELLE

Philosophy and Issues in African and the Black Diaspora 12, no. 1 (March 2009): 1–106. There is also a new collection including previously unpublished writings by Cooper, *The Portable Anna Julia Cooper*, ed. Shirley Moody-Turner (New York: Penguin Books, 2022).

34. Anna Julia Cooper, "The Status of Women in America," from *A Voice from the South* (1892), reprinted in *The Voice of Anna Julia Cooper*, ed. Charles Lamert and Esme Bhan (Lanham, MD: Rowman and Littlefield, 1998), 112. (Hereafter Cooper 1998.)

35. Cooper 1998, 236.

36. Cooper 1998, 236.

37. Cooper 1998, 169.

38. Cooper 1998, 173.

39. Wells gives an account of this in her autobiography, where she also notes that W. E. B. Du Bois in giving his report on the committee of forty excluded her name from the list. See *Crusade for Justice: The Autobiography of Ida B. Wells*, ed. Alfreda M. Barnett Duster (Chicago: University of Chicago Press, 1970), 324.

40. In spite of (or perhaps because of) the positive impact Wells had in bringing international attention to white terrorism in the form of lynching, she was harshly criticized by Black men who thought she should not be so out front on the issue.

41. When repeated petitions for participation in the World Fair in Chicago were denied, a protest was organized, and Wells, Frederick Douglass, Ferdinand L. Barnett, and Irvine Garland Penn compiled "The Reason Why the Colored American Is Not in the World's Columbian Exposition—The Afro-American's Contribution to Columbian Literature." See Alfreda M. Barnett Duster, "Introduction," *Crusade for Justice: The Autobiography of Ida B. Wells*, ed. Alfreda M. Barnett Duster (Chicago: University of Chicago Press, 1970). See Wells' account of the World's Fair and Douglass' role on pp. 115–120. Frederick Douglass did have the official role of being in charge of the Haiti building at the World's Fair. See Anna R. Paddon and Sally Turner, "African Americans and the World's Columbian Exposition," *Illinois Historical Journal* 88, no. 1 (Spring 1995): 19–36, and Ann Massa, "Black Women in the 'White City,'" *Journal of American Studies* 8 (1974): 319–337. Wells raised the money for the pamphlet and wrote the preface (which is printed in English, French, and German), plus five of the seven other sections in this publication, including: "Class Legislation," "The Convict Lease System," "Lynch Law," and the conclusion "To the Public."

SELECT GENEALOGY OF BLACK FEMINIST FRAMEWORKS 69

42. Fannie Barrier Williams, "A Northern Negro's Autobiography," *The Independent* 57, no. 2902 (July 14, 1904): 96. My citations of this text are from *Black Women in White America: A Documentary History*, ed. Gerda Lerner (New York: Vintage Books: A Division of Random House, Inc., 1992). (Hereafter Lerner 1992.)
43. Lerner 1992, 165.
44. Lerner 1992, 166.
45. Mary Church Terrell, "Lynching from a Negro's Point of View," *North American Review* 178, no. 572 (June 1904): 853–868. My citations of this text are from *Black Women in White America: A Documentary History*, ed. Gerda Lerner (New York: Vintage Books: A Division of Random House, Inc., 1992). (Hereafter Lerner 1992.) See Angela Davis, "Rape, Racism, and the Capitalist Setting," *The Black Scholar* 9, no. 7, *Blacks and the Sexual Revolution* (April 1978): 24–30. See also Angela Davis, "Rape, Racism, and the Myth of the Black Male Rapist," in *Women, Race, and Class* (New York: Vintage Books, 1981).
46. Lerner 1992, 207.
47. Lerner 1992, 207–209.
48. Lerner 1992, 207–209.
49. Lerner 1992, 210.
50. Terrell offers the following examples: "white women who apply the flaming torches to their [the lynch victims'] oil-soaked bodies"; "women who for generations looked upon the hardships and degradation of their sisters of a darker hue with few if any protests," (Lerner 1992, 209–210).
51. Lerner 1992, 210.
52. My citations of this text are from Lerner 1992, 461–467. The statement is signed by Mrs. Charlotte Hawkins Brown (President of North Carolina Federation of Women), Mrs. Marion B. Wilkinson (President South Carolina Federation of Women), Miss Lucy C, Lancey (Principal Haines Institutes and President of City Federation of Colored Women's Clubs, Augusta, GA), Mrs. Mary J. McCrorey (Chmn. Com. Of Management, Charlotte Branch, YWCA), Mrs. Janie P. Barrett (President of VA Federation of Colored Women's Clubs), Mrs. Booker T. Washington (Honorary President, National Association of Colored Women's Clubs), Mrs. R. R. Moton, Tuskegee Institute, Alabama), Mrs. John Hope (Dept. Neighborhood Works, National Federation of C. W. Clubs), Mrs. M.L. Crosthwait (Registrar, Fisk University, Nashville, TN), Mrs. Mary McLeod Bethune, Principal Daytona N. & I. School for Negro Girls, President of the Southern Federation of Colored Women's Clubs).
53. Lerner 1992, 462.

70 BEAUVOIR AND BELLE

54. Lerner 1992, 462.
55. Guy-Sheftall 1995, 81.
56. Guy-Sheftall 1995, 81.
57. Guy-Sheftall 1995, 96.
58. Guy-Sheftall 1995, 97–98. Alexander is among the first four Black women to earn a doctorate degree in the United States. The other three are Eva Dykes, Georgiana Simpson, and Anna Julia Cooper (discussed earlier).
59. Guy-Sheftall 1995, 98.
60. Ella Baker and Marvel Cook, "The Bronx Slave Market," *The Crisis: A Record of the Darker Races*, November 1935, 330. (Hereafter Baker and Cooke 1935.)
61. Baker and Cooke 1935, 330.
62. Baker and Cooke 1935, 340.
63. Baker and Cooke 1935, 340.
64. Esther Cooper, "The Negro Woman Domestic Worker in Relation to Trade Unionism" (MA thesis, Fisk University, 1940). (Hereafter Cooper 1940.) See also Erik McDuffie, "'No Small Amount of Change Could Do': Esther Cooper Jackson and the Making of a Black Left Feminist," in *Want to Start a Revolution?: Radical Women in the Black Freedom Struggle*, ed. Dayo F. Gore, Jeanne Theoharris, and Komazi Woodward (New York: New York University Press, 2009), 25–46. And see Shirley Chen's thesis: "'To work, write, sing, and fight for woman's liberation': Proto-Feminist Currents in the American Left, 1946–1961," 102n40: Esther Cooper described the "triple handicap" in 1940.
65. Cooper 1940, chapter 1.
66. "Work conditions faced by domestic workers constitute a serious problem for the thousands of individuals directly affected, as well as for society as a whole. Individuals and organizations, in attempting to shape a program for improving conditions of domestic workers, have come to the conclusion that organization of domestic work is one of the bases upon which higher standards might be maintained. In the efforts to unionize domestic workers, leaders had followed closely the experiences of other workers who have organized trade unions and have focused public opinion on their problems" (Cooper 1940, chapter 1).
67. Cooper, "Here on New York's street corners, women wait for housewives to come to them to bargain for a day's work" and later adding, "One of the worst types of human exploitation is the 'slave market' found in New York city, and one of its ugliest aspects is the way in which girls are shipped up in carloads from the South to stand on corners waiting for work at 25 to 35 cents an hour" (Cooper 1940, chapter 2 and conclusion).

SELECT GENEALOGY OF BLACK FEMINIST FRAMEWORKS   71

68. Cooper 1940, conclusion. McDuffie describes Cooper's thesis as "the most thorough sociological and historical study written on the working conditions and status of black women household workers and their efforts to unionize during the Depression" (Erik S. McDuffie, "Esther V. Cooper's 'The Negro Woman Domestic Worker in Relations to Trade Unionism': Black Left Feminism and the Popular Front," *American Communist History* 7, no. 2 (2008): 203–209), 203. He puts Cooper's thesis in context with the dominant white Communist feminism of the time, "By calling attention to the Bronx slave market, Cooper . . . in effect rejected the notion that 'woman' was a universal, ahistorical category, directly challenging ideas posited by some white Communist women theoreticians at this time that women were equally oppressed by patriarchy" (McDuffie 2008, 206).

69. Note that Jones' 1949 article will be taken up extensively in Chapter 2.

70. Claudia Jones, "For New Approaches to Our Work Among Women," *Political Affairs: A Magazine Devoted to the Theory and Practice of Marxism-Leninism* 27 (August 1948): 738–743. (Hereafter Jones 1948.) 1948), 738.

71. Jones 1948, 739.

72. Jones, 1948, 742–743.

73. Jones 1948, 742.

74. Guy-Sheftall 1995, 14.

75. See "Pronouns and Pauli Murray": https://www.paulimurraycenter.com/pronouns-pauli-murray (last accessed February 3, 2022.)

76. Guy-Sheftall 1995, 186.

77. Guy-Sheftall 1995, 192.

78. Guy-Sheftall 1995, 195.

79. Guy-Sheftall 1995, 197.

80. Guy-Sheftall 1995, 148.

81. Guy-Sheftall 1995, 148.

82. Guy-Sheftall 1995, 153.

83. According to Barbara Smith, the statement was first published in Zillah Einstein's edited collection *Capitalist Patriarchy and the Case for Socialist Feminism* (New York: Monthly Review Press, 1978). See Barbara Smith's prefatory remarks to "Combahee River Collective: A Black Feminist Statement," *Off Our Backs: A Women's Newsjournal* 9, no. 6, "AIN'T I A WOMON?" (June 1979): 6–8. "The Combahee River Collective Statement" (CRC) is published again in *Off Our Backs: A Women's Newsjournal* (June 1979), in *This Bridge Called My Back: Writings by Radical Women of Color* (Moraga and Anzaldúa, New York: Kitchen Table: Women of Color Press,

72 BEAUVOIR AND BELLE

1981), and in *All of the Women Are White, All of the Blacks Are Men, But Some of Us Are Brave* (Hull, Scott, and Smith, New York: The Feminist Press, 1982). It has also been anthologized, for example, in Beverly Guy-Sheftall's afroementioned *Words of Fire: An Anthology of African-American Feminist Thought* (1995).

84. See also Kristen A. Kolenz, Krista L. Benson, Judy Tzu-Chun Wu, Leslie Bow, Avtar Brah, Mishuana Goeman, Diane Harriford, Shari M. Huhndorf, Analouise Keating, Yi-Chun Tricia Lin, Laura Pérez, Zenaida Peterson, Becky Thompson, and Tiffany Willoughby-Herard, "The Combahee River Collective Statement: A Fortieth Anniversary Retrospective," *Frontiers: A Journal of Women Studies* 38, no. 3 (2017): 164–189); and Karina L. Cespedes, Corey Rae Evans, and Shayla Monteiro, "The Combahee River Collective Forty Years Later: Social Healing within a Black Feminist Classroom," *Souls: A Critical Journal of Black Politics, Culture, and Society* 19, no. 3 (2019): 377–389.

85. Keeanga-Yamahtta Taylor, *How We Get Free: Black Feminism and the Combahee River Collective* (Chicago: Haymarket Books, 2017), 15. (Emphasis added). (Hereafter Taylor 2017.)

86. Taylor 2017, 18.

87. Taylor 2017, 22.

88. Taylor 2017, 19.

89. For example, they state, "As Black women we see Black feminism as the logical political movement to combat the manifold and simultaneous oppressions that all women of color face" (Taylor 2017, 15).

90. Taylor explains: "It is difficult to quantify the enormity of the political contribution made by the women of the Combahee River Collective including Barbara Smith, her sister Beverly Smith, and Demita Frasier, because so much of their analysis is taken for granted in feminist politics today ... The Combahee River Collective did not coin the phrase "intersectionality"— Kimberlé Crenshaw did so in 1989—but the CRC did articulate the analysis that animates the meaning of intersectionality, the idea that multiple oppressions reinforce one another to create new categories of suffering" (Taylor 2017, 4).

91. Crenshaw 1989. Crenshaw is credited with coining the term "intersectionality," but Demita Frazier notes that before Crenshaw, "I said, 'You know, we stand at the intersection where our identities are indivisible.' There is no separation" (Taylor 2017, 123).

92. Crenshaw 1989, 139. (Crenshaw is referring to the title *All of the Women Are White, All of the Blacks Are Men, but Some of Us Are Brave: Black Feminist Studies.*)

SELECT GENEALOGY OF BLACK FEMINIST FRAMEWORKS 73

93. Crenshaw 1989, 139. (Emphasis added.)
94. Crenshaw 1989, 140. We can also find this single-axis framework operating in feminist philosophy and critical philosophy of race.
95. Crenshaw 1989, 140.
96. Crenshaw 1989, 140.
97. Crenshaw 1989, 140.
98. Crenshaw 1989, 149.
99. Crenshaw 1989, 149–150.
100. "Mapping the Margins: Intersectionality, Identity Politics, and Violence against Women of Color," *Stanford Law Review* 43, no. 6 (July 1991): 1241–1299. (Hereafter Crenshaw 1991.) Crenshaw's analysis also includes immigrant women of color and issues such as class, legal status, cultural barriers, and language barriers. It is worth noting that Crenshaw's account and critiques of identity politics ignoring intragroup difference seem misapplied when considering the notion of identity politics that we get from CRC (see Crenshaw 1991, 1242). It is also worth noting that Crenshaw is clear that, "intersectionality is not being offered here as some new, totalizing theory of identity" (Crenshaw 1991, 1244).
101. Crenshaw 1991, 1245. (Emphasis added.)
102. Crenshaw 1991, 1245.
103. Crenshaw 1991, 1251–1252.
104. Crenshaw 1991, 1245.
105. Crenshaw 1991, 1252.
106. Crenshaw 1991, 1252.
107. Crenshaw's concept of intersectionality is now over thirty years old, but it has persisted (if not dominated) as a Black feminist framework, discourse, and vocabulary well into the twenty-first century. To be sure, there have been a lot of of critiques of the concept. I have addressed some of them in previous publications. See Kathryn Sophia Belle (formerly Kathryn T. Gines), "Black Feminism and Intersectional Analyses: A Defense of Intersectionality," *Philosophy Today* 55, SPEP Supplement (2011): 275–284, and "Race Women, Race Men and Early Expressions of Proto-Intersectionality, 1830s–1930s," in *Why Race and Gender Still Matter: An Intersectional Approach*, ed. Namita Goswami, Maeve M. O'Donovan, and Lisa Yount (Brookfield, VT: Pickering and Chatto Publishers Limited, 2014), 13–25. See also Kathryn Sophia Belle, "Interlocking, Intersecting, and Intermeshing: Critical Engagements with Black and Latina Feminist Paradigms of Identity and Oppression," *Critical Philosophy of Race*, 8, nos. 1–2 (2020): 165–198.

2
Claudia Jones

"The Negro question in the United States is prior to, and not equal to, the woman question"

The year 1949 marked the publication of one of the most profound, insightful, and dynamic texts of the twentieth century, namely, Claudia Jones' "An end to the Neglect of the Problems of the Negro Woman!"—an essay that offered in-depth analyses of race, class, and gender with a sense of urgency and care, and placed a breadth of timely events within broader historical and international contexts, while also presenting a compelling call to action! This is one of numerous articles, critical essays, pamphlets, and poems that Black left internationalist feminist Claudia Jones published on Black liberation and women's liberation in general, as well as Black women's liberation in particular.[1] Here I am combining the terms "Black left feminism" and "Black internationalist feminism" to describe Jones' multifaceted theoretical and activist orientation. Mary Helen Washington is credited with coining the term "Black Left Feminism" in her essay "Alice Childress, Lorraine Hansberry, and Claudia Jones: Black Women With the Popular Front" (2003).[2] In *Sojourning for Freedom: Black Women, American Communism, and the Making of Black Left Feminism* (2011), Erik S. McDuffie cites Washington's trailblazing work and describes Black left feminism as "a path-breaking brand of feminist politics that centers working-class women by combining black nationalist and American Communist Party (CPUSA) positions on race, gender, and class with black women radicals' own lived experiences."[3] Cheryl Higashida uses the term "Black internationalist feminism" in her book, *Black Internationalist Feminism: Women Writers of the Black Left. 1945–1995* (2013).[4] She states, "What I call Black internationalist feminism challenged heteronormative and masculinist articulations of nationalism while maintaining the importance, even centrality, of

Beauvoir and Belle. Kathryn Sophia Belle, Oxford University Press. © Oxford University Press 2024.
DOI: 10.1093/oso/9780197660195.003.0003

national liberation movements for achieving Black women's social, political, and economic rights."[5] Furthermore, Higashida continues, "Women of the Black Left understood that essential to the liberation of African Americans, the Third World, and the worldwide proletariat was the fight against heteropatriarchy, which exacerbated oppressions within as well as between nations."[6]

In addition to her Black left internationalist feminism, in *Left of Karl Marx: The Political Life of Black Communist Claudia Jones* (2008), Carole Boyce Davies also reminds us that Jones was "a black feminist critic of Afro-Caribbean origin . . . a black communist woman very conscious of her location in history and of her contributions to advancing her particular understandings of anti-imperialism."[7] Davies emphasizes not only Jones' Afro-Caribbean origins and insights, but also how they informed her theories and practices: "Claudia Jones lived and organized at the intersection of a variety of positionalities (anti-imperialism and decolonization struggles, activism for workers' rights, the critique of appropriation of black women's labor, the challenge to domestic and international racisms and their links to colonialism) and was therefore able to articulate them earlier than many of her contemporaries."[8] This point is elaborated upon in her edited collection of Jones' writings, *Claudia Jones: Beyond Containment* (2011) where Davies describes Jones as someone who "consistently moved beyond all forms of containment—race, gender, national origin, place— and was definitely a transatlantic activist, a black radical intellectual from the Caribbean who revolutionized Marxism-Leninism particularly because she addressed in her time those issues that Marx and Lenin left unarticulated."[9]

The breadth and depth of Jones' Black left internationalist feminist analyses and activism include, but are not limited to, the issues of fascism, imperialism, capitalism, poverty, sexism, Black women (as Black, as women, and as workers; as militants, guardians, providers, protectors, mothers, domestic laborers, and more), Black women's health issues (including pregnancy and maternal death rates), slavery and rape, abolition and suffrage, Jim Crow and segregation, lynching, and police brutality. This chapter brings to the fore the crucial work of Claudia Jones and her special attentiveness to all of these themes and more as represented in her essay "An End to the Neglect of the Problems

76 BEAUVOIR AND BELLE

of the Negro Woman!" (1949), described by Davies as the "best and most easily available text for understanding Jones' significant contribution to black feminist theory" and as "pivotal for the history of black feminist theoretics."[10] I argue that Jones' triple-oppression analysis takes seriously the simultaneity of racial oppression, gender oppression, and class oppression in ways that explicitly center and make visible Black women's lived experience as well as their militant agency. Jones' analysis stands in sharp contrast to white feminist analyses that frequently implicitly universalize from one form of oppression (often white women's experiences of gender oppression), privilege gender oppression above others, collapse various forms of oppression into one and the same, and/or appropriate the oppressions and resistance efforts of others to advance their own resistance efforts—thereby ignoring and/or marginalizing other forms of interlocking oppressions that necessarily exceed white women's experiences of sexism and class oppression. I also argue that although Jones and Beauvoir take quite different approaches to the issues of their times, Jones must be credited for facilitating one of the earliest recoveries of *The Second Sex* in the US context.

In this chapter I am offering a close reading of Jones' "An End to the Neglect of the Problems of the Negro Woman!," underscoring the main themes and nuances of this article, which warrants far more attention than it has received, especially (but not exclusively) in the discipline of philosophy. I am intentionally centering a Black woman of Trinidadian descent who immigrated to the United States, where she audaciously centered Black women in her analyses and activism that transcended the United States. Just as Jones called for an end to the neglect of the problems of the Negro woman, I am calling for an end to the neglect of the writings of Black women in general and of Claudia Jones in particular. The chapter is organized into sections focused on several key themes from Jones' 1949 essay. In "Legacies of Slavery, Womanhood, and Motherhood" I examine how Jones takes up slavery in relationship to roles and representations of Black womanhood and Black motherhood, as well as her attentiveness to Black maternal death rates. In "The Economics of Women's Domestic Labor," I explore Jones' analysis of women's work—including women working inside and outside of the home, as well as her attention to disparities in wages along the lines of race and gender.

In "Black Women's Triple Oppression and Militant Agency," I examine her emphasis on Black women's militancy and agency despite triple oppression endured along the lines of race, class, and gender. Jones also brings attention to several prominent cases of injustice at that time (e.g., Dora Roberts, Rosa Lee Ingram, Amy Mallard, and the Trenton Six) and the significance of the Black Women's Club Movement. In "White Chauvinism, Male Chauvinism, and the Communist Party," I take up examples of chauvinism presented by Jones as well as the Party's approaches to white chauvinism and male chauvinism during this period. I also present Betty Millard's "Woman Against Myth" (1948), considering how Millard names, but does not really engage, the issue of triple oppression for Black women. Finally, in "Conclusion: . . . [Black] women think and write and speak," I note that Millard anticipates Simone de Beauvoir's arguments in some ways, I imagine a debate between Jones and Beauvoir on these overlapping issues taken up very differently in their respective 1949 texts, and I show how Jones was one of the earliest figures to recover *The Second Sex* in the US context.

Legacies of Slavery, Womanhood, and Motherhood

Jones is a trailblazer of critical analyses of Black women's experiences in slavery, tracing the persistent impact of slavery on the roles and representations of Black women from the slave trade to the mid-twentieth century in the United States.[11] Jones notes, "From the days of the slave traders down to present, the Negro woman has had the responsibility of caring for the needs of the family, of militantly shielding it from the blows of Jim-Crow insults, of rearing children in the atmosphere of lynch terror, segregation, and police brutality, and of fighting for an education for the children."[12] Jones identifies negative stereotypical representations of Black women going back to slavery—including the "traditional 'mammy' who puts the care of children and families of others above her own"—a "controlling image" that would continue to be re-examined decades later by Black feminists like Patricia Hill Collins.[13] Jones analyzes the intentions and impacts of these negative representations of Black women over time

78 BEAUVOIR AND BELLE

and argues, "This traditional stereotype of the Negro slave mother, which to this day appears in commercial advertisements, must be combatted and rejected as a device of the imperialists to perpetuate the white chauvinist ideology that Negro women are 'backward,' 'inferior,' and the 'natural slaves' of others."[14]

Offering a counter-narrative to the "mammy" stereotype, Jones explores Black womanhood and motherhood before and during slavery in the United States. She differentiates the historical status of Black women in Africa from the status of white women in Europe, asserting that positions of women in families in West African contexts were relatively higher than that of European women.[15] Jones also emphasizes Black mothers' love for their children, explaining, "There are numerous stories attesting to the self-sacrificial way in which East African mothers offered themselves to the slave traders in order to save their sons and Hottentot women refused food during famines until after their children were fed."[16] This is significant in part because it asserts a history of Black mothers that predates slavery, while also considering how Black mothers contended with the realities of the slave trade. As Davies explains, "Another of Jones' significant contributions in this essay is the link she makes between black women's roles in their families and the history of African women in matriarchal traditions . . . she demonstrates an advanced knowledge of African women beyond the stereotype and more in keeping with modern African feminist understandings."[17]

For Jones, slavery, race, gender, motherhood, labor, pregnancy, and family are not separable and/or merely analogous situations. Rather they are deeply interconnected in the lives of Black women. She asserts:

> It is impossible within the confines of this article to relate the terrible sufferings and degradation undergone by Negro mothers and Negro women generally under slavery. Subject to legalized rape by the slave owners, confined to slave pens, forced to march for eight to fourteen hours with loads on their backs and to perform back-breaking work even during pregnancy, Negro women bore a burning hatred for slavery, and undertook a large share of the responsibility for defending and nurturing the Negro family.[18]

Jones is showing the historical and contemporary impact of slavery on Black families. She analyzes the ways in which Black women took on familial responsibilities while also being subjugated to brutal degradation, legalized rape, and forced labor in slavery.

This is not a comparison of (white) womanhood and motherhood to slavery. It is an account of Black women's lived experiences of being literally and not metaphorically enslaved. This is not a reduction of Black women to the role of mother. It is a reclamation (rather than rejection) of the maternal by Black women over and against the denial of their familial ties in the context of chattel slavery, as well as a rejection of the prominent "mammy" stereotype that they repeatedly encountered in the aftermath of slavery. Far from reinforcing a patriarchal stereotype of (white) women as mothers, Jones is fighting the pervasive stereotypical representation Black women as "mammy" figures who care for white children to the neglect of their own. In the white imagination the Black "mammy" was not and could not be a "mother" who cares for her own children insofar as her children were not thought to need care and were not even considered her own. The institution of slavery rendered this an impossibility. Put another way, Black women were not considered "women" or "mothers." The enslaved mother, father, children, grandparents, aunts, uncles, cousins, etc. were not considered a traditional family within the structures and strictures of slavery. Rather, they were all considered property, often counted alongside cattle. This was their social and legal status, if not their ontological status. Thus, Jones is pushing back against historical and contemporary representations of the Black "mammy" who could never be a true "mother" by drawing on counter-examples of Black mothers who sacrificed for their children, and also by insisting that Black women defended and nurtured their families, even under the harshest conditions of slavery.

In her focus on Black mothers, Jones also calls attention to the neglected problem of their high maternal death rates, especially relative to white women: "Little wonder that the maternity death rate for Negro women is triple that of white women!"[19] And it is worth noting that the maternal death rate among Black and Indigenous women in the United States remains almost the same seven decades later! According to a press release from the Center for Disease Control (CDC) published in 2019, "Racial and Ethnic Disparities Continue in Pregnancy-Related Deaths: Black, American Indian/Alaska Native Women Most Affected."[20] These groups of women "are two to three times more likely to die from pregnancy-related causes than white women—and this disparity increases with age"[21] The CDC press release adds, "Most pregnancy-related deaths are preventable," and yet "Racial and ethnic disparities in pregnancy-related deaths have persisted over time."[22] Even accounting for education level, "The PRMR [pregnancy related mortality ratio] for black women with at least a college degree was 5.2 times that of their white counterparts."[23] Jones was ahead of her time in bringing attention to these issues, and we are still catching up to her insights about and attentiveness to the interconnections of race- and pregnancy-related mortality rates. She was similarly forward-thinking in analyzing differential wages disaggregated by gender and race when taking up the economics of women (e.g., their labor and wages), especially Black women, working within and outside of the home.

The Economics of Women's Domestic Labor

When Jones notes, "Not equality, but degradation and super-exploitation: this is the actual lot of Negro women!," she is not dealing with these matters in merely theoretical and abstract ways.[24] As Davies has argued, "Claudia Jones' position on the 'superexploitation of the black woman,' Marxist-Leninist in its formation, offered, for its time, the clearest analysis of the location of black women—not in essentialized, romantic, or homogenizing terms but practically, as located in U.S. and world economic hierarchies."[25] Davies not only situates this articulation of super-exploitation as "left of Marx," but she also reminds us that "Jones did not come up with her superexploitation analysis in isolation; it is in fact related to a pattern of analysis made by other black activist women."[26] In her examination of "economic hardships," Jones references a Bulletin of the Women's Bureau, US Department of Labor—*Handbook of the Facts for Women Workers* (1948, Bulletin 225). Drawing on this source material, while also adding her own analysis and insight, Jones offers statistical data about women working outside the home and their earnings, highlighting the differences between Black women and white women. Black women work outside of the home more often than their white counterparts.[27] White women receive higher earnings for their work outside of the home compared to their non-white counterparts (mainly Black women).[28] Likewise, the medium income for white families is higher than that of Black families.[29] Jones argues, "The super-exploitation of the Negro woman worker is thus revealed not only in that she receives, as woman, *less than equal pay for equal work with men*, but in that the majority of Negro women get *less than half the pay of white women*."[30]

When Jones takes up Black women and domestic labor, she has in mind Black women working outside of their own homes and earning an income by providing domestic labor in other people's homes (e.g., cooking, cleaning, and child care). But she is clearly aware that women working outside of the home are also burdened with domestic labor within their own homes. Jones explicitly states, "Many a domestic worker, on returning to her own household, must begin housework anew to keep her own family together."[31] Thus, her critiques about domestic labor are not about the experiences of housewives insofar as women working outside of the home to support themselves and their families are not "housewives."[32] Rather, Jones is critiquing the glorification of domestic labor that attempts to mask the economic exploitation of Black women domestic workers through low wages. Toward this end, she attunes readers to the neglect of the problems of Black women who are confined to low-wage domestic labor, and she refutes prevalent propaganda about the virtues of domestic work that seek to make it more "palatable."[33]

Jones is not only identifying neglected problems, but also offering tangible solutions and calling for concrete corrective action. For example, she pushes for trade unions to organize domestic workers ("the majority of whom are Negro women") and to fight for domestic workers to receive Social Security benefits.[34] She laments, "One of the crassest manifestations of trade-union neglect of the problems of the Negro woman worker has been the failure, not only to fight against relegation of the Negro woman to domestic and similar menial work, but to *organize* the domestic worker."[35] She is making a both/and argument. It is the case that Black women are often relegated to domestic labor and menial work even when they are qualified for other work

82 BEAUVOIR AND BELLE

opportunities. So it is necessary to expand work options and increase wages for Black women, in part by addressing the discrimination that limits their options and earning potential. And it is also the case that Black women domestic workers would benefit from trade-union organizing and from Social Security benefits, both of which would help to address the economic exploitation that domestic workers face. Again, Jones supports her position with statistics: "Only about one in ten of all Negro women workers is covered by present minimum-wage legislation, although about one-fourth are to be found in states having minimum-wage laws."[36]

Black Women's Triple Oppression and Militant Agency

Throughout this powerful 1949 article, Jones identifies Black women's triple oppression (as Black, as women, and as workers) as well as their militant agency, demonstrating how the former accelerated the latter. In the previous chapter ("Black Feminist Frameworks of Identity and Oppression"), I highlighted the "Triple Oppression Thesis" and presented examples from Ella Baker and Marvel Cooke ("The Bronx Slave Market," 1935), Louise Thompson ("Toward a Brighter Dawn," 1936), and Esther Cooper ("The Negro Woman Domestic Worker in Relation to Trade Unionism," 1940). We see Jones building on this legacy as she repeatedly situates Black women as simultaneously gendered (*woman/mother*), classed (*worker*), and raced (*Negro*). There are at least four explicit examples of this framing in the article. She states, "*As mother, as Negro, and as worker*, the Negro woman fights against the wiping out of the Negro family, against the Jim-Crow ghetto existence which destroys the health, morale, and very life of millions of her sisters, brothers, and children."[37] Here Jones is again situating Black women as political actors who are confronting attacks on multiple fronts. They are fighting for their families, communities, better living conditions, health and wellness, and the very existence of Black people. When Jones asserts, "Negro women—*as workers, as Negros, and as women*—are the most oppressed stratum of the whole population," she is making the case that Black women's specific lived experience with these triple identities leave them triply oppressed.[38] Black women workers are oppressed not only as workers, not only as Black, and not only as women—but as all three uniquely and simultaneously. Thus, special considerations are required for addressing (rather than neglecting) the needs of Black women at these intersections.

Jones reiterates this triple oppression in the contexts of job opportunities and the women's movement. Concerning the former she states, "Inherently connected with the question of job opportunities where the Negro woman is concerned, is the special oppression she faces *as Negro, as woman, and as worker*."[39] And concerning the latter, she asserts, "For the progressive women's movement, the Negro woman, who combines in her the status of *the worker, the Negro, and the woman*, is the vital link to this heightened political consciousness."[40] Here again Jones is returning to her framing of Black women as political actors and resisters, not merely victims of oppression. She situates Black women as a vital link to the heightened political consciousness of the women's movement if it is to be truly progressive and effective. This triple-oppression framework not only names the needs of Black women that often went neglected in 1949 and prior, but also anticipates activist and theoretical framings that would come decades later, such as *interlocking systems of oppression* (Combahee River Collective Statement), *imperialist-white-supremacist-capitalist-patriarchy* (bell hooks), and *intersectionality* (Kimberlé Crenshaw).

It cannot be overstated that Jones is intentional about repeatedly naming Black women's triple oppression, while also constantly emphasizing Black women as active agents rather than as passive victims. Connecting Black women's agency and militancy with Black liberation, she states, "An outstanding feature of the present stage of the Negro liberation movement is the growth in the militant participation of the Negro women in all aspects of the struggle for peace, civil rights, and economic security."[41] She supports this claim by noting, "Symptomatic of this new militancy is the fact that Negro women have become symbols of many present-day struggles of the Negro people."[42] Of course, Black women are not only symbols of Black struggle, but also militant actors. Jones points to the causal connections between increased oppression and increased militancy, "The intensified oppression of the Negro people, which has been the hallmark of the postwar

84   BEAUVOIR AND BELLE

reactionary offensive, cannot therefore but lead to an acceleration of the militancy of the Negro woman."[43] Thus, we see Jones presenting Black oppression, agency, militancy, liberation, peace, civil rights, and economics as deeply interconnected.

Jones makes her arguments with theoretical prowess, while also offering several specific compelling and concrete case studies. For example, Jones shows the replications of certain aspects of the aforementioned legacies of slavery and the contemporary exploitation of Black women's domestic labor with reference to the specific example of Dora Jones, a Black woman illegally enslaved for close to forty years.[44] Dora Jones of Alabama was a former student of Elizabeth Ingalls (then Myra Elizabeth Kimball of Massachusetts), a white woman teacher at Trinity Mission School in Alabama. Elizabeth (married to Walter P. Harman) moved to Washington, DC, where she had a daughter (Ruth). Elizabeth sent for Dora, a teenager, to come from Alabama to Washington, DC, to work as her maid and nanny. Elizabeth's first husband, Walter, sexually exploited and impregnated Dora, who was still a teenager. (This has been described by some as "seduction" or as an "affair," but neither of these descriptions captures the age difference or the power dynamics between Jones and Harman.) When Jones disclosed to Elizabeth what Walter had done, Elizabeth divorced Walter and forced Dora to get an illegal abortion, which Elizabeth arranged. Elizabeth coerced Dora to continue working for her (now without any compensation) in part by threatening to report her illegal abortion, threatening to send her to a mental institution, and intimidating her with guilt and shame about her "adultery."[45] Elizabeth remarried a man named Alfred Ingalls, who also participated in the ongoing enslavement of Dora. They transported Dora by car from Massachusetts to California. During their travels, Dora was forced to sleep in the car, on the floor, or in bathtubs. When their adult daughter Helen found Dora in the car among the luggage, she reported her parents to state and local authorities in California. In this case, the use of the word "slavery" is not symbolic or hyperbolic. In charging the jury, it was explained, "The indictment charges the defendants with the intent to hold Dora L. Jones as a slave. I shall, therefore define the word 'slave' for you. 'A slave is a person who is wholly subject to the will of another, one who has no freedom of action and whose person and services are

CLAUDIA JONES 85

wholly under the control of another, and who is in a state of enforced compulsory service to another.'"[46]

Claudia Jones also presents multiple cases of lynching, its impact on families, and resistance in the form of "protests against unpunished lynchings and the legal lynchings 'Northern style.'"[47] She underscores hypocrisy in America with regard to Black women and again reclaims their roles as mothers. Making a passing mention of President Truman's speech on the "'love and reverence' for all mothers of the land"—Jones names its contradictions, "The so-called 'love and reverence' for the mothers of the land by no means includes Negro mothers who, like Rosa Lee Ingram, Amy Mallard, the wives of the Trenton Six, or the other countless victims, dare fight back against lynch law and 'white supremacy' violence."[48] Jones begins with the Rosa Lee Ingram case: "Georgia keeps a widowed Negro mother of twelve children under lock and key. Her crime? She defended her life and dignity—aided by her two sons—from the attacks of a 'white supremacist.'"[49] Ingram (a forty-year-old widowed mother of fourteen children and sharecropper) and four of her sons (Charles age seventeen, Wallace age sixteen, Sammie Lee age fourteen, and James age twelve) were arrested for the death of their neighbor John Ethron Stratford, a "white would-be rapist" (age sixty-four and also a sharecropper).[50] Charles was tried separately and acquitted, and James was released. But Rosa Lee, Wallace, and Sammie Lee had a one-day trail (on January 26, 1948) in which the three were convicted by an all-white male jury and then sentenced to death (on February 7, 1948).

After years of protests and other interventions (e.g., fundraising and financial support, petitions, pamphlets, thousands of postcards and letters, legal defense, court appeals, prison visitations) coordinated by the Georgia Defense Committee, NAACP, Civil Rights Congress, Sojourners for Truth, Women's Committee for Equal Justice, and the Communist Left (those organizations often disagreeing with one another about strategies), the Ingrams' death sentences were commuted to life in prison. Then with ongoing coordinated resistance efforts, they were granted parole in August 1959.[51] McDuffie explains, "The Rosa Lee Ingram case represented the most important site of black women radicals' organizing during the late 1940s" and adds, "the Ingram campaign illustrates how black women radicals used familialism [i.e., emphasizing Ingram as widow and mother] as a basis for advancing a feminist agenda and contesting Cold War politics."[52] Support for the Ingram case was interracial and international.[53]

In addition to the Ingram case, Jones also calls attention to Amy Mallard, "the Department of Justice has greeted Mrs. Amy Mallard, widowed Negro school teacher, since her husband was lynched in Georgia because he had bought a new Cadillac and become, in the opinion of the 'white supremacists,' 'too uppity.'"[54] Jones is offering an example of what Ids B. Wells articulates earlier—that the crimes for lynching were often Black political and economic agency, not Black men raping white women. *The Pittsburgh Courier* reports that Robert Mallard was murdered in his car in front of Amy Mallard (his wife), their infant child, and two young companions, as well as before a band of fifty to seventy white men.[55] Motives for the murder included his political activity (his life was threatened to prevent him from voting) as well as his economic success and the purchase of this vehicle. *Atlanta Daily World* newspaper reported that Robert Mallard "had incurred the envy and jealousy of white residents in the community, that he had out-maneuvered white sales-men of advertising and trade supplies to Negro funeral homes."[56] Furthermore, officers from Tooms county, GA, described Mallard as a "'bad,' 'biggety,' and 'trouble-making' Negro."[57]

Although Mrs. Mallard told police that men in white robes shot and killed Mr. Mallard, Klan Dragon Green claimed to have done a "thorough investigation" confirming "that every Klan robe was under lock and key at the time of the murder."[58] To make matters worse, Mrs. Mallard was arrested for her husband's murder and taken into custody after her husband's funeral. Also arrested were the two young companions, William Tim Carter (age eighteen) and his sister Emma Lean Carter (age thirteen), as well as a white farmer and material witness Frank Brinson. Unfortunately, none of these injustices were shocking to this Black community in Georgia insofar as "Negro leaders earlier had predicted such a move as a means to cover up possible mob violence through intimidation of witnesses."[59] Eventually the charges were dropped, and Mrs. Mallard relocated to Harlem—during which time her house in Georgia was burned down by the KKK and funds in her bank account were stolen (reduced from $700 to $33).[60]

CLAUDIA JONES 87

Another important case cited by Jones is that of the Trenton Six, who were falsely accused of attacking William and Elizabeth Horner in a store owned by Mr. Horner (on January 27, 1948). He later died from the attack. According to Cathy Knepper, police units referred to as "Crime Crushers and the Trenton Gestapo . . . created a reign of terror in the black community" by frequently arresting and brutalizing Black men and then releasing them.[61] Eventually, six Black men (Collis English, McKinely Forrest, Ralph Cooper, Horace "Buddy" Wilson, James Thorpe, Jr., and John McKenzie), who by most accounts had nothing to do with the attack, were arrested, indicted, convicted for murder, and then sentenced to death (on August 6, 1948). As with other cases, the American Communist Party, Civil Rights Congress, and NAACP were involved in supporting the Trenton Six with legal counsel and raising awareness about the case. Again there were tensions and disagreements about strategies. Half of the defendants (English, Thorpe, and Cooper) went with Civil Rights Congress legal counsel, and the other half (Forrest, Wilson, and McKenzie) with NAACP legal counsel. English and Cooper accepted pleas and remained imprisoned until Cooper was released on parole in 1954 and English died after a heart attack in 1952. But the other four were acquitted (June 1951).

In addition to these specific cases, Jones also reminds readers of the powerful legacy and ongoing activism of the Black Women's Club Movement. In a section of the article subtitled "Negro Women in Mass Organizations," Jones notes, "The most prominent of their organizations are the National Association of Negro Women, the National Council of Negro Women, the National Federation of Women's Clubs, the Women's Division of the Elk's Civil Liberties Committee, the National Association of Colored Beauticians, National Negro Business Women's League, and the National Association of Colored Graduate Nurses."[62] To this list Jones also adds Black sororities, women's church committees, organizations among women of West Indian descent, and women's divisions of the NAACP and National Urban League. Jones explains, "These organizations play a many-sided role, concerning themselves with all questions pertaining to the economic, political, and social life of the Negro people, and particularly of the Negro family."[63] This itemization of Black women's organizing is presented to offer additional evidence of Black women's militant agency, but also to

88 BEAUVOIR AND BELLE

refute paternalistic attitudes about Black women's activist work. Jones asserts with frankness, "The disdainful attitudes which are sometimes expressed—that Negro women's organizations concern themselves *only* with 'charity work'—must be exposed as of chauvinist derivation, however subtle, because while the same could be said of many organizations of white women, such attitudes fail to recognize the *special character* of the role of Negro Women's organizations."[64] In the next section, I unpack Jones' choice of language here ("chauvinist") to characterize negative attitudes and actions toward Black women, while also offering a broader context for how chauvinism was being taken up within the Communist Party at the time.

White Chauvinism, Male Chauvinism, and the Communist Party

Jones explicitly references chauvinism several times in this article. In addition to the previous description of chauvinist attitudes toward Black women's organizing, she notes that the relegation of Black women to domestic work also contributes to the perpetuation and intensification of "chauvinism directed against *all* Negro women."[65] Concerning white women's interactions with Black women, Jones explains that "Chauvinism on the part of progressive white women is often expressed in their failure to have close ties of friendship with Negro women and to realize that this fight for equality of Negro women is in their own self-interest, inasmuch as the super-exploitation of oppression of Negro women tends to depress the standards of *all women*."[66] Here Jones is calling on progressive white women to confront their white chauvinism, cultivate friendships with Black women, and join the fight for Black women—even if only in self-interest, because all women are impacted by the oppression of any select group of women. And again, offering solutions, Jones calls on white progressives and Communists, especially white women, to step up by checking their chauvinism and becoming more trustworthy. She argues, "Persistent challenge to every chauvinist remark as concerns the Negro woman is vitally necessary, if we are to break down the understandable distrust on the part of Negro women who are repelled by the white chauvinism they often find expressed in progressive circles."[67] Put another way, white chauvinism is a white progressive problem, not a Black woman problem.[68]

Claudia Jones' articles (including but not limited to this 1949 article, "An End to the Neglect of the Problems of the Negro Woman!") were published when the Communist Party was in crisis concerning both "the Negro question" (at times framed in terms of "white chauvinism") as well as "the woman question" (at times framed in terms of "male chauvinism"). In fact, this particular article was featured in an issue of *Political Affairs* along with other articles explicitly naming white chauvinism in their titles—for example, "Destroy the Virus of White Chauvinism" by Pettis Perry and "Strengthen the Struggle Against White Chauvinism" by Bob Thompson. In *American Communism in Crisis: 1943–1957* (1972), Joseph Robert Starobin notes that the American Communist Party had a history of taking up the Negro question going back to 1919.[69] There was opposition to racial oppression, but the operating (and false) assumption was that racial oppression would be eliminated when class oppression was eliminated. He asserts, "As the American Communist Party staggered, they turned inward," and adds, "Probably the most symptomatic example of this 'turning inward' was the 1949–1953 campaign against 'white chauvinism.'"[70] For Starobin, "This frenzy marks one of the many points at which the experience of the American Communists two decades ago [late 1940s–early 1950s] offers a parallel and a precedent to the trauma affecting the new left in the late 1960s on the same issue—black and white relations."[71]

Kate Weigand examines the Party's approach to white chauvinism and the Negro question as well as to male chauvinism and the woman question in *Red Feminism: American Communism and the Making of Women's Liberation* (2001). The evolving conceptualization of and strategies for addressing the former had implications for the latter. She explains, "Their new approach to the Negro question redefined white chauvinism as a manifestation of ruling-class ideology that 'polluted the white workers of America'; and prevented the interracial unity that was necessary to achieve a revolutionary social transformation."[72] She elaborates, "In other words, they fully embraced the notion that white chauvinism impeded the interests of both white and black workers, that it betrayed revolutionary theory and practice by advancing the interests of the class enemy, and that it must be purged from the Party's ranks."[73] With this in mind, she traces how attitudes and strategies about the Negro question and the woman question shifted over time, noting, "Their regard for 'the woman question' in the 1920s was minimal and tokenistic compared with their attention to the 'ethnic question' and the 'Negro question,' but by the late 1930s Communists began using the lessons they had learned from their campaigns against ethnic fragmentation and racism between 1919 and 1936 to make gender issues a more central part of their program."[74]

Assessing how the Communist Party's approach to white chauvinism provided a blueprint that white women appropriated for their confrontation with male chauvinism, Weigand explains, "This insight set in motion changes that would ultimately make it possible for radical [white] women to emulate African American Communists and to organize on their own behalf."[75] Her account of white women's efforts to "emulate" Black strategies of resistance is reiterated again later when she states, "This became especially clear when some of the most radical women in the Communist Party such as the pioneering Communist feminist Mary Inman followed African American Communists' opposition to white chauvinism and denounced 'male chauvinism' in Party ranks and in their own families and relationships."[76] In addition to Inman, Weigand highlights other white women like Betty Millard in her analysis of "radical women," but she also names Claudia Jones. Presenting the Communist Party as unique in that historical moment, she explains, "But what made the Communist Party particularly unusual among other multicultural organizations working to improve women's status in this period before the Civil Rights movement burst on the national scene was that it attempted to analyze and respond to the particular problems that burdened black women along with class and gender oppression."[77]

To be sure, the intellectual, emotional, and activist labor of Black women provided the conditions for the possibilities for the Communist Party to take class, race, and gender seriously in their social and political agendas. Such attentiveness to the interconnections among various forms of oppression and the problems confronting Black women was neither accidental nor the result of Communist Party benevolence. Weigand acknowledges, "This work, inspired by the Party's leading black woman, Claudia Jones, made the Communist movement unique among feminist organizations that existed before the 1960s and shaped the ways that second-wave feminists would conceptualize the intersections between race and gender oppression in the 1970s and later."[78] Likewise Davies notes that Jones "challenged the limitations of CPUSA politics as she advanced positions that would influence the subsequent women's movement of the 1960s and 1970s."[79] And Angela Davis describes Jones as having a "constructive desire to urge her white co-workers and comrades to purge themselves of racist and sexist attitudes."[80] Living, working, and resisting at these intersections, Black women frequently, explicitly, and intentionally fought to dismantle what they identified as interconnected systems of oppression rather than confronting *either* one oppressive structure *or* any of the others. Weigand considers how Jones took this both/and approach insofar as she "capitalized on the Party's new commitment to women's liberation by framing many of the same issues as concerns about white chauvinism *and* male chauvinism."[81]

McDuffie also examines the Negro question and white chauvinism alongside the woman question and male chauvinism in the Communist Party. He reminds us that a separation of these frameworks assumes the maleness of Black people and the whiteness of women, without consideration for Black women confronted by both.[82] Like Weigand, McDuffie acknowledges that race often had a higher priority than gender in the Party.[83] We cannot take for granted that the Communist Party would have taken up the interconnected complexities of race, class, and gender oppression automatically or organically. Again, their initial operating assumption was that eliminating class oppression would also eliminate race and gender oppression. Black women disrupted the status quo by organizing to raise awareness about triple oppressions as well as strategies to confront them.[84] Arguing that Black women (and not working-class white men) were the vanguard center, they made explicit efforts to fight against interconnected systems of oppression globally.[85] There is one more explicit identification of chauvinism in this essay by Jones that warrants special attention. Jones states unequivocally, "A developing consciousness on the woman question today, therefore, must not fail to recognize that the Negro question in the United States is *prior* to, and not equal to, the woman question;

92   BEAUVOIR AND BELLE

that only to the extent that we fight all chauvinist expressions and actions as regards the Negro people and fight for the full equality of the Negro people, can women as a whole advance their struggle for equal rights."[86] I take Jones to be calling attention to Black women's situation as prior to and not equal to white women's situation and/or Black men's situation. As Anna Julia Cooper stated in 1892, the Black woman "is confronted by both a race question and a woman problem and is as yet an unknown or unacknowledged factor in both."[87] Davies notes that for Jones, "This perhaps controversial assertion ... is not as straightforward as the 'race first' assertion of black (male) nationalism."[88]

I also want to debunk assumptions that Jones is making a "race trumps gender" argument insofar as Black women are living at the intersections of Blackness and woman-ness and confronting racism and sexism simultaneously.[89] We know Jones is not taking a simple "race first" or "race trumps gender" position in part because of the aforementioned triple-oppression thesis that centers race, class, and gender identities and oppressions. Furthermore, she is also sure to name and critique Black men's chauvinism toward Black women and their problematic intra-racial gender politics. For example, she notes how "One freedman observed, during the Civil War, that many [Black] men were exceedingly jealous of their [Black women's] newly acquired authority in familial relations and insisted upon a recognition of their [Black men's] superiority over women."[90] Along similar lines, Jones is critical of the patriarchy of the Black Church, "which from the outset was under the domination of men, also tended to confirm the man's authority in the family."[91] But again, she underscores Black women's agency and resistance efforts to these affronts, for example, leaving their husbands and taking their children elsewhere.[92] For Jones, improving the conditions and status of Black people (as well as improving the status of women) necessarily entails improving the status of Black women, and especially Black women workers. Rather than privileging racism over sexism, Jones is calling for a fight against all forms of chauvinism that adversely impact the rights of Black people, women, and of course Black women.

Having said that, it is also the case that Jones is speaking directly to white women when she claims that the Negro question is prior to

CLAUDIA JONES 93

and not equal to the woman question. On this point, we can examine the specific example of Betty Millard's efforts to equate the Negro question with the woman question the previous year in her essay "Woman Against Myth" (1948). Weigand notes, "Partly in response to 'Woman Against Myth,' CP National Women's Commission secretary and best-known black woman leader Claudia Jones wrote her landmark article 'An End to the Neglect of the Problems of the Negro Woman.' "[93] Jones is refuting the efforts to equate racism with sexism. For example, Millard opens "Woman Against Myth" with the following quote from James Gordon Bennett (1852):

How did woman first become subject to man, as she is now all over the world? By her nature, her sex, just as the Negro is and always will be to the end of time, inferior to the white race, and therefore doomed to subjugation; but she is happier than she would be in any other condition, just because it is the law of nature.[94]

Beginning her essay in this way, Millard shows how white men (not just white women) compared the status and capacities of white women with Black men. This opening quote from Bennett serves the purpose of introducing a comparison of the condition and status of white women, Black men, and others that continues throughout Millard's essay. She argues that (white) woman's oppression is more subtle and harder to recognize than the pressing matters facing Black people, Jewish people, and anti-fascists. But Millard does not explicitly privilege (white) woman's oppression above anti-Black racism, antisemitism, or fascism. In fact, she seems to go in the opposite direction when she suggests that although (white) women are exploited by social structures, they do not constitute an oppressed people. It is in the context of claiming that women in general (i.e., white women) do not constitute an oppressed people that Millard names triple oppression as an important caveat concerning Black women in particular. She states, "All classes of the Negro people thus suffer, and the great majority of Negro women are triply oppressed as Negroes, women, and workers."[95]

94 BEAUVOIR AND BELLE

Although Millard names this triple oppression, she then moves quickly away from the insights of the triple-oppression thesis and ultimately defaults to an analogical approach equating racial and gender oppression. For example, she offers the following race/gender analogy: "Cut off from the productive process, they [white women] were confined to household drudgery, were uneducated and took no part in public life. Then, much as when Negroes are excluded from education they are then accused of being ignorant, [white] women were declared to have no brains worth mentioning."[96] Here Millard is comparing the lack of access to education and the resulting assumptions about white women's and Black men's ignorance. This race/gender analogy is followed by a slave/woman analogy: "Working fourteen hours a day for two or three dollars a week, [white] women found themselves in a new and more brutal kind of *slavery*; but at the same time, learning painfully the lesson of organization, they laid the groundwork for their freedom."[97] In these examples, Millard's analogical approach undermines the insights of the triple-oppression thesis that she previously acknowledged.

Millard returns to triple oppression again toward the end of the essay when states we, "struggle together with such organizations as the Congress of American Women for price and rent control, for the rights of the triply-oppressed Negro women, for nurseries, for protective legislation and equal pay—and the mobilization of millions of women for a progressive Third Party victory as a way of arresting the drive of the monopolists toward reaction and war."[98] In this way, Millard's "Woman Against Myth" is one prominent example of an essay by a white woman who names triple oppression and gestures at coalition. Nonetheless, she still reverts to analogies between white women's oppression and Black men's oppressions that the triple-oppression thesis is intended to disrupt and exceed. When we contrast Millard's essay with Claudia Jones' "An End to the Neglect of the Problems of the Negro Woman!" (as well as an earlier essay by Jones with similar themes and arguments, "For New Approaches to Our Work Among Women," 1948), we see the difference between simply naming triple oppression versus substantively engaging its impact while also offering strategies for mitigating it.[99] Millard does the former, Jones the latter.

Conclusion: ". . . [Black] women can think and speak and write!"

In reading Millard's "Woman Against Myth," I find it interesting that her analysis anticipates some of Simone de Beauvoir's rhetorical moves that we find in *The Second Sex* (e.g., the race/gender analogy, the slave/woman analogy, and the notion that white women do not constitute an oppressed group, or as Beauvoir puts it, women do not say "we"). And every time I read Jones' essay on women, published the same year as Beauvoir's essay on women, I am struck by the fact that Jones' essay has not received nearly the amount of critical attention that it warrants, especially when compared with the ink that has been spilled about *The Second Sex*—including, for example, an entire volume committed to the translation of that text and the placement (or not) of an indefinite article in Beauvoir's infamous sentence, "One is not born, but rather becomes, [a] woman."[100] I am not suggesting that Beauvoir does not warrant this level of attention (of course, many white feminists insist that she deserved *more* attention). Rather, I am asserting that it is scandalous that Jones has not garnered such attention. Perhaps this inattentiveness to Jones is evidence of the triple-oppression thesis that she simultaneously articulated and experienced.

On this point, Davies underscores the myriad ways in which Jones endeavored to "challenge the construction of black women as silenced and unthinking i.e., not intellectuals with agency—i.e., thinking, writing, speaking beings."[101] In a collection of Jones' writings edited by Davies, she opts for the title, ". . . [Black] women can think and speak and write!" for Jones' "Statement Before Being Sentenced To One Year And One Day Imprisonment By Judge Edward J. Dimok After A Nine Months Trail Of 13 Communist Leaders At Foley Square, New York, 1953." Davies derives this title from Jones' statement in which she proclaims, "You dare not, gentlemen of the prosecution, assert that Negro women can think and speak and write!"[102] Davies presents the US government's targeting and deportation of Jones as an example of the effort to erase Black women, especially Afro-Caribbean women, as thinkers and activists. She posits how Jones' problematic subjectivity is rendered non-existent, "Deported from the US during the McCarthy period, Claudia Jones was meant to be erased."[103]

96 BEAUVOIR AND BELLE

I have often considered how Claudia Jones' short but dense and comprehensive nineteen-page article "An End to the Neglect of the Problems of the Negro Woman!" might be in critical conversation with Simone de Beauvoir's long (almost one thousand pages in two volumes) encyclopedic book *The Second Sex*. There are several overlapping themes—for example, slavery, race, gender, motherhood, domestic labor, pregnancy, and family—taken up with decidedly different approaches by Jones and Beauvoir in these iconic texts that were both published in 1949. Jones centers Black women whose problems she ascertains have been neglected (in part because of the focus on Black men and white women). She situates Black women's lived experiences as mothers in the context of slavery and the persistent devaluation of Black women and the destruction of Black families as legacies of slavery. Beauvoir, who also has a lot to say about the aforementioned themes, centers white women and rarely mentions or acknowledges Black women in those discussions. She describes the burden and boredom of white women with motherhood and family, but Black women's efforts to defend and nurture their precariously positioned families during and after slavery do not register for her. In contrast with Jones, Beauvoir's engagement with slavery is more instrumental. She presents (white) women figuratively as slaves, but she does not really take on racialized chattel slavery or the situation of Black women who were literally and materially enslaved (in the US context and in the French colonial context).[104] Beauvoir describes (white) women as enslaved to their reproductive functions, but she does not acknowledge the ways that enslaved Black women and men were forced to "breed" by the men and women who held them and their children as property.

Contrasting Jones and Beauvoir in this way, it seems that Jones would have much to critique in Beauvoir (just as she pushed back on Millard). I am not aware of Jones ever publishing anything that explicitly engages Beauvoir, but she does have an interesting and important role in the recovery of *The Second Sex* in the United States. Jones not only intervened to prevent the publication of a negative review of the text in *Masses and Mainstream*, but she also later advocated for the publication of a more positive review in *Worker*.[105] More specifically, Jones helped Elizabeth Lawson publish a positive review of *The Second*

CLAUDIA JONES   97

Sex, "Woman: Second Sex" in *Worker* in 1954.[106] While Lawson offers a mostly favorable review, there are also some critiques.[107] On the more positive side, Lawson states, "to infuse the work from first to last with ardor for woman's freedom—this has been the rare achievement of the great French writer, Simone de Beauvoir, in her monumental work."[108] On the more critical side, Lawson notes, "Many criticism can be made of her work. Although she ably discusses the role of trade unions in the fight for woman's rights, there is far less than there should be on this vital aspect of the struggle. The book is overweighted with considerations of sex problems."[109] Lawson also critiques misstatements about the Soviet Union, Beauvoir's defaulting to psychoanalysis (despite her own critiques of it), the influence of idealist philosophy, as well as her materialist view.[110] Weigand notes, "Lawson published a laudatory review of Simone de Beauvoir's *The Second Sex*, which she called a 'magnificent contribution' and a 'trumpet call to women's liberation' that, despite its problems, progressives should read in order to benefit from its freshness, originality, and continuous revelations and delights.'"[111] Likewise, Shirley Chen explains, "when Lawson reviewed *The Second Sex* in the *Sunday Daily Worker* and declared that it 'was truly a great book, a magnificent contribution to the struggle for woman's rights,' she acted to rescue its significance for Communist women."[112]

Jones' connection to *The Second Sex* would also go beyond her roles with these reviews of the text. According to Chen, "In fact, prior to her [Lawson's] October review, Jones helped her put out a discussion document on the book through NWC [National Women's Commission]."[113] The discussion document offered a concise chapter-by-chapter summary of *The Second Sex* using quotations from the text, and Lawson "intended for the document to serve as a corrective to negative reviews in the press and as a substitute for those who could not obtain the 'very long and very expensive' book."[114] Both the discussion document and review were projects that came after the publication of Jones' article "An End to the Neglect of the Problems of the Negro Woman!" (1949) and just before Jones' deportation.[115] But given Jones' instrumental role in helping to get Lawson's summary and review of the text out to a Communist Party audience, I would say that she is one of the earlier contributors to the recovery work of Beauvoir and *The Second Sex* by Black women, though she remains neglected in the secondary

98   BEAUVOIR AND BELLE

literature on Beauvoir. Another prominent Black woman at the forefront of recovering Beauvoir and *The Second Sex* in the US context is Lorraine Hansberry (who is also frequently neglected in the secondary literature on Beauvoir). Claudia Jones worked with and at one point shared an apartment with Lorraine Hansberry, whose review of *The Second Sex* will be taken up in detail in the next chapter.[116]

Notes

1. Jones was a committed activist, strategic communist, insightful journalist, and brilliant theoretician. Born in Trinidad, Jones' family immigrated to the United States during her youth (when she was about eight years old). In *Left of Karl Marx: The Political Life of Black Communist Claudia Jones* (Durham, NC: Duke University Press, 2008), Carole Boyce Davies argues that Jones' identity not only as a Black woman, but more specifically as a Black immigrant woman from Trinidad, is important. (Hereafter Davies 2008.) Jones grew up in Harlem during the Great Depression and became active early on by joining the movement for the Scottsboro Nine. See also Erik S. McDuffie, *Sojourning for Freedom: Black Women, American Communism, and the Making of Black Left Feminism* (Durham, NC: Duke University Press, 2011). He notes, "above all, the Scottsboro case would enable the Communist Party to expand its presence in black communities and to recruit a new generation of black women," 57. (Hereafter McDuffie 2011.)

2. Mary Helen Washington, "Alice Childress, Lorraine Hansberry, and Claudia Jones: Black Women With the Popular Front," in *Left of the Color Line; Race, Radicalism, and Twentieth Century Literature of the United States,* ed. Bill Mullen James Smethurst (Chapel Hill: University of North Carolina Press, 2003). One of Washington's chapter subsections is titled "Lorraine Hansberry and Freedom: A Founding Text of Black Left Feminism." (Hereafter Washington 2003.)

3. McDuffie 2011, 3. In an earlier article, "Esther V. Cooper's 'The Negro Woman Domestic Worker in Relations to Trade Unionism': Black Left Feminism and the Popular Front," *American Communist History* 7, no. 2 (2008): 204, McDuffie notes, "Black left feminism paid special attention to the intersectional, transnational nature of African-American women's oppression and viewed them as key agents for transformative change. Committed to the Popular Front agenda of civil rights, trade unionism,

CLAUDIA JONES 99

anti-fascism, internationalism, and concern for women's equality, their work anticipated conclusions drawn by 'second wave' black feminism decades later." (Hereafter McDuffie 2008.)

4. Cheryl Higashida, *Black Internationalist Feminism: Women Writers of the Black Left. 1945–1995* (Urbana: University of Illinois Press, 2013). (Hereafter Higashida 2013.)

5. Higashida 2013, 2. Higashida elaborates, "This feminism was internationalist in two different but related senses. First, it held that self-determination for oppressed nations would bring about socialism for the working classes of all nations. Second, it linked the struggles of African Americans in the United States to struggle for national self-determination in the Caribbean, the Americas, Africa, Asia, and Australia" (Higashida 2013, 3).

6. Higashida 2013, 3.

7. Davies 2008, xiii–xiv. Davies also notes that unfortunately, "The fact is that she is not well known in the Caribbean, just as she is not remembered in the United States . . . But this lack of recognition is also related to the fact that women are not generally assigned importance as intellectual subjects" (Davies 2008, 25).

8. Davies 2008, 24–25.

9. *Claudia Jones: Beyond Containment*, ed. Carole Boyce Davies (Banbury: Ayebia Clark Publishing Limited, 2011), xxvii. (Hereafter Davies 2011.)

10. Davies 2008, 37. Claudia Jones' "An End to the Neglect of the Problems of the Negro Woman!" was originally published in *Political Affairs: A Magazine Devoted to the Theory and Practice of Marxism-Leninism* (28, no. 6. June 1949). (Hereafter Jones 1949.) The contents of this issue of the journal include: "Destroy the Virus of White Chauvinism" by Pettis Perry, "Strengthen the Struggle Against White Chauvinism" by Bob Thompson, "The Communist Party: Champion Fighter for Negro Rights" by James W. Ford, "An End to the Neglect of the Problems of the Negro Woman!" by Claudia Jones, "The People Organize to Re-Elect Ben Davis" by Herbert Whecidin and George Blake, "The Struggle for the Negro Labor Alliance" by Norman Ross, and "Consciousness of Negro Nationality: An Historical Survey" by Herbert Aptheker. My citations of this article are from a pdf of this essay, which describes Jones' article as "Reprinted from Political Affairs (June 1949) by National Women's Commission, C.P.U.S.A., 35 East 12th Street, New York 3, N.Y."

11. For example, in a section of her essay subtitled "Historical Aspects," Jones traces the persistent impact of slavery on the roles and representations of Black women from the slave trade to the mid-twentieth century in the

100 BEAUVOIR AND BELLE

United States. Angela Davis, bell hooks, Hortense Spillers, and others later build on this groundwork.

12. Jones 1949, 3.
13. Jones 1949, 7. See also Patricia Hill Collins, *Black Feminist Thought: Knowledge, Consciousness, and the Politics of Empowerment* (New York: Routledge, 1991).
14. Jones 1949, 7.
15. Jones 1949, 7.
16. Jones 1949, 7.
17. Davies 2008, 39. Davies also cites Ifi Amadiume's research on African matriarchy in *Male Daughters, Female Husbands: Gender and Sex in an African Society* (London: Zed Books, 1987) as well as in *Reinventing Africa: Matriarchy, Religion and Culture* (London: Zed Books, 1997). Davies adds in a footnote, "Moynihan clearly had not read Claudia Jones' essay" (Davies 2008, 248n20).
18. Jones 1949, 7.
19. Jones 1949, 5.
20. "Racial and Ethnic Disparities Continue in Pregnancy-Related Deaths: Black, American Indian/Alaska Native Women Most Affected" (September 5, 2019), https://www.cdc.gov/media/releases/2019/p0905-racial-ethnic-disparities-pregnancy-deaths.html, accessed August 6, 2020.
21. "Racial and Ethnic Disparities Continue in Pregnancy-Related Deaths: Black, American Indian/Alaska Native Women Most Affected."
22. "Racial and Ethnic Disparities Continue in Pregnancy-Related Deaths: Black, American Indian/Alaska Native Women Most affected."
23. "Racial and Ethnic Disparities Continue in Pregnancy-Related Deaths: Black, American Indian/Alaska Native Women Most Affected."
24. Jones 1949, 4.
25. Davies 2008, 2. Davies adds, "Jones' argument regarding the superexploitation of the black woman is clearly a position left of Karl Marx, since Marx himself did not account for race and gender and/or the position of the black woman" (Davies 2008, 3). Davies also explains, "Her superexploitation thesis rests on the fact that black women, by virtue of being located as they are in society, among the most exploited and most underpaid of workers, tend to be the ones whose value of their labor power various other fractions (including other exploited workers) benefit from" (Davies 2008, 43).
26. Davies 2008, 43.
27. "In 1940, two out of every five Negro women, in contrast to two out of every eight white women, worked for a living. By virtue of their majority status

CLAUDIA JONES 101

among the Negro people, Negro women not only constitute the largest percentage of women heads of families, but are the main breadwinners of the Negro family" (Jones 1949, 4–5).

28. "The Women's Bureau, U.S. Department of Labor, *Handbook of the Facts for Women Workers* (1948, Bulletin 225), shows white women workers as having median earnings more than twice as high as those of non-white women workers (mainly Negro women) as earning less than $500 a year!" (Jones 1949, 5). Note: The language of "white women" and "non-white women" is consistent with the publication that Jones is citing (though the publication does not indicate that not-white women workers are "mainly Negro women"). See *Handbook*, pp. 21–22.

29. "In three large Northern industrial communities, the median income of white families ($1,720) is almost 60 percent higher than that of Negro families ($1,095)" (Jones 1949, 5).

30. Jones 1949, 5. (Emphasis added.)

31. Jones 1949, 11.

32. Note: this issue is taken up later in Chapter 6, where I examine Beauvoir's analysis of the housework of housewives in *The Second Sex.*

33. Jones 1949, 5.

34. Jones 1949, 11.

35. Jones 1949, 10. (Emphasis original.)

36. Jones 1949, 11.

37. Jones 1949, 3–4. (Emphasis added.)

38. Jones 1949, 4. (Emphasis added.)

39. Jones 1949, 6–7. (Emphasis added.)

40. Jones 1949, 15. (Emphasis added.)

41. Jones 1949, 3.

42. Jones 1949, 3.

43. Jones 1949, 3.

44. Jones 1949, 11. See article on the case: https://ladailymirror.com/2018/08/02/black-l-a-1947-elizabeth-ingalls-to-pay-dora-jones-6000-in-slavery-case-sentenced-to-fine-and-probation/. And see: https://www.sandieg oreader.com/news/2017/mar/15/feature-slavery-trial-draws-all-eyes-san-diego/#. Also see: http://www.blackpast.org/aaw/jones-dora-1890-1972, accessed January 29, 2022.

45. Court records indicate that "She [Dora Jones] testified that she believed the defendant [Elizabeth Ingalls] could and would execute the threat frequently made and have her committed to prison if she left the defendant's service." *United States v. Ingalls* (1947). See https://law.justia.com/cases/federal/district-courts/FSupp/73/76/2125385/, accessed January 29, 2022.

102 BEAUVOIR AND BELLE

46. *United States v. Ingalls* (1947).

47. Jones 1949, 14.

48. Jones 1949, 4. I believe Jones is referencing Truman's Proclamation 2836—Mother's Day 1949 in which the third paragraph reads, "Whereas in accordance with the dictates of our hearts we have set that day aside for manifestations of our love and reverence for all mothers of the land"; https://www.presidency.ucsb.edu/documents/proclamation-2836-moth ers-day-1949, accessed January 29, 2022.

49. Jones 1949, 4.

50. McDuffie 2011, 161. For more on this case see Charles H. Martin, "Race, Gender, and Southern Justice: The Rosa Lee Ingram Case," *The American Journal of Legal History* 29, no. 3 (July 1985): 251–268. (Hereafter Martin 1985.) Major actors in this case included not only Claudia Jones, but also Thurgood Marshall, Elizabeth Gurley Flynn, Henry Wallace, Mary Church Terrell, Ada B. Jackson, Maude White, Maude White Katz, W. A. Scott, and W. E. B. Du Bois, Shirley Graham Du Bois, and Eslande Robeson. It is worth noting that a 1948 NAACP appeal was authored by Du Bois and presented by Mary Church Terrell. Martin notes, "Mrs. Alva Myrdal, U.N. Assistant Secretary General in the Department of Social Affairs, received the document. Myrdal thanked the group but cautioned that U.N. agencies did not normally consider individual cases" (Martin 1985, 263). Note: Martin and Jones state that Rosa Lee Ingram was the mother of twelve children. McDuffie states that she was the mother of fourteen children. Here I went with McDuffie in my description as his is the more recently published source. Note: Alva Myrdal will be taken up in more de- tail in Chapter 7.

51. Martin 1985, 266.

52. McDuffie 2011, 165.

53. McDuffie notes, "The Sojourners, together with the left-wing Emma Lazarus Federation of Jewish Women's Clubs, based in New York, issued a joint statement in June 1952 to the Fifteenth International Conference on Public Education in Geneva, sponsored by United Nations Educational, Scientific, and Cultural Organization (UNESCO)," (McDuffie 2011, 178). McDuffie notes, "Moreover, the groups' collaboration illustrates how the Sojourners enabled black left feminists for the first time to set the terms for the political discussion with white women radicals," (McDuffie 2011, 178). Furthermore, the Ingram case (building on the response to the Scottsboro case which came before it) would also inspire the response to Angela Davis' case that would come years later. McDuffie notes, "The Free Angela Davis movement resembled the colorful Scottsboro and postwar Popular Front

CLAUDIA JONES 103

movements of the 1930s around Rosa Lee Ingram and Willie McGee" (McDuffie 2011, 198).

54. Jones 1949, 4.

55. *The Pittsburgh Courier*, December 4, 1948.

56. "Mrs. Mallard Held in Husband's Slaying, Widow Taken into Custody After Funeral," *Atlanta Daily World*, November 28, 1948, beginning on page 1 (accessed through Proquest Historical Newspapers).

57. *Atlanta Daily World*, November 28, 1948, 4.

58. *Atlanta Daily World*, November 28, 1948, 1, 4.

59. *Atlanta Daily World*, November 28, 1948, 1.

60. *New York Amsterdam News*, "Amy Mallard's Georgia Homes Razed by Fire; Husband Lynched Near Lyons; Widow Now Resides in Harlem," October 15, 1949, 1 and 54.

61. Cathy Knepper, *Jersey Justice: The Story of the Trenton Six* (New Brunswick, NJ: Rivergate Books, 2011), 4. See also, Denise Lynn, "Before the Central Park Five, There Was the Trenton Six," https://www.aaihs.org/before-the-central-park-five-there-was-the-trenton-six/.

62. Jones 1949, 9.

63. Jones 1949, 9.

64. Jones 1949, 9. (Emphasis original.)

65. Jones 1949, 12. (Emphasis added.) She outlines several offenses toward Black women domestic workers from white progressives and communists, many of whom employ Black women domestic workers in their homes. These offenses include: "[1] exploiting Negro domestic workers . . . [2] refusing to hire them through the Domestic Workers' Union; (or [3] refusing to help in its expansion into those areas where it does not yet exist), and [4] generally of participating in the vilification of 'maids' when speaking to their bourgeois neighbors and their own families"; Jones 1949, 12. Jones continues, "Then there is the [5] expressed 'concern' that the exploited Negro domestic worker does not 'talk' to, or is not 'friendly' with, her employer, or [6] the habit of assuming that the duty of the white progressive employer is to 'inform' the Negro woman of her exploitation and her oppression which she undoubtedly knows quite intimately"; Jones 1949, 12. In today's parlance, Jones is describing the stereotype of the "angry Black woman" and the persistence of white progressives in "whitesplaining" and/or "mansplaining" exploitation and oppression to Black women experiencing it firsthand.

66. Jones 1949, 12. (Emphasis added.)

67. Jones 1949, 12.

104   BEAUVOIR AND BELLE

68. The framing here gestures at later framing that there is not a Negro problem: there is a white problem—as expressed by Richard Wright, Jean-Paul Sartre, and Gunnar Myrdal. That framework is taken up briefly in Chapter 5 (footnote 31) of this text.

69. Joseph Robert Starobin, *American Communism in Crisis: 1943–1957* (Berkley: University of California Press, 1972). (Hereafter Starobin 1972.)

70. Starobin 1972, 197 and 198.

71. Starobin 1972, 199.

72. Kate Wiegand, *Red Feminism: American Communism and the Making of Women's Liberation* (Baltimore: John Hopkins University Press, 2001), 19. (Hereafter Wiegand 2001.)

73. Wiegand 2001, 19

74. Wiegand 2001, 15–16. Still, "Not until the mid-1930s would Communists even begin to think about the woman question in earnest" (Wiegand 2001, 20).

75. Wiegand 2001, 20.

76. Wiegand 2001, 24.

77. Weigand 2001, 98–99.

78. Weigand 2001, 99. While I appreciate the point Wiegand is making about Jones' insights and impact here, it is important to note that Black feminism troubles the waters of representing feminism in waves. Anthologies like Beverly Guy-Sheftall's *Words of Fire* (1995) demonstrate that Black feminist activism and scholarship have their own rhythms that do not fit neatly into waves. McDuffie presents Esther Cooper as one example of someone whose "work and legacy offers an alternative narrative to the wave metaphor, for her activism highlights both the breaks and the continuities in Black feminist struggles from the 1930s through the 1980s" (McDuffie 2011).

79. Davies 2008, 30.

80. Angela Davis, *Women, Race, and Class* (New York: Vintage Books, 1981), 169.

81. Weigand 2001, 101. (Emphasis added.)

82. McDuffie provides two examples: (1) "The resolution of 1922 on the Negro Question framed black liberation in masculinist terms," and (2) "... *Theses of the Communist Women's Movement*, issued by the Comintern in 1920, elided black women's issues, articulating gender oppression narrowly in economic, deterministic terms" (McDuffie 2011, 36–37).

83. "Despite the latter resolution's [*Theses of the Communist Women's Movement*] call championing gender equality, support for the Woman Question in both the Communist International and the CPUSA during these years lacked priority" (McDuffie 2011, 37).

CLAUDIA JONES 105

84. McDuffie also names white women like Jeanette Pearl, author of "Negro Women Workers" in the *Daily Worker*, 1924 (McDuffie 2011, 49). He notes that her short and vague article "did not issue a call for the Workers Party to unionize black women or to recruit them into its ranks. Nor did she discuss how the interplay of race, gender, and class positioned African American women at the bottom of the U.S. labor force . . .The article's vagueness and the Comintern's inattention to black women were indicative of how Communist leadership at this moment understood all working women as white and all blacks as men" (McDuffie 2011, 49). In addition to Claudia Jones, McDuffie also presents earlier figures like Grace Campbell who contributed to "women in Current Topics," where she "examined how race, gender, class, and cultural biases shaped black women's relation to the criminal justice system," along with Fanny Austin, Bell Lamb, Maude White, Williana Burroughs, Hermina Dumont, Louise Thompson, Queen Mother Audley Moore, Thyra Edwards, Bonita Williams, Ella Baker, Rose Gaulden, and many others (McDuffie 2011, 49).

85. McDuffie 2011, 13, 27, 60, 92, 161, 173.

86. Jones 1949, 15. (Emphasis original.)

87. Anna Julia Cooper, "The Status of Women in America," from *A Voice from the South* (1892), reprinted by Charles Lemert and Esme Bhan (eds.), *The Voice of Anna Julia Cooper* (Lanham, MD: Rowman and Littlefield, 1998), 112–113.

88. Davies 2008, 48. Davies also explains, "This was not an easy position for Jones to advance, and it exposed her to a great deal of criticism from white women and the charge that she was guilty of 'reverse chauvinism' " (Davies 2008, 48).

89. See Charles Mills, "Intersecting Contracts," in *Contract and Domination*, by Charles Mills and Carole Pateman (Cambridge: Polity Press, 2007). See also a critique of Mills on this position in Kathryn Sophia Belle (formerly Kathryn T. Gines), "Black Feminist Reflections on Charles Mills's 'Intersecting Contracts,' " "Charles Mills," special issue, *Critical Philosophy of Race* 5, no. 1 (Spring 2017): 19–28.

90. Jones 1949, 8.

91. Jones 1949, 8.

92. Jones 1949, 8.

93. Weigand 2001, 101.

94. Betty Millard, "Woman Against Myth" (New York: International Publishers, 1948), 3. (Hereafter Millard 1948.) https://digital.library.pitt.edu/islandora/object/pitt%3A31735059397616/viewer#page/4/mode/2up

95. Millard 1948, 10–11.

106   BEAUVOIR AND BELLE

96. Millard 1948, 15.
97. Millard 1948, 15. (Emphasis added.)
98. Millard 1948, 23.
99. Claudia Jones, "For New Approaches to Our Work Among Women," *Political Affairs* 27 (August 1948): 738–743. This article was initially published in *Political Affairs: A Magazine Devoted to the Theory and Practice of Marxism-Leninism* (1948). The contents of this issue of the journal include: "Specific Features of American Imperialist Expansion" by William Z. Foster; "Resolution of the Information Bureau Concerning the Situation in the Communist Party of Yugoslavia"; "Statement on the Information Bureau Resolution Concerning the Situation in the C.P. of Yugoslavia" by William Z. Foster and Eugene Dennis; "The Yugoslav Leaders on the Path of Betrayal by V. J. Jerome; The 'Grand' Old Party" by Max Gordon; "The New State of Israel" by Alexander Bittelman; "A Few Thoughts on Our Perspectives" by Gil Green; "For New Approaches to Our Work Among Women" by Claudia Jones; "Against Opportunism in Practice" by Fred Fine; "National Group Work in California" by Pettis Perry; "The Menace of Social-Democracy and Our Fight Against Opportunism" by George Morris; and "On the Party's Responsibility for Work Among the Youth" by Marvin Shaw.
100. See *"On ne naît pas femme: on le devient . . . " The Life of a Sentence*, ed. Bonnie Mann and Martina Ferrari (Oxford: Oxford University Press, 2017). See Kathryn Sophia Belle, review of *"On ne naît pas femme: on le devient . . . " The Life of a Sentence* (ed. Bonnie Mann and Martina Ferrari), *Notre Dame Philosophical Review*, June 28, 2018, https://ndpr.nd.edu/news/on-ne-nait-pas-femme-on-le-deviant-the-life-of-a-sentence/.
101. Davies 2011, 4.
102. Davies 2011, 8.
103. Davies 2011, xxix.
104. Note: The slave/woman analogy will be taken up in more detail in Chapter 6.
105. Shirley Chen states, "In a letter to left-wing writer Eve Merriam some years later, Lawson recalled how she had prevented a negative review of *The Second Sex* from running in the Party's cultural journal *Masses and Mainstream*, and managed to get her review published in the *Worker* with the aid of Claudia Jones" (in " 'To work, write, sing and fight for women's liberation': Proto-Feminist Currents in the American Left, 1946–1961," thesis, University of Michigan, 2011, 79). (Hereafter Chen 2011.)

CLAUDIA JONES 107

106. Elizabeth Lawson, "Woman: Second Sex," *Worker*, October 24, 1954, 12. (Hereafter Lawson 1954.) Chen notes, "The Sunday edition of the Daily Worker was known as the Worker" (Chen 2011, 78n 21).
107. Lawson 1954, 12.
108. Lawson 1954, 12.
109. Lawson 1954, 12.
110. Lawson 1954, 12. Lorraine Hansberry wrote a review essay of *The Second Sex* in 1957 in which she critiqued Beauvoir's existentialism instead of her materialism, and many critiqued Beauvoir (and existentialism in general) as a philosophy of "miserablism"—far from idealist. Hansberry references one "positive but brief review" of *The Second Sex*—namely, this review by Elizabeth Lawson. Note: Hansberry's important review essay on *The Second Sex* is taken up in more detail in Chapter 3.
111. Weigand 2002, 128.
112. Chen 2011, 78. Chen also asserts that Lawson's "sudden advocacy for women's rights was sparked by French feminist existentialist Simone de Beauvoir's *The Second Sex* . . . in 1954 and promptly ended as the Party's internal crisis came to the forefront in 1956" (Chen 2011, 77–78).
113. Chen adds, "The 12-page mimeographed document 'went all over the country' and anticipated Lawson's laudatory review" (Chen 2011, 79).
114. Chen 2011, 79.
115. Lawson would follow Jones as the new "woman's affairs" columnist after Jones' deportation in 1955. Having been arrested in 1948 (under the 1918 Immigration Act) and again in 1951 (under the Smith Act), Jones went to trail in 1952, was found guilty in 1953, and was sentenced to prison as well as charged a large fine. Throughout her time of activism, arrests, trail, and imprisonment, her health deteriorated. When she was released from prison, efforts to prevent her deportation failed. Jones agreed to leave the United States voluntarily (though she was still officially deported) and relocated to London in 1955.
116. See Imani Perry, *Looking for Lorraine: The Radiant and Radical Life of Lorraine Hansberry* (Boston: Beacon Press, 2018), 52–53.

3

Lorraine Hansberry

"*The Second Sex* may well be the most important work of this century"

Beverly Guy Sheftall's *Words of Fire* (1995) features a previously un-published essay by Lorraine Hansberry on Simone de Beauvoir's *The Second Sex*. In a short but informative introduction to the essay, Margaret B. Wilkerson notes that Hansberry read *The Second Sex* in 1954 or 1955 and likely wrote this review in 1957. Offering some context for why this is significant, she explains, "it is a sign of her times, the 1950s, that she was apparently one of the few readers of either gender who paid close attention to Beauvoir's revolutionary analysis of 'the woman question.'"[1] Wilkerson describes Hansberry's critical commentary as "uncompromising in its critique of male supremacy wherever it appears, the concept of 'a woman's place,' and the failure of United States thinkers (particularly those of the Left) to take the book seriously enough to engage Beauvoir in a substantial and challenging dialogue."[2] I want to underscore a few points by Wilkerson here: (1) there was not significant uptake of Beauvoir's two-volume "revolutionary treatment" of the woman question in the United States in the 1950s, (2) Hansberry was one of the few close readers of any gender (and I would add, race) in the United States offering an analysis of *The Second Sex* at that time, and (3) Hansberry offers her own insights about and critiques of male supremacy, women's oppression, and the shortcomings of US thinkers on the Left concerning these issues at the time. It is also worth noting that like Claudia Jones, Hansberry was a Black left internationalist feminist.[3]

Imani Perry also offers insights on Hansberry's engagement with Beauvoir's text in *Looking for Lorraine: The Radiant and Radical Life of Lorraine Hansberry* (2018). Describing it as "her textbook," Perry notes, "In the marginalia of *The Second Sex*, Lorraine poured her

Beauvoir and Belle. Kathryn Sophia Belle, Oxford University Press. © Oxford University Press 2024.
DOI: 10.1093/oso/9780197660195.003.0004

ideas and engaged in a conversation with de Beauvoir, one that was passionate and enduring for the remainder of her life."[4] According to Perry, reading *The Second Sex* was "a bittersweet respite and ritual for Lorraine," later adding, "What she found in the book she kept returning to, calling it like a girlfriend; 'Simone' was both a testimony to her suffering and a shaft of light."[5] But it is also clear that Hansberry was not a passive receptacle of Beauvoir's ideas. Perry asserts, "She was a critical but captivated reader of de Beauvoir, and as was characteristic of Lorraine, her criticism was a sign of how seriously she took the work."[6] She surmises, "De Beauvoir gave Lorraine space to articulate a feminism that did not separate out sexuality and sexual desire for other women and also the inspiration to build a feminism that did not exclude race but treated it as a necessary part of understanding race, and race as a necessary part of understanding gender."[7]

Likewise, Wilkerson argues that Hansberry's essay demonstrates "the effect of Beauvoir's work on her thinking" and goes on to conclude, "Future readers of Hansberry's work must take into account her perspective on women as revealed in this commentary on *The Second Sex*."[8] I agree with Wilkerson on this point and I will add that readers of Beauvoir must likewise take into account Hansberry's analysis and recognize her as a trailblazer in the early recovery of Beauvoir's significance as an intellectual, thinker, and philosopher. She is one prominent example of a Black woman intellectual writing a substantive in-depth analysis of *The Second Sex* as early as the 1950s, and yet she has been largely ignored in the secondary literature on Beauvoir. Hansberry's unfinished essay was published in 1995, almost forty years after it was drafted. White feminist philosophers and Beauvoir scholars have had over two decades since its publication to read, cite, explore, analyze, and seriously engage this important contribution to the literature—but they have not yet done so. I find it outrageous that an activist, scholar, and writer of Hansberry's stature could be so thoroughly overlooked in the vast majority of philosophical secondary literature on Beauvoir for over two decades! As Hansberry might say, twenty-five years and one waits!

This chapter is first and foremost a celebration and amplification of Hansberry's brilliance and the insights that are presented in her essay on *The Second Sex*. I am intentionally and unapologetically centering

110   BEAUVOIR AND BELLE

Hansberry's voice, offering a close reading of her analysis of *The Second Sex*, and highlighting several key themes in her commentary. In addition to this celebration and amplification of Hansberry's voice, this chapter also offers a corrective to the aforementioned negligence of Hansberry's work, especially (but not exclusively) in the discipline of philosophy. This chapter is about Hansberry's reading of Beauvoir and what we learn when we take seriously the unique vantage point of this Black American woman writer who meticulously engaged a text by a white French woman writer, a text that (at the time) was not getting a lot of uptake in the United States. May future readers of Hansberry give her writing the time, care, and attention that she offers Beauvoir in her generous reading of *The Second Sex*.

In the first section of the chapter I examine Hansberry's critique of "The Biographical Imperative" approach to Beauvoir and *The Second Sex*. Next, I explore "Positive Readings of *The Second Sex* by Hansberry and Others" when it was first published and translated into English. This is followed by "Critiques of *The Second Sex*: Innocent, Ignorant Women and Hostile Men," which outlines Hansberry's impatience with surface and superficial critiques of the text. I argue that while Hansberry praises some of Beauvoir's insights, there are also points of disagreement and important differences between these two writers in these specific texts. For example, in "Hansberry's Critiques: Self-Adornment and Fashion" I show that there are some parts of Beauvoir's account of self-adornment that Hansberry finds insightful, but she pushes back on other aspects of Beauvoir's analysis of fashion. Furthermore, in "Hansberry's Critiques: Existentialism and Historical Materialism" I consider how Hansberry is critical of Beauvoir's existentialist framework, preferring a more historical-materialist approach.

There are also differences between Hansberry and Beauvoir in their perspectives on complicity. In "Complicity and Resistance of the Oppressed" I argue that unlike Beauvoir, who emphasizes woman's complicity and compares woman's oppression to other systems of oppressions (but ultimately privileges the former over the latter), Hansberry emphasizes the non-complicity and agitation of the oppressed and notes how class, colonial, and gender oppressions are interconnected systems to be resisted. And in "American Myths of the Liberated Woman: Diverse Experiences of 'Woman'" I argue that, to some extent, both Hansberry and Beauvoir name woman's experiences in various cultural and historical contexts while also making connections among the Negro question, the woman question, and Marxism—but they have different points of emphasis.

The Biographical Imperative

After contextualizing the timing of her own 1957 essay (eight years after the publication of the French editions of *The Second Sex* and four years after the first English translation), Hansberry opens with a quote from the "Introduction" of *The Second Sex* on the situation of woman as simultaneously free, autonomous, and Other: "'What peculiarly signalizes the situation of woman is that she—a free and autonomous being like all human creatures—nevertheless finds herself living in a world where men compel her to assume the status of the Other.'"[9] Hansberry states, "It is four years since those 732 pages of revolutionary treatment of the 'woman question' exploded upon the consciousness of a fragment of American book readers. Four years and one waits."[10] She has been waiting for serious engagement with Beauvoir's analysis of the situation of woman in *The Second Sex*, and in the absence of this long-awaited serious engagement with the text, Hansberry takes the time to offer the thinker and the text the level of engagement that she believed they deserved.

Contending that the gossip about Beauvoir's personal life prevented serious uptake of her ideas, Hansberry lays the groundwork for her own critical analysis by calling out the biographical imperative approach to Beauvoir and *The Second Sex*. I first encountered the phrase "biographical imperative" in Vivian May's *Anna Julia Cooper, Visionary Black Feminist: A Critical Introduction* (2007).[11] Drawing on work by Valerie Smith and Coco Fusco, May considers the myriad ways Black women's theoretical claims have been under-engaged or even dismissed because so much attention is given to their life stories.[12] What May describes as the "biographical imperative" is applied unequally to Black women theorists compared to their white male counterparts. In Hansberry's account of Beauvoir we find a critique of the ways that the biographical imperative has also been applied to white women theorists. May

112 BEAUVOIR AND BELLE

explains, "A critical discussion of major contributions of, for example, a well-known white male theorist does not *necessarily* begin with a lengthy reflection about his origins, his educational experiences and family life, and his life struggles. Questions of how or whether his race, class, or gender affected perception of his life work or presented obstacles (or, perhaps conduits) to success are not expected ... whether he was sufficiently close to his intellectual peers, or whether interpersonal tensions in his life loom so large that we should focus on them instead of his philosophical premises."[13]

May rightly points to biases in the intellectual engagement with the scholarship of Black women compared to white men (and following Hansberry we can also add white women). May is clear that she is not arguing against all biographical and historical contextualization of any major thinker, as long as they do not risk disengagement with that thinker's theories and ideas. I would add that we need to consider not only biographical and historical contextualization but also rigorous engagements with an intellectual's ideas, regardless of said intellectual's race, class, gender, sexuality, nationality, and so on. Put another way, I think May would agree that we should neither abandon a careful contextualization of Black women (and other Women of Color, as well as white women) nor neglect to offer such a contextualization of white men (as if they are universal, pure transcendence, and/or minds without particular bodies, biographies, and histories).

It is significant that Hansberry opens her own critical analysis of Beauvoir with a critique of the biographical imperative approach to this author and text. Hansberry underscores the irrelevance of Beauvoir's relationships with Sartre and others: "We have had to endure ... the exhaustive, casual, ill-informed, and thoroughly irrelevant commentary from our acquaintances on the lady's personal life: her 'affairs' with this or that famous Frenchman or American writer; unlimited debate as regards her marriage—or lack of it—to Jean-Paul Sartre; her alleged 'lesbianism.' "[14] Hansberry is clear that the focus on these relationships functions as deliberate distractions from Beauvoir's theoretical positions. She states, "to discuss whether such a woman has chosen to 'sanctify' her relationship to a man is to ignore a substantial part of her theories."[15] Furthermore, to focus on Beauvoir's marital status is to miss the point. Hansberry explains, "While she does not attack marriage, she does not anywhere accept the traditional views of its sacred place in the scheme of human development" and adds, "Therefore to discuss and 'accuse' this woman of not respecting marriage is quite like accusing a communist of not 'respecting' free enterprise."[16]

For Hansberry, the accuracy of the arguments advanced in *The Second Sex* are evidenced in part by the strategy to launch very personal attacks against the author rather than take her ideas seriously. As she puts it, "One may well begin by suggesting that the fact of such gossip about one who does appear to be the leading woman intellectual of our time is in itself something of a tribute to the accuracy of the thesis embodied in the title of Mlle. Beauvoir's two volumes on the status of woman."[17] Hansberry goes on to underscore the differential responses by readers in their approaches to the writings of women versus men: "It is impossible to conceive of any comparable volume of speculative fascination that could surround an equivalent male personality (the possible exception being that perhaps of homosexuality—which is also interesting)."[18] Readers tend to take a biographical imperative approach to women authors, while taking men authors more seriously and on their own terms. Hansberry does consider the exception of homosexuality here, suggesting that a similar biographical imperative approach is taken to the work of authors who are homosexual. But in general, audiences are encouraged to distinguish between a man's personal life and his work. She explains, "Tradition has accustomed us to assume that with regard to the writer, the artist, the theorist, the musician, the scientist—who is a man—that there are two aspects to his being: his work, which is important, and his personal life, which is really none of our business."[19] She laments that this tradition is not applied to women writers, authors, musicians, and scientists, in general—and certainly not to Beauvoir's case in particular.

In many ways, Hansberry anticipated similar critiques that would come decades later from white feminists in the United States like Margaret Simons and Nancy Bauer seeking a place for Beauvoir in the philosophy canon, or Toril Moi in France situating Beauvoir as an intellectual woman. But I have not seen citations of Hansberry in white feminist philosophical scholarship, including those actively recovering Beauvoir and her work, to date.[20] Again, Hansberry is a prominent

114 BEAUVOIR AND BELLE

Black woman intellectual who has written an insightful, mostly positive, but partly critical analysis of *The Second Sex*. Still, this work is either unknown or unacknowledged in the white feminist philosophical literature on Beauvoir, as far as I can tell.

Hansberry's Positive Readings of *The Second Sex*

To say that Hansberry offers a very positive reading of *The Second Sex* is an understatement. She suggests that it "may very well be the most important work of this century," and furthermore, "it is a victim of its own pertinence and greatness."[21] She is impressed with the answer to the call of the subject matter of woman: "Simone de Beauvoir has chosen to do what her subject historically demands; to treat of woman with the seriousness and dedication to complexity that any analysis of so astronomical a group as 'half of humanity' would absolutely seem to warrant."[22] She offers four specific anecdotal examples of women for whom the book had a positive impact:

(1) "To be sure, there was the playwright-actress who kept it open on her backstage dressing table reading aloud between curtains to the feminine half of the cast and 'indoctrinating' them, in the outraged and distressed opinion of the male director"; (2) "There is the woman reviewer writing in the *Daily Worker* a shamefully brief and limited, but nonetheless exuberant and intelligent review"; (3) "There is the young, lovely blonde and vaguely literate secretary sitting in her apartment with the weighty thing propped upon her thighs, dictionary but inches away, forcing herself with passionate dedication to endure and, as far as possible, absorb seven hundred pages of what she described as her 'liberation'"; (4) "And then, of course, there is the twenty-three-year-old woman writer closing the book thoughtfully after months of study and placing it in the most available spot on her 'reference' shelf, her fingers sensitive with awe, respect on the covers; her mind afire at last with ideas from France once again in history, *egalité, fraternité, liberté—pour tout le monde!*"[23]

I take Hansberry to be presenting these four examples to offer a sense of the range of women positively impacted by the book.

In addition to these women, she also notes that there were some men who respected the book, "It is not only fair but interesting to note the reverse: that *among men dedicated to equality* the book seemingly achieved respect and stature that many women have been unable to accord it."[24] While critical of male supremacy, Hansberry is open to potentially positive roles for men to be allies in eliminating the oppression of women. Hansberry outlines the evolution of man—from seeking to meet his individual needs, to seeking to meet the essential needs (like hunger) of the community, to seeking to meet the spiritual needs of the species.[25] She places the ethics of the woman question in this latter category of meeting the spiritual needs of the species, noting that there have been times when women found allies among men that restored faith in mankind. Asserting that there are examples from the past where woman "has found her most effective and telling champion among men," Hansberry adds, even "if by some miracle women should not utter a single protest against their condition there should still exist among men those who could not endure in peace until her liberation had been achieved."[26] This is an ethical call for men to commit to women's liberation.

Critiques of *The Second Sex*: Innocent, Ignorant Women and Hostile Men

Hansberry also analyzes negative reactions to *The Second Sex*. She puts these negative reactions into two categories: (1) women who are themselves innocent and ignorant, and (2) overtly hostile men. In the first group, she specifically identifies "The primary, negative attitude of legions of apparently *intelligent women* who are incapable of reading, let alone digesting, the heavy fabric of the writings."[27] She sees this as further evidence supporting Beauvoir's analysis of woman's oppression and "intellectual impoverishment."[28] She explains, "As a group they are unprepared and unable to accommodate a serious or profound discussion of their problems because of the very nature of their oppression."[29] Hansberry offers one general anecdotal example: "I have seen clear

116 BEAUVOIR AND BELLE

thinking, crisp American types of women (women intolerant and contemptuous of the more blatant codes of a male supremacist universe) puzzling briefly and inadequately over the work and then dismissing it."[30] In other words, even women who do not tolerate explicit male supremacy neglect to give *The Second Sex* the time and attention that Hansberry thinks it deserves.

The above example is followed by two more specific anecdotes: (1) "There is the attractive, young unmarried scientist who is vague but feels the author talked too much about 'sex' somehow," and (2) "[T]here is the married-new mother-engineer in her mid-twenties who has already contributed to the invention of breathtaking calculus machines but who was offended by the brutal and revolutionary discussions of motherhood and marriage—'All she seems to respect are career girls and lesbians.'"[31] I take Hansberry's point with these two specific examples to be that the aforementioned "ignorance" is not an issue of intellectual ability on the part of these two women readers (one a scientist and the other an engineer). The anecdotes offer examples of the uphill battle Beauvoir was facing even among an audience of otherwise intelligent women, such that "one wonders where the author might have begun."[32]

Hansberry frames the second group (of overtly hostile male readers) as "the enemy," those "within the ranks of the stalwarts of a male-dominated order" among whom "there is little struggle to appreciate the ideas of *The Second Sex*."[33] Still, she also contrasts men who do not even bother to engage the book with yet another category of men—those who "long adjusted to devastating argument, read it and properly attack it for its formidable solidity and undeniable brilliance."[34] And yet, having mentioned these attacks against the text, she also asserts that the major claims of *The Second Sex* have not been challenged substantively. This is not because the text has been embraced with open arms, but because "the ideological struggle to maintain a male-dominated society felt no real threat in a work which was not going to ever reach those masses of women who might most effectively make use of it."[35] The suggestion here is that Beauvoir's text could have been effectively used by masses of women at that time (if it ever reached them).

Hansberry expresses her frustration with American anti-intellectualism among women and men, noting, "the overwhelming

LORRAINE HANSBERRY   117

majority of American women (like the overwhelming majority of American men) do not read books," and adding, even the "microscopic section of our people who might be called the American woman intellectual—or even embracing the middle class woman with enough intelligence (leisure she has) to read—were [not expecting] to find a volume purportedly dealing with *their* problems in the alien idiom of a scholar, a thinker, an essayist."[36] To be sure, this is not educational elitism on the part of Hansberry. It is clear that her notion of "ignorance" is not about formal education or intellectual ability insofar as her examples of ignorance have included educated American women (e.g., the scientist, the engineer, the middle-class woman with intellect and opportunity to read by virtue of her leisure). Also recall that she previously (and favorably) mentioned the "vaguely literate secretary," perhaps less formally educated but committed to poring over the book with a dictionary. Finally, she sees the book as one that could be effectively used by masses of women (not just middle-class intellectual women). Thus, the ignorance that Hansberry describes is more about the idea that "we [American men and women] are a people, as oft noted elsewhere, who have grown accustomed to thought reduced on the tabloid sheet far below its least common denominator."[37] For her, there is ignorance in refusing to take the time to genuinely engage the ideas and arguments of this massive text insofar as there is a preference for arguments to be diluted and made more palatable.

Hansberry's Critiques: Self-Adornment and Fashion

Clearly, Hansberry is exasperated by many readers' failure to appreciate the theoretical rigor of *The Second Sex*, not to mention its practical relevance. But this does not amount to an uncritical endorsement of the text without reservations insofar as she presents some critiques of her own. One pertains to Beauvoir's analysis of woman's adornment and fashion. Hansberry remarks on woman's adornment practices early on in the essay, in the context of reports about women in the Soviet Union being urged to "become 'seductive' again."[38] Hansberry is critical of the American press for presenting these reports on women and seduction alongside "new fashions" in "our own over-fashion-conscious nation,"

118   BEAUVOIR AND BELLE

rather than offering "heavy theoretical work which would indicate a serious approach to the woman question in the Soviet Union."[39] From this starting point, she reflects on seduction and the symbolism of woman's adornment practices. Hansberry states, "Woman, the creature of seduction throughout her epochs of slavery, has sought to give the personal decorative arts some semblance of dignity beyond the obvious degrading truth, but it has only been a game."[40] Here she seems to consider woman's efforts to have agency (or at least dignity) in adornment practices, while also considering the "game" of self-deception, or what Beauvoir might call bad faith. On this point Hansberry notes, "The profoundest discussion of this fact will be found in the pages of *The Second Sex*, where the writer brilliantly destroys all myths of women's choice in becoming an ornament."[41] Beauvoir gives examples of the Hollywood star's painted nails, makeup, jewels, dress and ornaments, all of which, "were meant less to accentuate the woman's body's curves than to increase the body's powerlessness" (TSS 177). Observing Beauvoir's adornment practices, and perhaps even how Beauvoir has also become an ornament, Hansberry adds, "and the charm of it is the photograph then on the dust jacket which presents a quite lovely brunette woman, in necklace and nail polish—Simone de Beauvoir."[42]

Hansberry is far from dismissive of self-adornment practices, and she asserts that we need not "despair for the promotion of beauty anywhere."[43] She offers a critical analysis of beauty standards for woman without reducing all beauty practices to forms of oppression against woman. Hansberry explains, "Scent, jewelry, rouges have undoubtedly assumed some cultural identification with womanhood that hopefully, will henceforth be independent of an association of the centuries of slavery which has been the lot of woman."[44] She returns to fashion again later, noting, "This writer, for instance, finds the drab, colorless garb of men as distasteful as any other outrage of arbitrary fashion and is inclined to feel that the decorative traditions of woman's wear, whatever their origins, lend a desirable and attractive quality to life, to existence."[45] But she also gives this qualifier, "insofar as such fashions do not intrude on comfort, health, or safety."[46] In other words, self-adornment practices are not always about becoming an ornament or object. These practices can also be about self-expression and even self-actualization.

Pushing back more firmly, Hansberry describes Beauvoir as a soldier "occasionally given to the *expediencies* of warfare," and she suggests that "the question of fashion" is an unfortunate example of such expediency.[47] For Hansberry, fashion is not only a matter of taste, but also "another measure of freedom not to be discredited."[48]

Hansberry's Critiques: Existentialism and Historical Materialism

Another point of disagreement between Hansberry and Beauvoir pertains to the limits of existentialism and the import of historical materialism.[49] On the one hand, Hansberry is clear, "a great woman has made a great study and written, qualifications aside for the moment, a *great* book. And the world will never be the same again."[50] On the other hand, she calls for a more substantive reading and critique of existentialism, stating, "It remains for the writer who can with superior theories attack and demolish the forlorn and difficult roots of some of the existentialist thought of Mlle. Beauvoir, where it needs attack and demolition, and hopefully such a writer will necessarily emerge from the ranks of those who embrace a more far-reaching historical materialist view of life than Simone de Beauvoir."[51] Hansberry's relationship to Beauvoir and historical materialism is taken up by Soyica Diggs Colbert in *Radical Vision: A Biography of Lorraine Hansberry* (2021). Colbert explains, "Hansberry's criticism of de Beauvoir calls attention to the difference in their understandings of history, particularly histories of political struggle."[52] Unlike Beauvoir, "Hansberry's historical materialism accounts for the underground networks that sustain Black freedom struggles in periods of extreme political repression."[53]

There is a chapter in *The Second Sex* titled "The Point of View of Historical Materialism" in which Beauvoir critiques Friedrich Engels and the limits of historical materialism insofar as it takes for granted facts that it should explain. Hansberry is not denying that Beauvoir considers a historical materialist view. But she does advocate for a better, more expansive representation of this view. As with her earlier critiques of the biographical imperative approaches to Beauvoir and this text, here Hansberry anticipates later debates about existentialist, historical-materialist, and social-constructivist readings of *The Second Sex*.[54] Of course, there is value in reading Beauvoir through each of these lenses, and they need not be mutually exclusive or in competition with one another. I disagree with Hansberry on the forlornness and difficult roots of existentialism insofar as I have found existential analyses in general, and Black existential analyses of various intersecting identities and oppressions in particular exceeds the "miserablism" often associated with it.[55] While taking her critiques of Beauvoir's existentialism seriously, I also want to explore how Lewis Gordon, Cheryl Higashida, and Colbert productively read and engage Hansberry through an existential lens.

Existential themes have been identified across many of Hansberry's plays, but I will consider one play in particular, *Les Blancs*—which takes up issues of race, racism, colonialism, and anticolonial revolutionary violence (terror/terrorism)—as one example. There are several existentialist themes at work in *Les Blancs* including the gaze, the Other, freedom, responsibility, and authenticity.[56] Lewis Gordon, who has published several books on Blackness, anti-Black racism, and existentialism, engages Hansberry through a Black existentialist lens.[57] In *Bad Faith and Anti-Black Racism* (1995) Gordon theorizes race (and racism) existentially, describing the method of his study as a "descriptive ontology" or an "existential phenomenology."[58] For Gordon, "what is existential about racism is that it is a form of bad faith, which is a phenomenological ontological or existential phenomenological concept."[59] His analysis of race and existentialism in relationship to Sartre and Fanon is often cited, but I want to highlight his discussion of Hansberry in *Her Majesty's Other Children: Sketches of Racism from a Neocolonial Age* (1997), where he observes how both Fanon and Hansberry view race and racism as white constructions that persist in over-determining the lived experience of the Black.[60] Unfortunately, the importance of Hansberry as a philosophical figure has been largely overlooked by other philosophers.[61]

Higashida offers an in-depth analysis of existentialism, or more specifically existentialist feminism, in Hansberry's writings in "To Be(come) Young, Gay, and Black: Lorraine Hansberry's Existentialist Routes to Anticolonialism" (2008).[62] She sees affinities among Hansberry's *Les Blancs*, existentialist feminism, and the notion of reciprocal recognition in Beauvoir's *The Second Sex*.[63] Higashida argues, "Hansberry's overt engagement with existentialism focused on critiquing its nihilistic and solipsistic articulations of sexual and racial others. However, in countering Genet's vision of anticolonial struggle and its sexual politics, *Les Blancs* invokes ideas of mutual recognition that Hansberry had developed in thinking through gender and sexuality via Beauvoir."[64] Colbert also pays special attention to Hansberry's philosophical and existentialist interventions, noting that "Hansberry's writing affirms existentialist ideas of the individual's transformational capabilities *and* it challenges one of its central presumptions, that becoming emerges through individual antagonism."[65] Colbert later adds, "Hansberry's intervention into existentialist thought produces resistance to racism's slow structuring death through moments of political emergence that reveal underground forms of grassroots organizing and forecasts things yet to come."[66]

Complicity and Resistance of the Oppressed

In addition to the historical-materialism and existentialism debate in Hansberry's commentary on *The Second Sex*, another difference I see between Hansberry and Beauvoir pertains to complicity and resistance. I think the two would agree that woman is a human, a subject with transcendence—despite prescribed roles as Other, object, and immanence. Beauvoir tends to distinguish between the rebelliousness of "the Negro," "the Jew," and "the proletariat," on the one hand, and woman's complicity (or at least white bourgeois woman's complicity) with her own oppression, on the other hand.[67] But for Hansberry, all of these prescribed roles are unnatural, unstable, and impermanent.[68] At times Hansberry seems to echo Beauvoir on the issue of complicity, or at least woman's willingness to conform to certain roles. Hansberry notes that women "have been born into a cultural heritage which has instructed them of a role to play without question and in the main they are willing to do so."[69] However, contra Beauvoir, Hansberry asserts, "Woman like the Negro, the Jew, like colonial peoples, even in ignorance, is *incapable of accepting the role* with harmony."[70] She argues that woman would not accept the station assigned to her by choice any more than a man would accept such a station, and thus, "It must necessarily be imposed upon her—by force."[71] Hansberry states even more explicitly, "Woman, it may be said with some understatement to make the point, is oppressed."[72] Then she elaborates on her conceptualization of oppression and the nature of resistance against oppression: "A status not freely chosen or entered into by an individual or a group is necessarily one of oppression and the oppressed are by their nature (i.e., oppressed) forever in ferment and agitation against their condition and what they understand to be their oppressors."[73] Far from being in a state of complicity, Hansberry situates the oppressed as resistors seeking to change their position. This resistance may be overt or covert, conscious or unconscious, but it is always present. She asserts, "If not by overt rebellion or revolution, then in the thousand and one ways they will devise with and without consciousness to alter their position."[74]

Hansberry is well aware that women are expected to conform to gender roles and that at times women themselves reinforce certain gender roles and expectations. One example she considers is that of the housewife. But even in this example, she names the ways that women seek to flee from housework and rebel against their expected positions as housewives. Identifying the tensions between the objectification (specifically sexual objectification) of women on the one hand and the domestication of women (as mother or child raiser) on the other, Hansberry names the discontinuity between "wholesome" views of women's beauty in society and the "male sex publications where the glorification of woman as sex object has reached a new and inglorious height."[75] Hansberry observes, "it does not seem to occur to the overwhelming sections of our American males that, in maintaining woman as Sex Object and/or Child Raiser, the fraternity of social relationships other than sex must necessarily suffer to the extent of creating what is in fact an impossible social arrangement—as indeed must the sexual relationship itself."[76] There are contradictions between woman's expectations of herself and societal expectations of her. And in bad faith she tries to convince herself that she will be fulfilled by acquiescing to the roles prescribed by society. Hansberry explains, "She has gained the teasing expectation of self-fulfillment without the realization of it, because she is herself yet chained to an ailing social ideology which seeks

LORRAINE HANSBERRY   123

always to deny her autonomy and more—to delude her into the belief that that which imprisons her the more is somehow her fulfillment."[77]

Hansberry is aware that the confusion in the United States about "women and their place" is at times perpetuated and promoted by women. One example of this is from a 1956 speech by Agnes E. Meyer delivered at the Annual Meeting of the American Home Economics Association. Hansberry notes that Meyer draws on "Emerson's dubious and ambitious remark to the effect that 'civilization' is 'the power of good women.'"[78] Hansberry is paraphrasing Meyer's quotation of Emerson. I think she has in mind Emerson's essay "American Civilization," where he asserts:

> Right position of woman in the State is another index [of civilization]. Poverty and industry with a healthy mind read very easily the laws of humanity, and love them: place the sexes in right relations of mutual respect, and a severe morality gives that essential charm to woman which educates all that is delicate, poetic, and self-sacrificing, breeds courtesy and learning, conversation and wit, in her rough mate; so that *I have thought it a sufficient definition of civilization to say, it is the influence of good women.*[79]

Meyer critiques women's boredom with family responsibilities and their desire to take up positions in government and industry. According to Hansberry, Meyer "then proceeded (with only indirect justification, if any) to lay blame for much of woman's frustration at the door of the feminist movements of the past which, she declared, 'taught women to see themselves as the *rivals* of men rather than as partners.'"[80]

For Hansberry, housework and family care are required functions, "*things requisite to existence; to allowing oneself to do something else.*"[81] She notes, "there exists in the nature of 'homemaking' an indestructible contradiction to usefulness."[82] With this in mind, she elaborates, "And yet, therein hangs the problem: housework, 'homemaking,' are drudgery; it is inescapable, women flee it in one form or another."[83] In making these points, Hansberry includes two block quotes from *The Second Sex* that make passing mention of women and housework, "The domestic labors that fell to her lot because they were reconcilable

124 BEAUVOIR AND BELLE

with the cares of maternity imprisoned her in repetition and immanence."[84] Continuing an extended critical analysis, Hansberry presents the celebration of housewives and housework as a false narrative used to keep women in the position of performing undesirable but needed labor. Again focusing on resistance (even if unconscious), she explains, "They do not always understand their own rebellion, or why they want to rebel or why *they* deprecate, more than anyone else really, what the rest of the nation will always insist, so long as it does not have to do it, is the 'cornerstone' of our culture, the 'key' to our civilization and the 'bedrock foundation' of our way of life."[85] For Hansberry, "The ancient effort to glorify the care of the home into something it is not and cannot be is one of the greatest assaults against womanhood."[86]

American Myths of the Liberated Woman: Diverse Experiences of "Woman"

Hansberry also differs from Beauvoir in her attentiveness to particulars and differences between certain overlapping identities. Hansberry names a diverse range of woman's experiences in different cultural and historical contexts, while also making connections between the Negro question, the woman question, and American Marxism. One could argue that Beauvoir also does this, but Hansberry does it better. Beginning with her attention to particulars, Hansberry often qualifies her analysis of the woman question by explicitly situating it in an American context, rather than making universal claims. For Hansberry, one issue in America that contributes to the oppression of woman is the false claim that the American woman is not oppressed, or what she describes as the myth of the already liberated woman that undermines efforts to combat the systematic gender inequalities that persist precisely because these inequalities are concealed by this myth. According to Hansberry, "(This truth is hideously compounded, of course, in our own country, where the most devastating anti-equality myth of all is in the reign of our social order: the American myth of the *already* liberated American woman of all classes. And myth we shall see, is what it is)."[87] For Hansberry, one version of this myth is found in the representation of the American woman as the "free woman."[88]

It is worth noting that this analysis of the American woman as already liberated is included in a sub-section of Hansberry's commentary titled "AN AMERICAN MYTH: 'WE DON'T WEAR NO VEILS.'" This sub-heading (in all capital letters) coupled with her analysis in this section of the essay suggest that Hansberry is also refuting any claims that woman's freedom, liberation, and equality are about wearing (or not wearing) veils.

Having said that, Hansberry also takes up what she describes as the liberated attitude of the American woman noting, "It is only conjecture, but one cannot help but feel that though the American woman is far from enjoying anything remotely akin to 'equality' with men in her nation she is, subjectively speaking, possessed of a liberated attitude that must have a great deal to do with her historical experience in the New World."[89] Here we can also consider Hansberry's attention to the diverse historical experiences of woman in the "new world." She posits:

> We have been creatures of the frontier adventure; we have been the peasant girls off the ships from Ireland and Poland set loose in the industrial chaos of our social order; we have been even the black slave woman paradoxically assuming perhaps the most advanced internal freedom from a knowledge of the mythical nature of male superiority inherent in our experience as chattel. We have been the Jewish woman finding liberty in picket lines.[90]

Hansberry uses an inclusive "we" to describe woman's historical experience in America, but she is careful not to make it a universal "we" that ignores a diverse range of particular experiences. She names the paradox of "the advanced internal freedom" (what existentialists might call ontological rather than political freedom) of the enslaved Black woman who knows through her experience as chattel that male superiority (and I would add white superiority) is a myth. She names liberty found by the Jewish woman through picketing. And she shifts from the aforementioned ontological "inner" freedom to a more political (one might say "outer") freedom through franchise when she asserts, "We have not voted long, but we have a freedom in our gaits on the pavement that suggest almost an intuitive awareness of how that franchise was won."[91] Hansberry argues that these diverse women "have noisily,

126 BEAUVOIR AND BELLE

unscientifically, improperly, harmfully, hysterically, neurotically—and *heroically*—battled to place the question of the status of women in its proper place in the consideration of the most advanced thinking section of American political action and thought."[92] Here she takes qualities associated with "woman" and perceived as negative, and then re-appropriates and re-signifies them as positives, while also making the case that these women have fought to advance the question on the status of women through thought as well as action.[93]

Conclusion: The Negro Question, the Woman Question, and Marxism

This brings us to the connections among the Negro question, the woman question, and Marxism. Rather than rigidly framing Hansberry as a Communist, Perry reminds us, "By that time [1957] Lorraine was not officially a member of the Communist Party, although she still considered herself along the socialist-Communist spectrum."[94] We see this socialist-Communist spectrum evident earlier in the review when Hansberry notes, "As with the Negro question it seems American Marxists, Communists in particular, have been far in advance in the western world in their *recognition* of the 'woman question.' "[95] She also asserts, "American Communists have possessed the leisure . . . and a not-to-be-underestimated impetus (in the form of a collection of what must be the most vigorous and insurgent women anywhere in the world—American women Communists) to lift the woman question beyond the ordinary sphere of the 'battle-of-the-sexes'—type nonsense which is so tragically popular in our country."[96] Hansberry is building on these earlier observations when she highlights the diverse experiences of women in America and later argues, "It is this multi-experienced class from which American Communist women must be drawn."[97] She is simultaneously acknowledging that American Communists have already been taking up the Negro question and the woman question, while also calling for them to diversify their ranks and thereby expand their perspectives and impact.

Hansberry skillfully connects the woman question to other interlocking systems of oppression like racism, classism, and

LORRAINE HANSBERRY   127

colonialism without reducing them to one and the same. As Perry states, "She was a feminist, anticolonialist, and Marxist, and her sexuality became an essential part of her thinking through human relations."[98] Unlike Beauvoir, who compares woman's oppression to other systems of oppression, but ultimately privileges the former over the latter, Hansberry underscores how class, colonial, and gender oppressions are overlapping. She is very explicit on this point when she says, "It [the woman question] is, regardless of all other questions *barring* peace and liberation of the world's working classes and colonial peoples, the greatest social question existent; its depths and horrors and universality sometimes *overlapping*, even certain of those paramount issues mentioned above."[99] Here Hansberry identifies the woman question as the greatest social question, with two important caveats: (1) that it is not a higher priority than peace and liberation of the world's working classes and colonial peoples, and (2) that the woman question has depths and horrors that are overlapping with (not mutually exclusive from) the oppressions of violence and the lack of liberation for the working class and the colonized of the world. Hansberry's qualifiers signal her proto-intersectional approach rather than analogical approach to these various interlocking systems of oppression.[100] Recall that Claudia Jones (once roommates with Hansberry) took a similar approach in her 1949 essay, "An End to the Neglect of the Problems of the Negro Woman!," discussed in depth in the previous chapter.[101]

Notes

1. Margaret B. Wilkerson, "Lorraine Hansberry (1930–1965)," in *Words of Fire*, 126. (Hereafter Wilkerson 1995.) See also Wilkerson, "The Sighted Eyes and Feeling Heart of Lorraine Hansberry," *African American Review* 50, no. 4 (Winter 2017): 698–703.
2. Wilkerson 1995, 126.
3. See Mary Helen Washington, "Alice Childress, Lorraine Hansberry, and Claudia Jones: Black Women With the Popular Front," in *Left of the Color Line; Race, Radicalism, and Twentieth Century Literature of the United States*, ed. Bill Mullen James Smethurst (Chapel Hill: University of North

128 BEAUVOIR AND BELLE

Carolina Press, 2003). One of Washington's chapter subsections is titled "Lorraine Hansberry and Freedom: A Founding Text of Black Left Feminism." (Hereafter Washington 2003.) See also Cheryl Higashida, "Lorraine Hansberry's Existentialist Routes to Black Internationalist Feminism," in *Black Internationalist Feminism: Women Writers of the Black Left. 1945–1995* (Urbana: University of Illinois Press, 2013).

4. Imani Perry, *Looking for Lorraine: The Radiant and Radical Life of Lorraine Hansberry* (Boston: Beacon Press, 2018), 77. (Hereafter Perry 2018.) See also Soyica Colbert, "Practices of Freedom: Lorraine Hansberry, Freedom Writer," *Callaloo* 40, no. 2 (Spring 2017): 157–173. (Hereafter Colbert 2017.) Colbert notes, "In 'Myself in Notes' at age twenty-three Hansberry lists Simone de Beauvoir as a person she would like to meet" (Colbert 2017, 172n6). See also Colbert's *Radical Vision: A Biography of Lorraine Hansberry* (New Haven, CT: Yale University Press, 2021). (Hereafter Colbert 2021.)

5. Perry 2018, 75 and 77.

6. Perry 2018, 77.

7. Perry 2018, 78

8. Wilkerson 1995, 127.

9. Lorraine Hansberry, "Simone de Beauvoir and *The Second Sex*: An American Commentary," in *Words of Fire: An Anthology of African American Feminist Thought*, ed. Beverly Guy Sheftall (New York: The New Press, 1995), 128. (Hereafter Hansberry 1995.) Hansberry is quoting from TSS Parshley, xxxv; see also TSS Borde and Malovany-Chevallier, 17.

10. Hansberry 1995, 128.

11. Vivian M. May, *Anna Julia Cooper, Visionary Black Feminist: A Critical Introduction* (New York: Routledge, 2007). (Hereafter May 2007.) See also Kathryn Sophia Belle (formerly Kathryn T. Gines), review of *Anna Julia Cooper, Visionary Black Feminist: A Critical Introduction* by Vivian M. May (New York: Routledge, 2007); *Black Women's Intellectual Traditions: Speaking Their Minds*, ed. Kristin Waters and Carol B. Conaway (Burlington: University of Vermont Press, 2007); *Black Women in the Ivory Tower, 1850–1954: An Intellectual History*, ed. Stephanie Y. Evans (Gainesville: University Press of Florida, 2007); and *Daughter of the Revolution: The Major Nonfiction Works of Pauline E. Hopkins*, ed. Ira Dworkin (New Brunswick: Rutgers University Press, 2007) in *Signs: Journal of Wisdom and Culture*, Volume 34, No. 2, Winter 2009, pages 451–459.

12. May cites Valerie Smith, "Black Feminist Theory and the Representation of the 'Other,'" in *The Woman That I Am: Literature*

LORRAINE HANSBERRY 129

and Culture of Contemporary Women of Color, ed. D. Soyini Madison (New York: Routledge, 1998) and Coco Fusco, *English Is Broken Here: Notes on Cultural Fusion in the Americas* (New York: New Press, 1990).

13. May 2007, 39.
14. Hansberry 1995, 128.
15. Hansberry 1995, 129.
16. Hansberry 1995, 129.
17. Hansberry 1995, 128.
18. Hansberry 1995, 128.
19. Hansberry 1995, 128.
20. Essays on Hansberry in relationship to Beauvoir include Cheryl Higashida, "To Be(come) Young, Gay, and Black: Lorraine Hansberry's Existentialist Routes to Anticolonialism," *American Quarterly* 60, no. 4 (December 2008): 899–924 (hereafter Higashida 2008); Donna Dale Marcano, "Talking Back: bell hooks, Feminism and Philosophy," in *Critical Perspectives on bell hooks*, ed. Maria del Guadalupe Davidson and George Yancy (New York: Routledge, 2009); Mark Hodin, "Lorraine Hansberry's Absurdity: *The Sign in Sidney Brustein's Window*," in *Contemporary Literature* 50, no. 4 (Winter 2009): 742–774; and Kathryn Sophia Belle (formerly Kathryn T. Gines), "At the Intersections: Existentialism, Critical Philosophies of Race, and Feminism," in *The Routledge Companion to the Philosophy of Race*, ed. Paul C. Taylor, Linda Martín Alcoff, and Luvell Anderson (New York: Routledge, 2017) (hereafter Belle [formerly Gines] 2017). To my knowledge, none of these scholars identify as white feminists. More recently, Hansberry is cited in Kate Kirkparrick's *Becoming Beauvoir: A Life* (London: Bloomsbery, 2019).
21. Hansberry 1995, 129.
22. Hansberry 1995, 129.
23. Hansberry 1995, 130. The woman reviewer Hansberry is referencing Elizabeth Lawson, author of "Woman: Second Sex," which was published with the help of Claudia Jones in *Worker*, October 24, 1954, p. 12. (Hereafter Lawson 1954.) Lawson writes, "This book is a triumphant call to woman's liberation," but also notes, "Many criticisms can be made of her [Beauvoir's] work" (Lawson 1954, 12). See also Shirley Chen, " 'To work, write, sing and fight for women's liberation': Proto-Feminist Currents in the American Left, 1946–1961," honors thesis, University of Michigan, 2011. (Hereafter Chen 2011.) Chen notes, "The Sunday edition of the Daily Worker was known as the Worker" (Chen 2011, 78n21). Chen considers the differences in the ways that Hansberry and Lawson interpreted *The Second Sex*: "Lawson read *The Second Sex* as an essentially

130 BEAUVOIR AND BELLE

Marxist text with a militant argument for woman's right to work. In contrast Hansberry's essay reveals a more theoretically inclined feminism informed by Beauvoir's existentialist concept of the self. Whereas Lawson chided Beauvoir for dwelling on 'sex problems' and glossed over her chapter on lesbianism, these were paramount concerns to Hansberry" (Chen 2011, 89). Both Wilkerson and Perry read "twenty-three-year-old woman writer" as a self-description for Hansberry. See Wilkerson 1995, 226, and Perry 2018, 77.

24. Hansberry 1995, 129. (Emphasis added.)
25. Hansberry 1995, 140.
26. Hansberry 1995, 140. She adds, "Such we must always come to conclude is the nature of mankind, such is the glory of the human race of which the male is a magnificent half" (Hansberry 1995, 140),
27. Hansberry 1995, 129. (Emphasis added.)
28. These women "reflect what Beauvoir has shown to be their historical experience of utter intellectual impoverishment as a class" (Hansberry 1995, 129).
29. Hansberry 1995, 129. Hansberry asserts, "They cannot, therefore, be expected to assess the manner of men even that which might herald their ultimate emergence or transcendence into liberty any more than I should imagine a slave prior to the Civil War would have understood intellectually the nature of his bondage." (Hansberry 1995, 129). On this point I disagree with Hansberry, insofar as we have evidence of enslaved persons understanding their bondage experientially and intellectually, for example in the slave narratives of Frederick Douglass and Harriet Jacobs, to offer two prominent cases.
30. Hansberry 1995, 129.
31. Hansberry 1995, 129–130.
32. Hansberry 1995, 130.
33. Hansberry 1995, 129.
34. Hansberry 1995, 129.
35. Hansberry 1995, 132.
36. Hansberry 1995, 133. (Emphasis original.)
37. Hansberry 1995, 133.
38. Hansberry 1995, 131.
39. Hansberry 1995, 131.
40. Hansberry 1995, 131. Note that Hansberry, like Beauvoir, uses the term "slavery" here to describe the status of women in general rather the status of actually enslaved women in particular.
41. Hansberry 1995, 131.

LORRAINE HANSBERRY 131

42. Hansberry 1995, 131. Perry describes this as a moment when "She poked fun at Simone de Beauvoir's hypocrisy in harshly judging women's adornment" (Perry 2018, 87).
43. Hansberry 1995, 131. Perry notes that "Lorraine reveled in female beauty" (Perry 2018, 87).
44. Hansberry 1995, 131. Again, Hansberry, like Beauvoir, uses the term "slavery" here to describe the status of women in general rather the status of actually enslaved women in particular.
45. Hansberry 1995, 134.
46. Hansberry 1995, 134.
47. Hansberry 1995, 135.
48. Hansberry 1995, 135–136. For Hansberry, Beauvoir is "actually careless rather than reactionary when she implies that the initial martyrs of a cause do not serve an essential and expendable purpose" (Hansberry 1995, 135).
49. "Jean-Paul Sartre's writing" appears on a list of things Hansberry hates (Perry 2018, 95).
50. Hansberry 1995, 133.
51. Hansberry 1995, 133. She adds, "Until then *The Second Sex* will remain beyond the vague and shabby criticism of dogmatists of all persuasive shades" (Hansberry 1995, 133).
52. Colbert 2021, 15.
53. Colbert 2021, 15. Offering more context for Hansberry's activism, Colbert notes, "Hansberry's experience in the 1950s working simultaneously with the feminists of the Sojourners for Truth and Justice, the Black radicals on the journal *Freedom*, and leftists as a part of Camp Unity materialized her understanding of being together in difference" (Colbert 2021, 15).
54. For more on these debates, see *"On ne naît pas femme: on le devient... "The Life of a Sentence*, ed. Bonnie Mann and Martina Ferrari (Oxford: Oxford University Press, 2017).
55. Beauvoir wrote an essay responding to critics describing existentialism as "miserablism." See Simone de Beauvoir, "Existentialism and Popular Wisdom," in *Simone de Beauvoir: Philosophical Writings*, ed. Margaret Simons, Marybeth Timmerman, and Mary Beth Mader (Urbana: University of Illinois Press, 2004).
56. See also Belle (formerly Gines) 2017.
57. See Lewis Gordon, *Bad Faith and Anti-Black Racism* (Amherst: Humanity Books, 1995) (hereafter Gordon 1995); *Existence in Black: An Anthology of Black Existential Philosophy* (New York: Routledge, 1997a); *Her Majesty's Other Children: Sketches of Racism from a Neocolonial Age* (Lanham: Rowman & Littlefield Publishers, 1997b) (hereafter Gordon

132 BEAUVOIR AND BELLE

1997b); and *Existentia Africana: Understanding Africana Existential Thought* (New York: Routledge, 2000). See also *Fanon and the Crisis of European Man* (New York: Routledge, 1995); "Existential Dynamics of Theorizing Black Invisibility," (in Gordon1997a); and *Fanon: A Critical Reader*, ed. L. Gordon, T. D. Sharpley-Whiting, and R. T. White (Oxford: Blackwell Publishers, 1996). And see Lewis Gordon, "Racism as a Form of Bad Faith," *Newsletter on Philosophy and the Black Experience*, ed. Jesse Taylor and Leonard Harris, *American Philosophical Association Newsletters* 99, no. 2 (April 2000): 139–141; and "A Short History of the 'Critical' in Critical Race Theory," *Newsletter on Philosophy and the Black Experience*, ed. Richard Nunan and Jesse Taylor, *American Philosophical Association Newsletters* 99, no. 2 (April 2000): 151–154.

58. Gordon 1995, 5. He examines the resources within Sartre's writings (e.g., *Being and Nothingness*, 1943), for theorizing and combating the phenomenon of anti-Black racism. Gordon is also attentive to Fanon's existential insights on anti-Black racism—especially in *Black Skin, White Masks* and *The Wretched of the Earth*, two texts that are very influential on theoretical and material frameworks of race, racism, violence, and colonialism in the United States and elsewhere.

59. Gordon 1995, 135.

60. Gordon 1997b, 159. He notes "ironic similarities" between Hansberry and Fanon: "Although the two were six years apart in age and individuals from very different cultures, both were heavily influenced in their early adult years by direct engagement with revolutionary black voices in their communities: Fanon with Aimé Césaire; Hansberry with Paul Robeson and Du Bois. Both produced their first major work in their twenties; Fanon *Peau noire, masques blancs,* at age 26; Hansberry *A Raisin in the Sun* at age 28. Both works were complex explorations of black subjectivity in the face of attempting a dialectical relationship with the White World. (Nearly all of the themes in *Peau noire* emerge in *Raisin*, including the complex relation with negritude that marks a defensive strategy in the struggle for black liberation.) Both delivered important speeches on the role of the Black writer in 1959. Both devoted a portion of their last works to the question of violence in a liberation struggle. Both had white spouses who played crucial roles in their literary production. Both were revolutionary humanists. And as is well-known, both died very young" (Gordon 1997b, 153). See also Colbert 2017. Colbert notes, "While Fanon investigates how black maleness informs looking, Hansberry explicitly takes up the intersectionality of the gaze when deployed among women of different races and, perhaps, sexual interests" (Colbert 2017, 170).

LORRAINE HANSBERRY   133

61. I have heard conference papers on Hansberry by two philosophers, both Black women—Donna Dale Marcano (at a PhiloSOPHIA Conference at Penn State University in 2014) and V. Denise James (at a conference honoring Joyce Mitchell Cook at Yale University in 2015). James also discusses Hansberry in the interview, "Denise James on Political Illusions," in *Unmuted: Conversations on Prejudice, Oppression, and Social Justice*, ed. Myisha Cherry (New York: Oxford University Press, 2019).

62. See Higashida 2008. She describes Hansberry as intertwining anti-imperialist Black leftist politics with postwar European and US existentialism, but she is careful to note Hansberry's strong critiques of existentialism for sexual and racial othering, individualism, and solipsism, along with its association with despair and apathy (Higashida 2008, 899 and 901). In addition to the play *Les Blancs*, Higashida also considers Beauvoir's influence on the play *The Apples of Autumn*: "In her notes to this play, Hansberry borrows liberally from Beauvoir to describe the patriarchal social order constituting her female character's situation" (Higashida 2008, 906). Higashida also reads Beauvoir's existentialist insights in other plays by Hansberry such as *Flowers for the General* and *The Sign in Sidney Bruster's Window*, as well as in her critical commentary on Beauvoir's *The Second Sex* (Higashida 2013). See also Mark Hodin, "Lorraine Hansberry's Absurdity: The Sign in Sidney Brustein's Window," *Contemporary Literature* 50, no. 4 (Winter 2009): 742–774. For a more critical reading of Hansberry and existentialism, see Harold Cruse's section on Lorraine Hansberry in part 3 of *The Crisis of the Negro Intellectual* (New York: Morrow, 1967).

63. Higashida 2008, 905.

64. Higashida 2008, 911.

65. Colbert 2021, 6.

66. Colbert 2021, 16.

67. These themes are taken up some in Chapter 2 (Claudia Jones), and they are taken up in more detail in Chapter 5 (Beauvoir's race/gender analogies).

68. Hansberry 1995, 139–140.

69. Hansberry 1995, 137.

70. Hansberry 1995, 139. (Emphasis original.)

71. Hansberry 1995, 139

72. Hansberry 1995, 140

73. Hansberry 1995, 140

74. Hansberry 1995, 140

75. Hansberry 1995, 139. She adds, "In these publications men are encouraged and even shown how to relegate an entire sex to the level of one long,

134 BEAUVOIR AND BELLE

endless, if one is to believe the fantasies (and one might add, boring), animal relationship" (Hansberry 1995, 139).

76. Hansberry 1995, 139.

77. Hansberry 1995, 139.

78. Hansberry 1995, 137.

79. "American Civilization": is available here: https://www.theatlantic.com/magazine/archive/1862/04/american-civilization/306548/. (Emphasis added.) Emerson also makes other problematic claims, like, "The Indians of this country have not learned the white man's work; and in Africa, the Negro of today is the Negro of Herodotus."

80. Hansberry 1995, 137. (Emphasis original. Hansberry notes that this is Meyer's emphasis.)

81. Hansberry 1995, 138.

82. Hansberry 1995, 138.

83. Hansberry 1995, 137. But the rest of the quote focuses on how "Man's case is radically different"—he is transcendent, not limited, active, celebrated, proud, etc. (TSS Parshley, 63; TSS Borde and Malovany-Chevallier, 73). It is after these block quotes that Beauvoir returns to the import of existentialism, stating, "Thus an existential perspective has enabled us to understand how the biological and economic situation of primitive hordes led to male supremacy" (TSS Borde and Malovany-Chevallier, 75). It is interesting that Hansberry includes these extended block quotes that are a build-up to Beauvoir's claims about the importance of existentialism (which is an aspect of the text that Hansberry explicitly rejects, preferring historical materialism).

84. Hansberry 1995, 138. Hansberry is quoting and citing TSS Parshley, 63; see also TSS Borde and Malovany-Chevallier 73. Note, I go into more detail about Beauvoir's analysis of housewives and domestic labor in Chapter 6 (Beauvoir slave/woman analogies)

85. Hansberry 1995, 137. She continues, "The housewife says 'just a housewife' for all the reasons she would perhaps try to deny if she thought someone was attacking housework and 'homemaking' as drudgery was also attacking the cornerstone and key and bedrock foundation of her family, home, husband, nation, and world" (Hansberry 1995, 140).

86. Hansberry 1995, 140. Noting that women parroting men's views are often the ones "shouting such an argument," she attributes this to women's socialization. Woman is told by society, "from cradle to the grave that her husband, her home, her children will be the source of all rewards in life, the foundation of all true happiness" (Hansberry 1995, 140–141).

LORRAINE HANSBERRY 135

87. Hansberry 1995, 129. (Emphasis original.)
88. Hansberry 1995, 134.
89. Hansberry 1995, 131–132. To this she adds (not unproblematically), "(Distinguished, however, from the rest of the 'New World' excepting Canada perhaps, where the women of our America, chic and modern on the streets of Buenos Aires, Mexico City, and Rio de Janeiro, are nonetheless tied to a Latin and Catholic spirit of oppression that is horrifying to the most backward of the women of the United States)" (Hansberry 1995, 132).
90. Hansberry 1995, 132. This is not a comprehensive list insofar as it does not include, for example, Indigenous women (e.g., how they figure into and complicate the notion of "the frontier"), Latinas (named by Hansberry in the South American context but not the North American context), and Asian American women.
91. Hansberry 1995, 132.
92. Hansberry 1995, 132. (Emphasis original.)
93. See Anna Julia Cooper, "The Status of Woman in America," in *The Voice of Anna Julia Cooper: Including A Voice from the South and Other Important Essays, Papers, and Letters*, ed. Charles Lemert and Esme Bhan (New York: Rowman and Littlefield, 1998).
94. Perry 2018, 81. Perry adds, "But her politics were increasingly of her own critical fashioning" (Perry 2018, 81).
95. Hansberry 1995, 130. She adds, "One modifies to 'western' here because reports from and of China are gratifying if erratic and in some ways suspicious" (Hansberry 1995, 130). The Negro question, the woman question, and the Communist Party are taken up in more detail in Chapter 2 (Claudia Jones).
96. Hansberry 1995, 131.
97. Hansberry 1995, 132.
98. Perry 2018, 81.
99. Hansberry 1995, 133. (Emphasis added.)
100. For more on proto-intersectionality, see Kathryn Sophia Belle (formerly Kathryn T. Gines), "Race Women, Race Men and Early Expressions of Proto-Intersectionality, 1830s–1930s," in *Why Race and Gender Still Matter: An Intersectional Approach*, ed. Namita Goswami, Maeve M. O'Donovan and Lisa Yount (Brookfield, VT: Pickering and Chatto Publishers Limited, 2014), 13–25. Admittedly, Hansberry and Beauvoir are not that far apart on this issue, but I do see slight differences and more nuance in Hansberry's position.

136 BEAUVOIR AND BELLE

101. Perry notes that Hansberry "worked alongside other Communist Party activists like the Trinidad-born Claudia Jones (who was briefly roommates with Lorraine)" (Perry 2018, 52). According to Perry, "By July [1952], she shared an apartment with Claudia Jones at 504 West 143rd Street, unit 6A" (Perry 2018, 53).

4

Audre Lorde

"Difference is that raw and powerful connection from which our personal power is forged"

Audre Lorde's iconic essay "The Master's Tools Will Never Dismantle the Master's House" was delivered as a commentary for "*The Second Sex*—Thirty Years Later: A Commemorative Conference on Feminist Theory" held September 27–29, 1979, at New York University's Loeb Student Center (sponsored by the New York Institute for the Humanities and the Helena Rubinstein Foundation).[1] On the program, the conference coordinator is listed as Jessica Benjamin; the assistant to the coordinator is Margaret Honey; and the program committee includes Carol Ascher, Serafina Bathrick, Harriet Cohen, Muriel Dimen, Kate Ellis, and Sara Ruddick. Consultants listed are Charlotte Bunch, Joan Kelly, Gerda Lerner, Audre Lorde, Ryan Rapp, Adrienne Rich, and Catharine Stimpson. The three-day conference program features five sessions (all panels with multiple speakers, a moderator, and two commentators), two groups of workshops (with fifteen workshops in each group), and a poetry reading, as well as several lunch breaks, dinner breaks, and cocktail receptions. In addition to being identified as a consultant on the program, Lorde also appears as a commentator on the last panel session on Saturday, September 29, 1979, from 2:00 p.m. to 5:00 p.m., Session 5: The Personal and The Political. Panelists listed include Jessica Benjamin (*Starting from the Left and Going Beyond*), Camille Bristol and Bonnie Johnson (*Both and And*), Manuela Fraire (*How the Mother/ Daughter Relationship Influences the Method of Women's Liberation*), and Linda Gordon (*Individual and Community in the History of Feminism*), with Harriet Cohen as moderator and Barbara Ehrenreich listed as a second commentator after Lorde.

Offering some context for this historic event and commentary, Estelle B. Freedman notes in *The Essential Feminist Reader* (2007):

Beauvoir and Belle. Kathryn Sophia Belle, Oxford University Press. © Oxford University Press 2024.
DOI: 10.1093/oso/9780197660195.003.0005

138 BEAUVOIR AND BELLE

In the 1970s, women of color and lesbians in the United States called on feminist scholars to recognize their own discriminatory practices and to analyze the intersections of racial, sexual, and gender hierarchies. At an academic feminist conference commemorating the thirtieth anniversary of the publication of de Beauvoir's *The Second Sex*, the lesbian poet and literature professor Audre Lorde articulated the frustrations of women treated as tokens, the sole black or lesbian speaker invited to participate in a predominantly white movement. Her influential remarks impelled women's studies courses, programs, and conferences to expand their vision and embrace, rather than fear, differences among women.[2]

With this in mind, the current chapter takes up Lorde's influential (and, for some, incendiary) presence at the conference. Although the chapter is intentionally and specifically focused on Lorde's conference remarks and Benjamin's decades-later response, it is important to note that Lorde was anti-imperialist, leftist, and internationalist in her Third World Black diasporic feminist consciousness and politics.[3] Her impact and influence exceed the confines of this historic conference and commentary. Having said that, the chapter is presented in two main sections, the first unpacking the significance of Lorde's commentary at the Beauvoir conference and the second peeling back the layers of Benjamin's reflections on Lorde and this event in a published letter about two decades later.

In the first section of the chapter, "Audre Lorde: Difference, Representation, and Interdependence," I focus on Lorde in her own words in "The Master's Tools Will Never Dismantle the Master's House." I am intentionally amplifying Lorde's voice here, especially her insightful analyses of difference, representation, and interdependence. I argue that her philosophy of difference complicates monolithic assumptions about "woman" by insisting on attentiveness to other kinds of difference beyond the singular focus on gender. Explicitly naming race, sexuality, class, and age, Lorde also examines difference in relationship to survival, material conditions, representation, consciousness, mutuality, and interdependence. She argues that difference is a vital source of strength and critiques *The Second Sex* Conference organizers and speakers for the lack of difference reflected in the participants and the ideas presented at the event.

AUDRE LORDE 139

Next, I take up "Jessica Benjamin's Letter to Lester Olson: A Case Study." Here I examine conference coordinator Benjamin's reflections on Lorde and *The Second Sex* Conference over two decades later (2000) to show how, when Women of Color feminists—in this case, the self-identified Black lesbian feminist warrior poet Audre Lorde—request serious attentiveness to race, sexuality, class, and/or age within otherwise white feminist discourses, white women often accuse us of being angry and/or divisive, and/or playing "identity politics." It is ironic that Benjamin accuses Lorde of identity politics because this is one of many terms coined by Black feminist activists (in this case, Barbara Smith, Beverly Smith, and Demita Frazier's 1977 "The Combahee River Collective: A Black Feminist Statement") to denote their commitment to positive political work. Unfortunately, the concept has since been misappropriated, manipulated, and presented as pejorative. I argue that Benjamin's reflections offer a case study for problematic white feminist engagement with Black feminist thought and thinkers. Finally, in "Conclusion: 'Master's Tools' as Counter-Narrative to Analogical Approaches" I underscore the significance of the title "The Master's Tools Will Never Dismantle the Master's House" as a disruption of the white feminist default to analogies (e.g., the prostitution/marriage analogy explicitly critiqued by Lorde as well as the race/gender analogy and the woman-as-slave analogy), while also naming white feminism's frequent use and abuse of the master's tools more generally. Finally, in the conclusion, I argue that Lorde is attentive to her own insights in the organization of the "I AM YOUR SISTER CONFERENCE (1990), which brought together 1200 activists from twenty-three countries—especially in the face of strong critiques.

Audre Lorde: Difference, Representation, and Interdependence

Lorde begins "Master's Tools" by situating herself and the conditions under which she became a participant at this conference, noting, "I AGREED TO TAKE PART in a New York University Institute for the Humanities conference a year ago, with the understanding that I would be commenting upon papers dealing with the role of difference within

140 BEAUVOIR AND BELLE

the lives of american women."[4] And she is explicit about the types of difference that she had in mind, namely, "difference of race, sexuality, class, and age."[5] These are major themes for Lorde, who asserts that feminist claims that the personal is political must consider difference, and furthermore, that serious examinations of difference require input from various perspectives—especially the standpoints of "poor women, Black and Third World women, and lesbians."[6] Lorde is critical of the conference organizers for failing to have substantive difference represented on the conference program. She states, "I stand here as a Black lesbian feminist, having been invited to comment within the *only* panel at this conference where the input of Black feminists and lesbians is represented."[7]

Lorde elaborates on her conceptualization of difference throughout the essay, explaining, "Difference is that raw and powerful connection from which our personal power is forged."[8] She critiques the patriarchal socialization of women that entices them to ignore differences, "or to view them as causes for separation and suspicion rather than as forces for change."[9] Lorde also rejects the notion of tolerance, noting, "Advocating the mere tolerance of difference between women is the grossest reformism."[10] For her, difference has a positive and creative function, "Difference must not be merely tolerated, but seen as a fund of necessary polarities between which our creativity can spark like a dialectic."[11] Connecting difference and community with liberation, Lorde explains that community is necessary for liberation, adding that embracing difference as strength and as creative force is required both for community and for liberation.

Lorde continues to explain her expansive philosophy of difference, connecting it to survival, while also critiquing approaches to difference by society in general and white American academic feminist theory in particular. Again naming specific types of difference, she explains, "Those of us who stand outside of society's definition of acceptable women; those of us who have been forged in the crucibles of difference—those of us who are poor, who are lesbians, who are Black, who are older—know that *survival is not an academic skill*."[12] Having situated survival negatively (i.e., what survival is not), she goes on to situate it positively (i.e., identifying what survival means to her): "It [survival] is about learning how to stand alone, unpopular and sometimes reviled, and how to make common cause with those identified as outside the structures in order to define and seek a world in which we can all flourish."[13] Lorde also connects survival to her key concept of difference: "It [survival] is learning how to take our differences and make them strengths."[14]

Lorde is not thinking in merely abstract terms, but also in terms of material conditions. She asks, "If white american feminist theory need not deal with the differences between us, and the resulting difference in our oppressions, then how do you deal with the fact that the women who clean your houses and tend to your children while you attend conferences on feminist theory are, for the most part, poor women and women of Color? What is the theory behind racist feminism?"[15] Citing a talk from Adrienne Rich, she notes, "white feminists have educated themselves about such an enormous amount over the past ten years," then asks, "how come you have not also educated yourselves about Black women and the differences between us—white and Black—when it is key to our survival as a movement?"[16] Lorde warns, "The failure of academic feminists to recognize difference as a crucial strength is a failure to reach beyond the first patriarchal lesson."[17] Alternatively, taking our differences seriously enables us to see and address differential systems of oppression, while also empowering us to see our differences as sources of strength and creativity.

Lorde takes up to the issue of representation and participation later in the essay, again asking several pointed questions: "Why weren't other women of Color found to participate in this conference? Why were two phone calls to me considered a consultation? Am I the only possible source of names of Black feminists?"[18] Recall that Lorde is listed as a "consultant" on the conference program, but she is disclosing here that the consultation consisted of two phone calls. She is questioning superficial and performative participation as well as surface level consultation. In "The Personal, the Political, and Others: Audre Lorde Denouncing 'The Second Sex Conference,'" Lester C. Olson makes the following observations about Lorde's critique here: (1) "These remarks suggest underlying, interconnected techniques of domination in use at the conference"; (2) "To Lorde, the conference planners had appropriated her credibility as consultant by listing her as such on the program"; (3) "Moreover, the planners' use of this consultation

142   BEAUVOIR AND BELLE

superficially legitimated the program as inclusive, because she was a token black feminist and lesbian"; and (4) "Beyond this, her role as consultant implicitly may have excused the underrepresentation of black women and lesbians in the program."[19]

Lorde anticipates replies to her pointed questions, having heard them before. She states, "In academic feminist circles, the answer to these questions is often, 'We did not know who to ask.'"[20] Lorde describes this reply as an "evasion of responsibility" and "cop-out" that has negative consequences.[21] It "keeps Black women's art out of women's exhibitions, Black women's work out of most feminist publications except for the occasional 'Special Third World Women's Issue,' and Black women's texts off your reading lists."[22] Clearly, Lorde's critique here is not a call for symbolic or tokenistic representation. If that were the case, her presence at this conference and/or participation in the occasional special-issue publication would check off the "diversity" box. Lorde states, "To read this program is to assume that lesbian and Black women have nothing to say about existentialism, the erotic, women's culture and silence, developing feminist theory, or heterosexuality and power."[23] To be sure, Lorde is making a deeper claim, not only about representation among the panelists, but also about what differently situated women can contribute to these myriad issues. One way that she frames representation substantively is in terms of consciousness, "The absence of any consideration of lesbian consciousness or the consciousness of Third World women leaves a serious gap within this conference and within the papers presented here."[24]

Contra the master's tools of racism and patriarchy and the devaluation of difference, Lorde calls for difference, mutuality, and interdependence. She rejects "an either/or model of nurturing" that she noticed in one conference paper, "which totally dismissed my knowledge as a Black lesbian."[25] Lorde elaborates, "In this paper there was no examination of mutuality between women, no systems of shared support, no interdependence as exists between lesbians and women-identified women."[26] Rather than allowing the notion of nurturing to be manipulated by the master's tools ("the tools of racist patriarchy"), she asserts, "For women, the need and desire to nurture each other is not pathological but redemptive, and it is within that knowledge that our real power is rediscovered."[27] Building on her earlier analysis that

AUDRE LORDE 143

brings together difference and creativity for community and liberation, here Lorde connects interdependence with freedom and creativity. She explains, "Interdependency between women is the way to a freedom which allows the *I* to be, not in order to be used, but in order to be creative."[28]

Lorde explicitly connects her key concepts of difference and interdependence, noting that when we are not threatened by them we can see strength and security in them. Lorde asserts, "Only within that interdependency of different strengths, acknowledged and equal, can the power to seek new ways of being in the world generate, as well as the courage and sustenance to act where there are no charters."[29] She envisions empowering and creative new ways of being in the world that do not rely on the master's tools of domination and oppression. Lorde adds, "Within the interdependence of mutual (nondominant) differences lies that security which enables us to descend into the chaos of knowledge and return with true visions of our future, along with the concomitant power to effect those changes which can bring that future into being."[30] Thus, not only is she critiquing the limits of the conference for which she is a commentator and the myopic lens of white academic feminism, but she is also offering creative, expansive, and empowering alternatives.

Finally, Lorde is interested in what she calls a lesbian consciousness (as well as a consciousness of Third World women). Her notion of consciousness is interconnected with her insight about representation and difference, and the lack of attention to these issues in white academic feminism. According to Olson, "Difference became such a resource [for rhetorical invention for all women] by treating it as a creative tension. At the conference, Lorde's remarks enacted this transformation through her confrontational consciousness raising across the differences among women at the conference"[31] He explicitly connects Lorde's "Masters Tools" with Beauvoir's *The Second Sex* when he makes the case that, "At the conference, Lorde honored the achievements in *The Second Sex* by extending, modifying, and challenging Simone de Beauvoir's insights."[32] It is worth noting that Lorde's commentary does not explicitly take up *The Second Sex*. But Beauvoir's *Ethics of Ambiguity* is quoted in the commentary at the end: "Simone de Beauvoir once said: 'It is in the knowledge of the genuine conditions of our lives that

144   BEAUVOIR AND BELLE

we must draw our strength to live and our reasons for acting.'"[33] While I am not completely opposed to Olson's creative framing that connects "Master's Tools" with *The Second Sex*, I think it is also important to situate "Master's Tools" within a historical and philosophical Black feminist context, which I do in the next section.[34]

Jessica Benjamin's Letter to Lester Olson: A Case Study

Jessica Benjamin, the coordinator of the 1979 commemorative conference on *The Second Sex*, wrote "Letter to Lester Olson" (2000) in response to his article, "The Personal, the Political, and Others: Audre Lorde Denouncing 'The Second Sex Conference'" (2000). Her reply is both *defensive* (e.g., defending her choices as conference organizer) and *offensive* (e.g., recentering white women, disregarding Lorde's insights and critiques, and taking an overall condescending tone toward Lorde). While this would have been problematic even immediately after the 1979 conference (and there was another troublesome letter written at that time), the new letter reads as even more offensive now considering the fact that it was written and published about two decades later. Benjamin accuses Olson of decontextualizing Lorde's speech, defends her own position as a white feminist as well as her decisions as conference organizer, and takes up what she describes as emerging identity politics within the women's movement in general and in Lorde's speech in particular.[35] According to Benjamin, "the decontextualization of Audre Lorde's speech at that conference can serve to perpetuate the misunderstanding that underlay the destructive polarization that occurred at that time" and furthermore, "To accept her [Lorde's] view that the event was organized with no effort to include women of color by oblivious, racist, white women is surely not what happened."[36] With this in mind, she sets out to defend herself on multiple fronts.

Benjamin notes that there were bigger structural racial issues between Black and white women for which she should not be held responsible individually. She asserts, "In fact, the estrangement between white and black women at the time of the 'Second Sex Conference' had much deeper causes (the enduring structures of racism in our country) for which I believe no individual could be held responsible."[37] To this point, I would respond that while an individual may not be responsible for structural racism as a whole, individuals as well as institutional spaces like conferences certainly contribute to the myriad moving and interlocking parts of structural racism. Benjamin also suggests that Black women were simply not interested in feminism at the time. She attempts to support this claim with reference to two specific Black women, Mary Helen Washington ("For instance, Mary Helen Washington said she did not want to speak to an audience of all white women, and it was her experience that only white women came to feminist conferences") and Michele Wallace ("Indeed, at the time Michele Wallace, who probably would have been interested had she been available, was vociferously complaining about the lack of interest, indeed the rejection of feminism, among black women").[38] On my reading, Washington's point is not that Black women are not interested in feminism, but rather that she (and likely other Black women) had no interest in speaking to an audience of all white women.[39] It is also worth qualifying Wallace's point by noting that Black women were often not interested in a *white* feminism that frequently ignored and/ or devalued the experiences of Black women. What Benjamin misses in these anecdotes about Washington and Wallace is clearly articulated in Lorde's critical commentary at the conference. It is not the case that all Black women rejected feminism altogether. Rather there were (and still remain) good reasons to reject white feminists' focus exclusively on gender identity and oppression without regard for other forms of difference (e.g., race, class, sexuality, age) that are interlocking and intersecting with gender identities and oppressions. I am not claiming that all Black women identified as feminists in 1979 (any more than we do now). However, there is a persistent Black feminist (or if you prefer, Black proto-feminist) history in the United States that takes seriously race, class, and gender going back to Maria Stewart in 1831 (at least).[40] These were not new issues for Black women in 1979!

On the one hand, Benjamin claims, "The differences inside the women's movement that were most pressing politically and intellectually when this conference was planned (1978–1979) seemed to us to be the differences between heterosexual and lesbian women."[41] Put

146 BEAUVOIR AND BELLE

another way, race and class were not, in her estimation, political and intellectual priorities at that time. On the other hand, she bemoans audience members' responsiveness to Lorde as well as their emphasis on their own sexual identities and experiences. Benjamin states, "As each speaker ascended the microphone, she assigned herself a sexual identity (e.g., lesbian mother involved with an older woman) and from that vantage point expressed her personal sense of grievance and injustice, which was seen to be that of an excluded person, a silenced person and thus someone who fell into the same category of people Audre was speaking for (and, more importantly, not in the same category of the oppressors she was speaking against)."[42] Note that Benjamin frames "difference" in terms of heterosexual versus lesbian women, but she has a hard time holding space for more layered and nuanced differences as articulated by lesbian women at the conference. So in this example, when describing speakers responding to Lorde, Benjamin notes that they did in fact name their sexual identities (e.g., lesbian mother), just not exclusively in contrast to heterosexual identities. At one point Benjamin claims, "Difference was not yet a word that encompassed all these political issues."[43] However, she also adds, "But class, race, imperialism and colonialism were issues we took for granted since all of the organizers without exception, were women who had been in radical movements of the sixties dealing with those issues even before they had become feminists."[44] Lorde's remarks show how those differences that were taken for granted still remained largely excluded. As Alexis De Veaux explains in *Warrior Poet: A Biography of Audre Lorde*, " 'The Master's Tools' was an attack on the parochialism of feminist theory, its underlying racism, and racist feminist practices as unexamined dependence upon the patriarchy."[45] And furthermore, "As Lorde perceived it, by denying or excluding a forum for difference, white feminist academics duplicated rather than transformed systems of oppression: 'the master's tools.' "[46]

Another issue I want to raise pertains to Benjamin's problematic framing of identity politics. She makes at least three explicit references to identity politics in this published letter. First, she states, "We foresaw an increasing tendency away from political activism on behalf of feminist causes, as the movement splintered into ever-smaller groups concerned with maintaining cultural and personal homogeneity (what was to become identity politics)."[47] Here Benjamin presents "the movement" in a way that is presumed to be heterogenous and not homogenous. Yet "the movement" is also described as being splintered by ever-smaller groups, and the "ever-smaller groups" are depicted as seeking to maintain homogeneity. Put another way, a singular white feminist agenda is assumed to be heterogenous and all-encompassing, while explicitly multifaceted and diverse approaches such as those presented by Lorde (seeking to be not only attentive to gender issues, but also to the ways in which gender issues are impacted by race, class, sexuality, and age) are described as a move away from "political activism" and toward a homogenous "identity politics."

Second, Benjamin states, "the audience, fired by the content of Audre's speech, took its cue to use the open microphone as an opportunity to engage in a discourse that was brand new to all of us: that of identity politics."[48] Here, it is telling that this discourse is being framed as "new" to the white women present.[49] Again, Black women had been engaged in a multifaceted approach to feminism for almost 150 years by 1979. There were critiques of white-centered feminism (and male-centered Black nationalism) going back to abolition and suffrage, Jim Crow, Communism and socialism, imperialism and colonialism, civil rights and Black Power—all long before 1979. If the grievances of the audience members were new to the white feminists conference organizers, that is because they had not been paying attention or listening to Black women and other Women of Color for well over a century.

Third, Benjamin asserts, "The 'Second Sex Conference' has turned out to be a watershed event, a turning point, not only because of Audre's speech. It was the point from which we can date the formulation of identity politics, the idea of 'race, class, and gender,' and the enormous expansion of women's studies in the university bringing these ideas into fuller play."[50] This letter from Benjamin was written in 2000! For her to have the audacity assert that *The Second Sex* Conference in 1979 is the event, and date of the formulation of identity politics shows that she remained as ignorant about these matters at the turn of the twenty-first century as she had been two decades prior, when the conference took place and she claimed that the discourse was new to her. It is Benjamin who is engaging in a decontextualization

148 BEAUVOIR AND BELLE

here. As a corrective, I offer more context. The term "identity politics" dates back to "The Combahee River Collective: A Black Feminist Statement" (April 1977)—written by Barbara Smith, Beverley Smith, and Demita Frazier two years *prior* to the 1979 *The Second Sex* Conference.[51] According to Barbara Smith, the statement was first published in Zillah Eisenstein's edited collection *Capitalist Patriarchy and the Case for Socialist Feminism* (1978).[52] "The Combahee River Collective: A Black Feminist Statement" (CRC) is published again in *Off Our Backs: A Women's Newsjournal* (June 1979), in *This Bridge Called My Back: Writings by Radical Women of Color* (Moraga and Anzaldúa, 1981), and in *All of the Women Are White, All of the Blacks Are Men, But Some of Us Are Brave* (Hull, Scott, and Smith, 1982). It has also been anthologized in Beverly Guy-Sheftall's *Words of Fire: An Anthology of African-American Feminist Thought* (1995).

The CRC gave us the now well-known, even if frequently misunderstood and misused, concept "identity politics"—though some (including Benjamin) are not aware of this origin of the term. Smith, Smith, and Frazier explain, "We realize that the only people who care enough about us to work consistently for our liberation are us . . . This focusing upon our own oppression is embodied in the concept of *identity politics*."[53] They make a twofold case for identity politics. First, they assert, "We believe that the most profound and potentially most radical politics come directly out of our own identity, as opposed to working to end somebody else's oppression."[54] Second, they offer the following important nuance, "We realize that the liberation of *all* oppressed peoples necessitates the destruction of *all* the political-economic systems of capitalism and imperialism as well as patriarchy."[55] Barbara Smith elaborates on what they meant by identity politics: "What we were saying is that we have a right as people who are *not just* female, who are *not solely* Black, who are *not just* lesbians, who are *not just* working class, or workers—that we are people who embody *all of these identities*, and we have a right to build and define political theory and practice based upon that reality."[56] Unfortunately, this concept eventually got co-opted by the right.

Barbara Smith notes, "But however the right wing got ahold of identity politics and began using it as their whipping boy and their whipping girl, what we meant by identity politics when we originated the terminology was wholly different."[57] Once misappropriated, to be described as playing identity politics became an accusation, an assumption that you are subjectively centering your identity and lived experience in certain discussions and debates to the neglect of all others, that you are excluding anyone who does not share your identity from your political commitments. Identity politics came to be seen as a negative thing to be avoided at all costs, perhaps tantamount to a kind of essentialism. But Barbara Smith is very explicit about what identity politics is *not*, "We didn't mean that if you're not the same as us, you're nothing" and furthermore, "We were not saying that we didn't care about anybody who wasn't exactly like us."[58] She is emphatic about coalition building and solidarity with the struggles of socialist feminists, Men of Color workers, reproductive rights, and so on. Considering this background and context is important for showing how the term "identity politics" has been frequently taken out of context and misappropriated.

In the CRC statement, Smith, Smith, and Frazier are attentive to racial, sexual, heterosexual, and class oppression. They are also attentive to difference in ways that are compatible with how Lorde frames it in "The Master's Tools." While the white feminists at *The Second Sex* Conference may have been newly introduced to the idea that race, class, and gender were interlocking identities and oppressions, this was not the case for Lorde, who brings these concepts together in her speech, nor for the Black feminist traditions out of which Lorde (along with Smith, Smith, and Frazier) come and to which they contributed a great deal—not only as activists, intellectuals, writers, and speakers, but also as co-founders of the Kitchen Table: Women of Color Press (1980).[59] And let us not forget that Lorde was explicitly critiquing the conference organizers and presenters in part because of their inattention to "difference of race, sexuality, class, and age."

In addition to Benjamin's ignorance of Black feminist thought (historically, at the time of *The Second Sex* Conference, and even at the turn of the twenty-first century), what I also find troubling about Benjamin's letter to Olson is her condescending and paternalistic misrepresentation of Lorde and the "Master's Tools" critical commentary. We see a dismissive characterization of Lorde's speech as "inflammatory diatribe" rather than "substantive argument" when Benjamin

150 BEAUVOIR AND BELLE

states, "As for the substance of Audre's speech, it is surely debatable whether her paper should be taken as an inflammatory diatribe or a serious argument."[60] We see an effort to undermine Lorde's credibility by questioning her theoretical credentials when Benjamin states, "It is not clear to me that Audre ever studied any political theory, or had any acquaintance with the political revolutionaries of those different from herself."[61] It is worth noting that Lorde earned a BA from Hunter College with a major in American Literature and a minor in Philosophy and was well acquainted with theory—both her own and that of others. But notice that there is not only a general privileging of theory, but also the preference for a particular kind of theory by Benjamin—namely, that which has been generated by white men (without regard for other theories generated by non-white and non-male theorists). Benjamin is quite explicit about this when she claims, "Thus, I do not know whether she drew her conclusions from the experience of immersing herself in past *revolutionary theories by white males*. But it was no doubt a safe bet that nearly all past theories have been compliant with male domination and with racism—the question is whether such theory can be retooled."[62]

This privileging of white male theory is followed up with repeated paternalism toward and misrepresentation of Lorde. Benjamin asserts, "In my experience with political movements, radicals like Audre Lorde emerge time and again to express an opinion based on 'pure negation' of the existing relations, thus engaging in a reversal that in some measure keeps alive the enmity behind the very oppositions they would hope to challenge."[63] She adds, "I have also witnessed the fact that these proponents of radical reversal, who think that pure negation can work, often mobilize tremendous energy and so contribute a great deal."[64] This is a blatant misrepresentation of Lorde's remarks. When we take seriously Lorde's critical commentary, we see that far from offering "pure negation" or a "radical reversal" of existing relations, Lorde invited the audience to value difference as a creative force, embrace interdependence, and take seriously existing examples of cooperative and collaborative relations (e.g., women supporting women in community). Her aim was not to reverse the positions of the "masters" and the "slaves," but rather to envision a society in which everyone could be free.

When Benjamin declares, "I myself obviously belong to the group of feminist theorists who believe there is more to be learned by studying the dead white men of the past than by fully discarding them," and then adds, "My own belief regarding 'the master's tools,' that we must both bite and kiss the hand that has fed us, has remained," she clearly articulates her allegiances.[65] This alignment with "the dead white men of the past" is the subtext for Lorde's observations and critiques at *The Second Sex* Conference—namely, the issue of white feminist conference organizers and participants seeing the master's house as their only source of support and the master's tools as their only viable theoretical resources. On this point, it is important to note that Lorde's critical comments (which included references to existentialism, ontology, and the dialectic) are an affirmation of broader and more diverse sources of knowledge, not merely "pure negation" and/or "radical reversal" that dismisses theory altogether and/or advocates for fully discarding the study of dead white men.[66] Lorde explains what she means by "the master's tools and tactics" in part when she states:

> Women of today are still being called upon to stretch across the gap of male ignorance and to educate men as to our existence and our needs. This is an old and primary tool of all oppressors to keep the oppressed occupied with the master's concerns. Now we hear that it is the task of women of Color to educate white women—*in the face of tremendous resistance*—as to our existence, our differences, our relative roles in our joint survival. This is a diversion of energies and a tragic repetition of racist patriarchal thought.[67]

Thus, for Lorde, the tools of the master are not "thinking" and "theory." To presume so would be to presume (errantly) that only the master is capable of thinking and theorizing. Rather, Lorde explains that one tool of the oppressor is to redirect the efforts and energies of the oppressed toward the concerns of the master rather than toward their own liberation. She offers two examples: (1) the expectation that women educate men about the existence and needs of women, and (2) the expectation that Women of Color educate white women (who do not know in some cases, or do not want to know and do not care in other cases) about the existence, differences, and survival efforts

152   BEAUVOIR AND BELLE

of Women of Color, let alone joint survival strategies for *all* women. Benjamin's remarks about Lorde illustrate this second example Lorde offers. It is worth noting that Lorde's account of the master's tools has some affinity with one of Toni Morrison's famous observations about racism a few years earlier: "the function, the very serious function of racism . . . is distraction. *It keeps you from doing your work.* It keeps you explaining, over and over again, your reason for being."[68]

Long before writing this published "Letter to Lester Olson," Benjamin also wrote a letter to Audre Lorde after the conference. De Veaux states, "On behalf of several who served on the program committee, Jessica Benjamin sent a letter to Lorde a month later, citing Lorde's public anger at the failures in their vision as legitimate but divisive."[69] Again, there is a recentering of white women, particularly "the [conference] organizers who felt especially wounded" as well as "betrayed and disappointed" by Lorde's "legitimate" remarks.[70] This is yet another example of the master's tactics, that is, to draw attention away from Lorde's critiques and back toward the concerns of white women. De Veaux explains, "As they saw it, Lorde had acted out, disrupting a self-congratulatory moment for them and others."[71]

Lorde examines difference across race, gender, sexuality, class, and age. She emphasizes the value of difference and the inseparability of oppressive structures that attack various forms of difference, noting that we live "in a country where racism, sexism, and homophobia are inseparable."[72] In these ways, she also disrupts assumptions about women's experiences and oppressions as universal. But, "To their [*The Second Sex* Conference organizers'] ears, she'd privileged her identities as black and lesbian," and "In doing so, she had assumed a moral authority based on suffering; but suffering was a condition of all women, as they saw it, and they had envisioned a discussion that would push beyond the guilt-producing politics that so often arise from powerlessness."[73]

A copy of the letter is available in Lorde's papers archived at Spelman College where the following sentences are underlined by hand (presumably by Lorde): "<u>Because you are black and lesbian, you seemed to speak with the moral authority of suffering</u>." They explain to Lorde, "It was not, as you suggested, our intention to suppress the issue of racism at the conference." They continue (this part of the archived letter is

AUDRE LORDE   153

partially underlined by hand with two exclamation points added in the margins), "We failed to provide this arena in regard to racism because white women did not address the issue and black women did not choose to come." Concerning the recruiting of Women of Color to the conference, they state, "This situation is a natural outgrowth of the individualism and competitiveness of our circles, and the apolitical context in which such conferences get planned." (In the archived letter "our" is underlined by hand with the word "our" handwritten again in the margins and underlined three times with one exclamation point.)

In this earlier letter (as in the later open letter) there is a refusal to see the expansive and affirming notion of difference that Lorde offers. Instead, Lorde's remarks are reduced to a politics of suffering and guilt, while white women repeatedly re-center their own comfort. De Veaux notes, "They asserted that accusations of racism paralyzed, rather than permitted, any *comfortable* discussion of the topic."[74] Of course, this is not new insofar as there has been an ongoing historical lack (though not a total absence) of substantive analysis of race and racism by white women, especially as it manifests in white feminism. Furthermore, there have also been ongoing historical articulations and analyses of these issues by Black feminists. Nonetheless, as De Veaux explains, "Black women who did so were seen as betraying the calm to cause guilt in whites"[75]—again, a recentering of whiteness in an effort to get the oppressed to focus on the concerns of the oppressor. To be sure, at this point Lorde is well versed in these white feminist tactics, and she is not moved by Benjamin's initial letter. De Veaux states, "Her [Lorde's] response to Jessica Benjamin's letter had been anger, not hurt, as she was to admit, 'I had hoped for, but not expected, anything different.'"[76] I imagine Lorde would have similar sentiments about Benjamin's later open letter as well.

Conclusion: "Master's Tools" as Counter-Narrative to Analogical Approaches

I conclude this chapter with a consideration of Lorde's "Master's Tools" essay as a counter-narrative to white feminist analogical approaches to oppression and with the "I Am Your Sister" conference in 1990 where

154   BEAUVOIR AND BELLE

Lorde would have to confront critiques about its structure. Let us begin with the counter-narratives to analogical approaches to oppression. Take, for example, the analogy drawn between marriage and prostitution. Rejecting the marriage-as-prostitution analogy, Lorde asserts, "Poor women and women of color know there is a difference between the daily manifestations of marital slavery and prostitution because it is our daughters who line 42nd Street."[77] Put another way, the circumstances and material conditions confronting poor women and Women of Color sex workers on 42nd Street in New York City are not comparable to the circumstances and material conditions of middle-class married white women. Lorde both modifies and critiques analogical approaches to oppression and difference. As Olson observes, "Lorde modified analogies between sex and race in Beauvoir's book by concentrating on the overlapping concerns of black women ordinarily obfuscated by white feminists' development of such analogies."[78]

With this in mind, let us consider another aspect of the significance of Lorde's chosen title for her critical commentary: "The Master's Tools Will Never Dismantle the Master's House." Given the frequency with which white women (including Beauvoir) have analogized their gender oppression with racial oppression, specifically comparing their status as white women to the status of enslaved Black people, Lorde's "Master's Tools" is an important and necessary disruption to that analogical narrative.[79] Lorde provides an important counter-narrative. I agree with Olson's observation that "Lorde enacted a communicative process of rejecting simplistic binaries as master and slave, master and mistress, self and other, by treating them in combination and in overlapping senses."[80] We must take seriously how Black people (and more specifically Black women) and white women are situated differently within such analogies. De Veaux offers the following insight, "The notion that middle-class white women's intellectual and personal freedom was inflected with metaphors of bondage and depended on a modern day version of the mistress/indentured servant/slave relationship implicated contemporary white academics as accomplices in the historical narrative positioning white men (masters), white women (mistresses), and black people (slaves)."[81] Put another way, if the metaphor of slavery is to be used, rather than placing white women in the position of the slave, Lorde places them in the position of the mistress adjacent to and seeking to have a shared status with the master.

De Veaux notes, "From Lorde's perspective of the academy-as-plantation, its house was supported by deeply flawed, suspect means on the part of feminists."[82] Also highlighting how white women were situated in the position of masters across difference, Olson asserts, "Lorde's speech explored the ambiguities of the combined roles for white women in U.S. culture by evoking an understanding of their roles as masters across difference in race, class, and sexuality."[83] And De Veaux observes, "Lorde's essay, 'The Master's Tools Will Never Dismantle the Master's House,' framed a guerilla-tactics moment in which she struck at the unsuspecting 'mistresses' of the master's house."[84] This critique and counter-narrative implicate white feminism more generally as well as Beauvoir's *The Second Sex* more specifically. Again, De Veaux offers insight, "Further, this took place at just the moment when they were celebrating their own emancipation as configured by the impact of feminist analysis thirty years after Simone de Beauvoir's *The Second Sex*, a book many saw as shaping the modern age of feminist thought."[85] Thus, "The comparison of white women to white men as agents of oppression was a scathing one."[86]

Lorde would have to confront different (but related) critiques at her own celebratory, I AM YOUR SISTER CONFERENCE (dubbed a "celeconference"), which brought together 1200 activists from twenty-three countries in 1990. Following Lorde's lead, conference organizers were adamant about conference attendees being fifty percent Women of Color and fifty percent working class (allowing for overlaps between those categories). On the one hand, they noted that many white women complained bitterly when they were denied access to the conference to maintain those numbers and the commitment to difference that the numbers represented. On the other hand, they noted that among the conference attendees there were strong and valid critiques of inattentiveness to other forms of difference, especially language and disability. For example, there were translators for Spanish speakers (but not enough), the main stage for the event was not physically accessible for some, and the conference program was not made available in Braille. As ayofemi folayan states (in "I Am Your Sister: A Tale of Two Conferences"):

156 BEAUVOIR AND BELLE

Having a conference to honor Audre Lorde is a commendable achievement. Unfortunately, perpetuating patterns of oppression within our alliances is exactly what dooms our coalition efforts. As a black lesbian with disabilities, I felt tremendous pride as I realized that a coalition of women, with women of color providing the leadership, had made this conference happen. An equally deep swath of pain cut through me to understand that those same women could perpetuate ableism, attempt to render me invisible because of my disability, and in the same breath insist on their commitment to forging connections.[87]

Issues of invisibility and solidarity were also expressed by other conference attendees, e.g., women living with AIDS, women living in poverty, Asian women, Palestinian women, and Spanish speaking women.

For me, the issue is not that anyone should be expected to anticipate and accommodate *all* needs by *all* people at *all* times. Rather, I am interested in an openness to listening to critical feedback in a non-defensive way, acknowledging shortcomings, and making good faith efforts to make adjustments when possible. As folayan explains, "I am fairly forgiving of unconscious oppression . . . However, I am completely intolerant of someone who is so defensive as to insist that they would repeat the same oppressive behavior after they have been given specific information that it is oppressive."[88] Furthermore, it adds insult to injury when those pointing out limitations and requesting accommodations are then accused of being divisive. Lorde and the conference organizers reflect on this in the documentary by Jennifer Abod, "The Edge of Each Other's Battles: The Vision of Audre Lorde" (2002). They acknowledge rifts at the conference and their attempts to adjust real time. There was criticism of the conference organizers, and space was created to articulate and address (rather than altogether ignore) critiques. Lorde encouraged everyone to grow from the power and difficulties of difference and coalition building in this and other contexts. Lorde also admonished us to do our work, whatever that work is, while also recognizing that we have different ways of responding to what she called the terrors that haunt us.

Notes

1. This information is available on the original conference program, a copy of which was provided to me by Margaret Simons, who gave a paper ("A Tribute to *The Second Sex* and Simone de Beauvoir") for the 2:00–5:00 p.m. Opening Session—Simone de Beauvoir, September 27, 1979.
2. *The Essential Feminist Reader*, ed. Estelle B. Freedman (New York: Random House, 2007), 331.
3. In an interview with Keeanga-Yamahtta Taylor, Barbara Smith notes that Audre Lorde was part of the Combahee retreats and adds, "Audre definitely identified as a socialist as well. And she had had extensive political experience working in leftist movements prior to being involved with Combahee"; in Keeanga-Yamahtta Taylor, ed., *How We Get Free: Black Feminism and the Combahee River Collective* (Chicago: Haymarket Books, 2017), 57. (Hereafter Taylor 2017.) See also Cheryl Higashida, "Audre Lorde Revisited: Nationalism and Second Wave Black Feminism," in *Black Internationalist Feminism: Women Writers of the Black Left. 1945–1995* (Urbana: University of Illinois Press, 2013) and Lisa McGill, "Sister Outsider: African God(desse)s, Black Feminist Politics, and Audre Lorde's Liberation" in *Constructing Black Selves: Caribbean American Narratives and the Second Generation* (New York: NYU Press, 2005).
4. Audre Lorde, "The Masters Tools Will Never Dismantle the Master's House," in *Sister Outsider: Essays and Speeches by Audre Lorde* (Freedom: The Crossing Press, 1984), 110. (Hereafter Lorde 1984a).
5. Lorde 1984a, 110. Lorde names age along with race, sexuality, and class here. While she does not elaborate on age as a form of difference in this commentary, she does say more about it in "Age, Race, Class and Sex: Black Women Redefining Difference," in *Sister Outsider: Essays and Speeches by Audre Lorde* (Freedom: The Crossing Press, 1984). (Hereafter Lorde 1984b). In this essay, Lorde self-identifies as "a forty-nine year old Black lesbian feminist socialist mother of two, including one boy, and a member of an interracial couple," and she names ageism alongside racism, sexism, heterosexism, elitism, and classism (Lorde 1984b, 114). She notes, "ageism is another distortion of relationship which interferes without vision" (Lorde 1984b, 116–117). Beauvoir also takes up age in *The Second Sex* and *The Coming of Age*. For more on the issue of age in Beauvoir, see Penelope Deutscher, "Conversions of Alterity: Race, Sex, Age," in *The Philosophy of Simone de Beauvoir: Ambiguity, Conversion, Resistance* (Cambridge: Cambridge University Press, 2008), and "Beauvoir's Old

158 BEAUVOIR AND BELLE

Age," in *The Cambridge Companion to Simone de Beauvoir*, ed. Claudia Card (Cambridge: Cambridge University Press, 2003). (Hereafter Deutscher 2008.)

6. Lorde 1984a, 110.
7. Lorde 1984a, 110 (emphasis added).
8. Lorde 1984a, 112.
9. Lorde 1984a, 112.
10. Lorde 1984a, 111.
11. Lorde 1984a, 111. She asserts, "Without community there is no liberation, only the most vulnerable and temporary armistice between an individual and her oppression. But the community must not mean a shedding of our differences, nor the pathetic pretense that these differences do not exist." (Lorde 1984a, 112).
12. Lorde 1984a, 112 (emphasis original).
13. Lorde 1984a, 112.
14. Lorde 1984a, 112.
15. Lorde 1984a, 112.
16. Lorde 1984a, 113.
17. Lorde 1984a, 112.
18. Lorde 1984a, 113.
19. Lester C. Olson, "The Personal, the Political, and Others: Audre Lorde Denouncing 'The Second Sex Conference,'" *Philosophy and Rhetoric* 33, no. 3, *On Feminizing the Philosophy of Rhetoric* (2000): 259–285, here 272 (hereafter Olson, 2000).
20. Lorde 1984a, 113.
21. Lorde 1984a, 113.
22. Lorde 1984a, 113.
23. Lorde 1984a, 110.
24. Lorde 1984a, 111.
25. Lorde 1984a, 111.
26. Lorde 1984a, 111.
27. Lorde 1984a, 111. She adds, "It is this real connection which is so feared by a patriarchal world. Only with a patriarchal structure is maternity the only social power open to women" (Lorde 1984a, 111).
28. Lorde 1984a, 111.
29. Lorde 1984a, 111.
30. Lorde 1984a, 111–112.
31. Olson 2000, 269.
32. Olson 2000, 281.

AUDRE LORDE   159

33. Lorde 1984a, 113. Lorde is quoting Simone de Beauvoir, *The Ethics of Ambiguity* (New York: Kensington Publishing Group, 1948), 9.

34. For more on Simone de Beauvoir, Audre Lorde, and the notion of the erotic, see Sharon Patricia Holland, *The Erotic Life of Racism* (Durham, NC: Duke University Press, 2012) and Qrescent Mali Mason, "An Ethical Disposition toward the Erotic: The Early Autobiographical Writings of Simone de Beauvoir and Black Feminist Philosophy" (PhD diss., 2014). Holland makes also makes the following observation about queer theory, feminism, and race: "Queer theory's inheritance from [white] feminism is, for many queer theorists, to continue to denounce talk of race as identity politics and ignore 'racist practice' altogether, because these things are entirely disruptive to a theoretical project invested in the autonomy of (woman's) erotic preference, to echo Appiah. But, as postpositivist realist theory demonstrates, just because we eschew talk of race does not mean the racist effects vanish" (Holland 2012, 61).

35. Jessica Benjamin, "Letter to Lester Olson," *Philosophy and Rhetoric* 33, no. 3, *On Feminizing the Philosophy of Rhetoric* (2000): 286–290 (hereafter Benjamin 2000).

36. Benjamin 2000, 286.

37. Benjamin 2000, 286.

38. Benjamin 2000, 286.

39. I confirmed this in a direct conversation with Mary Helen Washington.

40. Note, I give an overview of the legacy of Black feminist frameworks in Chapter 1.

41. Benjamin 2000, 287.

42. Benjamin 2000, 289.

43. Benjamin 2000, 288.

44. Benjamin 2000, 288.

45. Alexis De Veaux, *Warrior Poet: A Biography of Audre Lorde* (New York: W.W. Norton & Company, 2004), 249 (hereafter De Veaux 2004).

46. De Veaux 2004, 249.

47. Benjamin 2000, 288.

48. Benjamin 2000, 289.

49. As De Veaux explains, "'The Master's Tools' identified and prophesied a new feminism—black feminism—that mainstream feminism could not see coming, or was ignoring" (De Veaux 2004, 250).

50. Benjamin 2000, 290.

51. Taylor 2017.

52. Zillah Eisenstien, ed., *Capitalist Patriarchy and the Case for Socialist Feminism* (Monthly Review Press, 1978). See Barbara Smith's prefatory

160 BEAUVOIR AND BELLE

remarks to "Combahee River Collective: A Black Feminist Statement," *Off Our Backs: A Women's Newsjournal* 9, no. 6, "AIN'T I A WOMON?" (June 1979): 6–8).

53. Taylor 2017, 18–19 (emphasis added).

54. Taylor 2017, 19.

55. Taylor 2017, 19 (emphasis added).

56. Taylor 2017, 61 (emphasis added).

57. Taylor 2017, 61.

58. Taylor 2017, 61.

59. For more on Kitchen Table: Women of Color Press, see Barbara Smith, "A Press of Our Own, Kitchen Table: Women of Color Press," *Frontiers: A Journal of Women's Studies* 10, no. 3, Women and Words (1989): 11–13); Jaime Grant, "Building Community-Based Coalitions from Academe: The Union Institution and the Kitchen Table: Women of Color Press Transition Coalition," *Signs: Journal of Women in Culture and Society* 21, no. 4, Feminist Theory and Practice (Summer 1996): 1024–1033); and Jennifer Gilley, "Ghost in the Machine: Kitchen Table Press and the Third Wave Anthology that Vanished," *Frontiers: A Journal of Women's Studies* 38, no. 3 (2019): 141–163.

60. Benjamin 2000, 289.

61. Benjamin 2000, 289.

62. Benjamin 2000, 289 (emphasis added).

63. Benjamin 2000, 290.

64. Benjamin 2000, 289.

65. Benjamin 2000, 289–290.

66. Benjamin 2000, 289–290.

67. Lorde 1984a, 113. (Emphasis added.)

68. Toni Morrison, "A Humanist View," speech from Portland State University's Public Speakers Collection: "Black Studies Center public dialogue Pt. 2," May 30, 1975. Morrison offers these examples, "Somebody says you have no language and you spend twenty years proving that you do. Somebody says your head isn't shaped properly so you have scientists working on the fact that it is. Somebody says you have no art, so you dredge that up. Somebody says you have no kingdoms and so you dredge that up. None of this is necessary. There will always be one more thing." (I would like to acknowledge and thank Michael E. Sawyer for the citation for this quote.)

69. De Veaux 2004, 250.

70. De Veaux 2004, 250.

71. De Veaux 2004, 250.

AUDRE LORDE 161

72. Lorde 1984a, 110.
73. De Veaux 2004, 250.
74. De Veaux 2004, 250. (Emphasis added.)
75. De Veaux 2004, 250. De Veaux also notes, "In the institutional milieu of black feminist and black lesbian feminist scholars—which was to crystalize in the late 1980s—and within the context of conferences sponsored by white feminist academics, Lorde stood out as an angry, accusatory, isolated black feminist lesbian voice" (De Veaux 2004, 247).
76. De Veaux 2004, 250.
77. Lorde 1984a, 112.
78. Olson 2000, 265.
79. Note these issues are taken up in more detail in Chapter 5 (Race/Gender Analogy), Chapter 6 (Slave/Woman Analogy), and Chapter 7 (abolition and suffrage).
80. Olson 2000, 265.
81. De Veaux 2004, 249.
82. De Veaux 2004, 250.
83. Olson 2000, 264–265.
84. De Veaux 2004, 248.
85. De Veaux 2004, 249.
86. De Veaux 2004, 249.
87. ayofemi folayan (author name lowercase in publication), "I Am Your Sister: A Tale of Two Conferences" (in *Off Our Backs*, December 1990, 20, No. 11, pages 1–5 and 9–11), 2. (Hereafter foloyan 1990.)
88. foloyan 1990, 2.

PART II
WHITE FEMINIST FRAMEWORKS

5

Simone de Beauvoir's
Analogical Approach

"There are deep analogies between the situations of women and blacks"

In *The Second Sex* (1949) Simone de Beauvoir offers various comparative and competing frameworks of oppression, including her use of the race/gender analogy as well as the more specific metaphor of woman as slave.[1] Focusing on woman's situation alongside other categories of identity and oppression, she makes the case that sexism (or what she calls "antifeminism"), on the one hand, and racism, antisemitism, classism, slavery, and colonialism, on the other hand, are comparative systems of oppression.[2] But when pointing to key differences between women and other groups, she sets up competing frameworks of oppression, privileging gender difference in ways that suggest that woman's subordination is a more significant and constitutive form of oppression than racism, antisemitism, class oppression, slavery, and/ or colonialism. In many cases the "woman" that Beauvoir describes is not a Black woman, a Jewish woman, a proletariat woman, an enslaved woman, or a colonized woman, but rather a white (and often bourgeois) woman. Furthermore, when she mentions "the Black," "the Jew," "the proletariat," "the slave," and "the colonized," these identities are often assumed to be male. In this way—using the term "woman" without qualifiers such as "white" and "French"—Beauvoir conceals the whiteness of the woman/women she is most often describing as Other while also frequently dismissing the gendered aspects of anti-Black racism, antisemitism, classism, slavery, and colonialism to which she compares white women's oppression.

In this chapter I examine Beauvoir's comparative and competing frameworks of oppression paying special attention to her use of the

Beauvoir and Belle. Kathryn Sophia Belle, Oxford University Press. © Oxford University Press 2024.
DOI: 10.1093/oso/9780197660195.003.0006

166 BEAUVOIR AND BELLE

race/gender analogy as well as her comparison of sexism with anti-Black racism, antisemitism, and classism. The chapter is divided into four main sections. In the first section, "The Race Gender Analogy (and the Question of Influence)," I offer a close reading of passages in *The Second Sex* where Beauvoir analogizes racial oppression with gender oppression, considering influences on her use of this analogy. In addition to pointing out several relevant quotes from *The Second Sex* in which these analogies appear, I also set these passages side by side with excerpts from Alva Myrdal, W. E. B. Du Bois, Richard Wright, Gunnar Myrdal, and Jean-Paul Sartre—all figures identified as influences on Beauvoir in select secondary literature.[3] In the second section, "Comparative and Competing Frameworks of Oppression," I focus on Beauvoir's comparisons between woman's situation (or more specifically the situation of sex workers) and the Jewish situation, her analysis of woman's complicity, her distinctions between the situation of the woman and the proletariat, as well as the ways she contrasts the working-class white woman with the bourgeois white woman.

In the third section, "Critiques of Beauvoir's Analogical Approach," I present critical analyses of the race/gender analogy in secondary literature by white feminists Sabine Broeck (2012), Elizabeth Spelman (1988), Margaret Simons (1999), and Penelope Deutscher (2008), along with critiques by Black feminist scholars Deborah King (1998) and Patricia Hill Collins (2017), as well as Latina feminist philosopher Stephanie Rivera Berruz (2012 and 2016). And in the fourth section, "The Potential and Pitfalls of Analogies," I take up Lorenzo Simpson's explorations of analogies as hermeneutical models for understanding across difference in *The Unfinished Project* (2001), and Gaile Pohlhaus, Jr.'s, critical engagement with Simpson on the use of analogies, as well as Trina Grillo and Stephanie Wildman's critiques of analogies between racial oppression and other forms of oppression.[4] I make the following arguments: (1) Beauvoir's comparative and competing frameworks of oppression pose at least two major problems—on the one hand, she collapses diverse systems of oppression as the same, and on the other hand, she distinguishes among these systems of oppression in a way that privileges gender difference and oppression above other forms of identity and oppression; (2) Beauvoir's utilization of the race/gender analogy omits the experiences and oppressions of Black women and

SIMONE DE BEAUVOIR'S ANALOGICAL APPROACH   167

other Women of Color who experience racial and gender oppression (as well as other forms of oppression) simultaneously; (3) even when white feminists critique Beauvoir's use of comparative and competing frameworks of oppression, including the race/gender analogy, often they do not cite Black and Latina feminist engagements with Beauvoir on these issues—or if they do, there is not substantive engagement with the arguments presented in the texts cited.

The Race/Gender Analogy (and the Question of Influence)

Let us first look at examples of comparative frameworks of oppression. Presenting woman as "Other" from the very beginning, Beauvoir describes *Otherness* as an "original category" and *alterity* as a "fundamental category" of human thought (TSS 6). She offers several examples of *Others*: "For the native of a country inhabitants of other countries are viewed as 'foreigners'; Jews are the 'others' for anti-Semites, blacks for racist Americans, indigenous people for colonists, proletarians for the propertied classes" (TSS 6).[5] In this way, Beauvoir presents women, "foreigners," Black people, Jewish people, Indigenous (colonized) people, and proletarians *comparatively* as Others. For her, the stereotype of "the eternal feminine" (TSS 4) corresponds to stereotypes about "the black soul" and "the Jewish character" (TSS 12). The justifications for creating inferior conditions for race, caste, class, or sex are not only comparable; they are actually the same (TSS 12). Examining these comparative frameworks more closely, my initial focus will be on Beauvoir's use of the race/gender analogy, followed by the question of influence with regard to her use of that analogy.

Simply stated, the race/gender analogy is the use of racial oppression as an analogy for gender oppression. Of course, analogical approaches to the interconnected systems of racial and gender oppressions are not new. White women have been analogizing their gender oppression with racial oppression and slavery going back at least to the late eighteenth century. Two prominent early examples of this argument by analogy include French playwright Olympe de Gouges and British philosopher Mary Wollstonecraft. In many ways, Beauvoir not only

168 BEAUVOIR AND BELLE

follows in this white European proto-feminist tradition that preceded her, but also further entrenches an analogical approach to oppression for white feminists coming after her. The analogizing of racial oppression with gender oppression frequently and problematically codes race as Black male and gender as white female, ignoring the ways in which Black women and other Women of Color experience racism and sexism—or racialized sexism and sexualized racism—simultaneously. This analogical framing also misses intraracial gender oppression (e.g., the sexism of Black men and other Men of Color) and intragender racial oppression (e.g., the racism of white women). Looking specifically at Beauvoir's comparisons of gender oppression against the white woman (as if all of the women are white) with racial oppression against Black men (as if all of the Blacks are men), I argue that this analogy does not account for the experiences and multiple simultaneous oppressions confronting Black women and other Women of Color (those of us who are brave).[6]

Beauvoir's analogical analysis emerges early in her introduction to *The Second Sex*, where she interrogates various disciplines and theories (e.g., religion, philosophy, theology, science, biology, experimental psychology) that have been used to prove women's inferiority. Comparing antifeminism to anti-Black racism, she turns suddenly to "separate but equal" doctrines as applied not only to race but also to gender (TSS 12).[7] Beauvoir explains that at most antifeminists were willing to "grant 'separate but equal' status to the *other* sex" and, comparing (white) women with Black (men). She also asserts that like Jim Crow racial segregation against Black American (men), gender segregation toward (white) women can only serve to support extreme forms of discrimination (TSS 12, emphasis original). For her, "This convergence"—that is, the use of so-called egalitarian segregation for gender as it has been used for race—"is in no way pure chance: whether it is race, caste, class, or sex reduced to an inferior condition, the justification process is the same" (TSS 12). Here we see not only the race/gender analogy, but also the comparison of race, caste, class, and sex oppression.

It is important to note that in the United States, "separate but equal" was not only a broad social practice (also known as *de facto* segregation), but also a legal practice (*de jure* segregation)—both having social

SIMONE DE BEAUVOIR'S ANALOGICAL APPROACH   169

and political implications and consequences. Jim Crow racial segregation was sanctioned by law with the *Plessy v. Ferguson* (1896) decision. The *Plessy* decision simultaneously reinforced the earlier *Dred Scott* (1857) decision (which declared that both enslaved and free Black people were not and could never be citizens and furthermore that we had no rights that needed to be recognized by whites), while also undermining the 14th Amendment (which was supposed to guarantee equal protection under the law), as well as the Civil Rights Act of 1866 (which mandated that all persons born in the United States, except American Indians, are citizens with full and equal benefits of all laws), and the Civil Rights Act of 1875 (which prohibited racial discrimination in public places). This is before the *Brown v. Board of Education* (1954) decision made racial segregation of public schools illegal (though public schools remained and are still racially and socioeconomically segregated decades after *Brown*). Having very briefly noted the significance of the notion of "separate but equal," let us turn back to Beauvoir and some of her influences.

The question of influence is one that is posed frequently in scholarship on Beauvoir. Some have argued that she was an important philosophical influence on Jean-Paul Sartre rather than the other way around.[8] Others have argued that Beauvoir was influenced by white male philosophers in the Western canon and/or appropriated their work in innovative ways to create her own unique philosophy.[9] It is not surprising that the question of influence also emerges in the specific context of the race/gender analogy. With this in mind, I explore the influences on Beauvoir concerning this analogy to show where she converges with and/or diverges from certain sources in her own analogical analyses of race and gender oppression. For example, there are similarities between Beauvoir's analysis of race and gender oppression in *The Second Sex* and Alva Myrdal's earlier observations in "A Parallel to the Negro Problem" (1944), appendix 5 in Gunnar Myrdal's *An American Dilemma*, volume 2.[10] Just as Beauvoir interrogates the disciplines and theories that offered "evidence" for (white) women's inferiority, A. Myrdal in her earlier essay explores arguments used to support problematic ideas about the inferiority of (white) women and Black (men). A. Myrdal states, "The arguments, when arguments were used, have been about the same: smaller brains, scarcity of geniuses

170 BEAUVOIR AND BELLE

and so on. The study of women's intelligence and personality has had broadly the same history as the one we record for Negroes."[11] Also presenting segregation as a form of both racial and gender discrimination, A. Myrdal states, "This close relation is no accident," while Beauvoir asserts, "this convergence is in no way pure chance" (TSS 12).[12]

Beauvoir itemizes several analogies between (white) women and Black (men) in her introduction, positing:

[T]here are deep analogies between the situations of women and blacks: both are liberated today from the same paternalism, and the former master caste wants to keep them "in their place," that is, the place chosen for them; in both cases, they praise, more or less sincerely, the virtues of the "good black," the carefree, childlike, merry soul of the resigned black, and the woman who is a "true woman"— frivolous, infantile, irresponsible, the woman subjugated to man. In both cases, the ruling class bases its argument on the state of affairs it created itself. (TSS 12)

Here Beauvoir explicitly names the "deep analogies" in the oppressive situations faced by (white) women and Black (men). Again, there are overlaps between Beauvoir's extended quote and A. Myrdal's appendix. A. Myrdal asserts, "Their [(white) women's and children's] present status, as well as their *history* and their problems in society reveal striking similarities to those of the Negroes."[13] She adds, "As the Negro [man] was awarded his 'place' in society, so there was a [white] 'woman's place.' In both cases the rationalization was strongly believed that [white] men, in confining them to this place, did not act against the true interest of the subordinate groups."[14]

Beauvoir and A. Myrdal identify similarities between racial subordination of Black (men) and gender subordination of (white) women— specifically the use of doctrines, theories, and academic disciplines to prove the inferiority of both groups, the paternalism applied to both groups, and the notion that both groups were expected to stay in their predetermined "place" in society. Also, both emphasize stereotypical representations of (white) women and Black (men). Beauvoir identifies the praise given to the "good black" (man) and the (white)

SIMONE DE BEAUVOIR'S ANALOGICAL APPROACH   171

"true woman"—insisting that in both cases these representations are rooted in conditions created by the ruling class. A. Myrdal asserts, "The myth of the [white] 'contented women,' who did not want to have suffrage or other civil rights and equal opportunities, had the same social function as the myth of the 'contented Negro'" (man).[15] But for her, "In both cases there was probably—in a static sense—often some truth behind the myth" of the contented (white) women and the contented Negro (man).[16]

Two additional overlapping issues we find in Beauvoir's introduction and A. Myrdal's appendix concern competition and the notion of superiority and inferiority complexes. Beauvoir notes that the competition of (white) women threatens (white) men in a similar way that the competition of Black people threatens white people (TSS 13). A. Myrdal discusses this comparative threat of competition in more detail:

> Women's competition has, like the Negro's, been particularly obnoxious and dreaded by men because of the low wages women, with their few earning outlets, are prepared to work for. Men often dislike the very idea of having women on an equal plane as co-workers and competitors, and usually they find it even more 'unnatural' to work under women. White people generally hold similar attitudes toward Negroes.[17]

Moving from competition to inferiority and superiority complexes, A. Myrdal considers how (white) women and Black (men) "have often been brought to believe in their inferiority of endowment."[18] But on this point Beauvoir shifts the paradigm when she explains, "in the United States a 'poor white' from the South can console himself for not being a 'dirty nigger'... Likewise, the most mediocre of males believes himself a demigod next to women" (TSS 13).[19] Noting the inferiority complexes in (white) men—rather than only in (white) women and Black (men)—Beauvoir explains that even in these cases, "no one is more arrogant toward women, more aggressive or more disdainful, than a man anxious about his own virility" (TSS 13).

Already in Beauvoir's introduction and A. Myrdal's appendix we see similarities in their language about race and gender oppression, as

172   BEAUVOIR AND BELLE

well as their presentation of women and Black people as if we belong to mutually exclusive groups. Neither of them are offering an account of Black women's simultaneous experiences of racial and gender oppression. But there are also subtle differences in their approaches to the race/gender analogy. I will return to these two figures later, but now I want to explore influences between Black male intellectuals and Beauvoir—specifically W. E. B. Du Bois and Richard Wright.

In *Beauvoir and the Second Sex: Feminism, Race, and the Origins of Existentialism*, Margaret Simons argues that Beauvoir also had significant influences on her work with regard to her use of racial oppression as an analogy for gender oppression in *The Second Sex*. She offers one of the earliest close examinations of W. E. B. Du Bois' and Richard Wright's philosophical influence on Beauvoir's theory of oppression. Describing Wright as "the intellectual heir" of Du Bois, Simons describes Du Bois' notion of double consciousness "as a model for Beauvoir's concept of woman as the Other in *The Second Sex*."[20] Let us examine these connections among Beauvoir, Du Bois, and Wright in more detail.

In the second volume of *The Second Sex*, when describing the experience of being revealed to oneself as alterity, Beauvoir states:

> It is a strange experience for an individual recognizing himself as subject, autonomy, and transcendence, as an absolute, to discover inferiority—as a given essence—in his self: it is a strange experience for one who posits himself for himself as One to be revealed to himself as alterity. That is what happens to the little girl when, learning about the world, she grasps herself as a woman in it. (TSS 311)

From this starting point of alterity as experienced by the little (white) girl grasping herself as (white) woman, Beauvoir describes a similar sense of alterity for American Black (men). She asserts:

> This is not a unique situation. American blacks, partially integrated into a civilization that nevertheless considers them an inferior caste, live it; what Bigger Thomas experiences with so much bitterness at the dawn of his life is this definitive inferiority, this cursed alterity

SIMONE DE BEAUVOIR'S ANALOGICAL APPROACH   173

inscribed in the color of his skin: he watches planes pass and knows
that because he is black the sky is out of bounds for him. (TSS 311)

Beauvoir then returns to the alterity experienced by the little (white)
girl, "Because she is woman, the girl knows that the sea and the poles, a
thousand adventures, a thousand joys are forbidden to her: she is born
on the wrong side" (TSS 311).[21]

Readers of Wright will recognize the reference to Bigger Thomas
(from *Native Son*) and may consider him the primary influence in
these passages.[22] But readers of W. E. B. Du Bois will also notice his
analysis of the strange experience of being perceived as a problem or
the peculiar sensation of double consciousness. In *The Souls of Black
Folk* (1903) Du Bois introduces this concept in "Of Our Spiritual
Strivings":

> It is a peculiar sensation, this double-consciousness, this sense of al-
> ways looking at one's self through the eyes of others, of measuring
> one's soul by the tape of a world that looks on in amused contempt
> and pity.[23]

For Du Bois, being revealed to oneself as alterity is an experience that
occurs in one's youth (as Beauvoir asserts later), though he speaks
of his own Black boyhood rather than of the little (white) girl about
whom Beauvoir speaks. He states, "It is in the early days rollicking
boyhood that the revelation first bursts upon one, all in a day, as it
were."[24] Furthermore, the notion that the little (white) girl is born on
the "wrong side" ("of the line" in the first English translation) is also
an allusion to Du Bois' analysis of the color line, which he famously
described as the problem of the twentieth century.[25]

Let us revisit A. Myrdal's appendix here insofar as she explicitly
names Du Bois, asserting, "Du Bois' famous ideological manifesto *The
Souls of Black Folk* is, to mention only one example, an ardent appeal
on behalf of women's interests as well as those of the Negro" (A. Myrdal
1944, 1076).[26] But A. Myrdal and Beauvoir have different positions
concerning the uniqueness of the situation of the (white) woman
and the Black (man) as well as the description of their situations as
"problems." A. Myrdal, whose appendix is part of G. Myrdal's massive

174 BEAUVOIR AND BELLE

two-volume study of the "Negro," denies the uniqueness of racial oppression. She explains:

> In studying a special problem like the Negro problem, there is always a danger that one will develop a quite incorrect idea of its uniqueness. It will, therefore, give perspective to the Negro problem and prevent faulty interpretations to sketch some of the important similarities between the Negro problem and the women's problem. In the historical development of these problem groups in America there have been much closer relations than is now ordinarily recorded.[27]

For A. Myrdal, the oppression of Black (men) is not unique because the oppression of (white) women has similar origins, ideologies, and consequences. She adds (contra G. Myrdal) that there is both a Negro problem and a women's problem: "both [Negroes and women] are still problem groups."[28]

But Beauvoir approaches these issues differently. Leading with the alterity experienced by the little (white) girl grasping herself as (white) woman in the world, Beauvoir asserts that it is the (white) girl's alterity (or the othering of gender oppression) that is not unique.[29] In contrast to A. Myrdal, for Beauvoir, there is not a *Negro problem* or a *women's problem*, rather there is a *white problem* and a *man problem*. Utilizing the frameworks of Richard Wright, G. Myrdal, and Jean-Paul Sartre, Beauvoir explains, "Just as in America there is no black problem but a white one, just as 'anti-Semitism is not a Jewish problem, it's our problem,' *so the problem of woman has always been a problem of men*" (TSS 148).[30] Finally, unlike A. Myrdal, who does not use the language of complicity in describing the status or situation of (white) women, Beauvoir underscores (white) woman's complicity and privilege. So Beauvoir not only pinpoints similarities between the little (white) girl grasping herself as a (white) woman and American Black (men), but she also names a "great difference" between the two: "the blacks endure their lot in revolt—no privilege compensates for its severity—while for the woman her complicity is invited" (TSS 311–312).

Returning to Wright and Beauvoir, we know that she read much of his literature, they traveled together in France and the United States, and she referenced his writings several times in *The Second Sex*.[31] In

SIMONE DE BEAUVOIR'S ANALOGICAL APPROACH   175

addition to the earlier example of Bigger Thomas from *Native Son* already discussed, Beauvoir also cites *Black Boy* in her chapter on "The Independent Woman" when she considers how the (white) woman can balance the tensions and contradictions confronting her. Comparing the situation of Black (men) from America and Black (men) from Africa with the situation of (white) women, Beauvoir references Wright at the end of the second volume of *The Second Sex*:

> Richard Wright showed in *Black Boy* how blocked from the start the ambitions of a young American black man are and what struggle he has to endure merely to raise himself to the level where whites begin to have problems; the blacks who came to France from Africa also have—within themselves as well as from the outside—difficulties similar to those encountered by women. (TSS 736–737)

Here Beauvoir is not only comparing the ways in which the ambitions of American Black (men) and (white) women are discouraged and/or denied altogether, she is also calling attention to the external and internal struggles within oppressed groups, specifically (white) women, Black American (men), and also Black African (men) who come to France. This is one of the few instances when Beauvoir's focus on the race/gender analogy is not primarily on Black (men) in America, insofar as she also names Black (men) from Africa coming to France. Still, she persists in contrasting the experiences of (white) women with Black (men) without mention of Black women. Before examining critiques of this analogical approach to racial and gender oppression, let us take up a few more considerations of the influences between Wright and Beauvoir, and then between G. Myrdal and Beauvoir.

In "Owned Suffering: Thinking the Feminist Political Imagination with Simone de Beauvoir and Richard Wright" (2000), Vikki Bell argues, "De Beauvoir's use of Wright is heuristic not sociological, rhetorical not empirical, and it is in this sense that the argument functions to strengthen de Beauvoir's point through association."[32] Unlike Bell, who emphasizes Wright's influence on Beauvoir in terms of "Wright's sociological thought" and "his broadly Marxist perspective," Margaret Simons emphasizes Wright's philosophical contributions and impact on Beauvoir.[33] She argues that "Wright's influence on Simone

176 BEAUVOIR AND BELLE

de Beauvoir's philosophy, [includes] . . . providing her with a theory of racial oppression and liberation that she utilized as a model in constructing the theoretical foundations for radical feminism in *The Second Sex*."[34] Simons reads Wright and Beauvoir as holding "a shared concept of the oppressed Other" as well as a similar "focus on the importance of social relations and recognition in the formation of the self."[35] Furthermore, both theorists use phenomenological descriptions of oppression in an effort to challenge pernicious stereotypes.[36]

For Simons (contra V. Bell), "Wright's phenomenological descriptions of black experience of oppression provide a methodological alternative to both [G.] Myrdal's objectifying social science methodology and the economic reductionism of Marxist orthodoxy."[37] Simons explains, "Wright's philosophical influence on Beauvoir is a subjectivist, phenomenological approach to the study of oppression . . . describing the lived experience of American racism from the standpoint of the oppressed."[38] And then she elaborates, "Wright provides a phenomenology of racial oppression to challenge the claims by segregationists that blacks are happy and contented with their naturally inferior place in society, much as Beauvoir, in the second volume of *The Second Sex* (entitled Lived Experience), relies on a phenomenological description of women's experience to challenge the oppressive stereotypes of popular myths and Freudian psychology."[39]

As with Beauvoir and A. Myrdal, there are noteworthy similarities and differences between Beauvoir and G. Myrdal. While Simons thinks that Wright probably introduced Beauvoir to *An American Dilemma*, biographer Deirdre Bair points out that Beauvoir received a copy of the text from Nelson Algren in 1947.[40] Beauvoir writes about the text in letters to Algren in which she reflects on what she learns from G. Myrdal about Black people and notes the analogies between Black people and women.[41] Simons notes similarities between Beauvoir and G. Myrdal, including their use of analogies with racism, how they draw on the notion of caste and social constructionism (rather than biological racial categories), their connection to African American intellectual traditions, and the encyclopedic scope of their texts.[42] In *Outsider Citizens: The Remaking of Postwar Identity in Wright, Beauvoir, and Baldwin* (2006), Sarah Relyea cites Simons' important work on the influences of Wright and G. Myrdal on Beauvoir, but Relyea puts more

SIMONE DE BEAUVOIR'S ANALOGICAL APPROACH 177

emphasis on the latter's influence and asserts, "close comparison of the two works [*An American Dilemma* and *The Second Sex*] shows that Beauvoir adopts other fundamental concepts and arguments from Myrdal's analysis of race, which she recasts in terms of existential philosophy as an analysis of gender."[43]

Penelope Deutscher in *The Philosophy of Simone de Beauvoir: Ambiguity, Conversion, Resistance* (2008) also explores G. Myrdal's influences on Beauvoir, especially her writing on sexism and racism. She posits that the initial scope of Beauvoir's book on the "woman question" might have been closer to that of Sartre's short book on the "Jewish question," but after reading *An American Dilemma*, Beauvoir expands her project.[44] Describing some influences as important interventions, Deutscher asserts, "Beauvoir's engagement with American racism, and particularly with the analysis of race relations offered by Wright, John Dollard, and [G.] Myrdal constituted, therefore, a decisive intervention into her reflections on relations between the sexes."[45] She also draws important distinctions between G. Myrdal and Beauvoir. On the one hand, she reads Beauvoir as using a more interrogated interdisciplinary method than G. Myrdal—taking cues from his interdisciplinarity and also enhancing it by registering multiple voices that work both with and against the disciplines in question.[46] On the other hand, Deutscher notes that Beauvoir does not always utilize the diverse resources of Black scholarship available in G. Myrdal's study, that is, she does not closely examine G. Myrdal's references to Black writers—especially writers whose alternative analyses could have called into question her more problematic presuppositions about race and racism that we find in *The Second Sex*.[47]

Up to this point, I have outlined examples of the race/gender analogy at work in *The Second Sex*, focusing on the comparative aspects of Beauvoir's analysis of racial and gender oppression, and making connections with A. Myrdal, Du Bois, Wright, and G. Myrdal. We see these influences in the very framing of the comparisons between racial and gender oppression. We also see how she converges with Wright, Sartre, and G. Myrdal in framing the issues of oppression as *oppressor* problems rather than problems caused by the *oppressed*. But she diverges from A. Myrdal's formulation of racial oppression as a Negro problem and gender oppression as a women problem. A. Myrdal

178 BEAUVOIR AND BELLE

and Beauvoir also offer divergent perspectives on the uniqueness of racial and gender oppression—A. Myrdal emphasizing the lack of uniqueness of racial oppression and Beauvoir underscoring the lack of uniqueness of gender oppression. When we pay closer attention to these influences and analogical analyses of oppression, the ways that they conceal the simultaneous racial oppression and sexual oppression experienced by Black women become more evident.

Comparative and Competing Frameworks of Oppression

In addition to analogizing the oppression of (white) women with the oppression of Black (men), Beauvoir also makes controversial comparisons between women (more specifically, sex workers) and Jewish people. She asserts that the situation of prostitutes and "the Jews' [situation] were often rightly compared" (TSS 113).[48] Concerning the perception of Jewish people and prostitutes by the church, Beauvoir asserts, "usury and money lending were forbidden by the church exactly as extra-conjugal sex was; but society can no more do without financial speculators than free love, so these functions fell to the damned castes" (TSS 113). There is an implicit description of Jewish people as financial speculators and of prostitution as free love here. She also compares the ways in which prostitutes, like Jews, experienced residential restrictions and limitations placed on their movement.[49] Beauvoir then adds, "Like Jews, [prostitutes] had to wear distinctive signs on their clothes," and furthermore, "They [prostitutes] were *by law* taxed with infamy, had no recourse whatsoever to the police and the courts, and could be thrown out of their lodgings on a neighbor's simple claim. For most of them, life was difficult and wretched" (TSS 113). There is also Beauvoir's description of unmarried peasant women as "pariahs." She states, "There are still many social strata where she is offered no other perspective; for peasants, an unmarried woman is a pariah; she remains the servant of her father, her brothers, and her brother-in-law; moving to the city is virtually impossible for her; marriage chains her to a man and makes her mistress of a home" (TSS 443). The comparison between Jewish people and prostitutes, as well as between pariahs

SIMONE DE BEAUVOIR'S ANALOGICAL APPROACH 179

and unmarried peasant women, suggests that the women she has in mind are white (or at least not Jewish), and the Jewish people she has in mind are presumably male.

An additional problematic comparison is presented in Beauvoir's extended analysis of the conditions endured by the (white) bourgeois housewife tending to domestic duties—framed as a battle of good versus evil, "The housewife wears herself out running on the spot; she does nothing; she only perpetuates the present; she never gains the sense that she is conquering a positive Good, but struggles indefinitely against Evil" (TSS 474). She elaborates on this good-versus-evil theme, "All doctrines of transcendence and freedom subordinate the defeat of evil to progress toward good. But the wife is not called to build a better world; the house, the bedroom, the dirty laundry, the wooden floors, are fixed things: she can do no more than rout out indefinitely the foul causes that creep in; she attacks the dust, stains, mud, and filth; she fights sin, she fights with Satan" (TSS 476). And then there is Beauvoir's glib depiction of the destruction of women's housework as "small holocausts" when she asserts, "For her to consent to it [housework] without regret, these small holocausts must spark some joy or pleasure somewhere" (TSS 483).

While I have not found any critiques of this problematic holocaust language as a descriptor for the plight of the housewife, there is pointed criticism of Beauvoir's good-versus-evil framing of domestic work. In "Womanism: The Dynamics of the Contemporary Black Female Novel in English" (1985), Chikwenye Ogunyemi distinguishes the projects of Black womanism and white feminism and writing. In doing so she presents Beauvoir as one example of the differences between them. After quoting Beauvoir's above observation of woman's domestic work ("But woman is not called upon to build a better world: her domain is fixed and she has only to keep up the never ending struggle against the evil principles that creep into it; in her war against dust, stains, mud, and dirt she is fighting sin, wrestling with Satan"[50]), Ogunyemi pushes back on this framing. She explains, "In couching woman's war in domestic and religious terms, de Beauvoir is playful and somewhat Puritanical; her account does not cover the experience of the black woman for whom Satan is not a metaphysical concept but a reality out there, beyond her home, where she must willy-nilly go to obtain

180   BEAUVOIR AND BELLE

the wherewithal for descent survival as well as for a 'better world.'"[51] Ogunyemi is not talking about the burden of domestic labor for the housewife, rather, she is drawing attention to the sexual exploitation of Black women working as domestic workers in white homes.[52]

In making these various comparisons, Beauvoir also underscores differences, particularly the different responses to oppression by (white) women versus other groups (e.g., Black people, Jewish people, and the proletariat). As previously noted, she asserts that women are complicit—women do not resist or revolt against their oppressors. To this she also adds that women do not posit themselves as subjects (thereby turning their oppressors into objects) and offers several examples. There is the aforementioned example from the race/gender analogy in which Beauvoir identifies several similarities between (white) women and Black (men), but also asserts, "The great difference is that the blacks endure their lot in revolt—no privilege compensates for its severity—while for the woman her complicity is invited" (TSS 311–312).[53] She continues this line of argument, contrasting the complicity of (white) women with the revolts and calls for eliminativism among Black people, Jewish people, and the proletariat. She states that while fanatic Jews or Blacks may seek to eliminate their oppressors in order to make all of humanity Jewish or Black, "a woman could not even dream of exterminating males" insofar as a "cleavage of society by sex is not possible" (TSS 9).

Beauvoir insists that unlike the proletariat, which "has always experienced its condition in revolt" with the goal "to cease to exist as a class," the (white) woman's situation is different, "specifically because of the community of life and interests that create her solidarity with man, and due to the complicity he encounters in her: she has no desire for revolution, she would not think of eliminating herself as a sex: she simply asks that certain consequences of sexual differentiation be abolished" (TSS 66).[54] To be clear, Beauvoir is noting that white bourgeois women are satisfied with their race and class status. They only seek to abolish the gender oppression they experience from their white bourgeois male counterparts. And when considering subjectivity, Beauvoir notes that (white) women do not generally say "we" like proletarians and Black people—positing themselves as subjects and transforming the bourgeois or whites as objects (TSS 8). So having compared the

SIMONE DE BEAUVOIR'S ANALOGICAL APPROACH   181

oppression of (white) women to Black people, Jewish people, and the proletariat, Beauvoir also contrasts the differential responses to oppression by (white) bourgeois women (namely, their complicity) and these other groups (namely, revolt, eliminitivism, and subjectivity).[55]

Moving away from comparative frameworks of oppression and the differing responses to oppression by women and other Others, we find that competing frameworks of oppression also emerge in *The Second Sex*. This becomes clear when Beauvoir contrasts antifeminism with racism, antisemitism, colonialism, and class oppression based on reciprocity, numerical minority status, and historical events of oppression. Beauvoir differentiates the significance of gender subordination from other oppressions by asserting that reciprocity is absent in gender difference, suggesting that other categories of difference and corresponding forms of oppression do allow for reciprocity in a way that gender does not.[56] According to Beauvoir, "whether one likes it or not, individuals and groups have no choice but to recognize the reciprocity of their relation" (TSS 7). But she goes on to pose the question, "How is it, then, that between the sexes this reciprocity has not been put forward, that one of the terms has been asserted as the only essential one, denying any relativity in regard to its correlative, defining the latter as pure alterity?" (TSS 7). Likewise, when exploring the relationship between oppression and minority status, Beauvoir observes that absolute domination of one group by another for shorter or longer periods of time often resulted from numerical inequality or a majority dominating a minority. But women are not minorities like other groups: "women are not a minority like American blacks, or like Jews: there are as many women as men on earth" (TSS 7).

When looking at historical events of oppression, Beauvoir insists that there is not a specific event in history to which women can trace their oppression. She singles out women's subordination as a constitutive form of oppression when arguing that unlike other oppressions, which are traceable to a historical event, there have always been women, and they have always been subordinate to men.[57] She presents the following examples of events in history that resulted in subordination: often, the two opposing groups concerned were once independent of each other; either they were not aware of each other in the past, or accepted each other's autonomy; and some historical event

182 BEAUVOIR AND BELLE

subordinated the weaker to the stronger: the Jewish Diaspora, slavery in America, and colonial conquests are facts with dates. In these cases, for the oppressed there was a *before*: they share a past, a tradition, sometimes a religion, or a culture (TSS 7–8). Again, her point is that women cannot pinpoint a historical event that decisively resulted in their being subordinated by men.

Underscoring the ongoing oppression of women with no specific historical event to which they can point, Beauvoir contrasts the situation of (white) women with the proletariat along the same lines. Initially she does see a possible comparison between women and the proletariat: both are oppressed despite the fact that they are not a numerical minority.[58] But she immediately pushes back on this comparison when thinking about offering a historical account of oppression. She explains, "However, not *one* event but a whole historical development explains their [proletarians] existence as a class and accounts for the distribution of *these* individuals in this class" (TSS 8). Continuing to contrast the situation of women to proletarians, Beauvoir asserts, "There have not always been proletarians: there have always been women; they are women by their physiological structure; as far back as history can be traced, they have always been subordinate to men; their dependence is not the consequence of an event or a becoming, it did not *happen*" (TSS 8).[59]

Thus, Beauvoir is clear, the dependence and subordination of women—unlike Jews, the enslaved, the colonized, or the proletariat—is not the result of a particular event or fact in history. For her, "Alterity here [in the case of women, but not the other groups] appears to be an absolute, partly because it falls outside the accidental nature of historical fact" (TSS 8).[60] Women have no past, history, religion, solidarity, or even space of their own to make communities (TSS 8). Beauvoir again highlights what she sees as the uniqueness of woman's oppression toward the end of the introduction: "But what singularly defines the situation of woman is that being, like all humans, an autonomous freedom, she discovers and chooses herself in a world where men force her to assume herself as Other: an attempt is made to freeze her as an object and doom her to immanence, since her transcendence will be forever transcended by another essential and sovereign consciousness" (TSS 17).

It is worth noting that in addition to contrasting the situation of the (white) "woman" and the situation of "the proletariat" (man), there are also moments when Beauvoir contrasts the status of the white working-class woman with the white bourgeois woman across different historical contexts—asserting that the former experiences more gender equity than the latter. I will offer three brief examples. First, going back to feudalism, she asserts, "From feudality to today, the married woman is deliberately sacrificed to private property," and furthermore, "The greater the property the greater this servitude" (TSS 110). But she claims that this is not an issue for small, poor rural communities where "spouses live on an equal footing; woman is neither a thing nor a servant: those are the luxuries of a rich man; the poor man experienced reciprocity of the bond that attaches him to his other half; in freely contracted work, woman wins concrete autonomy because she has an economic and social role" (TSS 110).[61] Second, she contrasts the white working-class woman with the white bourgeois woman when reflecting on the status of women in France. Beauvoir explains, "In such conditions it is clear how rare it was for a wife to act or merely to make her presence felt: among the working classes, *economic oppression cancels out sexual inequality*; but it deprives the individual of opportunities; among the nobility and bourgeoisie, the wife is abused because of her sex; she has a parasitic existence; she is poorly educated; she needs exceptional circumstances if she is to envisage and carry out any concrete project" (TSS 114–115, emphasis added).[62] Third, she differentiates between working-class women and bourgeois women during the *ancien régime*, noting that working-class women enjoyed more independence.[63] Thus, the working-class woman is described by Beauvoir again as "oppressed on an economic and not on a sexual level" (TSS 126). Despite notable rallies for freedom among bourgeois women (e.g., Olympe de Gouges), Beauvoir states that "these efforts are abortive" (TSS 127).[64] Nevertheless, Beauvoir is hopeful that "When economic power falls into the hands of the workers, it will be possible for the working woman to gain the capacities that the parasitic woman, noble or bourgeois, never obtained" (TSS 127). Of course, even though Beauvoir does take up class differences among white women, it is still the case that Black women and other Women of Color

184   BEAUVOIR AND BELLE

impacted by race, class, gender, and colonialism are not considered in these analyses and analogies.[65]

In this section I have outlined Beauvoir's troubling use of comparative and competing frameworks of oppression in *The Second Sex*. Most often the woman that Beauvoir refers to as the Other is a white woman whose subordination is being compared to or juxtaposed with the subjugations of men through different forms of oppression—for example, anti-Black racism, antisemitism, and classism. According to Beauvoir, white women's oppression is similar to anti-Black racism, antisemitism, and classism because in all of these cases they are stereotyped, offered similar justifications for their inferior treatment, segregated, and/or singled out in certain ways. But Beauvoir also insists that white women's oppression is fundamentally different from these other oppressions because women have no reciprocity, there is not a historical event to account for their oppression, and women are complicit with rather than resistant to their oppression. Unfortunately, the subjugation of non-white women is obscured, not only in their experiences of what Beauvoir calls antifeminism, but also as a salient aspect of anti-Black racism, antisemitism, and/or classism that women within these groups experience simultaneously. These critiques are not altogether new. In the next section, I examine the secondary literature critiquing Beauvoir's analogical approaches to oppression in *The Second Sex*.

Critiques of Beauvoir's Analogical Approach

In "Re-reading de Beauvoir 'After Race': Woman-as-Slave Revisited" (2011), Sabine Broeck problematizes Beauvoir's analogical analyses of gender and race along with the secondary literature she interprets as supporting them. Broeck identifies two shortcomings of the race/gender analogy: (1) it presents gender struggles as parallel to and yet in competition with anti-colonial and Black struggles, and (2) it forsakes possibilities for acknowledging the epistemic leadership of Black female subject positions, especially in efforts to create coalitions between white and Black women aiming at destroying both gender oppression (suppression of the female human) and racial oppression

SIMONE DE BEAUVOIR'S ANALOGICAL APPROACH 185

(abolishment of thingification and abjection of the Black male and female).[66] Broeck explains, "My interest is to engage this transportation of race to gender as a problematic epistemic ground" including "an epistemic default orbit of women's interests, in which whiteness as racialization does not factor."[67] I agree with Broeck's critiques and insights about the narrowing impact of this analogical approach in white feminism. But I also want to nuance some of these critiques as applied to specific scholars. For example, Broeck seems more sympathetic to Elizabeth Spelman and Margaret Simons as secondary sources that acknowledge Beauvoir's indebtedness to Black intellectuals concerning discourses on race, but she critiques Penelope Deutscher as a supporter of Beauvoir's analogical arguments and describes her as one who "clearly sees the analogy of race and gender relations as a worthwhile."[68] Taking a slightly different position from Broeck on this particular point, I show where Spelman, Simons, and Deutscher are each critical of Beauvoir's analogies of different systems of oppression.

Spelman is among the earlier critics of Beauvoir (and white feminism more generally) and the use of the race/gender analogy, along with other comparative and competing frameworks of oppression. Spelman notes that when Beauvoir compares "women" with other groups while simultaneously ignoring women within those other groups, "she expresses her determination to use 'woman' only in reference to those females not subject to racism, anti-Semitism, classism, imperialism."[69] She elaborates, "As we have seen, on the one hand she refers to what she herself takes to be significant differences among women; but on the other, she dismisses those differences as irrelevant to understanding the condition of 'woman,' insofar as she takes the story of 'woman' to be that provided by examination of the lives of women *not* subject to racism, classism, anti-Semitism, imperialism, and so forth."[70] For Spelman, the question is not whether these comparisons are historically accurate, but rather that these comparisons obscure the existence of women within the groups to which woman's situation gets compared.[71] She argues that this is not so much ignorance on the part of Beauvoir, who had the theoretical resources available to present a far more nuanced analysis of "woman" than is offered in *The Second Sex*.[72] To be clear, Beauvoir had insights about the multiple positions of women and the differential political consequences of those

186 BEAUVOIR AND BELLE

multiple positions, yet she undermines these insights in her comparison of white women to other groups (while frequently disregarding the status of non-white women within those groups).[73] Unfortunately, as Spelman asserts, "Beauvoir sabotages her insights about the political consequences of the multiple locations of women" in her very comparison of women to other groups.[74]

Although Simons is among Beauvoir's ardent defenders, she too problematizes these analogical accounts of oppression as well as her Eurocentrism. For Simons, "separating racism and sexism as distinct, though analogous, analytical categories can be problematic, denying the experience of African American women, for instance, for whom the effects of racism and sexism are often inseparable."[75] Furthermore, as Simons explains in "Beauvoir and the Problem of Racism" (2002), "Beauvoir's understanding of racism is central to her philosophical project in *The Second Sex*; but racism and ethnocentrism are also problems for her . . . In her study of women in history, Beauvoir elects to focus solely on the West, and more specifically France, dispensing with the rest of women's history in a footnote."[76]

Likewise, Deutscher articulates the limits of Beauvoir's approach to race, racism, and colonialism, asserting: "Conceptually, Beauvoir does not consider the plurality of race and cultural difference as mediating, dividing, or fragmenting a subject in an ongoing way . . . as if the intersections of each [woman or man] with race and culture wait politely outside the door while their exchange as 'sexed' takes place."[77] Deutscher describes ambiguity as an untapped theoretical resource for Beauvoir for "thinking about what it means to be simultaneously sexed and raced."[78] Spelman, Simons, and Deutscher each critique the limits of Beauvoir's feminism and her use of the race/gender analogy. Having said that, Broeck, Spelman, Simons, and Deutscher do not include Black feminist and/or Latina feminist literature on Beauvoir in the works cited here.[79] As a corrective to this, I want to highlight critiques of the race/gender analogy presented by Black feminist scholars Deborah King and Patricia Hill Collins, as well as Latina feminist philosopher Stephanie Rivera Berruz.

King explicitly takes up Beauvoir in her writings, but as far as I can tell, she has remained unacknowledged in secondary literature on Beauvoir for over thirty years. She critiques the race/gender analogy in white feminism in her famous and frequently anthologized essay "Multiple Jeopardy, Multiple Consciousness: The Context of a Black Feminist Ideology" (1988), where she asserts: "Among the first and perhaps most widely used approaches for understanding women's status in the United States has been the race-sex analogy. In essence, the model draws parallels between the systems and experiences of domination for blacks and those for women, and, as a result, it assumes that political mobilizations against racism and sexism are comparable."[80] King identifies the limits of this analogy in white feminism in general, but she names specific white feminists who use of the analogy, including Beauvoir. She notes, "Feminist theorists including Simone de Beauvoir, Kate Millett, Mary Daly, and Shulamith Firestone have all drawn extensively on this analogy in their critiques of the patriarchy."[81] Pinpointing the limitations of this approach, King states, "We learn very little about black women from this analogy."[82]

In "Simone de Beauvoir, Women's Oppression and Existential Freedom," Patricia Hill Collins takes up *The Second Sex* (along with *Ethics of Ambiguity* and *America Day By Day*) to offer an account of Beauvoir's arguments about freedom and oppression, while also interrogating her use of analogies. Collins distinguishes between analogies that present *oppositional difference* and *relational difference*. She explains, "A race/gender analogy framed within assumptions of oppositional difference would ask: how are racism and sexism alike and unlike one another? In contrast, a race/gender analogy framed within assumptions of relational difference would ask: what do comparisons of racism and sexism reveal not only about the separate systems but also about how they shape one another?"[83] Placing Beauvoir's analogies in the former category of oppositional difference, she argues, "by uncritically relying upon a seemingly hegemonic, analogical method grounded in oppositional difference of equating Black people, children, poor people, animals, and women, Beauvoir's work . . . suggests an uncritical reliance on these analogies as shortcuts to build her case about oppression."[84] The result is the separating and privileging of gender oppression as distinct from and somehow above these other systems of oppression.[85] Hill Collins asks pointedly, "What are the implications for Beauvoir's depiction of freedom that views gender oppression as something that merits analysis via the race/

188 BEAUVOIR AND BELLE

gender analogy, but that renders race, age, class, and ethnicity as self-evident, descriptive forms of oppression that can be invoked yet not engaged?"[86]

Stephanie Rivera Berruz explicitly takes up Beauvoir and the race/gender analogy in at least two publications and should also be cited in the secondary literature on Beauvoir.[87] In a 2012 commentary Berruz asserts, "Works like that of Gines' [now Belle] . . . are of utmost importance in opening a new theoretical terrain that considers the importance of black feminist thought and its utility in thinking through race, gender, and sexuality within different philosophical traditions."[88] However, she also calls for a more extensive examination of the "disanalogy" between race and gender in *The Second Sex*. Berruz offers a more in-depth critical engagement with Beauvoir in her later article "At the Crossroads: Latina Identity and Simone de Beauvoir's *The Second Sex*" (2016), where she argues that Latinas are rendered imperceptible in *The Second Sex*. This is true not only for the race/gender analogy (operating within a Black-white binary in which race is coded as Black man and gender as white woman), but also throughout the entire text, which offers no considerations of Latina identity, experience, and oppression. Berruz argues, "Beauvoir's use of the race/gender analogy functions to occlude the possibilities of articulating the multiplicitous character of identities," "presumes a separation between race and gender that cannot account for multiplicity," and "fails to provide a framework from which to explore the 'other' who cleans houses, cooks, crosses boarders, the other who is always multiple."[89] Offering an intervention in Beauvoir's approach, Berruz asserts, "Reflecting on what it means to be Latina in the US context sheds light on some deeper seated troubles with the comparative and competing structure of Beauvoir's framework for understanding the situation of woman and her oppression."[90]

Clearly, there have been strong and compelling critiques of Beauvoir's comparative and competing frameworks of oppression, including her use of analogies. Generally speaking, Beauvoir takes what I have described as an analogical approach to understanding oppression. I have offered several examples in which she does not name the whiteness of the women she has in mind when discussing the situation of "woman," and she simultaneously ignores the existence and

SIMONE DE BEAUVOIR'S ANALOGICAL APPROACH   189

experiences of women who are not white within these other groups to which she compares and contrasts white woman's situation. Despite the persistence of this approach throughout *The Second Sex*, there a few moments when Beauvoir acknowledges the limits and problems with comparative/competing frameworks of oppression, noting the overlaps between gender, race, and class, on the one hand, with the very different experiences of gender oppression and class oppression, on the other hand. Concerning the overlaps of race, class, and gender, we can return to the introduction. Beauvoir actually names white bourgeois women and Black women when she observes, "As bourgeois women, they are in solidarity with bourgeois men and not with women proletarians; as *white* women, they are in solidarity with *white* men and not with *black* women" (TSS 8, emphasis added). This is one of the few places where she explicitly names not only class, but also white women and Black women. Beauvoir's observation here shows her awareness that race, class, and gender operate together (and not just analogically). She also recognizes the existence of proletarian (white) women as well as Black women and the challenges of coalitions between women across difference. Unfortunately, this awareness and recognition presented in the introduction are abandoned in her broader analogical approach throughout the text. As Kathy Glass observes in "Calling All Sisters: Continental Philosophy and Black Feminist Thinkers" (2010), "For all its strengths, Beauvoir's study fails to fully explore the racism integral to white women's historical reluctance to align themselves politically with black women . . . Beauvoir stops short of interrogating the whiteness that has made possible white women's lack of empathy for their Black counterparts."[91]

Again, Beauvoir has resources within her own theoretical framework to know better and do better. For example, concerning the differences between gender oppression and class oppression, Beauvoir critiques Engels because "He tried to reduce the opposition of the sexes to a class conflict" (TSS 66). She describes his thesis as "indefensible" and adds, "woman cannot in good faith be regarded only as a worker; her reproductive function is as important as her productive capacity, both in the social economy and in her personal life" (TSS 66). She insists that it is impossible to consider the woman as a solely productive force: for man she is a sexual partner, a reproducer, an erotic

190 BEAUVOIR AND BELLE

object, an Other through whom he seeks himself (TSS 67). Beauvoir offers several counterpoints to Engels' position (TSS 66): gender oppression is not equivalent to class conflict; division of labor by sex and resulting oppression should not be confused; and there is no biological basis for division by class (which suggests a biological basis for division by gender). How much more powerful could Beauvoir's analysis have been if she combined these observations? How might *The Second Sex* have been different if she sustained the insights that white bourgeois women are in solidarity with white bourgeois men and not with women proletarians or Black women, and furthermore that one form of identity and oppression cannot be distilled into others? Beauvoir correctly argues that the oppression of the sexes cannot be reduced to class conflict. Likewise, racial and class oppression cannot be reduced to gender oppression. The analogical approach does not work in part because race, class, and gender oppressions are not parallel, rather they are intersecting. An intersectional approach is more conducive to building coalitions across various differences.

The Potential and Pitfalls of Analogies

Before concluding, I want to consider a few arguments and counterarguments pertaining to the positive potential of analogies, as well as the pitfalls and failures of analogies. For this purpose, I am taking up *The Unfinished Project: Toward a Post-Metaphysical Humanism* (2001) by Lorenzo Simpson, "Understanding Across Difference and Analogical Reasoning in Simpson's *Unfinished Project*" (2009) by Gaile Pohlhaus, Jr., and "Obscuring the Importance of Race: The Implication of Making Comparisons between Sexism and Racism (or Other Isms)" by Trina Grillo and Stephanie Wildman.[92] Simpson's *The Unfinished Project* explores the interconnection of humanity through globalization as well as the pitfalls and possibilities for building community that are not limited to the binaries of homogeneity or cultural division. Rather than attempting to erase cultural differences, he seeks to build bridges across difference through common aesthetics, ethical standards, and sensitivity. Simpson is seeking not only general understanding across difference, but more specifically "mutual understanding," which for him requires "reversibility of perspectives."[93] He explains that this latter concept "does not require mutual identification or even necessarily take such identification to be an ideal."[94] The mutual understanding he has in mind "does not entail an objectionable ethnocentrism" insofar as we can expand our experience to include not only that which concerns us, but also that which concerns others (e.g., "love, sexuality, religion, power, natality, mortality, etc.").[95] Thus, he takes up the import of analogies as hermeneutical models for understanding across difference.

According to Simpson, analogizing allows for the possibility of understanding others as well as the possibility of having a new understanding of oneself. Positing that analogies can minimally provide a starting point for developing mutual understanding, he argues that they offer a common ground for understanding, or a point of contact among worldviews that expands tools for understanding one another's concerns in dialogue. He cautions that *false analogies* may stymie understanding, but *proper analogies* can expand understanding. To arrive at proper analogies, we might ask, "What category of phenomena, or what topics, do *we* treat similarly, or address in *some* way that can be intelligibly connected by us to the way—that *they're* addressing X?"[96] He considers two lines of inquiry regrading analogies: "In the first case, we are asking, Which of the topics with which we are familiar is analogous to what they're addressing, such that the best case can be made for what they are doing? In the second case, we are asking more generally, *Is* there for them something analogous to our X?"[97] He goes on to acknowledge that in the use of analogies, "There is thus a sense in which some degree of ethnocentrism is epistemologically unavoidable."[98] He revisits analogies again in an extended footnote in the epilogue. Referencing Wittgenstein on "the importance of finding examples that mediate between two terms," Simpson asserts, "the production of the analogical framework that allows the intermediate cases to be appreciated as intermediate cases, mediating between one's own position and that of the other, is *ipso facto* an expansion of both horizons, for it renders intelligible to both sides an intelligible application of their term that they were not in a position to entertain prior to their collaborative work."[99]

192   BEAUVOIR AND BELLE

Of course, I am both suspicious and critical of analogizing between racism and other forms of oppression, especially by white people who do not experience racism (and are actually benefiting from structural racism), while simultaneously seeking to compare their oppressions (e.g., sexism, classism) to racism in general and anti-Black racism in particular. I present Simpson's case for analogies here because I want to take seriously a counter-argument to my more critical position on analogical approaches to understanding systems of oppression. There are some points raised by him with which I agree. For example, I agree that understanding across cultural differences without erasing cultural differences is desirable. I also agree that false analogies hinder rather than help cross-cultural understanding. I would even agree that proper analogies might in some select cases provide a starting point for mutual understanding across cultural differences. But the analogies between racism and sexism—especially in white feminism in general and in Beauvoir's *The Second Sex* in particular—often fall into the category of *false analogies* layered with invidious ethnocentrism. These white feminist analogical approaches to racial and gender oppressions are not *proper analogies* enabling understanding across cultural differences, rendering a deeper understanding, and/or expanding horizons.

In "Understanding Across Difference and Analogical Reasoning in Simpson's *Unfinished Project*" (2009), Gaile Pohlhaus, Jr., replies to Simpson and the analogical path to understanding. She notes, "While I agree that in a certain sense we always begin where we are, I do not think this necessarily means we must make analogies to what we already know, that is, that we must find in others similarities to ourselves, in order to understand them (and even ourselves anew)."[100] For Pohlhaus, analogies have the possibility of being helpful to understand differently socially situated others, but they are neither necessary nor sufficient.[101] In contrast to Simpson's emphasis on analogies for understanding across difference, Pohlhaus calls for practical relations to arrive at understanding across difference. Pohlhaus is clear that she not rejecting analogies altogether. She asserts, "While certainly not wishing to rule out the use of analogies entirely, it is important to note that this way of understanding has in fact been criticized for leading precisely to misunderstanding."[102] She elaborates in a footnote, "I concede that analogies can be extraordinarily helpful . . . [but] even when

SIMONE DE BEAUVOIR'S ANALOGICAL APPROACH 193

an analogy is apt it can sometimes do more harm than good in the effort to build mutual understanding across differences."[103] Pohlhaus turns to the essay "Obscuring the Importance of Race: The Implication of Making Comparisons between Sexism and Racism (or Other Isms)" by Trina Grillo and Stephanie Wildman to show how analogies often result in a *false* sense of understanding (rather than what Simpson describes as mutual understanding).[104]

Grillo and Wildman examine the various ways in which making analogies between different systems of oppression fail.[105] They argue that there are "dangers inherent in the use of analogies," especially "analogizing sex discrimination to race discrimination."[106] And it is the use of analogies themselves (not just false analogies or less apt analogies) that contribute to a failure to acknowledge and understand the *differences* between the experiences of oppression being analogized.[107] They explain, "Comparing sexism to racism perpetuates patterns of racial discrimination by marginalizing and obscuring the different roles that race plays in the lives of people of color."[108] Grillo and Wildman elaborate, "The comparison minimizes the impact of racism, rendering it an insignificant phenomenon—one of a laundry list of other -isms or oppressions that society must suffer."[109] They identify several problematics of analogies between race and sex discrimination, especially when deployed by white analogizers: (1) analogizers often equate their situations with others; (2) analogizers forget the differences between her experiences and the experiences of others; (3) analogizers center themselves and their own experiences rather than attempting to acknowledge and understand experiences of others; (4) analogizers present women and People of Color as mutually exclusive categories, ignoring the existence and experiences of Women of Color; (5) analogizers appropriate the pain of others and assume the position of one who suffers; and/or (6) analogizers actually deny the existence of suffering of others.[110]

Having convincingly outlined these myriad failures of analogies, the co-authors do not dismiss them altogether insofar as, "analogies are necessary tools to teach and explain, so that we can better understand each others' experiences and realities."[111] Still, they offer the caveat, "Instead of drawing false inferences of similarities from analogies; it is important for whites to talk about white supremacy."[112] We might

194   BEAUVOIR AND BELLE

summarize these points by saying that while it may be *possible* to reach an understanding of differently situated others through analogies, it is also very *probable* that analogies will fail in several ways, including: the false understanding of others' experience/suffering, the displacement of others' experience/suffering, and/or the denial of others' experience/ suffering. We find each of these failures in Beauvoir's use of analogies in *The Second Sex*.

Conclusion

In this chapter I have problematized Beauvoir's analogical analyses in *The Second Sex*, arguing that her utilization of the race/gender analogy omits the experiences and oppressions of Black women. I provided a more extensive examination of how the analogy is functioning in the text and a more nuanced exploration of Beauvoir's influences—noting where she converges and diverges from these influences. I have also explored other comparative and competing frameworks of oppression in *The Second Sex* alongside divergent secondary literature on this figure and text. She presents various systems of oppression as similar but separate—identifying similarities in the motives and strategies of oppression and then proceeding in a way that suggests these oppressions are generally separate and/or separable. But this is not the case for Black women, Jewish women, colonized women, and/or proletarian women (especially proletarian Women of Color) within the groups to whom Beauvoir compares the situation of the white bourgeois "woman."

When Beauvoir says that there are deep analogies between the situations of women and Blacks, what is not stated is that she is presenting the situations of white women and Black men, while also erasing Black women. When she talks about Black Americans and racist Americans, she is not mentioning French Black people and anti-Black racism among the French. When she compares the situations of prostitutes to Jews, she does not mention that sex workers were not systematically targeted for actual obliteration through a literal holocaust, which is also quite different from her figurative description of the destruction of women's housework as "small holocausts." When

SIMONE DE BEAUVOIR'S ANALOGICAL APPROACH   195

she asserts that Blacks, Jews, and proletarians (often assumed to be white men) resist and revolt while women (often assumed to be white) are complicit, she minimizes the experiences of oppression for women who are Black, Jewish, and/or proletariat as well as the agency among these women for resistance or revolt. When she insists that there have always been women and women have always been subordinate to men, she imposes a Western narrative of gender formation that has been and continues to be challenged by Women of Color feminists. Additionally, considering select secondary literature that takes up these issues, I noted that white feminists have neglected to cite and *actually engage* Women of Color literature on Beauvoir. To be sure, since I have been bringing attention to these problematic citational practices, calling attention to the lack of citations of Black women and other Women of Color in Beauvoir studies, some white women are beginning to at least mention some of the major figures I have been highlighting. But they still fail to actually engage with the substantive arguments of this literature. As a corrective to this lack of citation and engagement, I presented and engaged critical commentaries by King, Hill Collins, and Berruz— whose writings on Beauvoir have remained largely unacknowledged and unengaged in the secondary literature by white feminists.

Notes

1. Note that I am distinguishing between the race/gender analogy and the related woman-as-slave metaphor. In this chapter I focus on the race/gender analogy and other comparative and competing frameworks of oppression. The woman-as-slave metaphor will be taken up later in Chapter 6.
2. Note that I am focusing on Beauvoir's comparisons of the woman to the Black, the Jew, and the proletariat in this chapter. I take up the issue of colonialism in Chapter 8 (coloniality of gender).
3. See Margaret Simons, *Beauvoir and the Second Sex: Feminism, Race, and the Origins of Existentialism* (Lanham, MD: Rowman and Littlefield, 1999). (Hereafter Simons 1999.) Penelope Deutscher, *The Philosophy of Simone de Beauvoir: Ambiguity, Conversion, Resistance* (Cambridge: Cambridge University Press, 2008.) (Hereafter Deutscher 2008.) Sabine Broeck "Re-reading de Beauvoir 'After Race': *Woman-as-Slave* Revisited,"

196 BEAUVOIR AND BELLE

International Journal of Francophone Studies 14, nos. 1 and 2 (2011): 167–184. (Hereafter Broeck 2011.)

4. Many thanks to Linda Martín Alcoff for urging me to read Simpson and Pohlhaus on the issue of analogies, and to Pohlhaus for the citation of Grillo and Wildman.

5. Note that Beauvoir specifically names racist Americans and not French racists. In this description she misses interconnections between anti-Black racism and colonialism as forms of alterity and systems of oppression.

6. See *All of the Women Are White, All the Blacks Are Men, But Some of Us Are Brave*, ed. Gloria Hull, Patricia Bell Scott, and Barbara Smith (New York: The Feminist Press at CUNY Graduate Center, 1982).

7. The translators note that in the French Beauvoir writes "L'égalité dans la différence," which has a literal translation of "different but equal" rather than "separate but equal" (TSS 12n6).

8. Kate and Edward Fullbrook *Simone de Beauvoir and Jean-Paul Sartre: The Remaking of a Twentieth Century Legend* (New York: Basic Books A Division of Harper Collins Publishers, 1994); Simons 1999. See also *Beauvoir and Sartre: The Riddle of Influence*, ed. Christine Daigle and Jacob Golomb (Bloomington: Indiana University Press, 2009).

9. Nancy Bauer, *Simone de Beauvoir, Philosophy, and Feminism* (New York: Columbia University Press, 2001.) (Hereafter Bauer 2001.) Fredrika Scarth *The Other Within: Ethic, Politics, and the Body in Simone de Beauvoir* (New York: Rowman and Littlefield Publishers, Inc., 2004.) (Hereafter Scarth 2004.)

10. Simons 1999; Deutscher 2008; Broeck 2011. Alva Myrdal, "A Parallel to the Negro Problem" (1944), appendix 5 in Gunnar Myrdal, *An American Dilemma: The Negro Problem in Modern Democracy*, vol. 2 (New York: Routledge, 1944, 2017). (Hereafter A. Myrdal 1944.) Alva Myrdal was a Swedish sociologist, politician, and 1982 Nobel Peace Prize recipient (and married to Gunnar Myrdal).

11. A. Myrdal 1944, 1077 · A. Myrdal continues, "As in the Negro problem, most men have accepted as self-evident, until recently, the doctrine that women had inferior endowments in most of those respects which carry prestige, power, and advantages in society, but that they were, at the same time, superior in some other respects" (A. Myrdal 1944, 1077)—perhaps acknowledging white women's "superior" advantages.

12. A. Myrdal 1944, 1076.

13. A. Myrdal 1944, 1073.

14. A. Myrdal 1944, 1077.

15. A. Myrdal 1944, 1077.

SIMONE DE BEAUVOIR'S ANALOGICAL APPROACH 197

16. A. Myrdal 1944, 1077.
17. A. Myrdal 1944, 1077.
18. A. Myrdal 1944, 1077.
19. Fanon in *Black Skin, White Masks*, uses the language of inferiority and superiority complexes and an analysis of the phrase "dirty nigger." See also Amy Victoria Atkins, "Black/Feminist Futures: Reading Beauvoir in *Black Skin, White Masks*," *The South Atlantic Quarterly* 112, no. 4 (Fall 2013): 697–723.
20. Simons 1999, 176.
21. The idea that the girl is born on the "wrong side" ("of the line" in the first English translation) is similar to Du Bois' analysis of the color line. See Beauvoir, *The Second Sex*, trans. Howard Madison Parshley (New York: Knopf, 1953), 298.
22. For example, Vikki Bell focuses on the connection with Wright, but not the connection with Du Bois. See "Owned Suffering: Thinking the Feminist Imagination with Simone de Beauvoir and Richard Wright," in *Transformations*, ed. Sarah Ahmed, Jane Kilby, Celia Lury, Maureen McNeil, and Beverley Skeggs (London: Routledge, 2000). (Hereafter V. Bell 2000.) V. Bell offers the following critique: "At this point, all I wish to contend is that de Beauvoir's use of the unlikely figure of Bigger Thomas serves us particularly poorly as an image of shared modalities of suffering and equally bad as an image of oppositional politics. She uses Bigger Thomas as a way of suggesting that the suffering experienced by women, the position of being objectified while remaining necessarily a subject, is one that is fictionalized by Richard Wright in a different context" (V. Bell 2000, 69). Bell adds the following critical note, "But her effort to make this rhetorical move becomes highly problematic, and tends toward both a form of essentialist psychology, positing women and black people as separate, but parallel, modes of subjectivity; identifying sexism and racism as comparable modes of oppression; and perhaps more importantly, suggesting an *ought* which has feminism based on revolt in the manner of Bigger Thomas" (V. Bell 2000, 69).
23. Du Bois 1997, 38.
24. Du Bois 1997, 37–38.
25. See Beauvoir, *The Second Sex*, trans. Howard Madison Parshley (New York: Knopf, 1953), 298.
26. I would not describe *The Souls of Black Folk* as an ardent appeal for women's interests. A. Myrdal may be thinking of Du Bois' *Darkwater: Voices from Within the Veil* (1920), which includes his pro-feminist essay "The Damnation of Women."

198 BEAUVOIR AND BELLE

27. A. Myrdal 1944, 1073.

28. A. Myrdal 1944, 1077.

29. V. Bell (who does not take up the connections between Beauvoir and A. Myrdal, but does take up connections with Wright) notes that "Tracing these as moments at which de Beauvoir draws parallels and makes comparisons between gender and 'race' enables a consideration of the ways in which her argument illuminates some of the difficulties of fixing certain concepts central to feminist argument as peculiar to the conditions of womanhood" (V. Bell 2000, 64).

30. In *Anti-Semite and Jew*, Sartre correctly attributes to Wright the claim that America does not have a Negro problem but rather a white problem. He states: "Richard Wright, the Negro writer, said recently: 'There is no Negro problem in the United States, there is only a White Problem.' In the same way we must say that anti-Semitism is not a Jewish problem; it is our problem" (Sartre 1995, 152). In *An American Dilemma*, G. Myrdal also takes this position, asserting, "The Negro problem is primarily a white man's problem" (G. Myrdal 1944, 669).

31. For more on these connections see, Kathryn Sophia Belle (formerly Kathryn T. Gines), "The Man Who Lived Underground: Jean-Paul Sartre and the Philosophical Legacy of Richard Wright," *Sartre Studies International* 19, no. 2 (2011): 42–59, and "At the Intersections: Existentialism, Critical Philosophies of Race, and Feminism," in *The Routledge Companion to the Philosophy of Race*, ed. Paul C. Taylor, Linda Martín Alcoff, and Luvell Anderson (New York: Routledge, 2017).

32. V. Bell 2000, 65.

33. V. Bell 2000, 71.

34. Simons, 1999, 168.

35. Simons 1999, 176–177.

36. Simons 1999, 178.

37. Simons 1999, 176.

38. Simons 1999, 178.

39. Simons 1999, 178.

40. See Deirdre Blair, *Simone de Beauvoir: A Biography* (New York: Summit Books, 1990), 364, 368. *An American Dilemma* is also frequently referenced by Sartre in "Revolutionary Violence" (from *Notebooks for an Ethics*), where he offers an analysis of oppression, racism, and slavery in the United States. It is likely that Sartre had access to this text (along with *What the Negro Wants* edited by Rayford Logan, which Sartre also references) through Beauvoir.

SIMONE DE BEAUVOIR'S ANALOGICAL APPROACH 199

41. These letters are available in *A Transatlantic Love Affair: Letters to Nelson Algren*, ed. Sylvie Le Bon Beauvoir, trans. Ellen Gordon Reeves (New Press, 1998).

42. Simons states, "Myrdal can thus be seen as influencing Beauvoir's theoretical framework in *The Second Sex* in four ways: by encouraging the use of an analogy with racism, providing a model for the encyclopedic scope of *The Second Sex*, introducing the concept of caste as a substitute for the biological category of race, and grounding her understanding of social constructionism in science and in the African American intellectual tradition" (Simons 1999, 171).

43. Sarah Relyea, *Outsider Citizens: The Remaking of Postwar Identity in Wright, Beauvoir, and Baldwin* (New York: Routledge, 2006), 47. Relyea offers a close reading of *The Second Sex* alongside *America Day By Day* and *An American Dilemma* to point to overlaps and influences across the three texts. It is also interesting that Relyea seeks to defend G. Myrdal against Simons' critiques of his "paternalistic liberalism" (see Simons 1999, 170–173, and Relyea 2006, 47–48). I also find it curious that Relyea makes no mention of Alva Myrdal's appendix.

44. Deutscher 2008, 80. According to Deutscher, "The response to [G.] Myrdal is excited and identificatory. She is drawn to the breadth, multidisciplinary nature, and size of his project and states her attraction to the idea of being the object of that kind of extended intimacy with the reader" (Deutscher 2008, 80). As Beauvoir herself notes in a letter to Nelson Algren, "I should like to write a book as important as this big one about Negros" (Deutscher 2008, 80).

45. Deutscher 2008, 78.

46. Deutscher 2008, 81.

47. Deutscher, "Making mention of a greater diversity of African American writers than appears in *The Second Sex*, it [*An American Dilemma*] is a reserve offering unexplored possibilities with the potential to resist and tacitly challenge the use she did make of [G.] Myrdal. This use could be seen as an excess to her writing, containing resources for questioning some of her suppositions" (Deutscher 2008, 137).

48. The French edition reads: "*On à rapproché justement leur situation et celle des Juifs ausquels elles étaient souvent assimilées*" (LDS 1 170).

49. Beauvoir states, "they [prostitutes] were relegated to ghettos or reserved neighborhoods. In Paris, loose women worked in pens where they arrived in the morning and left after the curfew had tolled; they lived on special streets and did not have the right to stray, and in most other cities brothels were outside town walls" (TSS 113).

200 BEAUVOIR AND BELLE

50. Chikwenye Ogunyemi, "Womanism: The Dynamics of the Contemporary Black Female Novel in English," *Signs: Women in Culture and Society* 11, no. 1 (1985): 76. (Hereafter Ogunyemi 1985.)

51. Ogunyemi 1985, 76–77.

52. In contrast to Ogunyemi, Beauvoir's discussion of domestic labor is often focused on the white bourgeois housewife's burden of motherhood and boredom with family. Quoting Balzac's *The Physiology of Marriage*, "'The married woman is a slave who must be seated on a throne,'" Beauvoir explains that this is considered the lot of the bourgeois woman (TSS 129). Again, the white bourgeois woman is presented as complicit with her oppression, so comforted by her class status that she does not resist her gender status. Beauvoir describes it in this way: "It is hoped that, thus duped, seduced by the ease of their condition, they will accept the role of mother and housewife to which they are being confined" (TSS 129–130). She concludes, "And in fact, most bourgeois women capitulate . . . The bourgeois woman clings to her chains because she clings to her class privileges" (TSS 130). In her chapter titled "The Married Woman," Beauvoir is clear that marriage is not an equally beneficial arrangement for men and women. The woman gets the lesser deal in this arrangement, sacrificing her freedom and transcendence for social status and material comforts. For example, when Beauvoir asserts, "Woman is destined to maintain the species and care for the home, which is to say, to immanence," this is both an example of the white bourgeois housewife in particular and of the immanent inessential woman as object (in contrast to the transcendent essential man as subject) in general (TSS 443).

53. In addition to this passage, Beauvoir emphasizes woman's complicity earlier when she states: "The man who sets the woman up as *Other* will thus find in her a deep complicity" (TSS 10). With regard to this passage and the previous mention of Bigger Thomas, Vikki Bell sees Beauvoir as framing Black (men) as more authentic because they respond to their situation in revolt, and (white) women as inauthentic because they are complicit with their situation (Bell 2000, 66–67). Relyea also takes up this analysis of revolt versus complicity, the citation of Bigger Thomas, and the "contrasting of Bigger's 'resentment' and 'revolt' with woman's 'complicity' in her oppression"—noting, "She [Beauvoir] argues that women have often consented to the feminine myth, worshipping the mysteries of love and motherhood, whereas blacks assume an attitude of revolt" (Relyea 2006, 42).

SIMONE DE BEAUVOIR'S ANALOGICAL APPROACH   201

54. Additional examples of resistance that Beauvoir mentions include the proletarian revolution in Russia, Blacks in Haiti, and the Indo-Chinese fighting in Indochina. See TSS 8.

55. Of course, Claudia Jones and Lorraine Hansberry offer analyses of Black women's militancy that challenge Beauvoir's account of woman's complicity. Note that these issues are taken up in Chapters 2 (Claudia Jones) and 3 (Lorraine Hansberry).

56. For more on reciprocity in Beauvoir's *The Second Sex*, see Penelope Deutscher, "Conversions of Reciprocity," chapter 5 of *The Philosophy of Simone de Beauvoir: Ambiguity, Conversion, Resistance* (Cambridge: Cambridge University Press, 2008), 159–183. Deutscher identifies several uses of the term "reciprocity" in Beauvoir's work. One is that "my perception of the other as (racially, or via some collectivity or identity) marginal or not the norm should ideally be equalized and thus inflected by my sense that I, too, must sometimes take up a position as potentially suspect and conspicuous" (ibid., 162). Additional meanings of reciprocity in *The Second Sex* include: "mutual need or dependency; legal and economic equality, particularly the kind that allows one to enter into a contractual relationship on a fair footing; mutual obligation; exchanging the role of 'other'; exchanging the role as other in the more specific sense of that which is foreign, importantly different, and elusive to one's grasp; subjects serving as both subject and object for each other, occupying positions as simultaneously subject and object; the idea of a constant tension produced by the mutual attempt to subordinate, without this necessarily producing the entrenched subordination of any individual or group, a tension that can be seen in both friend and enemy relations; and the mutuality of generosity and friendship between subjects, which can be seen as a supreme human accomplishment" (ibid., 163–164).

57. Note that this claim will be revisited with regard to the coloniality of gender in Chapter 8 (coloniality of gender).

58. "Proletarians are not a numerical minority either, and yet they have never formed a separate group" (TSS 8).

59. Again, Beauvoir's claim that there have always been women, and women have always been subordinated, gets taken up and problematized in more detail in Chapter 8 (coloniality of gender).

60. The French edition reads: "C'est en partie parce qu'elle échappé au caractère accidentel du fait historique que l'alterité apparaît ici comme un absolu" (LDS 1, 17).

202 BEAUVOIR AND BELLE

61. On the one hand, Beauvoir highlights woman as servant for the rich man. On the other hand, she notes the idleness of the rich woman, which she says is paid for with submission (TSS 110). Beauvoir asserts, "The sixteenth century sees the codification of the laws perpetuated throughout the ancien régime; by that time feudal habits and customs had totally disappeared, and nothing protects women from men's claims that they should be chained to the household" (TSS 111). Also, it seems that for Beauvoir, reciprocity is possible between man and woman within poor rural communities.

62. Overall, Beauvoir explains, "the wife's legal status remained practically unchanged from the early fifteenth century to the nineteenth century; but in the privileged classes her concrete condition does change" (TSS 117). Some of the conditions that she has in mind include access to informal and formal education opportunities, particularly among noble women.

63. From business and trade to working at home, she had the means for more freedom, and she is partner and equal to her husband (TSS 126).

64. Beauvoir concludes, "Bourgeois women were too integrated into the family to find concrete grounds for solidarity with each other; they did not constitute a separate caste capable of forcing their demands: on an economic level, they existed as parasites" (TSS 127). Here is white woman's dilemma, "while women could have participated in events in spite of their sex, they were prevented by their class, and those from the agitating class were condemned to stand aside because they were women" (TSS 127).

65. For an in-depth analysis of Black women as women, as Black, and as workers, see Claudia Jones, "An End to the Neglect of the Problems of the Negro Woman!," *Political Affairs: A Magazine Devoted to the Theory and Practice of Marxism-Leninism* (1949). Note this essay by Jones is taken up in Chapter 2.

66. Broeck 2011, 181.

67. Broeck 2011, 169.

68. Broeck 2011, 168.

69. Elizabeth Spelman, *Inessential Woman: Problems of Exclusion in Feminist Thought* (Boston: Beacon Press, 1988), 65. (Hereafter Spelman 1988.)

70. Spelman 1988, 71. (Emphasis added). She also states here: "According to [Beauvoir], the situation of 'woman' must be contrasted to that of Blacks, Jews, the working class."

71. Spelman 1988, 65.

72. Spelman 1988, 58.

73. Spelman 1988, 64.

74. Spelman 1988, 64.

SIMONE DE BEAUVOIR'S ANALOGICAL APPROACH 203

75. Simons, 1999, 169–170.
76. Simons, "Beauvoir and the Problem of Racism," *Philosophers on Race: Critical Essays*, ed. Julie K. Ward and Tommy L. Lott (Malden, MA: Blackwell Publishers Ltd., 2001), 260. These critiques and challenges are also applicable to Beauvoir's comparison between women and slaves taken up in Chapter 6 (slave/woman analogy).
77. Deutscher 2008, 134.
78. Deutscher 2008, 135.
79. I am focusing specifically on critiques of the race/gender analogy in *The Second Sex* by Deborah King (whose essay is published the same year are Elisabeth Spelman's book) as well as Patricia Hill Collins (whose essay was published after Broeck's article) and Stephanie Rivera Berruz (whose commentary and article are both published after Broeck's article).
80. Deborah King, "Multiple Jeopardy, Multiple Consciousness: The Context of a Black Feminist Ideology," *Signs: Journal of Women in Culture and Society* 14, no. 1 (1988): 43. (Hereafter King 1988.)
81. King 1988, 44.
82. King 1988, 45.
83. Patricia Hill Collins, "Simone de Beauvoir, Women's Oppression and Existential Freedom," in *A Companion to Simone de Beauvoir*, ed. Laura Hengehold and Nancy Bauer (Wiley and Sons, 2017), 325–338, here 328. (Hereafter Collins 2017.)
84. Collins 2017, 328.
85. Collins notes, "Beauvoir's claim that women's oppression is universal, fundamental, and unique is explicit" (Collins 2017, 331).
86. Collins 2017, 331.
87. Stephanie Rivera Berruz, "Ressenha: GINES, Kathryn T. [now Kathryn Sophia Belle]—Sartre, Beauvoir, and the Race/Gender Analogy: A Case for Black Feminist Philosophy," *Sapere Aude, Belo Horizonte* 3, no. 6 (2012): 504–507. (Hereafter Berruz 2012.) Stephanie Rivera Berruz, "At the Crossroads: Latina Identity and Simone de Beauvoir's *The Second Sex*," *Hypatia* 31, no. 2 (2016), 319–333. (Hereafter Berruz 2016.)
88. Berruz 2012, 505.
89. Berruz 2016, 320. Here Berruz is referencing a quote from Mariana Ortega's "Phenomenological Encuentros: Existential Phenomenology and Latin American & US Latina Feminism," where Ortega urges more attention to "This so called other ... writing theory, teaching, cleaning houses, cooking, crossing boarders" (Ortega 2006, 61).
90. Berruz 2016, 325.

204   BEAUVOIR AND BELLE

91. Kathy Glass, in "Calling All Sisters: Continental Philosophy and Black Feminist Thinkers," in *Convergences: Black Feminism and Continental Philosophy*, ed. Maria del Guadalupe Davidson, Kathryn Sophia Belle (formerly Kathryn T. Gines), and Donna Dale Marcano. (New York: SUNY Press, 2010), 229.

92. Lorenzo Simpson, *The Unfinished Project: Toward a Post-Metaphysical Humanism* (New York: Routledge, 2001). (Hereafter Simpson 2001.) Gaile Pohlhaus, Jr., "Understanding Across Difference and Analogical Reasoning in Simpson's Unfinished Project," *Journal for Peace and Justice Studies* 19, no. 1 (2009): 37–49. (Hereafter Pohlhaus 2009.) Trina Grillo and Stephanie Wildman, "Obscuring the Importance of Race: The Implication of Making Comparisons between Sexism and Racism (or Other Isms)," *Duke Law Journal* 1991, no. 2 (April 1991): 397–412. (Hereafter Grillo and Wildman 1991.)

93. Simpson 2001, 79.

94. Simpson 2001, 79.

95. Simpson 2001, 90.

96. Simpson 2001, 90. (Emphasis original.)

97. Simpson 2001, 90. (Emphasis original.)

98. On this point he distinguished between "'transcendentally' necessary ethnocentrism" and "contingent, empirical, and possibly invidious ethnocentrism." (Simpson 2001, 91.)

99. Simpson 2001, 161n5. (Emphasis original.)

100. Pohlhaus 2009, 41.

101. She explains (and I agree), "while in some cases it can be helpful, it is not necessary to use analogies in order to understand another who does not share one's social position, culture, or worldview, and perhaps more importantly, it is never sufficient" (Pohlhaus 2009, 37).

102. Pohlhaus 2009, 42.

103. Pohlhaus 2009, 49n6.

104. Pohlhause cites Trina Grillo and Stephanie Wildman, "Obscuring the Importance of Race: The Implication of Making Comparisons between Sexism and Racism (or Other Isms)," in *Critical Race Feminism*, ed. Adrien Katherine Wing (New York: New York University Press, 1997). I am citing the earlier version of the article, Grillo and Wildman 1991.

105. These co-authors are not only considering analogies from a theoretical and abstract perspective, but also drawing on observations at professional conferences with racially mixed groups. They note, "When a speaker compared sexism and racism, the significance of race was

SIMONE DE BEAUVOIR'S ANALOGICAL APPROACH 205

marginalized and obscured, and the different role that race plays in the lives of people of color and of whites was overlooked. The concerns of whites became the focus of attention, even when the conversation had been supposedly centered on race discrimination" (Grillo and Wildman 1991, 399).

106. Grillo and Wildman 1991, 400.
107. Grillo and Wildman 1991. 403–404.
108. Grillo and Wildman 1991, 401.
109. Grillo and Wildman 1991, 401.
110. Grillo and Wildman 1991, pages 398, 401. See also Pohlhaus 2009, 44. She states, "At the very least such a reflection suggests that analogies are particularly likely to lead one to a failure to understand when they are thought of as the crux of understanding" (Pohlhaus 2009, 46).
111. Grillo and Wildman 1991, 398.
112. Grillo and Wildman 1991, 410.

6

Slavery and Womanhood

"Assimilating woman to the slave is a mistake"

In *The Second Sex* (1949) Simone de Beauvoir frequently takes an analogical approach to oppression, including her frequent use and abuse of the race/gender analogy as well as the slave/woman analogy, also referred to as the woman-as-slave metaphor. This chapter will focus on the slave/woman analogy rather the race/gender analogy (which I examined at length in the previous chapter). While these analogies are sometimes presented as synonymous, a closer reading of *The Second Sex* reveals that they are neither always already the same nor necessarily mutually exclusive.[1] Beauvoir compares the situation of woman and that of slaves throughout *The Second Sex*. Her discussion of slavery includes, but is not limited to, analogy and metaphor. There are points early in the text where she seems to be describing institutional slavery or forced slave labor even as she is considering the implications of slavery for the status of women who are not enslaved. There are also moments when Beauvoir portrays woman as enslaved by man, enslaved by domestic duties, and enslaved by the body's reproductive functions for the species. Additionally, she analyzes and appropriates Hegel's master-slave dialectic as a theoretical framework for examining the subjugation of woman. But in each of these cases when Beauvoir is talking about slavery, she does not focus on racialized slavery in the United States or slavery in European (including French) colonial contexts. Even when she explicitly takes up anti-Black racism in the text, her examples tend to focus on issues like racial segregation in the United States *post*-emancipation.

In this chapter, I argue that Beauvoir's historical and metaphorical accounts of slavery do not adequately address racialized slavery or the oppressive experiences of enslaved Black women. As a corrective, I examine critiques of her use of the slave/woman analogy while

Beauvoir and Belle. Kathryn Sophia Belle, Oxford University Press. © Oxford University Press 2024.
DOI: 10.1093/oso/9780197660195.003.0007

also taking seriously the exploitation experienced by enslaved Black women. The chapter is presented in four sections. In the first section, "Woman as Slave," I begin with Alva Myrdal's use of the slave/woman analogy in "A Parallel to the Negro Problem" (1944), appendix 5 in *An American Dilemma*, volume 2. From here I turn to Beauvoir's use of the slave/woman analogy early on in *The Second Sex*. In the second section, "Beauvoir's Use of Hegel's Master-Slave Dialectic," I examine her allusions to and appropriations of Hegel, her awareness of the differences between Hegel's account and the situation of woman, and the ways that her engagements with Hegel have been taken up in the secondary literature (e.g., by Nancy Bauer, Frederika Scarth, and Sabine Broeck). In the third section, "Interventions: Reimagining Subject, Object, and Abject," I explore how the slave/woman analogy is intertwined with the philosophical concepts of "subject" and "object," while also analyzing "abject" as an important and overlooked third term brought in by Broeck. This section also highlights critiques of the subject/object dynamic in white feminism, women's studies, and postcolonial studies more generally (e.g., by Norma Alarcón and Malini Johar Schueller). In section four, "Critical Interrogations: Slave/Woman Analogy Problematics," I highlight critiques of the slave/woman analogy persuasively presented by Angela Davis, bell hooks, Kimberlé Crenshaw, and Patricia Hill Collins. And finally, in "Conclusion: Exploitation of Enslaved Black Women Beyond Analogy," I move away from the slave/woman analogy to analyses of the exploitation of enslaved Black women by Davis and hooks. I also return to Broeck, who contextualizes the significance of Beauvoir's adverse influence in signifying and shaping white feminist epistemologies in these analogical ways.

Woman as Slave

Let us begin with Alva Myrdal's analysis of race and gender oppression in "A Parallel to the Negro Problem." I explored connections between A. Myrdal and Beauvoir in the previous chapter, but here I will focus specifically on A. Myrdal's comparison of the status of (white) women to (Black male) slaves in the US context, before turning to

208   BEAUVOIR AND BELLE

Beauvoir (who largely ignores racialized slavery in the US context). For A. Myrdal, there is some awareness of important *differences* in the status of and sentiments toward the (white) woman, the (white) child, and the (Black male) slave. A. Myrdal acknowledges there are distinctions, "both in actual status of these different groups and in the tone of sentiment in the respective relations."[2] Furthermore, she notes, "In the decades before the Civil War, in the conservative and increasingly antiquarian ideology of the American South, [the white] woman was elevated as an ornament and looked upon with pride, while the Negro slave became increasingly a chattel and a ward."[3]

Nonetheless, A. Myrdal insists on claiming that these groups also share a similar status to one another. For A. Myrdal, the (white) woman, the (white) child, and the (Black male) slave—the latter described as "a sort of family member" in some ways—are all similarly situated under the power of the *pater-familias*.[4] She quotes slavery advocate George Fitzhugh's *Sociology for the South* (1854) in which various other groups are also described as slaves: "The kind of slavery is adapted to the men enslaved. Wives and apprentices are slaves, not in theory only, but often in fact. Children are slaves to their parents, guardians, and teachers. Imprisoned culprits are slaves. Lunatics and idiots are slaves also."[5] But A. Myrdal is especially interested in the "parallel" in the oppression of white women and enslaved Black men. For her, these parallels go "considerably deeper" to include: (white) women lacking the same rights as "all free white citizens of full age" (i.e., white men) and the notion that (white) women and "negroes" are similarly subordinated—here she attributes a quote to Dolly Madison claiming that "the Southern wife was 'the chief slave of the harem.'"[6] With this in mind, A. Myrdal insists, "From the very beginning, the fight in America for the liberation of the Negro slaves was, therefore, closely coordinated with the fight for women's emancipation."[7]

As in the previous chapter, which took up the similarities and differences between A. Myrdal's and Beauvoir's uses of the race/gender analogy, here I also want to note one major difference between them in their use of the slave/woman analogy. Whereas A. Myrdal explicitly references racialized slavery in her comparison of the status of white women, white children, and enslaved Black men, Beauvoir does not do the same. Beauvoir speaks of slavery in more general terms, both

SLAVERY AND WOMANHOOD   209

historically and with reference to Hegel's master/slave dialectic. For example, within the first one hundred pages of *The Second Sex*, Beauvoir offers a broad narrative about the history of slavery and the changing perception and status of woman. She explains:

> Man wanted to exhaust the new possibilities opened up by new technology: he called upon a servile workforce, and he reduced his fellow man to slavery. Slave labor being far more efficient than work that women could supply, she lost the economic role she played within the tribe. And in his relationship with the slave, the master found a far more radical confirmation of his sovereignty than the tempered authority he exercised on woman. Venerated and revered for her fertility, being *other* than man and sharing the disquieting image of the *other*, woman, in a certain way, kept man dependent on her even while she was dependent on him; the reciprocity of the master-slave relationship existed in the present for her, and it was how she escaped slavery. (TSS 86. Emphasis original.)[8]

Beauvoir is describing in very general terms the emergence of the oppression of "woman" and of "fellow man." She differentiates slave labor (suggested to be a male slave labor force) from woman's labor (which is distinct from slave labor here) and describes the former as more efficient than the latter. In this context, the "woman" and the "slave" are presented as mutually exclusive and as having different relationships to the master. Woman is able to "escape" slavery through the establishment of a servile workforce, or the reduction of man to slavery. She also suggests that the circumstances faced by the slave are worse than those of woman, though both suffer. Beauvoir explains, "As for the slave, *he* had no taboo to protect *him*, being nothing but a servile *man*, not just different, but inferior: the dialectic of the master-slave will take centuries to be actualized; within the organized patriarchal society, the slave is the only beast of burden with a human face: the master exercises tyrannical authority over *him*; this exalts his [the man/master's] pride: and *he* [the man/master] turns it against the woman" (TSS 86–87, emphasis added).[9] Again, this account assumes slave labor is all male and/or ignores the woman who is also subjugated to slave labor.

210   BEAUVOIR AND BELLE

As with the earlier examples of comparative and competing frameworks of oppression in *The Second Sex*, we see both a comparison and a contradistinction drawn between the subjugation of slaves and of women. Comparatively, Beauvoir notes that like all oppressed people dependent on a master's whims (from slave to servant to indigent), women too "have learned to present [the master] with an immutable smile or an enigmatic impassivity; they carefully hide their real feelings and behavior" (TSS 271). This façade of the oppressed is framed as the "Mystery" of the Other—whether "feminine Mystery" or mystery of "the Black" or "the Yellow" or "the slave" – considered "absolutely as the inessential Other." (TSS 271).[10] However, Beauvoir previously underscored an especially significant distinction between woman and slave. She asserts that woman does not become conscious of herself against the man, unlike the slave who "becomes conscious of himself against the master" (TSS 66).

In addition to this comparison and contradistinction between woman and slave, Beauvoir also presents woman as slave or as enslaved. In her introduction, Beauvoir initially stops short of describing woman as slave and opts instead to use the term "vassal."[11] But throughout *The Second Sex* we find multiple references to woman as enslaved, including her portrayal of woman as enslaved by man and enslaved by the body's reproductive functions for the species. Woman's enslavement to man is sometimes conceptualized by Beauvoir in terms of property; for example, woman is bought like a head of cattle or a slave, woman is property like a slave, beast of burden, or thing.[12] She contends that man clearly wants to enslave woman, particularly as he imagines himself to be her benefactor, liberator, or redeemer.[13] But the irony of man's success in enslaving woman is that "in doing so, he robbed her of what made possession desirable" (TSS 204).

In addition to being enslaved by man, Beauvoir underscores the ways in which woman's reproductive function enslaves her to the species with significant limitations imposed upon her. She insists, "Woman's enslavement to the species and the limits of her individual abilities are facts of extreme importance; the woman's body is one of the essential elements of the situation she occupies in this world" (TSS 48). She also contends, "The fundamental reason that woman, since the beginning of history, has been consigned to domestic labor and

SLAVERY AND WOMANHOOD 211

prohibited from taking part in shaping the world is her enslavement to the generative function" (TSS 136). Beauvoir is pointing to both the bodily impositions of pregnancy and birth as well as the existential implications of maternity and its impact on being in the world and shaping the world. These reflections on white women being enslaved by their reproductive functions do not include any reference to the experiences of enslaved Black women and men forced to "breed" in order to expand the slave labor of white masters.

Beauvoir discusses the "sexual initiation" of (white) women as almost always an experience of rape, stating, "In any case, however differential and courteous a man might be, the first penetration is always a rape" (TSS 395).[14] But she does not name the sexual exploitation of Black women in the context of slavery and beyond. It is not that she is not aware of the phenomenon, rather she chooses to frame it quite differently. In Beauvoir's words, "Fiercely racist [white] American men in the South have always been permitted by custom to sleep with black women, before the Civil War as today, and they exploit this right with a lordly arrogance; a white woman who had relations with a black man in the times of slavery would have been put to death, and today she would be lynched" (TSS 386). Let us unpack this a bit. First, note that Beauvoir does not use the term "rape" in this context, despite the fact that she uses the term "rape" elsewhere in the same chapter (TSS Volume 2, Part 1, Chapter 3, including in the two pages before this quote). Rather than naming what Claudia Jones refers to as white men's "legalized rape" of Black women, Beauvoir describes this as a "custom"—even if one that is "exploited . . . with lordly arrogance" by "fiercely racist men." Also note these men's whiteness is not named here, though perhaps it is assumed by the "racist" qualifier. Even more puzzling is the fact that Beauvoir mentions penalties against white women for sleeping with Black men—death during slavery and lynching today—without any mention of the lynching of Black men, women, and children![15]

Beauvoir's Use of Hegel's Master-Slave Dialectic

Another place where white woman's conditions get compared with slavery is through Beauvoir's allusions to and appropriations of Hegel's

212 BEAUVOIR AND BELLE

master-slave dialectic. She uses this dialectic as a theoretical framework for examining the subjugation of the white woman within the white male/white female power dynamic. On the one hand, Beauvoir asserts, "Certain passages where Hegel's dialectic describes the relationship of master to slave would apply far better to the relationship of man to woman" (TSS 74). On the other hand, she acknowledges that the woman is not the same as the slave, even if there are women who are enslaved. Beauvoir states:

> Assimilating the woman to the slave is a mistake; among slaves there were women, but free women have always existed, that is, women invested with religious and social dignity: they accepted man's sovereignty, and he did not feel threatened by a revolt that could transform him in turn into an object. Woman thus emerged as the inessential who never returned to the essential, as the absolute Other, without reciprocity. (TSS 160; LDS 1 239)

Here she explicitly acknowledges that "among slaves there were women," but she does not take up the situation of enslaved women. Instead she moves quickly to "free women" who (unlike enslaved women) are "invested with religious and social dignity." It is puzzling that this insight is explicitly named by Beauvoir and then consistently ignored throughout the text. As Elizabeth Spelman observes in *Inessential Woman*, Beauvoir "sometimes contrasts 'women' to 'slaves' . . ., but she never really talks about those women who according to her own categories belonged to slave populations—for example, Black female slaves in the United States."[16]

Beauvoir is cognizant of important differences between Hegel's "slave" and the situation of woman. For Hegel, she explains, "the Master's privilege . . . arises from the affirmation of Spirit over Life in the fact of risking his life: but in fact the vanquished slave has experienced this same risk [of his own life]" (TSS 74). In contrast to Hegel's slave, Beauvoir states: "the woman is originally an existent who gives *Life* and does not risk *her* life; there has never been combat between the male and her" (TSS 74, emphasis original). Also, unlike Hegel's slave and the master, woman aspires to and recognizes man's values rather than pitting her values against his (TSS 74–75). In the dialectic, "Each

SLAVERY AND WOMANHOOD 213

one [master and slave] tries to accomplish itself by reducing the other to slavery. But in work and fear the slave experiences himself as essential, and by a dialectical reversal the master appears the inessential one" (TSS 159). This reversal between the master and slave has not occurred between man and woman. Man has remained essential and woman has remained inessential. Beauvoir presents the possibility for an outcome between man and woman that differs from the dialectic between master and slave. Rather than reversing the position of essential and inessential or subject and object, Beauvoir posits, "The conflict can be overcome by the free recognition of each individual in the other, each one positing both itself and the other as object and as subject in a reciprocal movement" (TSS 159). Highlighting the challenge that this possibility entails, she adds, "But friendship and generosity, which accomplish this recognition of freedoms concretely, are not easy virtues" (TSS 159).

As with the previous comparisons of woman's oppression to other forms of oppression (racism, antisemitism, colonialism, classism), Beauvoir's comparison of woman to slave along with her presentation of woman as enslaved is problematic. Again, Beauvoir sabotages her own insights. She herself notes that it is a mistake to assimilate woman to the slave. She understands that among slaves there were women and that free women (invested with religious and social dignity) have always existed. And yet, enslaved women remain largely ignored in Beauvoir's analysis. It is also noteworthy that the issue of slavery as presented in *The Second Sex* has not been a central point of emphasis in much of the secondary literature. When slavery in this text is examined in the literature, it is often taken up in the context of Beauvoir's engagement with Hegel's master-slave dialectic. But the issue of slavery as explicitly connected to institutional slavery, or the history of racialized colonial enslavement is under-engaged in the literature. I will briefly explore examples of both the connection of slaves to Hegel's master-slave dialectic and the connection of slaves to institutional slavery in select secondary literature.

When analyzing Beauvoir's relationship to the master-slave dialectic, some readers critique her use of Hegel and suggest that she takes up his position uncritically, while others assume that she simply adopts Jean-Paul Sartre's reading of Hegel.[17] In *Simone de*

214 BEAUVOIR AND BELLE

Beauvoir, Philosophy, and Feminism (2001), Nancy Bauer rejects these approaches, examining Beauvoir's use of Hegel and seeking to distinguish Beauvoir's analysis from Hegel's and Sartre's in terms of appropriation and transformation, rather than application.[18] Put another way, Bauer argues that Beauvoir appropriates and transforms Hegel's master-slave dialectic rather than simply applying it to the dynamic between man and woman. In *The Other Within: Ethics, Politics, and the Body in Simone de Beauvoir* (2004) Fredrika Scarth, like Bauer, insists that Beauvoir's analysis of the master-slave dialectic offers alternatives to both Hegel and Sartre.[19] For Scarth, rather than simply apply the dialectic to man and woman or use it as an analogy, Beauvoir appropriates it and transforms it by changing the meaning of risk that drives the dialectic.[20] But neither of these readings of Beauvoir's use of Hegel mention or account for actual enslaved persons as a reference point for Hegel's or Beauvoir's analyses of slavery.[21]

These central issues are also raised by Sabine Broeck ("Re-reading de Beauvoir 'After Race': *Woman-as-Slave* Revisited," 2011), who makes significant interventions in this discussion. Concerning the master-slave dialectic, Broeck notes that "Among white philosophers in France in the late 1940s and 1950s, 'slavery' if anything, had an entirely Hegelian/Kojevean horizon. There was no slave trade historiography that had made its way into a wider discourse."[22] But Broeck insists that such "white epistemic isolation" must be called into question in the cases of Beauvoir (and Sartre, given their intellectual exchanges and personal relationships with figures like Frantz Fanon, Aimé Césaire, and Richard Wright). For Broeck, despite these transnational, multi-ethnic, anti-racist intellectual friendships, Beauvoir's writing, "in its insistence on a creative re-employment of Hegelian allegory, has obscured rather than illuminated a positioning of the subject of gender vis-à-vis its colonial and enslavist implications in the history of modern Europe."[23] So we might read Beauvoir as successfully deploying (or appropriating or transforming) Hegel's master/slave dialectic, but Broeck warns that we must also take into consideration the problematics of that dialectic as it relates to the histories of enslaved people of African descent.

SLAVERY AND WOMANHOOD 215

Interventions: Reimagining Subject, Object, and Abject

Broeck goes beyond Hegel's master/slave dialectic and argues that the woman-as-slave analogy, the logic of which has deeply racist effects, is one that has been used from early modern feminism (e.g., Wollstonecraft and Olympe de Gouges) through second-wave feminism (e.g., Millet and French feminists).[24] She asserts, "What appeared as a new philosophical pre-figuration was actually a re-configuration of an allegorical trope with a long history: the rhetorical construction that casts woman as slave in opposition to man as master has long allowed white western women to enter critical negotiations of subjectivity in western (post)-Enlightenment thought."[25]

Broeck describes this geometrically as a triangle in which white Man figures as *Subject*, white Woman figures as *Object*, and Black Slave, a seemingly gender-neutral and invisible third position, figures as *Abject*. Broeck argues:

> Hegelian allegory and western modern philosophy in its wake knows the subject only as masterful opponent to the object. There is no subject model in western thought that would not require a subject that is one precisely because it masters its object other, which in turn may dialectically strive to become a subject of mastery. This binary opposition, however, can only work because of its unspoken third term: the position of being abjected from this struggle, namely the early modern position of factually enslaved people of African origin. This triangle, however invisible, enables the notorious Hegelian opposition: the position of the abjected is the one that any given object may differentiate itself against, thus aspiring to, or actually becoming, a subject (however "lesser").[26]

This triangle presented by Broeck is significant. She describes it as the driving dynamic of transatlantic modernity. Taking seriously this triangle, it seems that feminist interventions by Beauvoir and others have not destroyed the subject-object binary, and the universal Man as subject has not capitulated. Rather, (white) woman has sought to

216 BEAUVOIR AND BELLE

gain more recognition from (white) man and tried to move closer to subjectivity by appropriating the suffering of the abject (enslaved Black people) while also avoiding being seen as or reduced to the abject.

According to Broeck, the goal of *The Second Sex* is in part "to establish a philosophical positioning of woman in the most universalizing and general sense, to counter the white patriarchal mythology of woman as lack, as absence, and at best an ornamental and empirical object."[27] But this is also an important point of contention for Broeck insofar as Beauvoir's text (and its critical reception) problematically puts white women in the epistemic default position while simultaneously ignoring the racialization of white women.[28] And despite Beauvoir's use of history and accounts of her own lived experience, Broeck asserts that she actually also turns away from these details "in order to create a counter-space for woman as a generalization, as occupying a universal subject position that philosophy can recognize."[29] Simply put, Broeck claims that Beauvoir's ultimate goal is to insert white women into philosophy (as subjects rather than objects).[30]

Let us also take seriously Norma Alarcón's earlier insights about this dynamic in "The Theoretical subject(s) of *This Bridge Called My Back* and Anglo-American Feminism" (1994).[31] Juxtaposing the approach to subjectivity in *This Bridge Called My Back* (1981) with the approach of Anglo-American Feminism in general and Simone de Beauvoir's *The Second Sex* in particular, Alarcón describes *Bridge* as a project that "gives voice to the contradictory experiences of women of color" and in so doing also develops "a theory of subjectivity and culture that would demonstrate the considerable differences between them and Anglo-American women, as well as between them and Anglo-European men and men of their own culture."[32] In contrast, Alarcón notes, "Simone de Beauvoir and her key work *The Second Sex* have been most influential in the development of [white] feminist standpoint epistemology. She may even be responsible for the creation of Anglo-American feminist theory's 'episteme': a highly self-conscious ruling class white Western female subject locked in a struggle to death with 'Man.'"[33]

For Alarcón, it is problematic that the *person* in feminist theory is conceptualized as a self-sufficient individual adult (drawing on Flax) and that the *subject* is constituted as individual and individualist (drawing on Spivak). The result is the construction of a feminist subject

SLAVERY AND WOMANHOOD 217

of consciousness that parodies masculine subject consciousness with "ethnocentric liberal underpinnings."[34] She elaborates, "With gender as the central concept in feminist thinking, epistemology is flattened out in such a way that we lose sight of the complex and multiple ways in which the subject and object of possible experience are constituted. The flattening effect is multiplied when one considers that gender is often solely related to white men."[35] Alarcón pushes back on the inclinations (and practices) in Anglo-American feminism (and women's studies more generally) that construct and maintain a universal, unitary, or even "common denominator" category of *woman* that ignores, denies, downplays, flattens out, or silences complexities and differences.[36] She explains, "The inclusion of other analytical categories such as race and class becomes impossible for a subject whose consciousness refuses to acknowledge that 'one becomes a woman' in ways that are much more complex than in a simple opposition to men . . . [insofar as] one may also 'become a woman' in opposition to other women."[37] Consequently, "the freedom of women of color to posit themselves as multiple-voiced subjects is constantly in peril of repression precisely at that point where our constituted contradictions puts us at odds with women different from ourselves."[38]

Of course, there are resources in the writings of Women of Color to approach these issues very differently. Alarcón is clear that "*Bridge*, along with the 1980s writings by many women of color in the United States, has problematized many a version of Anglo-American feminism, and has helped open the way for alternative feminist discourses and theories . . . however the impact among most Anglo-American theorists appears to be more cosmetic."[39] She explains, "Notwithstanding the power of *Bridge* to affect the personal lives of its readers, *Bridge's* challenge to the Anglo-American subject of feminism has yet to effect newer discourse . . . Anglo feminist readers of *Bridge* tend to appropriate it, cite it as an instance of difference between women, and proceed to negate that difference by subsuming women of color into the unitary category of woman/women."[40] Put another way, even if Women of Color are taught in select courses and cosmetically represented on reading lists (e.g., in women's studies or even philosophy) there seems to be a resistance among Anglo-American feminists "to include the voices of 'women of color' into feminist discourse."[41]

218   BEAUVOIR AND BELLE

Similar observations and insights can also be seen in Malini Johar Schueller's "Analogy and (White) Feminist Theory: Rethinking Race and the Color of the Cyborg Body" (2005). Approaching these issues from the perspectives of both postcolonial studies as well as gender and sexuality studies, Schueller describes "Incorporation by analogy" as the "dominant paradigm of the imperialist incorporation of women of color in contemporary gender and sexuality studies."[42] Noting that "Postcolonial theory has already revealed how analogy and metaphor have been fundamental in constituting colonial discourse" (here she mentions Edward Said on woman as metaphor for the Orient, and binaries analogizing children and primitives), Schueller encourages readers to thoroughly investigate "the role of racial analogy, resemblance, and metaphor within feminist/gender theory."[43] I would also add the discipline of philosophy to postcolonial studies and women's, gender, and sexuality studies here.

On the one hand, Schueller gently suggests, "the analogizing move within white feminist theory, working . . . through assimilation and the incorporation of racial difference, *may* constitute a neocolonial moment *more dangerous* than the earlier absence of race and, thus, *may* need close scrutiny."[44] On the other hand, she also takes even stronger positions, asserting that "racial analogy in white feminist/gender/sexuality studies functions as a colonial fetish that enables the (white) theorist to displace the potentially disruptive contradictions of racial difference onto a safer and more palatable notion of similarity, thus offering theory that can be easily assimilated within the politics of liberal multiculturalism."[45] Building on Homi Bhabha's notion of fetish, Schueller adds, "inclusion by analogy functions fetishistically to exclude the disturbing and troubling aspects of racial difference by mimicking the politics of liberal multiculturalism."[46] In the final analysis, "racial analogy within (white) feminist theory helps whiteness retain its privilege by being uninterrogated."[47]

Critical Interrogations: Slave/Woman Analogy Problematics

In *Women, Race, and Class* (1981), Angela Davis takes up the slave/ woman analogy (also described interchangeably as "the analogy of slavery" and "the metaphor of slavery"). She notes, "White women in the North—the middle-class housewife as well as the young 'mill girl'—frequently invoked the metaphor of slavery as they sought to articulate their respective oppressions."[48] Davis differentiates between the slavery metaphors used by middle-class versus working-class white women. In her estimation, if the metaphor was to be used, the latter had a stronger claim to its use than the former. She elaborates in this extended quote:

> Well-situated women began to denounce their unfulfilling domestic lives by defining marriage as a form of slavery. For working women, the economic oppression they suffered on the job bore a strong resemblance to slavery . . . As between women who were workers and those who came from prosperous middle-class families, the former certainly had more legitimate grounds for comparing themselves to slaves. Although they were nominally free, their working conditions and low wages were so exploitative as to automatically invite the comparison with slavery. Yet it was the women of means who invoked the analogy of slavery most literally in their efforts to express the oppressive nature of marriage . . . primarily for the shock value of the comparison.[49]

Davis explains that the problematic implications of this comparison, namely, the suggestion that slavery was no worse than marriage and that the conditions of white middle-class women were comparable to the harsh labor, brutal punishments, and sexual exploitation endured by enslaved Black women and men.

In *Ain't I a Woman: Black Women and Feminism* (1981), bell hooks also critiques the woman-as-slave analogy, or white women presenting their conditions as "synonymous" with enslaved Black people. For hooks, this claim was not at all helpful for those enslaved. She notes, "there was very little if any similarity between the day-to-day life experiences of white women and the day-to-day experiences of the black slave."[50] At one point she grants, "Theoretically, the white woman's legal status under patriarchy may have been that of 'property,' " but quickly adds, "she was in no way subjected to the dehumanization and brutal oppression that was the lot of the slave."[51]

220 BEAUVOIR AND BELLE

In the final analysis, hooks makes this critical observation, "When white women reformers made synonymous the impact of sexism on their lives, they were not revealing an awareness of or sensitivity to the slave's lot; they were simply appropriating the horror of the slave experience to enhance their own cause."[52] In this way, both Davis and hooks anticipate Broeck's later critique of white women's use of this analogy as an appropriation and exploitation of the suffering of the enslaved.

In "Understanding Across Difference and Analogical Reasoning in Simpson's *Unfinished Project*" (2009),[53] Gaile Pohlhaus, Jr., also cautions against the use of such analogies. She references Kimberlé Crenshaw's critiques of white feminists analogizing racism and sexism, including the slave/woman analogy which, "highlights the issue pertaining to the oppression of white women while making invisible the bulk of what African Americans suffered under slavery."[54] Pohlhaus elaborates:

> Because the analogy began with the lives of white women, the range of things that could be seen using this analogy was set by the experiences of white women, so that the majority of what was suffered under slavery disappears in the comparison ... As Crenshaw notes, analogy in such a case results in at least two harms. First, it uses those to whom one is analogizing only to return to the origin of the analogy. Second it makes invisible those aspects of that to which one analogizes that are not present in the place analogized from.[55]

Crenshaw's critique of the slave/woman analogy (as cited by Pohlhaus) focuses on the disappearing act that it enables. On the one hand, the analogy strategically exploits the suffering of the enslaved to advance the cause of white women. On the other hand, the analogy attempts to make invisible the suffering of the enslaved while bringing greater visibility to the experiences of white women.

Patricia Hill Collins also problematizes Beauvoir's use of the woman-as-slave metaphor in "Simone de Beauvoir, Women's Oppression and Existential Freedom" (2017).[56] She explains, "Beauvoir returns frequently to the metaphor of women as slaves as the core trope for women's oppression, an idea made intelligible through her analogical thinking about Black people."[57] She elaborates, "By using metaphorical

SLAVERY AND WOMANHOOD   221

shortcuts to make her points, Beauvoir often conflates stereotypes of Black people as enslaved, incarcerated, ignorant, unaware of their own unfreedom and happy with their predicament."[58] Connecting the race/gender analogy to the woman-as-slave metaphor, Collins argues, "Via the race/gender analogy, Beauvoir uses Black people to invoke slavery, a metaphor that references an unexamined racial framework, in support of claims about women's oppression."[59] I would nuance this by reiterating my earlier assertions that in *The Second Sex*, Beauvoir more specifically uses Black men to invoke slavery and racial oppression in an effort to call attention to the gender oppression of white women. Collins is clear that although Beauvoir knew better, she did not do better.[60] With this in mind, in this last section of this chapter, let us move beyond slave/woman analogy to take seriously the lived experiences of enslaved Black women as examined by Davis and hooks.

Conclusion: Exploitation of Enslaved Black Women Beyond Analogy

In "Reflections on the Black Woman's Role in the Community of Slaves" (1971), Angela Davis cites Beauvoir's *The Second Sex* for a very specific purpose. She does not draw on Beauvoir's race/gender analogy, slave/woman analogy, or even her analysis of the woman question more generally. Rather, Davis quotes Beauvoir's accounts of the sexual relations of animals to contextualize the sexual assaults endured by enslaved Black women from white male slave masters. Davis' analysis provides an implicit refutation of Beauvoir's slave/woman analogy insofar as she centers the experiences of enslaved Black women whom she argues were simultaneously genderless and gendered. On the one hand, enslaved Black women were denied a gendered identity when it came to slave labor. On the other hand, they were gendered through rape, "the white master could endeavor to reestablish her [enslaved Black woman's] femaleness by reducing her to the level of her *biological* being."[61] Davis continues, "Aspiring with his sexual assaults to establish her as a female *animal*, he would be striving to destroy her proclivities toward resistance."[62] It is in this context that Davis quotes Beauvoir's accounts of the sexual relations of animals from *The Second Sex*:

It is unquestionably the male who *takes* the female—she is taken. Often the word applies literally, for whether by means of special organs or through superior strength, the male seizes her and holds her in place; he performs the copulatory movements; and among insects, birds, and mammals, he penetrates . . . Her body becomes a resistance to be broken through.[63]

According to Davis, the white slave master used "openly terroristic" rape to treat enslaved Black women as animals and to temper their resistance efforts.[64]

Davis builds on and significantly expands this analysis of enslaved Black women as both genderless and gendered in *Women, Race, and Class*. Again, from the standpoint of labor, Black women were treated as genderless, "Since women, no less than men, were viewed as profitable labor-units, they might as well have been genderless as far as the slaveholders were concerned."[65] But when it came to terroristic sexual assault, Black women were reduced to their gender. Davis explains, "In this sense, the oppression of women was identical to the oppression of men. But women suffered in different ways as well, for they were victims of sexual abuse and other barbarous mistreatment that could only be inflicted on women."[66] She adds, "Expediency governed the slaveholders' posture toward female slaves: when it was profitable to exploit them as if they were men, they were regarded, in effect, as genderless, but when they could be exploited, punished and repressed in ways suited only for women, they were locked into their exclusively female roles."[67] Contrasting enslaved Black women to white women, Davis notes that prevalent ideologies of femininity, motherhood, and womanhood did not apply to enslaved Black women. In this way, "'Woman' became synonymous in the prevailing propaganda with 'mother' and 'housewife,' and both . . . bore the fatal mark of inferiority. But among Black female slaves, this vocabulary was nowhere to be found."[68] Having offered a brief account of Davis' insights concerning the experiences of enslaved Black women, let us now turn to bell hooks' related analysis. They both provide pertinent counter-narratives that are absent in Beauvoir's analysis.

Returning to *Ain't I a Woman*, hooks (who cites Davis' 1971 article) argues that Black women's oppression in slavery was intensified by the combination of racism and sexism. According to hooks, "The brutal treatment of enslaved black women by white men exposed the depths of male hatred of woman and woman's body."[69] Citing Paige Smith's *Daughters of the Promised Land* (1970) as one example, hooks also argues that the sexual exploitation of enslaved Black girls and women has been minimized by modern historians (of the 1970s) who casually present it as "boys will be boys" and even suggest submissive complicity among those enslaved.[70] Rejecting this revisionist history, hooks cites *American Slavery: As It Is* (1839), compiled by scholars and activists Angela and Sarah Grimké.[71] The Grimké sisters, in accordance with the times, often spoke in Victorian veiled references. But hooks notes, "Had Angelina and Sarah Grimké lifted the veil of private life any higher they would have exposed not only slaveowners siring children by black women, but sadistic misogynist acts of cruelty and brutality that went far beyond seduction—to rape, to torture, and even to orgiastic murder and necrophilia."[72] She explains, "black women have always been seen by the white public as sexually permissive, as available and eager for the sexual assaults of any man, black or white. The designation of all black women as sexually depraved, immoral, and loose had its roots in the slave system."[73] Consequently, "A devaluation of black womanhood occurred as a result of the sexual exploitation of black women during slavery that has not altered in the course of hundreds of years."[74] These histories and experiences are rendered invisible by white feminists like Beauvoir in their use and abuse of the slave/woman analogy.

In "Calling All Sisters: Continental Philosophy and Black Feminist Thinkers" (2010), Kathy Glass underscores yet another way in which Beauvoir herself demonstrates the excesses of the comparison of the status of white women to the status of slaves, namely her awareness of white women's pro-slavery stances in the US context as well as their unflinching support of other oppressive causes across multiple international contexts. Beauvoir notes, "If she [the white woman] belongs to the privileged elite that profits from the given social order, she wants it unshakable" (TSS 641). She adds the following specific examples:

224　BEAUVOIR AND BELLE

> Among the Southerners during the Civil War, no one was more pas-
> sionately in favor of slavery as the women; in England during the
> Boer War, and in France against the Commune, it was the women
> who were the most enraged; they seek to compensate for their inac-
> tion by the force of feelings they display; in victory they are as wild
> as hyenas against the neaten enemy; in defeat they bitterly refuse any
> arrangements; as their ideas are only attitudes, they do not mind
> defending the most outdated causes: they can be legitimists in 1914,
> tsarists in 1949. (TSS 641–642)

Glass argues that although Beauvoir is clearly aware of "white women's fear-based investment in the status quo," she fails to name and interrogate the benefits of whiteness for women—especially the ways in which "racial supremacy yielded white women power over nineteenth-century blacks of both sexes."[75] Glass also points out the need to offer correctives to these narratives in *The Second Sex*—in which "the signifier 'woman' remains tightly bound, more often than not, to the signified 'white woman'"—insofar as this text has deeply influenced the white feminism that has followed it. Glass asserts, and I agree, "Beauvoir's book impacted decisively on the politics of white American feminists, who gained access to the English translation of *The Second Sex* in 1953; as the record shows, mainstream feminist writings reproduced Beauvoir's oversights throughout the 1960s."[76] And I would add that these oversights have persisted into the twenty-first century.

I conclude with Broeck and Collins. Like Glass, Broeck affirms the philosophical significance of Beauvoir and *The Second Sex*, arguing, "The signifying and repertoire-building power of de Beauvoir's texts has, by way of their continuous dissemination and reception, pre-ordained feminist epistemology until today."[77] In this way Broeck situates the gravity of Beauvoir's (and her readers') problematic analogies among different systems of oppression and appropriations of the suffering of others. Not only does Broeck assert that Beauvoir appropriated Black suffering endured in slavery to advance her philosophical discussion of woman's situation, but she also posits that

SLAVERY AND WOMANHOOD 225

Beauvoir's readers seem to readily accept this appropriation.[78] In the end, "Beauvoir's analysis remained anchored in that binary philosophy, which does not have any critical interest in the 'thingification' of the enslaved in modern, enlightened history."[79] Consequently, white women seeking subjectivity by appropriating and yet differentiating from Black abjectivity ultimately miss opportunities for coalitions and solidarity with Black women and men.[80] And as Collins concludes, "I can only imagine how much more robust her [Beauvoir's] analysis of existential freedom might have been had she not relied so heavily on the race/gender analogy . . . Understanding women's oppression through intersectional analysis of race, class, age, ethnicity, and sexuality might have provided a new angle of vision on freedom."[81] Thus, the implications of the woman-as-slave analogy, like the other comparative and competing frameworks operating throughout *The Second Sex*, warrant more critical attention.

Notes

1. For examples of how the slave/woman and race/gender analogies at times overlap, see Sabine Broeck, "Re-reading de Beauvoir 'After Race': *Woman-as-Slave* Revisited," *International Journal of Francophone Studies* 14, nos. 1–2 (2011), 167–184. (Hereafter Broeck 2011.)
2. Alva Myrdal, "A Parallel to the Negro Problem" (1944), appendix 5 in Gunnar Myrdal, *An American Dilemma: The Negro Problem in Modern Democracy*, vol. 2 (New York: Routledge, 1944, 2017), 1073. (Hereafter A. Myrdal 1944.)
3. A. Myrdal 1944, 1073.
4. A. Myrdal states, "We do not intend to follow here the interesting developments of the institution of slavery in America through the centuries, but merely wish to point out the paternalistic idea which held the slave to be a sort of family member and in some way—in spite of all differences—placed him beside woman and children under the power of the *pater-familias*" (1073).
5. A. Myrdal 1944, 1073.
6. A. Myrdal 1944, 1074, 1075.
7. A. Myrdal 1944, 1075.

226 BEAUVOIR AND BELLE

8. Early on (TSS 70–87), Beauvoir suggests that she is describing labor, woman, and slavery during what she calls the "primitive period" (TSS 87). Here she seems to have in mind more ancient forms of slavery than the transatlantic slave trade. She makes further references to Apollo in Aeschylus' *Eumenides*, as well as seventeenth-century cosmologies of Assyro-Babylonians, in discussing the shift away from matrilineal to paternal rights. She also mentions Sparta, describing it as the only city-state where women were treated almost equally to men, not jealously enslaved by a master (TSS 96–97); free women, slaves, and prostitutes in Greece; and Asian slaves prostituted near Athens (TSS 97).

9. Beauvoir elaborates, "Everything he wins, he wins against her; the more powerful he becomes, the more she declines. In particular, when he acquires ownership of land, he also claims woman as property" (TSS 87).

10. Beauvoir continues, "the fact is that rich America and the male are on the side of the Master, and Mystery belongs to the slave" (TSS 87).

11. Beauvoir states: "Now, woman has always been, if not man's slave, at least his vassal; the two sexes have never divided the world up equally; and still today, even though her condition is changing, woman is heavily handicapped" (TSS 9). There are other references to woman as vassal throughout the text (TSS 9, 149, 189, 243, 264, 270, 341, 423, 440, 656–657, 691, 726, and 733). This distinction was first brought to my attention by Debra Bergoffen at a conference, but she also references woman as vassal in "Why Rape? Lessons from *The Second Sex*," in *A Companion to Simone de Beauvoir*, ed. Laura Hengehold and Nancy Bauer (Hoboken: Wiley-Blackwell, 2017).

12. "He buys her like a head of cattle or a slave, he imposes his domestic divinities on her: and the children she conceives belong to her spouse's family" (TSS 90). "Since she is his property like the slave, the beast of burden, or the thing, it is natural for a man to have as many wives as he wishes . . . polygamy" (TSS 91).

13. "Clearly man wants woman's enslavement when fantasizing himself as a benefactor, liberator, or redeemer" (TSS 201).

14. For more of Beauvoir's analysis of rape, see also TSS 384–385, 394–396, 403, 455, 459.

15. Ida B. Wells and others wrote extensively on the issue of lynching. (I have not been able to find sources about white women being lynched for sleeping with Black men.)

16. Elizabeth Spelman, *Inessential Woman: Problems of Exclusion in Feminist Thought* (Boston: Beacon Press, 1988), 65.

SLAVERY AND WOMANHOOD   227

17. For example, Kathy Ferguson states: "De Beauvoir's self is very like Hegel's, an empty ego traveling on a journey filled with conflict and danger from others. She sees human subjectivity as characterized by 'the imperialism of the human consciousness,' always needing to conquer"; Kathy E. Ferguson, *The Man Question: Visions of Subjectivity in Feminist Theory* (Berkley: University of California Press, 1993), 58. Ferguson also discusses essentialism (see "Essentialism?," in "Praxis Feminism," ch. 3 of *The Man Question*, pp. 81–91) and mentions Black women and Black feminism, but not enslaved Black people (in relation to Hegel or other contexts). See also Mary O'Brien, *The Politics of Reproduction* (London: Routledge, 1983). For a reading on Beauvoir and slavery looking at historical philosophers and republicanism before Hegel, see Susan James, "Complicity and Slavery in *The Second Sex*," in *The Cambridge Companion to Simone de Beauvoir*, ed. Claudia Card (Cambridge University Press, 2006), 149–167.

18. Bauer argues, "Beauvoir, on my view, is not simply gesturing at the master-slave dialectic as a source of inspiration for and illumination of her own view. Rather, she wants what she has to say about women to *contest*, on philosophically internal ground, the generic picture of human relations we get in the dialectic . . . between Hegel and Sartre" (Nancy Bauer, *Simone de Beauvoir, Philosophy, and Feminism* [New York: Columbia University Press, 2001], 182).

19. For Scarth, "[Beauvoir] suggests that hostility is only one possible reaction to the presence of free others; there will always remain the possibility of conversion and reciprocal recognition"; Fredrika Scarth, *The Other Within: Ethics, Politics, and the Body in Simone de Beauvoir* (Lanham, MA: Rowman and Littlefield, 2004), 104.

20. Scarth asserts, "But Beauvoir doesn't precisely apply the dialectic to the relation between men and women. It would be more accurate to say that she appropriates it. By this I mean that Beauvoir doesn't simply use the master-slave dialectic as an analogy of the relations between men and women, in which masters are to slaves as men are to women. Rather, she transforms the dialectic by changing the meaning of risk that drives it" (Ibid.). Scarth notes the following differences: "One difference is that the risk that men take, for Beauvoir, is not simply the risk of life in the struggle with another, but more generally the risk of asserting themselves as free, the risk of creating something new in the world" (Ibid., p. 108). Another difference is this: "The salient fact about woman as Other is that she allows man to escape 'that implacable dialectic of master and slave which has its source in the reciprocity between beings'" (ibid.).

228 BEAUVOIR AND BELLE

21. Bauer does note the issue of slavery in Beauvoir's *The Ethics of Ambiguity*; see Simone de Beauvoir, *Pour une morale de l'ambigüité* (Paris: Gallimard, 1947); *The Ethics of Ambiguity*, trans. Bernard Frechtman (New York: Citadel Press, 1976). She observes, "In the *Ethics*, for example, Beauvoir briefly discusses the predicament of African-American slaves in the antebellum American South" (Bauer, *Simone de Beauvoir, Philosophy, and Feminism*, 175). However, this is not taken into consideration in Bauer's analysis of the master-slave dialectic in *The Second Sex*.

22. Broeck 2011, 171.

23. Broeck 2011, 172. She later elaborates, "For de Beauvoir, as for post-Enlightenment thinkers in the Hegelian tradition, the subject is thought of as such because it masters the other who is thus structurally always already in the submissive 'slave' position. Consequently, (and despite her knowledge of history) if de Beauvoir wants to install woman as the primary antagonist to man, she has to signify her as the Hegelian type 'slave'; she narrates the figure of woman as emblematic of the species 'slave' by giving woman a consciousness of the slavish who is in need of being put next to freedom, thereby to become a resistant object to a subject, and eventually, a subject herself" (Broeck 2011, 178).

24. Broeck 2011, 171, 178.

25. Broeck 2011, 171.

26. Broeck 2011, 178.

27. Broeck 2011, 177.

28. Broeck 2011, 169.

29. Broeck 2011, 177.

30. "De Beauvoir's ultimate goal therefore, is not to create a counter-ethnography of certain groups of women in certain historical, cultural, social and political situations, but to insert *woman* into philosophy" (Broeck 2011, 177).

31. Norma Alarcón, "The Theoretical Subject(s) of *This Bridge Called My Back* and Anglo-American Feminism," in *The Postmodern Turn: New Perspectives on Social Theory*, ed. Steven Seidman (Cambridge: Cambridge University Press, 1994). (Hereafter Alarcón 1994.) It is worth noting that Alarcón also appears on the program at the aforementioned "*The Second Sex*—Thirty Years Later: A Commemorative Conference on Feminist Theory" held September 27–29, 1979, at New York University. See also Chapter 4 (Audre Lorde).

SLAVERY AND WOMANHOOD 229

32. Alarcón 1994, 140. See *This Bridge Called My Back: Writings By Radical Women of Color*, ed. Cherríe Moraga and Gloria Anzaldúa (New York: Kitchen Table: Women of Color Press, 1981).

33. Alarcón 1994, 145–146.

34. Alarcón 1994, 142.

35. Alarcón 1994, 147.

36. Alarcón 1994, 144–145, 147.

37. Alarcón 1994, 145.

38. Alarcón 1994, 150.

39. Alarcón 1994, 141.

40. Alarcón 1994, 143.

41. Alarcón 1994, 145.

42. Malini Johar Schueller's "Analogy and (White) Feminist Theory: Rethinking Race and the Color of the Cyborg Body," *Signs: Journal of Women in Culture and Society* 31, no. 1 (2005): 65. (Hereafter Schueller 2005.)

43. Schueller 2005, 67.

44. Schueller 2005, 68. (Emphasis added.)

45. Schueller 2005, 72.

46. Schueller 2005, 74.

47. Schueller 2005, 82.

48. Angela Davis, *Women, Race, and Class* (New York: Vintage Books, 1981), 33–34. (Hereafter Davis 1981.)

49. Davis 1981, 33–34.

50. bell hooks, *Ain't I a Woman: Black Women and Feminism* (Boston: South End Press, 1981), 126. (Hereafter hooks 1981.)

51. hooks 1981, 126.

52. hooks 1981, 126.

53. Gaile Pohlhaus, Jr., "Understanding Across Difference and Analogical Reasoning in Simpson's Unfinished Project," *Journal for Peace and Justice Studies* 19, no. 1 (2009): 37–49. (Hereafter Polhaus 2009.)

54. Pohlhaus 2009, 46. (Pohlhaus is citing Kimberlé Crenshaw's "The Obama Phenomenon" for *The Future of Minority Studies Colloquium*, Cornell University).

55. Pohlhaus (drawing on Crenshaw) 2009, 46.

56. Patricia Hill Collins, "Simone de Beauvoir, Women's Oppression and Existential Freedom," in *A Companion to Simone de Beauvoir*, ed. Laura Hengehold and Nancy Bauer (Hoboken: Wiley-Blackwell, 2017). (Hereafter Collins 2017.)

57. Collins 2017, 328.

58. Collins 2017, 329.

230   BEAUVOIR AND BELLE

59. Collins 2017, 328–329.
60. Collins notes, "Beauvoir is certainly aware of the power of ideology and details its pernicious effects in *The Second Sex*" (Collins 2017, 328). She later observes, "Beauvoir herself recognizes the limits of analogies, but cannot seem to extract herself from them" (Collins 2017, 329).
61. Angela Davis, "Reflections on the Black Woman's Role in the Community of Slaves," *The Black Scholar* 3, no. 4 (December 1971): 2–15, 13. (Emphasis original.) (Hereafter Davis 1971.)
62. Davis 1971, 13. (Emphasis original.)
63. Davis 1971, 13.
64. Davis 1971, 13.
65. Davis 1981, 5.
66. Davis 1981, 6. It is important to note that enslaved Black men were also raped and sexually exploited. For a more detailed analysis of this, see Thomas A. Foster's *Rethinking Rufus: Sexual Violations of Enslaved Men* (Athens: University of Georgia Press, 2019).
67. Davis 1981, 6.
68. Davis 1981, 12.
69. hooks 1981, 29.
70. hooks 1981, 28–29.
71. For hooks, because the sisters' "brother had fathered children by a black female slave," consequently, "they were particularly concerned about the sexual exploitation of black female slaves" (hooks 1981, 27).
72. hooks 1981, 28.
73. hooks 1981, 52.
74. hooks 1981, 53.
75. Kathy Glass, "Calling All Sisters: Continental Philosophy and Black Feminist Thinkers," in *Convergences: Black Feminism and Continental Philosophy*, ed. Maria del Guadalupe Davidson, Kathryn Sophia Belle (formerly Kathryn T. Gines) and Donna Dale Marcano. (New York: SUNY Press, 2010), 230. (Hereafter Glass 2010.)
76. Glass 2010, 231.
77. Broeck 2011, 171.
78. Broeck 2011, 169, 171, 178. "Bolstered by this evasion, the engagement of feminism with post-Enlightenment rhetorical structures of modern subjectivity, which has consistently positioned woman as 'slave' in a subject-object antinomy, must be considered a productive and generative rhetorical move to maneuver white western women into a position of claimant to the subject. This is true for Wollstonecraft and de Gouges as for de Beauvoir: the threat of being a 'slave' became the horizon of degradation

SLAVERY AND WOMANHOOD 231

from which the object-subject negotiations about rights and freedom could be differentiated successfully" (Broeck 2011, 179).

79. Broeck 2011, 179.
80. Broeck 2011, 181.
81. Collins 2017, 337.

7

Abolition and Suffrage in the United States

"They undertook a campaign in favor of blacks"

In "A Parallel to the Negro Problem" (1944) Alva Myrdal asserts, "[White] women suffragists received their political education from the Abolitionist movement. Women like Angelina Grimké, Sarah Grimké, and Abby Kelly began their public careers by speaking for Negro emancipation and only gradually came to fight for women's rights. The three great suffragists of the nineteenth century—Lucretia Mott, Elizabeth Cady Stanton, and Susan B. Anthony—first attracted attention as ardent campaigners for the emancipation of the Negro and the prohibition of liquor."[1] Concerning suffrage, Myrdal claims that white women had to suppress their pursuit of rights in the interest of "Negro" (men). She explains, "The women's movement got much of its public support by reason of its affiliation with the Abolitionist movement: the leading male advocates of woman suffrage before the Civil War were such Abolitionists as William Lloyd Garrison, Henry Ward Beecher, Horace Greeley, and Frederick Douglass. The women had nearly achieved their aims, when the Civil War induced them to suppress all tendencies distracting the federal government from the prosecution of the War. They were apparently fully convinced that victory would bring the suffrage to them as well as to the Negroes."[2]

In a stunning turn of events, Myrdal laments, "The Union's victory, however, brought disappointment to the women suffragists. The arguments 'the Negroes hour' and 'a political necessity' met and swept aside all their [white women's] arguments for leaving the word 'male' out of the 14th Amendment and putting 'sex' alongside 'race' and 'color' in the 15th Amendment."[3] For Myrdal, white and Black male abolitionists abandoned white women when it came to the issue of

Beauvoir and Belle. Kathryn Sophia Belle, Oxford University Press. © Oxford University Press 2024.
DOI: 10.1093/oso/9780197660195.003.0008

ABOLITION AND SUFFRAGE IN THE UNITED STATES 233

suffrage. She states, "Even their [white women's] Abolitionist friends turned on them, and the Republican party shied away from them."[4] Myrdal adds, "Even a few Negroes, invited to the women's convention of January 1869, denounced the women for jeopardizing the black man's chances for the vote. The War and Reconstruction Amendments had thus sharply divided the women's problem from the Negro problem in actual politics. The deeper relation between the two will, however, be recognized up till this day."[5]

Beauvoir also takes up these issues in *The Second Sex* when offering an account of (white) women's rights in America. Of course, Beauvoir states very explicitly that "Among the Southerners during the Civil War, no one was more passionately in favor of slavery as the [white] women" later in *The Second Sex* (TSS 641). But earlier in the text, like Myrdal before her, Beauvoir situates (white) women's early political engagements within the abolitionist movement. She explains, "Some women began to claim their political rights around 1830. They undertook a campaign in favor of blacks. As the antislavery congress held in 1840 in London was closed to them, the Quaker Lucretia Mott founded a feminist association" (TSS 144).[6] She also describes Harriet Beecher Stowe's *Uncle Tom's Cabin* (1852) as a text known for "arousing the public in favor of blacks" (TSS 144).[7] According to Beauvoir, "The [white] American women united around Harriet Beecher Stowe aroused public opinion to fever pitch against slavery; but the real reasons for the Civil War were not sentimental" (TSS 150). The events from the Civil War to the drafting of the 14th and 15th Amendments are summarized by Beauvoir in this way: "When the Civil War broke out, [white] women ardently participated; but in vain they demanded that the amendment giving [male] blacks the right to vote be drafted as follows: 'The right . . . to vote shall not be denied or abridged . . . on account of race, color, *sex*'" (TSS 144, emphasis original). In addition to Lucretia Mott and Harriet Beecher Stowe, Beauvoir also names Susan B. Anthony and Mary Baker Eddy—but not Angelina Grimké, Sarah Grimké, Abby Kelly, or Elizabeth Cady Stanton (all named by Myrdal). Beauvoir draws the following conclusions from this history: "women's entire history has been written by men" and furthermore, "never did women form a separate caste" or seek "to play a role in history as a sex" (TSS 148–149).[8]

234 BEAUVOIR AND BELLE

In "An End to the Neglect of the Problems of the Negro Woman" (1949), Claudia Jones also discusses the abolition and suffrage movements, offering different perspectives and contexts from both Myrdal and Beauvoir. On the one hand, Jones recalls a legacy of white women's activism, noting, "But white women, today, no less than their sisters in the abolitionist and suffrage movements, must rise to challenge this lie and the whole system of Negro oppression."[9] On the other hand, Jones is critical of white women's ongoing failure to recognize how various forms of oppression are interconnected. She argues, "But it was the historic shortcoming of the women's suffrage leaders, predominantly drawn as they were from the bourgeoisie and the petty-bourgeoisie, that they failed to link their own struggles to the struggles for the full democratic rights of the Negro people following emancipation."[10] The "linking" that Jones has in mind is coalitional, not analogical.

These insights by Jones were also presented earlier by scholar-activist Ida B. Wells (*Crusade for Justice: The Autobiography of Ida B. Wells*, 1970) and later by Angela Davis (*Women, Race, and Class, 1981*), bell hooks (*Ain't I a Woman: Black Women and Feminism, 1981*), Paula Giddings (*When and Where I Enter: The Impact of Black Women on Race and Sex in America*, 1984), and Deborah King ("Multiple Jeopardy, Multiple Consciousness: The Context of a Black Feminist Ideology," 1988). Put another way, Black women have been correcting this white woman savior narrative about abolition and suffrage for decades.

This chapter will explore the aforementioned claims made by Myrdal and Beauvoir about the abolition and suffrage movements in the United States. Both Myrdal and Beauvoir present versions of events that repeatedly center white women, marginalize Black men, and ignore Black women. Their narratives present several issues that I want parse out. In the first section, "White Women Abolitionists: Political Consciousness and Contradictions," I take up the claim that white women gained political consciousness through their abolitionist efforts before turning to the issue of suffrage. In the second section, "Seneca Falls: Significance and Shortcomings," I explore what has been described as the myth of Seneca Falls along with the claim that white women fought for the freedom of Black men through abolition only

ABOLITION AND SUFFRAGE IN THE UNITED STATES   235

to have to suppress the issue of woman's suffrage. In the third section, "Suffrage and Suppression: Pitfalls of Expediency Arguments," I examine the myriad manifestations of white abolitionists' and suffragists' racism (anti-Black, anti-immigrant, and anti-Indigenous) about which Myrdal and Beauvoir are silent in their narratives on abolition and suffrage. Following the insights of Jones, I offer a more expansive counternarrative with attention to the intersections of gender, race, and class in abolition and suffrage—focusing primarily on Davis, but also with references to hooks, Giddings, Wells, and King. I argue that a more nuanced and inclusive understanding of the abolition and suffrage movements in the United States is made possible when we shift from the narrowness of Myrdal's and Beauvoir's analogical approach (i.e., their analogizing between the conditions of the white middle-class woman and the conditions of the enslaved Black man) to the intersectional approaches offered by Davis, hooks, Giddings, Wells, and King (i.e., their attention to the intersections of gender, race, and class within abolition and suffrage efforts).[11] Again, there is a long history of Black women's experiences and confrontations with slavery, abolition, suffrage, and analogies.

White Women Abolitionists: Political Consciousness and Contradictions

Let us begin with the claim that white women gained political consciousness of their subordinate status in society through their abolitionist efforts before turning to women's rights and the issue of suffrage. Davis agrees that white women gained political experience through their abolitionist efforts, "As Eleanor Flexner's outstanding study of the women's movement reveals, women abolitionists accumulated invaluable political experiences, without which they could not have effectively organized the campaign for women's rights more than a decade later."[12] Likewise, Deborah King asserts, "The social movements for racial equality in the United States, whether the abolitionist movement in the nineteenth century or the civil rights movement in the mid-twentieth century, were predecessors, catalysts, and prototypes for women's collective action."[13] She adds, "A significant segment of

236 BEAUVOIR AND BELLE

feminist activists came to recognize and understand their own oppression, as well as to develop important organizing skills through their participation in efforts for racial justice."[14] On this issue, bell hooks notes a comment by Abby Kelly: " 'We have good cause to be grateful to the slave for the benefit we have received to ourselves in working for him. In striving to strike his irons off, we found most surely that we were manacled ourselves.' is often quoted by scholars as evidence that white women became conscious of their own limited rights as they worked to end slavery."[15] But hooks adamantly disagrees. For her, "despite popular 19th century rhetoric, the notion that white women had to learn from their efforts to free the slave of their own limited rights is simply erroneous. No 19th century white woman could grow to maturity without an awareness of institutionalized sexism."[16]

Both Davis and Giddings consider the roles of race, gender, and class in abolition activism. Davis situates the birth of the abolitionist movement within the context of the Nat Turner revolt.[17] She asserts that a Black woman (unnamed by Davis) created the first female anti-slavery society (in Salem, MA, in 1832) and, "By 1833, when the Philadelphia Female Anti-Slavery Society was born in the wake of the founding convention of the American Anti-Slavery Society, enough white women were manifesting their sympathetic attitudes toward the Black people's cause to have established the basis for a bond between the two oppressed groups."[18] Davis notes that white women, including both working-class women and middle-class housewives, were drawn to the abolitionist movement in the 1830s.[19] Housewives "had acquired leisure time, which enabled them to become social reformers—active organizers of the abolitionist campaign. Abolitionism, in turn, conferred upon these women the opportunity to launch an implicit protest against their oppressive roles at home."[20] And although white middle-class housewives were more visible in the movement, Davis reminds us that "white working women were also among those who readily agreed with Garrison's militant and anti-slavery position" and furthermore, "factory women lent decisive support to the abolitionist cause."[21]

Whereas Myrdal groups together Lucretia Mott, Susan B. Anthony, Angelina Grimké, Sarah Grimké, and Elizabeth Cady Stanton (Beauvoir mentions Mott and Anthony), Davis points to key

ABOLITION AND SUFFRAGE IN THE UNITED STATES   237

differences among these white women's backgrounds and approaches to abolition and suffrage. For example, while Elizabeth Cady Stanton and Susan B. Anthony might have been new to the abolition cause in the 1840s, abolitionist women like Lucretia Mott, Angelina Grimké, and Sarah Grimké had almost a decade of work and experience ahead of them. Mott was a Quaker minister committed to abolitionism in practice (e.g., through the Underground Railroad and by personally helping an enslaved woman escape in a carriage). Mott also attended the founding convention of the American Anti-Slavery Society (1833) and then went on to organize the founding meeting of the Philadelphia Female Anti-Slavery Society.[22] Davis pays particular attention to Sarah and Angelina Grimké as positive examples of white women allies.[23]

The Grimké sisters gained some male support, and much male opposition (including criticism by clergymen) for their activism.[24] Davis explains, "Their main priority had been to expose the inhumane and immoral essence of the slave system and the special responsibility [white] women bore for its perpetuation. But once the male supremacist attacks against them were unleashed, they realized that unless they defended themselves as women—and the rights of women in general—they would be forever barred from the campaign to free the slaves."[25] Being put in a position to have to defend themselves as women in order to engage in abolitionist work, the Grimké sisters responded: "What then can woman do for the slave, when she herself is under the feet of man and shamed into silence?"[26] This did not result in an either/or campaign to fight either for white women's rights or to fight against slavery. Rather they took a both/and approach, "Since the abolition of slavery was the most pressing political necessity of the times, they urged women to join in that struggle with the understanding that their own oppression was nurtured and perpetuated by the continued existence of the slave system."[27] For Davis these systems of oppression and fights for liberation are dialectical, not hierarchical or analogical. She explains, "Because the Grimké sisters had such a profound consciousness of the inseparability of the fight for Black Liberation and the fight for Women's Liberation, they were never caught in the ideological snare of insisting that one struggle was absolutely more important than the other. They recognized the dialectical character of the relationship between the two causes."[28]

238   BEAUVOIR AND BELLE

In a similar vein, rather than comparing the status of white women to the status of enslaved Black people, Giddings explores the ways in which white supremacy and patriarchy worked together, "The Victorian family ideal also carried a specific consequence for women. White southern women found themselves enmeshed in an interracial web in which wives, children, and slaves were *all* expected to obey the patriarchal head of the household, as historian Anne Firor Scott observed."[29] She continues, "As it was often asserted by slavery apologists, a change in the role of women *or* Blacks would contribute to the downfall not only of slavery, but of the family and society as well."[30] Giddings attributes some of the discord between Black and white women abolitionists to class differences as well as to the "bitter legacy" of the cult of true womanhood, which "soured potential alliances not only between middle-class White reformers and working-class women, but also among Black women of all classes."[31] She notes the irony of white women abolitionists' racist stance and explains, "For Whites, though, abolitionist activism was primarily a means of releasing their suppressed political energies—energies which they directed toward the goal not of Black liberation, but of their own."[32] Giddings states even more explicitly, "As both the race and feminist issues intensified in the 1840s and 1850s, it was inevitable that Black and White women abolitionists would come to a parting of the ways. The parting was due not only to White racism, but also to the primacy of race or sex issues in their respective struggles."[33]

For hooks, it is necessary to differentiate between abolitionists being *anti-racist* and being *anti-slavery*.[34] According to hooks, "Because many 19th century white women's rights advocates were also active in the abolitionist movement, it is often assumed they were antiracist . . . [But] In actuality, most white abolitionists, male and female, though vehement in their anti-slavery protest, were totally opposed to granting social equality to black people."[35] She continues:

> They attacked slavery, not racism . . . That they were not demanding social equality for black people is an indication that they remained committed to white racist supremacy despite their anti-slavery work. While they strongly advocated an end to slavery, they never advocated a change in the racial hierarchy that allowed their caste

ABOLITION AND SUFFRAGE IN THE UNITED STATES 239

status to be higher than that of black women or men. In fact, they wanted that hierarchy to be maintained.[36]

hooks reminds us that at the end of the day, "white women wanted to see no change in the social status of blacks until they were assured that their demands for more rights were met."[37]

While hooks considers white abolitionist racism in more general terms, Davis offers more specific examples. Davis presents the Grimké sisters as positive examples of white women who saw and sought to dismantle the dialectical qualities of sexism and racism as structures of oppression, but she is very critical of the racism of other white women like Elizabeth Cady Stanton. Davis underscores the contradictions of white womanhood and presents Stanton as one example. Emphasizing her class privilege Davis notes, "Elizabeth Cady Stanton's life exhibited all the basic elements, in their most contradictory form, of the middle-class woman's dilemma" (e.g., white middle-class women's intellectual achievements neutralized by marriage and motherhood).[38] Davis is especially critical of Stanton's revisionist history about the roles of Black abolitionist men. Stanton names the white male abolitionists William Lloyd Garrison and Nathaniel P. Rogers as the only men to join the women in the gallery at the 1840 World Anti-Slavery Conventions, but she fails to name the Black male abolitionist Charles Remond. Remond wrote of his choice to refuse his seat at the convention in *Liberator* (October 16, 1840), but Stanton excludes him from her historical account.[39] Davis asserts, "Why the Black male abolitionist Charles Remond is not mentioned in Stanton's description of the events is rather puzzling."[40] She also considers the racism of white abolitionists toward Frederick Douglass' daughter, Rosetta Douglass.[41] Rosetta was admitted to Seward Seminary, a girls' seminary in Rochester, New York, but was formally prohibited from attending classes with white girls by the principal of the school, a white abolitionist woman. Davis laments, "That a white woman associated with the anti-slavery movement could assume a racist posture toward a Black girl in the North reflected a major weakness in the abolitionist campaign—its failure to promote a broad anti-racist consciousness."[42] Returning to the positive example of the Grimké sisters, and also transitioning to the suffrage movement, Davis asserts, "This serious shortcoming, abundantly criticized by the

240 BEAUVOIR AND BELLE

Grimké sisters and others, was unfortunately carried over into the organized movement for women's rights."[43]

Seneca Falls: Significance and Shortcomings

The Seneca Falls Convention (initially called the Woman's Rights Convention) was held at Wesleyan Chapel in Seneca Falls, New York, on July 19–20, 1848.[44] The event is described by many as the first convention with an explicit focus on women's suffrage rights. One of the familiar narratives (versions of which are repeated by Myrdal and Beauvoir) is that women (including Lucretia Mott and Elizabeth Cady Stanton) were denied seats at the World's Anti-Slavery Convention (London, 1840). Then Mott and Stanton worked together to organize the Women's Convention at Seneca Falls eight years later, which launched the women's rights and suffrage movements. Lisa Tetrault troubles this constructed memory in *The Myth of Seneca Falls: Memory and the Women's Suffrage Movement, 1848–1898* (2014). She notes:

> One could anchor the beginning of the women's rights movement in the United States in many events—some before, some after Seneca Falls. One could begin with the Grimké sisters' practical and theoretical defenses of women as public actors in the 1830s. With Black women's resistance to slavery and to the systematic raping of their bodies. With the Lowell Mill textile operatives and their 1834 and 1836 strikes for fair treatment and decent wages . . . Women's rights had many beginnings. And for much of the early to mid-nineteenth century, people commonly invoked a variety of events when they spoke about the origins of women's rights.[45]

Tetrault's analysis of the carefully constructed myth of Seneca Falls (a myth that was created over decades after the actual event) complicates Beauvoir's aforementioned conclusions that women's entire history has been written by men and that women never sought to play a historical role as a sex (TSS 148–149).[46]

Of course, Davis maps out all of these early fights against gender, race, and class oppression, highlighting the significance of the Seneca

Falls Convention and describing its manifesto, the *Declaration of Sentiments*, as a symbol of the first wave of white women's feminism. Adapting language from the *Declaration of Independence*, the *Declaration of Sentiments* states, "We hold these truths to be self-evident; that all men and women are created equal; that they are endowed by their Creator with certain inalienable rights; that among these are life, liberty, and the pursuit of happiness; that to secure these rights governments are instituted, deriving their just powers from the consent of the governed." The document goes on to outline the government's "abuses and usurpations" against women. It declares, "The history of mankind is a history of repeated injuries and usurpation on the part of man toward woman having in direct object the establishment of an absolute tyranny over her." There are also more problematic claims, including the notion that, "He has withheld from her rights which are given to the most ignorant and degraded men—both natives and foreigners."

This articulation of white middle-class women's sense of superiority over "ignorant and degraded" men including "natives and foreigners" suggests that just as the Declaration of Independence did not mean all men, it meant white men—similarly, the Declaration of Sentiments did not mean all women, it meant white women. Acknowledging the import of the meeting and the manifesto, Davis states, "The inestimable importance of the Seneca Falls Declaration was its role as the *articulated consciousness of women's rights* at midcentury."[47] Revisiting the consciousness and contradictions of white middle-class women reflected in the Seneca Falls Declaration, Davis offers the following critique: "as a rigorous consummation of the consciousness of white middle-class women's dilemma, the Declaration all but ignored the predicament of white working-class women, as it ignored the condition of Black women in the South and North alike."[48]

Davis reminds us that in the late 1820s, white working-class women—mill women—"staged 'turn-outs' and strikes, militantly protesting the double oppression they suffered as women and as industrial workers."[49] Put another way, working-class white women were organizing and protesting long before middle-class white women became involved in abolition and suffrage activism. She adds, "By the summer of 1848, when the Seneca Falls Convention took place,

242 BEAUVOIR AND BELLE

conditions in the mills—hardly ideal to begin with—had deteriorated to such an extent that the New England farmers' daughters were fast becoming a minority in the textile labor force."[50]

Davis also expounds on the inattention to Black women's conditions at this historic meeting on women's rights. Black women were not in attendance at the Seneca Falls Convention, and there are no references to them in the relevant documents. She posits, "In light of the organizers' abolitionist involvement, it would seem puzzling that slave women were entirely disregarded."[51] In addition to previous abolition work, Davis reminds us that earlier the Grimké sisters explicitly articulated and critiqued these problematic practices: "The Grimké sisters had previously criticized a number of female anti-slavery societies for ignoring the condition of Black women and for sometimes manifesting blatantly racist prejudices."[52] She traces the continuity of middle-class white women ignoring the plight of Black women going back to abolition efforts and persisting with the fight for suffrage. Davis notes, "As early as 1837 the Grimké sisters chastised the New York Female Anti-Slavery Society for failing to involve Black women in their work . . . The absence was all the more conspicuous in light of their [Black women's] previous contributions to the fight for women's rights."[53] With this in mind, it is disappointing but perhaps not surprising that middle-class white women would increasingly embrace anti-Black, anti-immigrant, and anti-Indigenous sentiments (e.g., against the "ignorant and degraded" men, "natives and foreigners") in the interest of expediency to advance a white women's suffrage agenda decades later.

Recall that Myrdal mentions several men who advocated for both abolition and suffrage, including William Lloyd Garrison, Henry Ward Beecher, Horace Greeley, and Frederick Douglass. Here, I am especially interested in Douglass, who attended the Seneca Falls Convention and was also a signatory to the Declaration of Sentiments. During the convention, Stanton insisted on raising the issue of suffrage while her husband and Mott both opposed. But Douglass stood with Stanton on this issue.[54] Douglass reports on the Women's Right's Convention at Seneca Falls in "The Rights of Women" (1848), a short article published in his anti-slavery paper *The North Star* (one of the few periodicals to

ABOLITION AND SUFFRAGE IN THE UNITED STATES   243

advertise the convention). It seems that Douglass was the only Black person in attendance among the white and mostly female suffragists, and he intervened at a key moment of the convention so that the resolution on women's suffrage would pass.[55] In Douglass' article he argues for equal political rights for men and women and declares, "Our doctrine is that 'right is of no sex.'"[56] He also helped at a Rochester meeting a month later. Davis notes, "During those early days when women's rights was not yet a legitimate cause, when woman suffrage was unfamiliar and unpopular as a demand, Frederick Douglass publicly agitated for the political equality of women."[57]

The Seneca Falls Convention in 1848 would be followed up by other meetings in 1850, including women's rights conventions in Salem, Ohio, and in Worchester, Massachusetts. And, of course, there is the 1851 meeting in Akron, Ohio, where Sojourner Truth is said to have delivered the famous "Ar'n't I a Woman" remarks. While there has been controversy surrounding the words that have been attributed to Truth, several accounts attest that Truth shared experiences from her own life to impact her audience. This lived experience included the forced physical labor she endured (born in New York, where she was enslaved until she escaped in 1826) and her giving birth to several children who were also enslaved, some of whom were held in indentured servitude as late as the 1850s (long after emancipation in New York in 1827).[58]

Davis contextualizes Truth's intervention, "As the only Black woman attending the Akron convention, Sojourner Truth had done what not one other of her timid white sisters was capable of doing"—that is, challenge the male-supremacist logic and weaker-sex arguments that women could not vote because they needed men to aid them in stepping over puddles and getting into carriages.[59] Davis notes how Truth "exposed the class-bias and racism of the new women's movement."[60] She also explicitly criticized Black male patriarchy toward Black women, arguing that Black men's rights should not be prioritized over Black women's rights and asserting "if colored men get their rights, but not colored women get theirs, there will be a bad time about it."[61] Annual national meetings for women's rights continued for the following decade, until the outbreak of the Civil War in 1861.

Suffrage and Suppression: Pitfalls of Expediency Arguments

Now let us consider the suggestion by Myrdal and Beauvoir that white women fought for the freedom of Black men as abolitionists, only to have to suppress the issue of woman's suffrage. Stanton articulates these grievances in an 1865 letter to the editor of the *New York Standard* in which she states, "The representative women [i.e., middle-class white women] of the nation have done their uttermost for the last thirty years to secure the freedom of the negro . . . but now . . . it becomes a serious question whether we had better stand aside and see 'Sambo' walk into the kingdom first."[62] Yes, she did write "Sambo." We find that Stanton is suddenly, if only rhetorically, interested in the plight of Black women when she describes the state of emancipated Black women as another form of slavery. She writes, "In fact, it is better [for Black women] to be the slave of an educated white man, than of a degraded, ignorant black one."[63] It seems that Stanton assumed the "prize" for white women's abolitionist work would be suffrage for white women ahead of Black men and women. Davis describes the letter in this way, "Its indisputably racist ideas indicate that Stanton's understanding of the relationship between the battle for Black Liberation and the struggle for women's rights was, at best, superficial."[64] And hooks offers this insight: "Ardent white women's rights advocates like Elizabeth Cady Stanton who had never before argued for women's rights on a racially imperialistic platform expressed outrage that inferior 'niggers' should be granted the vote while 'superior' white women remained disenfranchised."[65]

Davis repeatedly centers the interconnections among race, class, and gender in the abolition and suffrage movements. It is clear that attention to these interlocking systems of oppression was lacking among most white women advocates for abolition and suffrage, despite explicit articulation of these interconnections by Black women like Truth and even white women like the Grimké sisters. Davis notes, "The leaders of the women's rights movement did not suspect that the enslavement of Black people in the South, the economic exploitation of Northern workers, and the social oppression of women might be systematically related."[66] Despite the limitations of the Seneca Falls Convention and even the explicitly racist contents of Stanton's 1865 letter, there was still

ABOLITION AND SUFFRAGE IN THE UNITED STATES   245

an attempt at suffrage coalition through the American Equal Rights Association formed in 1866, whose leadership included Mott as president with Stanton and Douglass as co-vice presidents.[67] The constitution of the organization stated its aims were to "secure Equal Rights to all American Citizens, especially the right of suffrage irrespective of race, color, or sex." But for Davis, it is clear that Stanton and others "perceived the organization as a means to ensure that Black men would not receive the franchise unless and until white women were also its recipients."[68]

The debates and battles for woman's suffrage would continue for decades. Douglass' ongoing commitments to women's suffrage and rights are expressed in two later speeches, "Give Women Fair Play" (March 1888) and "I Am a Radical Woman Suffrage Man" (May 1888). In the address "Give Women Fair Play" he goes beyond the issue of political rights and asserts that women have the ability and the agency to articulate their own cause, their problems, and the best way for those problems to be remedied. Consequently, men "can neither speak for her, nor vote for her, nor act for her, nor be responsible for her."[69] Douglass adds, "I say of her, as I say of the colored people, 'Give her fair play, and hands off.'"[70] He makes similar claims in "I Am a Radical Woman's Suffrage Man," where he asserts that to help the cause of the woman the man is expected "to get out of the way, to take his obstructive forces of fines of imprisonment and his obstructive usages out of the way, and let woman express her sentiments at the polls and in the government, equally with himself."[71] By this Douglass is not claiming that men should not be involved in or support the women's movement, but rather, he is arguing that men are not to determine *what* women's issues are and *how* they are to be addressed.[72]

To be sure, middle-class white women expressed their expectation for the right to vote with (or ahead of) Black men in a myriad of problematic ways. As Davis points out, "one thing seems clear: their defense of their own interests as white middle-class women—in a frequently egotistical and elitist fashion—exposed the tenuous and superficial nature of their relationship to the postwar campaign for Black equality."[73] Not surprisingly, the American Equal Rights Association dissolved. Douglass made efforts to appeal to white women with "vivid visual imagery [that] demonstrated that the former Black slaves suffered

246 BEAUVOIR AND BELLE

an oppression that was qualitatively and brutally different from the predicament of white middle-class women."[74] Nonetheless, Stanton and Anthony successfully argued for the dissolution of the association. Giddings notes that "The 1869 AERA [American Equal Rights Association] meeting was a contentious one, resulting in the split of the AERA into two suffrage organizations."[75] These two organizations included the National Woman Suffrage Association and the American Woman Suffrage Association. The two later merged to form the National American Woman Suffrage Association in 1890.

Davis is clear that Stanton and Anthony had the experience and resources to make different choices at this historical juncture—both through their experience with abolition and through their interactions with Douglass and others like Ida B. Wells. Wells (a scholar, educator, race woman, and clubwoman) fought against gender and racial oppression using an intersectional approach. She encouraged women to become active in local and national issues through civic organizations. Wells is best known for her anti-lynching journalism and activism, including her publications like *Southern Horrors: Lynch Law in All Its Phases* (1892), *The Red Record* (1865), *Mob Rule in New Orleans* (1900), "Lynch Law in America" (1900), and "Lynching, Our National Crime" (1909)—all of which demonstrate her insights into lynching in America as an issue with intersecting economic, political, racial, and gendered implications. But it is also important to recognize Wells' impactful suffrage work. In 1913 she founded the Alpha Suffrage Club in Chicago—identified by Guy-Sheftall as "the first Black woman suffrage organization, committed to enhancing Black women's civic profile by encouraging them to vote for and help elect Black candidates."[76] She adds, "Ignoring or minimizing the political work and writing of African American women such as Ida Wells-Barnett renders invisible the important ways these women have contributed to a broad range of social justice initiatives, such as the passage of antilynching legislation, the attainment of voting rights for women regardless of race and national origin, and the election of Black officials."[77]

Wells criticized white women suffragists, particularly Susan B. Anthony, for neglecting to publicly acknowledge links between racism and sexism.[78] We get insights into the complexities of Wells' relationship with Anthony in *Crusade for Justice: The Autobiography*

ABOLITION AND SUFFRAGE IN THE UNITED STATES   247

of Ida B. Wells. On the one hand, Wells considered Anthony a friend. She recalls that Anthony fired a secretary who refused to take dictation from her.[79] On the other hand, Wells is clear that she challenged Anthony on her racist expediency tactics. As previously mentioned, Anthony acknowledges that "Frederick Douglass, the ex-slave, was the only man who came to their [Seneca Falls 1848] convention and stood up with them."[80] But Anthony also discloses that she did not want Douglass to attend the Equal Suffrage Association meeting in Atlanta, GA. She tells Wells, "I myself asked Mr. Douglass not to come. I did not want to subject him to humiliation, and I did not want anything to get in the way of bringing the southern white women into our suffrage organization."[81] Anthony also admitted that she declined to aid a group of Black women "in forming a branch of the suffrage association . . . on the ground of that same expediency."[82] Wells informs Anthony that her expediency tactics are wrong, noting, "although she may have made gains for suffrage, she had also confirmed white women in the attitude of segregation."[83] Anthony wrongly assumed that all would change for the better when white women got the right to vote.[84]

Davis notes that this conversation between Wells and Anthony takes place in 1894 and puts it in historical context: "Racism was objectively on the rise during this period and the rights and lives of Black people were at stake. By 1894 the disfranchisement of Black people in the South, the legal system of segregation and the reign of lynch law were already well established."[85] With this in mind, Davis argues, "The increasingly influential 'expediency' argument proposed by Anthony and her colleagues was a feeble justification for the suffragists' indifference to the pressing requirements of the times."[86] The uncamouflaged violence visited upon Black people during the 1890s was often met with expediency arguments or even outright betrayals of democracy by white women suffragists who "might as well have announced that if they, as white women of the middle-class and bourgeoisie, were given the power of the vote, they would rapidly subdue the three main elements of the U.S. working class: Black people, immigrants and the uneducated native white workers."[87]

On a similar note, Giddings explains, "White women, including suffragists who should have been their [Black women's] natural allies, often became their most formidable adversaries. For White suffrage leaders either acquiesced to, or took advantage of, the anti-Black sentiment in the period."[88] White women adapted/adopted white supremacy in an effort to expedite their suffrage. Like Davis, Giddings is clear, "The aim of this strategy was to prove that the enfranchisement of White women would further, rather than impede, the power of a White ruling class that was fearful of Black and immigrant domination."[89] Giddings cites a declaration from the 1893 NAWSA convention:

> Resolved, that without expressing any opinion on the proper qualifications for voting, we call attention to the significant facts that in every State there are more women who can read and write than all negro voters; more American women who can read and write than all foreign voters; so that the enfranchisement of such women would settle the vexed question of rule by illiteracy whether of home-grown or foreign-born production.[90]

White women became more explicit and intentional in separating themselves from Black liberation; in fact, they implicitly and explicitly supported subjugation of others.[91] But there were several pitfalls to this approach. Despite the increase of anti-Black and anti-immigrant positions within white women's organizations, they were still met with sexism. Giddings notes, "White antisuffragists harped on the theme of true womanhood in its many variations."[92] And Davis argues that white women's insistence on an taking oppressive stance toward others actually reinforced their own oppression and was self-defeating. She states,

> As racism developed more durable roots within white women's organizations, so too did the sexist cult of motherhood creep into the very movement whose announced aim was the elimination of male supremacy. The coupling of sexism and racism was mutually strengthening. Having opened its doors to the prevailing racist ideology more widely than ever before, the suffrage movement had opted for an obstacle course which placed its own goal of woman suffrage in continuous jeopardy.[93]

ABOLITION AND SUFFRAGE IN THE UNITED STATES   249

While the issue of suffrage is often framed in terms of white women versus Black men, we must also remember the suffrage work being done by Black women. I have already mentioned Truth and Wells, but there were many more. For example, Mary Ann Shadd Cary (former abolitionist and first Black women to publish a newspaper, *Provincial Freeman*) was asked by the National Colored Labor Union (NCLU) "to address the convention on women's rights and suffrage."[94] Giddings notes that NCLU became stronger on women's rights than white labor unions. She also reminds us of the national work Black women were doing for suffrage: "By the 1900's, Black suffrage clubs were to be found all over the country, including Tuskegee, St. Louis, Los Angeles, Memphis, Boston, Charleston, and New Orleans, and there were state suffrage societies in Delaware, Idaho, Montana, North Dakota, Texas, New York, and Maryland, among others."[95] She adds, "A number of women worked in the recently created suffrage department of the NAACP."[96] And Giddings reminds us that "Harriet Tubman and Frances Ellen Harper continued to address suffrage meetings. So did Mary Church Terrell."[97] She frames Black women's suffrage activism as "one of several flash points at which Black women were confident in their abilities as a group, and they were both prepared and compelled to demand the rights of full citizenship, economically, socially, politically."[98] Rejecting the either/or binary, Giddings reminds us that, "For Black women, suffrage was both a feminist and a racial demand for equality."[99]

It is also worth noting that the white women who pushed aside Black men and women in the interest of expediency and white supremacy eventually circled back to Black women for support. By 1917, there seemed to be more favor for the Anthony Amendment, and white suffragists sought support from Black women. Giddings states, "NAWSA even went to the extraordinary length of taking a stand against lynching in 1917."[100] Black women were justifiably suspicious of white women on the basis of their prior record of racism and explicit expressions of white supremacy. Giddings explains:

> The Black women's suspicions [of white suffragists seeking support] were verified by 1918, the year the Anthony Amendment, with the support of President Wilson, passed the House with the

250   BEAUVOIR AND BELLE

exact two-thirds majority required. Now the suffrage bill had to get through the southern-dominated Senate. At this point, the pretense of racial solidarity was dropped. Immediately after the House vote, the southern racists came out of the woodwork, and White suffragists hoisted their tattered flag of "expediency." Beginning in 1918, several congressmen . . . proposed amendments to the suffrage bill so that only White women would be allowed to vote.[101]

In the end, despite all of the white women suffragists' anti-Black and anti-immigrant politicking and expediency posturing, Southern States still did not support the cause of white woman's suffrage. Davis notes, "When the votes on the Nineteenth Amendment were tallied, the Southern States were still lined up in the opposition camp—and, in fact, almost managed to defeat the amendment."[102]

Conclusion: The Import of a Black Feminist Ideology Rooted in Our Reality

The issues of abolition and suffrage offer historical case studies for the possibilities as well as the problematics of coalitional work across race, class, and gender differences toward a common cause of liberation across difference. This chapter has taken up and troubled Myrdal's and Beauvoir's claims that white women gained political consciousness through their abolitionist efforts before turning to the issue of suffrage, as well as their claims that white women fought for the freedom of Black men through abolition only to have to suppress the issue of woman's suffrage. I have also shown how Myrdal's and Beauvoir's accounts do not consider white abolitionists' and suffragists' racism (anti-Black, anti-immigrant, and anti-Indigenous). It is important to correct the myth of Seneca Falls, the corresponding narrative perpetuated by Myrdal and Beauvoir, and the limits of their aforementioned race/gender and slave/woman analogies. Black women, from Ida B. Wells to Claudia Jones to Angela Davis to bell hooks to Paula Giddings to Deborah King, have been offering counternarratives and correctives to this white feminist myth for decades. As King summarily argues,

ABOLITION AND SUFFRAGE IN THE UNITED STATES   251

In the case of the struggle for suffrage in the nineteenth century again is an instructive example of the complexity of multiple jeopardy and its politics. Initially, there was an alliance of blacks and women for universal suffrage. However, as the campaign ensued, opponents of universal suffrage and of any extension of voting privileges, were successful in transforming the debate into one of whom should receive the vote—women or black males. Many prominent white suffragists . . . abandoned the alliance and demanded a 'women only' enfranchisement . . . More damning however, were their politics of expediency. They cooperated with avowed racists in order to gain the southern vote and liberally used racial slurs and epithets arguing that white women's superior character and intellect made them more deserving of the right to vote than blacks, Native Americans, and Eastern Europeans and Asian immigrants.[103]

Against all of these odds, Black women continued to organize and fight for universal suffrage. Jones, Davis, Giddings, and King all emphasize Black women's multifaceted approach to identity and oppression that takes seriously the interconnections of race, class, and gender in the battles for abolition and suffrage. Again, it is worth quoting King at length:

> The basis of *our feminist ideology is rooted in our reality*. To the extent that the adherents of any one ideology insist on separatist organizational forms, assert the fundamental nature of any one oppression, and demand total cognitive, affective, and behavioral commitment, that ideology and its practitioners exclude black women and the realities of our lives . . . It is in confrontation with multiple jeopardy that black women define and sustain a multiple consciousness essential for our liberation, of which feminist consciousness is an integral part.[104]

I have highlighted more expansive counternarratives to those offered by Myrdal and Beauvoir by turning our attention to Wells, Jones, Davis, hooks, Giddings, and King—each of whom is attentive to the intersections of gender, race, and class in relationship to abolition and suffrage. I have demonstrated that a more nuanced and inclusive

252   BEAUVOIR AND BELLE

understanding of the abolition and suffrage movements in the United States is made possible when we shift from the narrowness of Myrdal's and Beauvoir's analogical approach (i.e., their analogizing between the conditions of the white middle-class woman and the conditions of the enslaved Black man) to the intersectional approaches offered by Wells, Jones, Davis, hooks, Giddings, and King (i.e., their attention to the intersections of gender, race, and class with abolition and suffrage). Thus, this chapter is also an elaboration and extension of my argument problematizing analogies that have sought to and/or functioned to marginalize and erase the Black women's experiences and activism in the dominant white-woman-washed narratives about slavery, abolition, and suffrage.

Notes

1. Alva Myrdal, "A Parallel to the Negro Problem" (1944), appendix 5 in Gunnar Myrdal, *An American Dilemma: The Negro Problem in Modern Democracy*, vol. 2 (New York: Routledge, 1944, 2017), 1075. (Hereafter A. Myrdal 1944).
2. A. Myrdal 1944, 1075.
3. A. Myrdal 1944, 1075.
4. A. Myrdal 1944, 1075–1076.
5. A. Myrdal 1944, 1076.
6. Beauvoir incorrectly dates the Seneca Falls Convention on July 18, 1840 (TSS 144), but as the translators note, it actually took place July 19–20, 1848.
7. In *Women, Race, and Class* (New York: Vintage Books, 1981), Angela Davis notes that *Uncle Tom's Cabin* was "One of the most popular pieces of abolitionist literature" and even agrees that it "rallied vast numbers of people—and more women than ever before—to the anti-slavery cause," 27. (Hereafter Davis 1981.) But she also offers a very different perspective on the text and its multiple shortcomings. For Davis, "the enormous influence her [Stowe's] book enjoyed cannot compensate for its utter distortion of slave life" (Davis 1981, 27). Davis explains that the text is "pervaded with assumptions of both Black and female inferiority" (Davis 1981, 31). But beyond these issues, "The glaring contradiction between the reactionary content and the progressive appeal of *Uncle Tom's Cabin* was not

ABOLITION AND SUFFRAGE IN THE UNITED STATES 253

so much a flaw in the author's individual perspective as a reflection of the contradictory nature of [white] women's status in the nineteenth century" (Davis 1981, 31). Toni Morrison also takes on this text in her published Harvard lectures *The Origin of Others* (Cambridge, MA: Harvard University Press, 2017). (Hereafter Morrison 2017.) In the chapter titled "Romancing Slavery," Morrison explains, "Control, benign or rapacious, may ultimately not be necessary. See? Says Harriett Beecher Stowe to her (white) readers. Calm down, she says. Slaves control themselves. Don't be afraid. Negroes only want to serve. The slave's natural instinct, she implies, is toward kindness—an instinct that is disrupted only by vicious whites who, like Simon Legree (significantly, a Northerner by birth), threaten and abuse them. The sense of fear and disdain that white people may have, one that encourages brutality, is, she implies, unwarranted. Almost. Almost. Yet there are in *Uncle Tom's Cabin* signs of Stowe's own fear, literary protection, as it were" (Morrison 2017, 9–10). Morrison continues (citing passages from the text), "The natural beauty Stowe is at pains to describe is cultivated, welcoming, seductive, and excessive" and adds, "These are carefully demarcated passages intended to quiet the fearful white reader" (Morrison 2017, 11 and 13). Morrison is clear, "Harriet Beecher Stowe did not write Uncle Tom's Cabin for Tom, Aunt Chloe, or any black people to read. Her contemporary readership was white people, those who needed, wanted, or could relish the romance [of slavery]" (Morrison 2017, 13–14).

8. Beauvoir explains, "For the most part, women resign themselves to their lot without attempting any action; those who did try to change attempted to overcome their singularity . . . When they intervened in world affairs, it was in concert with men and from a masculine point of view" (TSS 149).

9. Claudia Jones, "An End to the Problem of the Neglect of the Negro Woman," *Political Affairs: A Magazine Devoted to the Theory and Practice of Marxism-Leninism* 28, no. 6 (June 1949): 15. (Hereafter Jones 1949.) She also discusses strategies used to divide Black and white women's coalitions, offering this example, "The suffragists, during their first jailings were purposely placed on cots next to Negro prostitutes to 'humiliate' them" (Jones 1949, 15).

10. Jones 1949, 15.

11. With the exception of Paula Giddings, most of these writers are not historians in the traditional sense, but each of them offers theoretical frameworks that have significantly shaped how these historical events are perceived and analyzed. For more historical accounts, see: Eleanor Flexner and Ellen Fitzpatrick, *Century of Struggle: The Woman's Rights Movement in the United States* (Cambridge, MA: Harvard University Press, 1959);

254 BEAUVOIR AND BELLE

Shirley J. Yee, *Black Women Abolitionists: A Study in Activism, 1825–1860* (Knoxville: University of Tennessee Press, 1992); Ann D. Gordon with Bettye Collier-Thomas, eds., *African American Women and the Vote, 1837–1965* (Amherst: University of Massachusetts Press, 1997); Julie Roy Jeffery, *The Great Silent Army of Abolition: Ordinary Women in the Antislavery Movement* (Chapel Hill: University of North Carolina Press, 1998); Rosalyn Terborg-Penn, *African American Women and the Struggle for the Vote, 1850–1920* (Bloomington: Indiana University Press, 1998); Lisa Tetrault, *The Myth of Seneca Falls: Memory and the Woman's Suffrage Movement, 1848–1898* (Chapel Hill: University of North Carolina Press, 2014); Ann D. Gordon with Bettye Collier-Thomas, eds., *African American Women and the Vote, 1837–1965* (Amherst: University of Massachusetts Press, 1997); and Martha S. Jones, *Vanguard: How Black Women Broke Barriers, Won the Vote, and Insisted on Equality for All* (New York: Basic Books, 2020).

12. Davis 1981, 39. See Eleanor Flexner, *Century of Struggle: The Women's Rights Movement in the US* (New York: Atheneum, 1973). Shirley Chen notes that Eleanor Flexner was involved in the Communist Party before writing her book about women's suffrage in *"'To Work, Write, Sing and Fight for Women's Liberation': Proto-Feminist Currents in the American Left, 1946–1961"* (MA thesis, University of Michigan, 2011, 76). (Hereafter Chen 2011.) Flexner had no graduate training or academic background (Chen 2011, 95). She adds, "Tellingly, by the 1970s, Flexner also grew disillusioned with the women's movement due to the 'extraordinary blind spot that the 'lib' crowd is developing where history is concerned—*our* history, women's history. In her eyes, these younger radical feminists were consumed with theoretical analyses and had neglected to give credit to the very real struggles that women before them had fought for and won" (Chen 2011, 99–100.) See Flexner letter to Gerda Lerner, February 8, 1971, Gerda Lerner papers, Schlesinger Library.

13. Deborah King, "Multiple Jeopardy, Multiple Consciousness: The Context of a Black Feminist Ideology," *Signs: Journal of Women in Culture and Society* 14, no. 1 (1988): 44. (Hereafter King 1988.)

14. King 1988, 44.

15. bell hooks, *Ain't I a Woman: Black Women and Feminism* (Boston: South End Press, 1981), 126. (Hereafter hooks 1981.)

16. hooks 1981, 126.

17. "In 1831, the year of Nat Turner's revolt, the organized abolitionist movement was born," (Davis 1981, 32–33).

18. Davis 1981, 34.

ABOLITION AND SUFFRAGE IN THE UNITED STATES   255

19. Davis 1981, 34.
20. Davis 1981, 37. We might hear echoes of Beauvoir's analysis in *The Second Sex* when Davis asserts, "As workers, [white] women had at least enjoyed economic equality, but as wives, they were destined to become appendages to their men, servants to their husbands. As mothers, they would be defined as passive vehicles for the replenishment of human life. The situation of the white housewife was full of contradictions" (Davis 1981, 32).
21. Davis 1981, 36.
22. Davis 1981, 37–38.
23. They were allies insofar as they "most consistently linked the issue of slavery to the oppression of women," though (again) with a coalitional rather than analogical approach (Davis 1981, 40).
24. She notes, "on July 28, 1837, the Council of Congregationalist Ministers of Massachusetts issued a pastoral letter severely chastising them for engaging in activities which actively subverted women's divinely ordained role" (Davis 1981, 41). She adds, "some of the leading men of the abolitionist campaign claimed that the issue of women's rights would confuse and alienate those who were solely concerned about the defeat of slavery" (Davis 1981, 42).
25. Davis 1981, 42.
26. Davis 1981, 43.
27. Davis 1981, 44.
28. Davis 1981, 44. Davis notes that they also perceived the import of class issues. Sarah Grimké acknowledged plight of poor women (Davis, WRC 57). And Angelina Grimké, "In her speech ['Address to the Soldiers of Our Second Revolution'] she proposed a radical theory and practice which could have been realized through an alliance embracing labor, Black people, and women" (Davis, WRC 68–69) . See also Gerda Lerner, *The Grimké Sisters from South Carolina: Pioneers for Woman's Rights and Abolition* (New York: Schocken Books, 1971).
29. Paula Giddings, *When and Where I Enter: The Impact of Black Women on Race* (New York: Harper Collins, 1984), 42–43 (Emphasis original.) (Hereafter Giddings 1984.)
30. Giddings 1984, 43. (Emphasis original.)
31. Giddings 1984, 54.
32. Giddings 1984, 55.
33. Giddings 1984, 55. Giddings offers even more context, "All Black women abolitionists (and most of the leading Black male abolitionists) were feminists. But when it came to a question of priorities, race, for most of them, came first" (Giddings 1984, 55).

256 BEAUVOIR AND BELLE

34. It is worth noting that hooks and others have been using the term "anti-racist" for decades. It has become part of the popular lexicon again with public uptake of the more recent book: Ibram X. Kendi, *How to Be An Antiracist* (New York: One World, 2019).

35. hooks 1981, 124.

36. hooks 1981, 125.

37. hooks 1981, 126.

38. Davis 1981, 49.

39. Davis 1981, 48.

40. Davis 1981, 48.

41. Rosetta Douglass went on to become a teacher, activist, and founding member of the National Association for Colored Women.

42. Davis 1981, 59.

43. Davis 1981, 59.

44. White women organizers of the Convention included Elizabeth Cady Stanton, Lucretia Mott, Mary M'Clintock, Martha Coffin Wright, and Jane Hunt.

45. Lisa Tetrault, *The Myth of Seneca Falls: Memory and the Women's Suffrage Movement, 1848–1898* (Chapel Hill: University of North Carolina Press, 2014), 5. (Hereafter Tetrault 2014.)

46. Beauvoir explains, "Never did women form a separate caste: and in reality they never sought to play a role in history as a sex . . . For the most part, women resign themselves to their lot without attempting any action; those who did try to change attempted to overcome their singularity . . . When they intervened in world affairs, it was in concert with men and from a masculine point of view" (TSS 149). Tetrault "locates the origins of the Seneca Falls story in the post-Civil War years, some twenty to thirty years after the actual meeting, arising from the messy, contentious world of post-Civil War politics" and "examines the consequences of this development for the women's rights movement (Tetrault 2014, 3). And in her essay "Discrimination Against Afro-American Women in the Women's Movement, 1830–1920," in *The Afro-American Woman: Struggles and Images*, ed. Sharon Harley and Rosalyn Terborg-Penn (Baltimore, MD: Black Classic Press, 1997) Rosalyn Terborg-Penn notes, "Furthermore, in the *History of Woman Suffrage*, volume six, editor Ida Husted Harper included only passing reference to the role of black women in the movement from 1900 to 1920. The historical fallacy has been perpetuated by feminists in the 1960s and 1970s as well. In repeating what history has taught them, they have assumed that black women heretofore have been uninterested in women's rights issues. In describing the current

ABOLITION AND SUFFRAGE IN THE UNITED STATES 257

participation of black women in the feminist struggle as a recent development or in describing black women merely as objects of discrimination in the women's movement or in neglecting the participation of black women entirely, these feminist writers grossly distort reality" (Terborg-Penn 1997, 27).

47. Davis 1981, 53. (Emphasis original.)
48. Davis 1981, 54.
49. Davis 1981, 54–55.
50. Davis 1981, 55. They were being replaced by "immigrant women who, like their fathers, brothers and husbands, were becoming the industrial proletariat of the nation. These [immigrant] women—unlike their predecessors, whose families owned land—had nothing to rely upon but their labor power. When they resisted, they were fighting for their right to survive" (Davis 1981, 55).
51. Davis 1981, 57.
52. Davis 1981, 57.
53. Davis 1981, 58.
54. Davis notes, "Frederick Douglass was the only prominent figure who agreed that the convention should call for women's right to vote" (Davis 1981, 50).
55. Beverly Guy-Sheftall, *Words of Fire: An Anthology of African American Feminist Thought* (New York: The New Press, 1995), 4. There are not any Black women in attendance on record.
56. See *Traps: African American Men on Gender and Sexuality*, ed. Beverly Guy-Sheftall and Rudolph Byrd (Bloomington: Indiana University Press, 2001), 28. (Hereafter Douglass 2001.) Despite his strong support of women's political rights, he would eventually part ways with white feminists due to disagreements about the order of priorities regarding race and gender. Angela Davis has noted that Susan B. Anthony "pushed Douglass aside for the sake of recruiting white Southern women into the movement for woman suffrage" and "she refused to support the efforts of several Black women who wanted to form a branch of the suffrage association" (Davis 1981, 111). Davis later asks, "How could Susan B. Anthony claim to believe in human rights and political equality and at the same time counsel the members of her organization to remain silent on the issue of racism?" (Davis 1981, 121).
57. Davis 1981, 51.
58. Nell Irvin Painter has framed and theorized much of the controversy surrounding the problematic images and representations of Truth by figures such as Olive Gilbert and Frances Titus (publishing editions of her

258 BEAUVOIR AND BELLE

Narrative) as well as Harriet Beecher Stowe and Frances Dana Gage, who published essays appropriating Truth for their own purposes. See Nell Painter, "Sojourner Truth in Life and Memory: Writing the Biography of and American Exotic," *Gender and History* 2 (1990): 3–19. (Hereafter Painter 1990.) *Sojourner Truth: A Life, A Symbol* (New York: W. W. Norton and Company, 1997); and her "Introduction," in *Narrative of Sojourner Truth* (New York: Penguin Classics, 1998), vii–xx. *Narrative of Sojourner Truth* (New York: Penguin Classics, 1998); Harriett Beecher Stowe, "Libyan Sibyl," *Atlantic Monthly* 6, no. 66 (April 1863): 473–481.

59. Davis 1981, 61.

60. Davis 1981, 63.

61. Sojourner Truth, "When Woman Gets Her Rights Man Will Be Right" (Guy Sheftall 1995, 37). Kimberlé Crenshaw references Truth in her article "Demarginalizing the Intersection of Race and Sex: A Black Feminist Critique of Antidiscrimination Doctrine, Feminist Theory and Antiracist Politics" (*University of Chicago Legal Forum* 139, no. 1 (1989): article 1, 139–167. (Hereafter Demarginalizing).

62. Cited by Davis 1981, 70.

63. Cited by Davis 1981, 70.

64. Davis 1981, 71.

65. hooks 1981, 127. "At the beginning of the 20th century, white women suffragists were eager to advance their own cause at the expense of black people" (hooks 1981, 127).

66. Davis 1981 66.

67. Davis 1981 75.

68. Davis 1981 75.

69. Douglass 2001, 30.

70. Douglass 2001, 30.

71. Douglass 2001, 40.

72. We can certainly celebrate Douglass' strong stand for women's rights, but there is no mention of the particular situation of Black women or the contributions of Black women to women's suffrage activism here. Furthermore, in these speeches the conditions of women are either compared to or contrasted with the conditions of slavery or of "the Negro" in a way that erases Black women from the category of "woman" and the category of "Negro." His arguments for women's equality, rights, and suffrage present racism and sexism as related but separate systems of oppression. He does not emphasize the ways that these systems work together, mutually reinforce one another, and present unique issues for Black women who experience both simultaneously and differently than

ABOLITION AND SUFFRAGE IN THE UNITED STATES 259

white women and/or Black men. In fact, there is no explicit mention of Black women in the "Rights of Women" article or the later speeches. And Brittany Cooper has pointed out in *Beyond Respectability: The Intellectual Though of Race Women* (Urbana: University of Illinois Press, 2017), "Douglass's relationship to Black women intellectuals was not uncomplicated. Despite his relationships, he acted as a racial gatekeeper for women seeking racial leadership" (Cooper 2017, 61).

73. Davis 1981, 76.
74. Davis 1981, 82.
75. Giddings 1984, 67.
76. Beverly Guy-Sheftall, "1909–1914: The Black Public Intellectual," in *Four Hundred Souls: A Community History of African America, 1619–2019*, ed. Ibram X. Kendi and Keisha N. Blain (New York: One World, 2021), 276. She adds, "By 1916, the Alpha Suffrage Club had nearly two hundred members and published a newsletter entitled The Alpha Suffrage Record," page 276. (Hereafter Guy-Sheftall 2021.)
77. Guy-Sheftall 2021, 276–277. She adds, "Black freedom struggles and women's liberation movements since then would not have been possible without the courageous and visionary leadership of Ida Wells-Barnett and the brilliant strategizing of women's organization such as the Alpha Suffrage Club in the early twentieth century" (Guy-Sheftall 2021, 277).
78. Angela Davis explains: "Wells' admiration for Anthony's individual stance against racism was undeniable . . . But she unhesitatingly criticized her white sister for failing to make her personal fight against racism a public issue of the suffrage movement" (Davis 1981, 111).
79. Ida B. Wells, *Crusade for Justice, The Autobiography of Ida B. Wells*, ed. Alfreda M. Duster (Chicago: University of Chicago Press, 2020). (Hereafter Wells 2020.) The secretary told Anthony, "It is all right for you, Miss Anthony, to treat Negros as equals, but I refuse to take dictation from a colored woman" (Wells 2020, 229).
80. Wells 2020, 229.
81. Wells 2020, 230.
82. Wells 2020, 230.
83. Wells 2020, 230.
84. Wells disagreed, asserting, "Knowing women as I do, and their petty outlook on life, although I believe that it is right that they should have the vote, I do not believe that the exercise of the vote is going to change women's nature nor the political situation" (Wells 2020, 230).
85. Davis 1981, 112.

260 BEAUVOIR AND BELLE

86. Davis 1981, 112. "However racist these early postures of the women's movement may seem, it was not until the last decade of the nineteenth century that the woman suffrage campaign began to definitively accept the fatal embrace of white supremacy" (Davis 1981, 115).
87. Davis 1981, 116.
88. Giddings 1984, 123.
89. Giddings 1984, 124.
90. Giddings 1984, 124
91. 1899 NAWSA convention in Grand Rapids, MI—"It was at that convention that Anthony helped put the NAWSA on record as saying that woman suffrage and the Black question were completely separate causes" (Giddings 1984, 127). Also, "In 1903, again in deference to southern delegates, a NAWSA convention recognized the principle of states' rights by allowing individual state affiliates to determine their own qualifications for membership" (Giddings 1984, 127). There were attempts to segregate a suffrage march in 1913 and put the Black women (including Wells and the Alpha Suffrage Club) in the rear of the march. But Wells got into line with white women anyway (Giddings 1984, 127–128).
92. Giddings 1984, 119.
93. Davis 1981, 122.
94. Giddings 1984, 69. Mary Ann Shadd Cary was a student at Howard Law School by 1870. "In 1871, Cary tested her case and she successfully registered to vote, becoming one of the few women to do so in the period" (Giddings 1984, 71). For more on Mary Ann Shad Cary, see *Mary Ann Shad Cary: The Black Press and Protest in the Nineteenth Century* by Jane Rhodes (Bloomington: Indiana University Press, 1998 and more recently, *Mary Ann Shad Cary: Essential Writings of a Nineteenth Century Black Radical Feminist*, edited by Nneka D. Dennie (Oxford: Oxford University Press, 2023).
95. Giddings 1984, 129.
96. Giddings 1984, 129–130.
97. Giddings 1984, 129–130.
98. Giddings 1984, 131.
99. Giddings 1984, 159.
100. Giddings 1984, 159
101. Giddings 1984, 159.
102. Davis 1981, 148.
103. King 1988, 58–59.
104. King 1988, 71–72. (Emphasis added.)

PART III

FRAMEWORKS BEYOND THE BLACK/WHITE BINARY

8

The Coloniality of Gender and the Other Others

"The category of *Other* is as original as consciousness itself"

Throughout *The Second Sex* (1949), Simone de Beauvoir offers an extensive analysis of the myriad ways in which woman is situated as "Other."[1] This analysis includes not only her critiques of the limits of biology, psychoanalysis, and historical materialism (which for her do not offer an adequate account of woman's situation as Other) but also her own extensive gathering of the history, facts, and myths that she asserts have contributed to situating woman as Other. She argues that a more accurate account of woman's situation as Other requires an existential analysis. Recall that Beauvoir presents woman as "Other" early on in the introduction to *The Second Sex*, where she describes *Otherness* as an "original category" and *alterity* as a "fundamental category" of human thought (TSS 6). Focusing on white men and white women (but not explicitly naming whiteness), Beauvoir contrasts their relationship to and their existential statuses with one another, stating, "She [white woman] is determined and differentiated in relation to [white] man, while he is not in relation to her; she is the inessential in front of the essential. He is the Subject; he is the Absolute. She is the Other" (TSS 6).[2]

So, for Beauvoir, white woman is determined and differentiated in relationship to white man. She is rendered inessential, object, and Other. But white man is *not* determined and differentiated in relationship to white woman. He is *not* inessential, object, and Other. Rather, he is essential, Subject, Absolute, Self. It is worth noting that these contrasting situations are not limited to relations between the sexes,

Beauvoir and Belle. Kathryn Sophia Belle, Oxford University Press. © Oxford University Press 2024.
DOI: 10.1093/oso/9780197660195.003.0009

264 BEAUVOIR AND BELLE

and these differential categories are not exclusively gendered. Beauvoir asserts:

> The category of *Other* is as original as consciousness itself. The duality between Self and Other can be found in the most primitive societies, in the most ancient mythologies; this division did not always fall into the category of the division of the sexes, it was not based on an empirical given: this comes out in works like Granet's on Chinese thought, and Dumézil's on India and Rome ... [A]lterity is the fundamental category of human thought. No group ever defines itself as One without immediately setting up the Other opposite itself. (TSS 6, emphasis original)[3]

Put another way, the Self/Other and One/Other dynamic in human relationships (or relationships between consciousnesses) and group interactions have a long history that is not unique to white woman and white man. Here Beauvoir points to this dynamic in what she calls primitive societies and ancient mythologies. She also mentions Chinese thought, India, and Rome. But for Beauvoir, the main difference with the dynamic between white woman and white man (in contrast to the dynamics between other groups) has to do in part with reciprocity, or the lack thereof.[4]

Beauvoir posits that if, following Hegel, "a fundamental hostility to any other consciousness is found in consciousness itself; the subject posits itself only in opposition; it asserts itself as the essential and sets up the other as inessential, as the object" (TSS 7). She continues, "But the other consciousness has an opposing reciprocal claim: traveling, a local is shocked to realize that in neighboring countries locals view him as a foreigner; between villages, clans, nations, and classes there are wars, potlatches, agreements, treaties, and struggles that remove the absolute meaning from the idea of the *Other* and bring out its relativity; whether one likes it or not, individuals and groups have no choice but to recognize the reciprocity of their relation" (TSS 7). Again, for Beauvoir, one difference in dynamics between the white man and the white woman, versus other groups of subjects/objects, essentials/inessentials, absolutes/others, is about relativity and reciprocity. She asks, "How is it, then, that between the sexes this reciprocity has not

THE COLONIALITY OF GENDER AND THE OTHER OTHERS   265

been put forward, that one of the terms has been asserted as the only essential one, denying any relativity in regard to its correlative, defining the latter as pure alterity? Why do [white] women not contest male sovereignty?" (TSS 7). She then asserts, "No subject posits itself spontaneously and at once as the inessential from the outset; it is not the Other who, defining itself as Other, defines the One; the Other is posited as Other by the One positing itself as the One. But in order for the Other not to turn into the One, the Other has to submit to this foreign point of view. Where does this submission in [white] woman come from?" (TSS 7).

Of course, Beauvoir gives several additional examples of other Others: "For the native of a country inhabitants of other countries are viewed as 'foreigners'; Jews are the 'others' for anti-Semites, blacks for racist Americans, indigenous people for colonists, proletarians for the propertied classes" (TSS 6).[5] I am calling attention to the situation and status of the other Others that appear and/or are disappeared in *The Second Sex*, and that are often overlooked or disregarded by some of her readers.[6] It is not that Beauvoir is completely oblivious to these nuances. For example, much later in the text (in "The Woman in Love" chapter), when discussing the adolescent girl's wish to identify with the male, she notes, "it is not the individuality of one man or another that seduces her; she is in love with man in general" (TSS 684). But then Beauvoir offers several qualifiers concerning the race, class, and even colonial status of this "man in general":

> Of course, the man must belong to the same class and the same race as her own: *the privilege of sex works only within this framework*; for him to be a demigod, he must obviously be a human being first; for the daughter of a colonial officer, the native is not a man; if the young girl gives herself to an "inferior," she is trying to degrade herself because she does not think she is worthy of love. (TSS 664, emphasis added)

Here we see that Beauvoir is very much aware that the dynamics of race, class, gender, and colonial status are operative in interpersonal (and I would add social and political) relationships. She is quite explicit about the non-human, non-man, and inferior status assigned to

266 BEAUVOIR AND BELLE

the "native" (male). But these insights that show up in rare moments of the text are not applied evenly across the text. They are acknowledged and then systematically (or perhaps carelessly) ignored. And, of course, Black women and other Women of Color remain absent from the discussion and analysis represented by this blunt example of the (white) girl who can only really be in love with a white man of the same class and colonial status as her own without degrading herself.[7]

In this chapter (as with earlier chapters), I am interested in both critical and positive readings of *The Second Sex*. I go beyond often cited white feminist approaches and appropriations in an effort to disrupt the typical readings of this figure and text that avoid and/or defend problematic issues operating at the intersections of race, colonialism, religion, culture, gender, and so on. I examine what I will refer to as the other Others that appear in *The Second Sex* but are often overlooked and/or disregarded by many readers. More specifically, I consider how orientalism, the colonial gaze, and the coloniality of gender contribute to Beauvoir's problematic representations of Indians, Asians (she uses the term "Orientals"), Arabs, and Muslims in *The Second Sex*, on the one hand, as well as what Stephanie Rivera Berruz identifies as the imperceptibility of Latinas in this text, on the other hand. I also consider the coloniality of gender and the denial of the status of "man" and "woman" to the colonized, on the one hand, as well as the imposition of Western sex/gender categories in contexts in which they do not actually apply, on the other hand. The chapter is presented in five sections.

In the first section, "The Limits of Biology, Psychoanalysis, and Historical Materialism," I explore Beauvoir's insistence on an existential analysis that goes beyond the limits of biology, psychoanalysis, and historical materialism and her claim that these latter approaches to "woman" and her situation as Other are not sufficient. In the second section, "Problematic Historical Narratives: Perpetual Primitive Past in Present," I examine Beauvoir's grand historical narratives about the oppression of the white Western woman and juxtapose them with her problematic claims about Indians, Asians, Arabs, and Muslims— terms that at times seem to be used interchangeably. I argue that when Beauvoir explicitly takes up non-white, non-Western women in the text, this uptake is often presented through a colonial gaze and

THE COLONIALITY OF GENDER AND THE OTHER OTHERS   267

imaginary that seeks to lock these other Others into a perpetual primitive past, even in her present moment. In the third section, "Orientalism, Colonialism, Asian Female-ness, and the Imperceptibility of Latinas," I turn to insightful analyses of Beauvoir presented by Sally Markowitz (who critiques her orientalism) and Alia Al-Saji (who critiques her colonial tourist gaze and colonial dissonance). Next, I explore Kyoo Lee's more generous readings and productive appropriations of Beauvoir for her own examination of "Asian woman-ness" and Asian female stereotypes. I also takes seriously Stephanie Rivera Berruz's critiques of *The Second Sex* and what she identifies as the "imperceptibility of Latinas" in that text, before turning to Mariana Ortega, who presents examples of Latina feminists who have been influenced by Beauvoir's existentialism and phenomenology.

Although Beauvoir analogizes and contrasts woman's oppression with colonial oppression, outside of the aforementioned colonial "woman in love" example, she does not really emphasize colonialism as a core contributing factor in the conceptions of gender and gender oppression in *The Second Sex*. In the final two sections of the chapter, I turn to the counter-narratives offered by María Lugones' insightful account of the coloniality of gender and the importance of decolonial feminisms, as well as Oyèrónké Oyewùmí's critical analysis of colonialism and gender impositions from the West. In section four, "The Coloniality of Gender and Decolonial Feminisms," I argue that Beauvoir does not offer an account of the impact of colonialism on gender formation and gender oppression, nor does she reflect critically on her own colonial subjectivity or the condescending colonial gaze that undergirds her grand historical narratives and analogical approaches to various systems of oppression. Although Lugones does not explicitly name Beauvoir, I argue that her concept of the coloniality of gender, her critiques of white feminist indifference to Women of Color, and her call for decolonial feminism all have implications for the limits and problematics of *The Second Sex*. Finally, in section five, "The Invention of Women and the Imposition of Western Gender Categories," I take up Oyèrónké Oyewùmí's examination of the imposition of Western gender categories onto Yorùbá discourse. As with Lugones' insights explored in the section that precedes it, in this section

268   BEAUVOIR AND BELLE

I argue that Oyewùmí's critiques of Western feminist assumptions about gender and sex difference are applicable to Beauvoir's *The Second Sex*.

The Limits of Biology, Psychoanalysis, and Historical Materialism

In Volume 1 of *The Second Sex*, Beauvoir explores the "great historical defeat of the female sex," which is attributed in part to new tools disrupting the gendered division of labor, the domination of men, paternal rights replacing maternal rights, and the advent of patriarchal family structures founded on private property. In the opening chapters of the text, Beauvoir offers observations about biology and psychoanalysis, arguing that neither offers adequate answers to the question of why woman is situated as Other. Beginning with biology, Beauvoir examines body as situation, woman's "enslavement" to the species through procreation, and the ways that the body is subjected to various taboos and laws. For her, it is not through the biological body, but rather through social impositions upon the body, that "the subject gains consciousness of and accomplishes himself" (TSS 46–47). Part of the point Beauvoir is making is that biology does not determine primacy and physiology cannot ground values (TSS 47).[8] Again, a biological account is not sufficient insofar as "biology alone cannot provide an answer to the question that concerns us: why is woman the *Other*?" (TSS 48).[9] With this in mind she charts out an alternative course of inquiry, "Thus we will clarify the biological data by examining them in light of ontological economic, social, and psychological contexts" (TSS 48).

For Beauvoir, psychoanalysis is also insufficient. She notes, "psychoanalysts in particular define man as a human being and woman as a female: every time she acts like a human being, the woman is said to be imitating the male" (TSS 60). She asserts, "For us woman is defined as a human being in search of values within a world of values, a world where it is indispensable to understand the economic and social structure" (TSS 61). In addition to biology and psychoanalysis, she argues that Engels' historical materialism also has its limits. While it

THE COLONIALITY OF GENDER AND THE OTHER OTHERS   269

may be helpful to show how "private property appears" and the corresponding "great historical defeat of the female sex" (TSS 63), Beauvoir cautions that "it is impossible to *deduce* woman's oppression from private property" (TSS 65). Using the inclusive word "we," she asserts, "So we reject Freud's sexual monism and Engles' economic monism for the same reason" (TSS 68). Beauvoir does not to altogether reject biology, psychoanalysis, and historical materialism. Rather, for her, these accounts tell an incomplete story that is made more complete with existentialism.

Thus, an existential analysis is required to go beyond these limits. Beauvoir argues, "Underlying the personal emotional conflicts [psychoanalysis] as well as the economic history of humanity [historical materialism] there is an existential infrastructure that alone makes it possible to understand in its unity the unique form that is a life" (TSS 68). She explains, "To discover woman, we will not reject certain contributions of biology, psychoanalysis, or historical materialism: but we will consider that the body, sexual life, and technology exist concretely for man only insofar as he grasps them from the overall perspective of existence" (TSS 68). This marks a shift from Volume 1, Part 1: "Destiny" to Volume 1, Part 2: "History." But before turning my attention to "History" in the text, I want to point to problematic claims about "Indian tribes" that begin in the "Biological Data" chapter and continue in later parts of the text.

Problematic Historical Narratives: Perpetual Primitive Past in Present

In her "Biological Data" chapter, Beauvoir references "Indian tribes" and remarks in passing that, "If customs desire—as in some Indian tribes—that girls choose husbands, or if it is the father who decides on the marriages, the male's sexual aggressiveness does not grant him any initiative, any privilege" (TSS 48). Although she is making the case for putting biological data (if male sexual aggressiveness is to be counted as biological data) *in context* (i.e., "clarifying the biological data by examining them in light of ontological economic, social, and psychological context"), this is one of several passing references

270 BEAUVOIR AND BELLE

to "Indian tribes" offered by Beauvoir *without context*. For example, it is not always clear what "Indian tribes" she has in mind. In some cases she seems to be talking about people in India, and in other cases she seems to be referencing Indigenous people in the United States. She seems not to know (or not to care) that she is presenting "Indian tribes" in non-distinct ways, blurring and collapsing different peoples, places, and times.

Later in the text Beauvoir discusses women's and men's roles in clans, society, agriculture, and procreation—as well as their connections to land and to property. This is often presented as a grand historical narrative that looks back at non-specified "primitives" across centuries of history. There are several instances when Beauvoir shifts from general claims about "primitives" to specific examples of groups that she deems to be perpetually primitive. That is, she represents some groups and their behaviors as primitive both historically and in her present moment (i.e., in the mid-twentieth century, when she is writing this book). For example, Beauvoir asserts, "Such beliefs [about the feminine body as a mysterious source of life] are *still alive today* among numerous Indian, Australian, and Polynesian tribes, and become all the more important as they match the practical interests of the collectivity" (TSS 78, emphasis added). In a footnote she elaborates, "For the Bhantas of India, or in Uganda, a sterile woman is considered dangerous for gardens . . . In India of yore, naked women pushed the plow through the field at night. Indians along the Orinoco left the sowing and planting to the women" (TSS 78).[10] Here we see references to various "tribes" (Indian, Australian, Polynesian—with Uganda in Africa added in for good measure). There is an overgeneralized grouping together of these vastly diverse other Others as perpetually primitive, not only in the past, but also "still today."

This grand historical narrative continues with Beauvoir's ongoing descriptions of how woman is oppressed by family obligations and reproduction, followed by an account of various forms of "sacred prostitution." Again going from historical to contemporary examples of "primitive people," she states, "Religious prostitution *has continued to our day* among Egyptian alma's and Indian *bayadères*, who make up respectable castes of musicians and dancers" (TSS 97, first emphasis added, second emphasis original). Beauvoir adds, "But most often in

THE COLONIALITY OF GENDER AND THE OTHER OTHERS   271

Egypt, India, and Western Asia, sacred prostitution slipped into legal prostitution, the priestly class finding it profitable" (TSS 97).[11] Again, there is an overgeneralized grouping together of these vastly diverse geographical locations, cultural expressions, religions, and people in her analysis of family obligations, reproduction, and prostitution.

Continuing with her analysis of procreation as a primary source of oppression for women, she notes that "Some civilizations prohibit early marriage; Indian tribes are cited where women are guaranteed a two-year rest period between births; but in general over the centuries, women's fertility has not been regulated" (TSS 136). Beauvoir's analysis of menstruation is also considered through a grand historical narrative of "primitive societies."[12] In a footnote she cites Lévi-Strauss, who "points out that 'young Winnenbago Indians' visit their mistresses and take advantage of the privacy of the prescribed isolation of these women during their menstrual period" (TSS 167). And when describing the use of menstrual blood in ceremonies, she notes, "*Still today*, when some Indians go off to fight spectral monsters haunting their rivers, they place a fiber wad filled with menstrual blood on the bow of their boat: its emanations are harmful to their supernatural enemies" (TSS 168, emphasis added). Again, the "primitive" past is perpetually present (at least for certain groups who are alienated from Beauvoirian futurity).

There are a more mentions of "Indians" in Volume 2 of *The Second Sex*. For example, in the chapter on "The Married Woman," Beauvoir describes how young girls learn domestic roles like cooking from their female elders. But the pleasures of such activities dissipate with repetition. On this point she notes, "For Indians who get their nourishment essentially from tortillas, the women spend half of their days kneading, cooking, reheating, and kneading again identical tortillas, under every roof, *identical through the centuries*: they are hardly sensitive to the magic of the oven" (TSS 481, emphasis added). And in the chapter on "The Mother," she critiques the church for being inconsistent on killing (e.g., authorizing killing in war, but not in cases of abortion). Beauvoir offers the following example of the church condoning massacre while condemning abortion: "If a council authorized it, he would not protest against the pious massacre of the Indians any more than the good old days. The truth is that this is a conflict with a stubborn old

272　BEAUVOIR AND BELLE

tradition that has nothing to do with morality" (TSS 526). I take it that her point is to defend abortion, not to condone war or the "pious massacre of the Indians."[13] But it is yet another problematic comparison, and one that follows an earlier reference to abortion access for Arab women (and assumptions about their lack of maternal sentiments): "In North Africa the Arab woman has no recourse to abortion: out of ten children she gives birth to, seven or eight die, *and no one is disturbed because painful and absurd childbirth has killed maternal sentiments*" (TSS 525, emphasis added).[14]

In addition to the above commentaries, there are also multiple mentions of "Oriental" peoples and attitudes. In one of Beauvoir's discussions of marriage customs, she takes up society's treatment of widows, including expectations that they marry the brother of the deceased ("This custom called levirate is found among many Oriental peoples") or that they kill themselves (the more "radical solution . . . to sacrifice them on their husbands' tombs") (TSS 93). In her overview of representations of the "good wife" she notes, "For Orientals, a wife should be fat: everyone sees that she is well fed and brings respect to her master" (TSS 193).[15]

Beauvoir also offers an extensive analysis of the feminine myth as presented in the works of Montherlant, D. H. Lawrence, Claudel, Breton, and Stendhal. In the section on Montherlant, he is described as belonging "to the long male tradition of adopting the arrogant Manichaeism of Pythagoras" (TSS 214). She also notes that he finds it "suitable for woman to be purely flesh" (TSS 218). Along these lines she adds, "Montherlant approves the Oriental attitude: as an object of pleasure, the weak sex has a place—modest, of course, but worthwhile—on earth; the pleasure it gives man justifies it, and that pleasure alone" (TSS 218). But she also contrasts Motherlant with what she describes as "Oriental" attitudes: "However, Montherlant is in no way an Oriental sultan; in the first place he does not have the sensuality . . . The Oriental relishes woman voluptuously, thereby bringing about carnal reciprocity between lovers: the ardent invocations of the Song of Songs, the tales of *The Thousand in One Nights*, and so much other Arab poetry attest to the glory of the beloved; naturally, there are bad women; but there are also delicious ones, and sensual man lets himself go into their arms confidently, without feeling humiliated"

THE COLONIALITY OF GENDER AND THE OTHER OTHERS 273

(TSS 218). There are seemingly interchangeable references here to "Oriental" attitudes on the one hand and "Arab" poetry on the other. In addition to "Indians" and "Orientals," we see that Beauvoir also problematically references "Arabs" and "Muslims" as fixed (and yet somehow interchangeable) negative stereotypes. Returning to her discussion of family, she notes that when patrimony is the basis of society "woman also remains totally alienated" and adds, "This is what has happened in the Muslim world" (TSS 91–92). Examining the ways in which various religions and religious texts have been used to subjugate women, Beauvoir repeatedly associates Muslims with woman's oppression. She describes the religion as one "that was created when the Arab people were warriors and conquerors professed the utmost disdain toward women" (TSS 92). She also asserts, "The Muslim woman, veiled and shut in, is still today a kind of slave in most levels of society" (TSS 92). Here Beauvoir recounts seeing four women squatting in a cave in Tunisia, doomed to the private realm, "no other universe but the murky cave from which they emerge only at night, silent and veiled" (TSS 92).

Hypersexualizing Muslim men, in her efforts to reinforce the oppressed status of Muslim women, she states,

> For Muslims, woman is reduced to a state of abjection because of the feudal structure of society that does not allow recourse to the state against the family and because of religion, expressing this civilization's warrior ideal, that has destined man to death and stripped woman of her magic: What would anyone on earth, ready to dive without any hesitation into the voluptuous orgies of the Muhammadan paradise, fear? (TSS 184–185).[16]

This fixed representation of Muslims also emerges later in her chapter on "The Married Woman." Beauvoir laments the reduction of "woman" to "desperate housewives" confined to mindless repetition of housework. She then makes this observation:

> The loneliness of the household weighs on the woman just as routine tasks leave her head empty. She is happy when, in Midi towns, she can sew, wash, and peel vegetables while chatting on her doorstep;

274 BEAUVOIR AND BELLE

fetching water from the river is a grand adventure for half-cloistered Muslim women: I saw a little village in Kabyle where the women tore down the fountain an official had built on the plaza; going down every morning to the wadi flowing at the foot of the hill was their only distraction. All the time they are doing their marketing, waiting in lines, in shops, on street corners, they talk about things that affirm their 'homemaking worth' from which each one draws the sense of her own importance; they feel they are part of a community that— for an instant—is opposed to the society of men as the essential to the inessential. (TSS 479)

One wonders how Beauvoir moves so carelessly between the "desperate housewives" and the "half-cloistered Muslim women" in these passages.

Orientalism, Colonialism, Asian Female-ness, and the Imperceptibility of Latinas

As I have noted elsewhere, Beauvoir frequently talks about "woman" in general, even universal terms, when she means something more specific, like white middle-class woman. For example, she states, "This very ambivalence of the Other, of the Female, will be reflected in the rest of her history; until our times she will be subordinated to men's will" (TSS 89). She continues, "one of the problems he will seek to solve is how to make his wife both a servant and a companion; his attitude will evolve throughout the centuries, and this will also entail an evolution in woman's destiny" (TSS 89). These seem to be more general yet universalized claims about the status of "woman." But in a footnote to this claim about the centuries-long evolution of woman's destiny, Beauvoir narrows her scope. Beauvoir states, "We will examine this evolution in the Western world. *The history of the woman in the East, in India, and in China was one of long and immutable slavery.* From the Middle Ages to today, *we will center this study on France, where the situation is typical*" (TSS 89, emphasis added). On the one hand, this is an example of Beauvoir explicitly specifying that she is focusing on the Western, French woman (not some universal woman,

THE COLONIALITY OF GENDER AND THE OTHER OTHERS   275

though it is simultaneously claimed that this situation is "typical"). On the other hand, we cannot overlook the blanket overgeneralizations, not to mention conflations, of the East, India, and China as unevolved and unchanged throughout history. The condescending colonial gaze represented in this footnote persists in her problematic references to other Others.

In "Oriental Dreams: Orientalism and History in *The Second Sex*" (2009), Sally Markowitz describes the above footnote as "jarring" and states, "One may interpret this passage generously, overlooking Beauvoir's easy generalizations about non-Western cultures, but later in the book one encounters this troubling explanation of what makes gender relations in the modern West so special."[17] The troubling explanation Markowitz has in mind is Beauvoir's assertion that "The Oriental man who is unconcerned with his own destiny is satisfied with a female who is his pleasure object; but Western man's dream, once elevated to consciousness of the singularity of his being, is to be recognized as a foreign docile and freedom" (TSS 188). Markowitz argues, "In this brief rather astounding passage, Beauvoir manages not only to rehearse the major theoretical categories of her work—self/other, subject/object, individuality, freedom, reciprocity—but also to situate them squarely and explicitly within the wider discourse of what Edward Said has famously called orientalism."[18] She attributes this orientalism to Western philosophy in general and Hegel's (and Marx's) influence on Beauvoir in particular.[19] For Markowitz, the surprise is not so much that Beauvoir perpetuates this narrative, which is common among Western intellectuals of her time, but rather that so little attention has been paid to these passages in the contemporary secondary literature on *The Seconds Sex*. She notes, "Indeed, even those relatively few critics who have discussed Beauvoir's treatment of race have overlooked these passages."[20] Critiquing both Beauvoir and her readers, Markowitz continues, "Indeed, Beauvoir herself does not shrink away from explicitly invoking the oriental male, even if her contemporary readers ignore this invocation."[21] She concludes, "In any case, we should not continue to ignore Beauvoir's orientalism."[22]

To be sure, there are readers of Beauvoir who are calling attention to these and other problematic passages in *The Second Sex*. For example, in "Material Life: Bergsonian Tendencies in Simone de Beauvoir's

276 BEAUVOIR AND BELLE

Philosophy," Alia Al-Saji argues that there are "fault lines in Beauvoir's theory of oppression" specifically in the cases of "Muslim and Arab women in both *The Ethics of Ambiguity* and *The Second Sex*."[23] Like Markowitz, Al-Saji notes how certain groups are presented by Beauvoir as being stuck in a perpetual past, and names this as a project of colonialism. She argues, "Islam and Arab cultures in general are seen as without progress; they are stuck in a homogenous, perpetual past—projected backward in the linear colonial construction of time, which Beauvoir repeats in her narrative and which was part of the self-justification of French colonialism."[24] She elaborates, "the very way in which Beauvoir conceives *the* Muslim world to be stuck in the past precludes its becoming a cultural resource for resistance."[25] Al-Saji also underscores how little attention has been paid to these problematic passages: "This dimension in Beauvoir's texts is underdeveloped in the secondary literature and her readers might be excused for wanting to avoid it: For how could a philosopher who resisted flattening existence to a single register of sense fail so utterly when it came to the lives of Muslim and Arab women who were her contemporaries— especially since so many were the very *indigènes* living under French colonial rule, the colonized peoples in revolt whose colonial and racial oppressions her texts deployed to analogize 'women's' oppression?"[26] Thus, Al-Saji invites readers to confront Beauvoir's disturbing colonial tourist gaze, "Actively ignoring her own positionality as colonial traveler—and aside from the assumption that her tourist's anecdote is representative of culture, let alone a religion with many cultures and historical empires—the disturbing element of this reasoning is its conflation of past and present, across 1,400 years of civilizational history."[27] She notes how Muslim and Arab women are strategically used to recenter Western women in the text: "The abjection of Muslim and Arab 'female' life forms the vital backdrop—the material foil—to modern, Western 'women's' existence."[28]

Anticipating certain defenses of Beauvoir, Al-Saji is clear that Beauvoir's work to help Djamila Boupacha does not excuse these passages in *The Second Sex*. Al-Saji retorts, "Yet Beauvoir's radical awareness of her colonial positionality and complicity—which she makes explicit in her interventions on behalf of Boupacha—does not seem to have led to a revision in her views on Islam."[29] She also warns,

THE COLONIALITY OF GENDER AND THE OTHER OTHERS   277

"we should be wary of assuming that reading Beauvoir from the lens of a philosophy of life, as a material feminism, would save her philosophy from this racializing and colonial dissonance."[30] Put another way, both Markowitz and Al-Saji implore readers of *The Second Sex* to pay attention to and critique these problematic passages rather than ignoring them, pretending they do not exist, and/or making excuses for them—and I concur.

But there are more generous readers of Beauvoir on some of these points. Kyoo Lee, for example, positively (though not altogether uncritically) engages Beauvoir's *The Second Sex* in several articles.[31] Rather than critiquing Beauvoir on the aforementioned issues, she appropriates theoretical resources in Beauvoir for analyzing race, ethnicity, culture, gender, and the body. For example, in "Should My Bum Look Bigger in This?—Re-dressing the Beauvoirian Femme" (2012), she takes up the two English translations of the famous sentence in *The Second Sex*.[32] Lee states, "I am rehearsing—hearing—Simone de Beauvoir, of *The Second Sex*, whose pivotal formulation on femme remains oddly un/re/translatable: 'On ne naît pas femme: on le devient'" (Beauvoir 1949, 285–286).[33] She pushes notions of *double* and *triple* rhetorically: "Femme always already does a double (or triple) job of being herself while becoming herself for herself (as well as the other); for a woman, to be herself is to become herself and vice versa."[34] Lee similarly pushes *second* and *third*:

> Here, I am banking on a certain third vision, a more formal compositional, Beauvoirian dynamics of gender construction. What I have in mind is the elliptical, elastic, enduring quasi-geometry of a third perspective that enables the very observation and articulation of the perpetual second(ari)ness of the second sex, something akin to "a recovered literary formalism, a formalism *otherwise*," as Marjorie Garber puts it in her theoretical modeling of "third-person interruption."[35]

Lee returns to language and translation, seconds and doubles, again in "Second Languaging *The Second Sex*, Its Conceptual Genius: A Translingual Contemporization of 'On ne naît pas femme: on le devient,'" where she asserts, "Bringing a kind of

278   BEAUVOIR AND BELLE

meta-narrative second(-order) perspective to bear on the traditional and particularly phenomenological body of *philosophia*, Beauvoir, in her double consciousness, is second-languaging philosophy without secondarizing it: rather, I might as well say, she is 'seconding' it as in vocally supporting or activating it, actively echoing it."[36]

And in "Why Asian Female Stereotypes Matter to All: Beyond Black and White, East and West" (2013), Lee draws on Beauvoir (and many others) as she continues to examine *second* and *third* in her analysis of "Asian woman-ness." She cites DuBois' *Souls of Black Folk* ("How does it feel to be a problem?"), thinking with DuBois as well as Hurston, Ahmed, Bayoumi, and Morrison about how it feels to be a problem.[37] She is also thinking with Beauvoir on this question. Lee notes, "Here, I also recall Simone de Beauvoir's 'irritation' over and 'hesitation' around the question not just of woman but of being a woman (philosopher), noted at the very beginning of *The Second Sex*: 'I hesitated a long time before writing a book on woman. The subject is irritating, especially for women; and it is not new.' "[38] Lee is grappling with Asian female stereotypes as a problem across contexts—from white feminisms that are not attentive to race and ethnicity, to race theories that do not go beyond the Black/white binary, to the constructed dichotomies of East versus West.

On this point Lee is more critical, stating, "I set out to describe the Asian woman-ness as 'a problem,' as distinct although not entirely different from, say, the 'white European' womanness of the second sex, which seems to remain a secondary concern for de Beauvoir, or African American woman under multiple appropriative oppressions, as powerfully focalized by Morrison on the layered legacies of slavery in U.S. history as traceable in literary moments, figures, and voids."[39] Lee clarifies her objectives in this essay as follows: "Advanced below is, in brief, a note toward a case for the social ontological centrality of this issue of Asian gender stereotypes to feminist and critical race theories, especially in the transnational U.S. social imaginary: the double intersections of the black/white binary on the one hand, and the gendered rhetoric of East-meets-West, on the other hand, the very point that tends to get crossed out in the form of invisibility or hypervisibility."[40] With this in mind, she names several stereotypes ("'China Doll,' 'Dragon Lady,' 'Geisha Girl,' 'Lotus Flower,' 'Madame

THE COLONIALITY OF GENDER AND THE OTHER OTHERS   279

Butterfly,' etc., etc., etc. . . . let me then start with some of those Orientalized Asian female stereotypes materializing in readymade nicknames or metonyms, 'altered names' ").[41] She also calls attention to the contradictions of these stereotypes—"Asian [American] woman a China Doll/Dragon Lady (with often 'No Joy, No Luck'), and Asian man, sexless/perverse, and so on."[42]

Invoking Beauvoir's book title and famous sentence, Lee complicates the notion of "the second sex" and asserts, "When one is not born but *becomes* an Asiatic woman, she comes to belong to something other/less/more than the second sex, the female, the woman, the feminine subject, of and through which Simone de Beauvoir speaks in *The Second Sex*."[43] Asian women exceed Beauvoir's formulation of the second: "Rather again, the Asiatic woman, still and often existing in ominous caricatures, in their second names, appears to embody and enact something like the third sex a la and contra Beauvoir: the second sex of the Third World, the secondary second sex."[44] Lee invites us to consider this third woman that is not adequately accounted for in white feminism, that does not appear when race is conceived as operating only within a Black/white binary, and when gender is limited to a male/female binary.[45]

The issue of moving beyond the Black/white binary is also taken up in Stephanie Rivera Berruz's article "At the Crossroads: Latina Identity and Simone de Beauvoir's *The Second Sex*" (2016), where she argues that Latinas are rendered imperceptible in *The Second Sex*.[46] Berruz critiques Beauvoir's use of the race/gender analogy as well as the slave/woman analogy, while also calling attention to the limits of the Black/white binary.[47] Whereas Lee considers how we need to go beyond the Black/white binary to account for Asian women, Berruz makes a similar case against these analogies and the Black/white binary insofar as they do not account for the multiplicitous identities and experiences of Latinas. She explains, "In other words, the case of Latina identity highlights the shortcomings with respect to Beauvoir's framework in *The Second Sex* because it exceeds the black-white binary and requires a multidimensional approach for naming its experiences."[48] Berruz argues, "Working along an enunciation of the black-white binary that ties gender problematically to whiteness and enslavement to blackness renders the possibility of a multidimensional identity like that

280 BEAUVOIR AND BELLE

of Latina imperceptible within the architecture of *The Second Sex*."[49] She elaborates, "Latina identity falls through the cracks. The structure reinscribes the indeterminate status of Latina identity through the black-white binary."[50] Clarifying expectations and stakes, Berruz asserts, "At minimum, I am calling for an active consideration of this shortcoming as a way of attempting to read *The Second Sex* more responsibly" and adds, "At stake in this discussion is whose oppression and lived experiences can be named and identified as meaningful."[51] Agreed.

Like Lee, rather than critique Beauvoir on these issues, Mariana Ortega offers examples of how Beauvoir, specifically her existential phenomenology, has been appropriated in other Latin American and Latina feminisms.[52] In "Phenomenological Encuentros: Existential Phenomenology and Latin American & U.S. Latina Feminism" (2006), Ortega begins her discussion of existentialist and phenomenological traditions with Martin Heidegger.[53] She argues, "Heideggerian existential phenomenology remains largely ignored by Latin American feminists due to their preference for more Marxist and Sartrean philosophies. But its [Heideggerian existential phenomenology] influence can be felt through the work of thinkers such as Beauvoir and Irigaray who have had a great impact on Latin American feminists' involvement in political movements and theories."[54] Ortega provides several examples of this influence on Graciela Hierro (former coordinator of the Center for Feminist Studies at Universidad Nacional Autónoma de México) and María Luisa Femenías (Philosophy Department at the Universidad Nacional de la Plata, Argentina).

According to Ortega, "One Latin American feminist who has been influenced by Beauvoir's work and in turn has had a great influence in feminist thought in Latin America is Graciela Hierro . . . Her texts . . . demonstrate a life-long commitment to the study of women in a patriarchal society."[55] Ortega adds, "Inspired by Beauvoir, Hierro denies the essentialism some attribute to women . . . She defends the position that gender is socially constructed and that, consequently, society can provide an education that allows girls and women to occupy spaces other than domestic ones."[56] Concerning María Luisa Femenías, Ortega explains that she "analyzes the role of Beauvoir's thought in the development of feminist theories in the later part of the

THE COLONIALITY OF GENDER AND THE OTHER OTHERS 281

twentieth century . . . [including] Beauvoir's contribution to philosophy and feminism and her critiques against Marxism and Freudian psychoanalysis."[57] Ortega continues:

> Femenías concludes that "identity or difference" is a false antithesis and argues instead for "difference and identity" . . . In the end, she reminds us that theories that appeal to difference are tied to norms and values that are universalizable, and thus there is an interrelatedness between identity and difference that cannot be overlooked if we are to start thinking of the terms . . . as instruments for action and change for women's conditions rather than theoretical, abstract principles.[58]

Finally, Ortega highlights the significant import of existentialism, phenomenology, and experience in the scholarship of Latina feminists such as María Lugones, Gloria Anzaldua, Linda Martín Alcoff, Ofelia Shutte, and Paula Moya. In the next section I turn my attention to Lugones in particular, exploring her theoretical framework of the colonially of gender, her call for decolonial feminism, and implications for *The Second Sex.*

Coloniality of Gender and Decolonial Feminism

Ortega explores the impact of Beauvoir, existentialism, and phenomenology on Latina philosophers including María Lugones. Although Lugones does not explicitly engage Beauvoir and *The Second Sex* in the essays I am taking up here, her analysis has implications for Beauvoir's framing of gender and woman as Other. One of the most striking omissions in *The Second Sex* (in addition to the imperceptibility of Latinas named by Berruz) is the lack of analysis of colonialism's impact on gender formation and oppression (beyond the "woman in love" example). I have in mind not only Beauvoir's own colonial subjectivity and gaze, but also the aforementioned grand historical narratives about gender roles and gender oppression that ignore what Lugones terms the coloniality of gender. Beauvoir is so ensnared in her analogical approach along with her comparative and competing frameworks

282 BEAUVOIR AND BELLE

of oppression (e.g., her comparison of gender oppression with racism, colonialism, antisemitism, classism) that she often misses important ways in which these various oppressions intersect with and reinforce one another (again, beyond the "woman in love" example already mentioned). As a corrective to these oversights in Beauvoir's analogical analysis that centers white women, I turn to Lugones' insights about the coloniality of gender and her call for decolonial feminism.

Using Anibal Quijano's concept of coloniality of power (and simultaneously expanding and complicating his approach), Lugones analyzes how gender, race, sexuality, heterosexism, and capitalism intersect in "Heterosexism and the Colonial/Modern Gender System" (2007). She argues that heterosexism plays an important role in the fusing of gender with race through colonial power.[59] Instead of emphasizing patriarchy, Lugones historicizes gender to demonstrate that "heterosexuality, capitalism, and racial classification are impossible to understand apart from each other."[60] Critiquing white feminist theory, practice, and indifference—especially white feminist philosophy, Lugones argues, "There has been a persistent absence of the deep imbrication of race into the analysis that takes gender and sexuality as central."[61] She asserts, white feminists "understood women as inhabiting white bodies but did not bring that racial qualification to articulation or clear awareness . . . they did not understand themselves in intersectional terms, at the intersection of race, gender, and other forceful marks of subjection or domination."[62] These insights are relevant for *The Second Sex*, which offers an analogical analysis of race and gender (e.g., comparing the oppression of white women to the oppression of Black men, or noting that the white woman could not give herself over to the "native" without degrading herself) that does not adequately account for the myriad ways that Black women and other Women of Color have experienced these various forms of identity and oppression simultaneously.

Lugones chooses to root her approach in the feminisms offered by Women of Color. She states, "I am interested in investigating the intersection of race, class, gender, and sexuality in a way that enables me to understand the indifference that persists in much [white] feminist analysis" and adds, "The framework that I introduce is wholly

THE COLONIALITY OF GENDER AND THE OTHER OTHERS 283

grounded in the feminisms of women of color and women of the Third World and arises from within them."[63] Lugones leverages Quijano's account of gender, demonstrating how "The logic of structural axes shows gender as constituted by and constituting the coloniality of power" and positing, "In a sense, there is no gender/race separability."[64] We see examples of this indifference by white feminists in *The Second Sex* where Black women and other Women of Color are in some cases not represented at all, and in other cases problematically misrepresented, as has already been shown in the previous sections of this chapter.

In "Toward a Decolonial Feminism" (2010), Lugones continues to question the construction and organization of the world into "atomic, homogeneous, separable categories" and presents intersectionality as one way of resisting and exceeding this type of categorization imposed by colonial modernity.[65] She explains, "Contemporary women of color and third-world women's critique of feminist universalism centers the claim that the intersection of race, class, sexuality, and gender exceeds the categories of modernity."[66] Lugones describes the coloniality of gender as "what lies at the intersection of gender/class/race as central constructs of the capitalist world system of power."[67] She also asserts that "'colonized woman' is an empty category: no women are colonized; no colonized females are women."[68] Part of her point is that the category of "woman" is reserved for the colonizer woman insofar as colonized "females" are not considered "women." (Again, in the "woman in love" example, Beauvoir makes a similar point about the native "male" who is non-human, non-man, and inferior in the colonial system. But the native woman is not considered in that example.)

Lugones is clear that her methodological move from Women of Color feminisms to a decolonial feminism is a praxical task that "enact[s] a critique of racialized, colonial, and capitalist heterosexualist gender oppression as a live transformation of the social."[69] The decolonial feminist sees the colonial difference; emphatically resists her epistemological habit of erasing it; sees the world anew; requires herself to drop her enchantment with "woman," the universal; and begins to learn about other resisters to the colonial difference.[70] Rather than relegating other Others to a perpetual primitive past like Beauvoir, Lugones takes seriously past and present colonial impositions of race,

284 BEAUVOIR AND BELLE

class, heterosexism, and gender oppression, while also being attentive to present and future possibilities through coalitional decolonial feminisms.

The Invention of Women and the Imposition of Western Gender Categories

One of the key theorists and texts that Lugones engages and cites as she develops her theory of the coloniality of gender is Oyèrónké Oyewùmí's *The Invention of Women: Making An African Sense of Western Gender Discourses* (1997). In this text Oyewùmí describes "the epistemological shift occasioned by [the transatlantic slave trade, colonialism, and] the imposition of Western gender categories on Yorùbá discourse."[71] She is clear, "This book is not about the so-called woman question. The woman question is a Western-derived issue—a legacy of the age-old somato-centricity in Western thought."[72] This is the case in part because "the fundamental category 'woman'—which is foundational in Western gender discourses—simply did not exist in Yorùbáland prior to its sustained contact with the West."[73] Looking at what she calls "the Yorùbá case" in particular, Oyewùmí offers counter-examples showing that "the human body need not be constituted as gendered."[74] She interrogates Western impositions of gender onto a gender-free Yorùbá language to make her point:

> The problem of gender and its constructs in Yorùbá language, literature, and social practice calls for immediate attention. Yorùbá language is gender-free . . . There are no gender-specific words denoting son, daughter, brother, or sister. Yorùbá names are not gender-specific... Given that anatomic categories are not used as social categories, it is clear that apprehending the gender of particular individuals or personages in a different time period and across space is at best an ambiguous adventure.[75]

While Oyewùmí is calling out the imposition of Western gender categories in the very specific context of Yorùbáland, her analysis has broader implications. She is offering a cautionary tale: "Yorùbá society,

THE COLONIALITY OF GENDER AND THE OTHER OTHERS 285

like many other societies worldwide, has been analyzed with Western concepts of gender on the assumption that gender is a timeless and universal category."[76] Thus, Oyewùmí identifies (and challenges) several assumptions about sex difference in Western feminist writings:

1. Gender categories are universal and timeless and have been present in every society at all times.
2. Gender is a fundamental organizing principle in all societies and is therefore always salient. In any given society, gender is everywhere.
3. There is an essential, universal category "woman" that is characterized by the uniformity of its members.
4. The subordination of woman is a universal.
5. The category of "woman" is pre-cultural, fixed in historical time and cultural space in antithesis to another category—"man."[77]

Again, the Yorùbá case study offers a cautionary tale about the problems of imposing Western gender categories and assumptions about sex difference that have implications for Beauvoir's overgeneralizations about "woman" in *The Second Sex*. In other words, some of these assumptions outlined by Oyewùmí are present in *The Second Sex*.

I am not claiming that Beauvoir states that gender is universal and timeless. On the contrary, she explores how (white) woman has been treated at different points in history, paying attention to how other factors like class position impact (white) woman's experience. Beauvoir also does not claim that the category of "woman" is pre-cultural. I have already shown that she presents some cultures and the conditions of other Others within those cultures as fixed in historical time and cultural space (e.g., in her aforementioned representations of Indians, Asians, Muslims, and Arabs that are "still today" stuck in a primitive past). But there is an explicit claim and operating assumption in *The Second Sex* that gender categories have been present in every society at all times, that gender is an organizing principle in all societies, that gender is everywhere, and that the subordination of woman is universal. For example, in the introduction Beauvoir presents gender as a binary (even if one that may eventually disappear). She asserts, "And the truth is that anyone can clearly see that humanity is split

286   BEAUVOIR AND BELLE

into two categories of individuals with manifestly different clothes, faces, bodies, smiles, movements, interests, and occupations; these differences are perhaps superficial; perhaps they are destined to disappear" (TSS 4). Beauvoir also asserts, "The division of the sexes is a biological given, not a moment in human history" (TSS 9).

Furthermore, Beauvoir claims on several occasions throughout *The Second Sex* that there have *always* been women and women have *always* been subordinate. Again, in the introduction Beauvoir asserts, "there have always been women; they are women by their physiological structure; as far back as history can be traced, they have always been subordinate to men; their dependence is not the consequence of an event or a becoming, it did not *happen*" (TSS 8, emphasis original). Her point is that there is not a singular event that has rendered woman as Other. She explains, "Alterity here [in the case of woman] appears to be an absolute, partly because it falls outside the accidental nature of historical fact" (TSS 8). These claims are representative of the assumptions about sex difference in Western feminist writings that Oyewùmí critiques.

Of course, many would argue that Beauvoir is not an essentialist when it comes to gender. In fact, she is often credited with theorizing sex and gender as distinct categories—whether from the perspective of social construction or from the perspective of existential phenomenology. For example, *"On ne naît pas femme: on le devent . . .": The Life of a Sentence*, edited by Bonnie Mann and Martina Ferrari, is a robust collection of essays that examine the philosophical and feminist implications of Beauvoir's most famous sentence in that text (*"On ne naît pas femme: on le devient . . ."*)—including the perceived consequences of translating the sentence with the indefinite article ("One is not born, but rather becomes, a woman") as Parshley does versus translating the sentence without the indefinite article ("One is not born, but rather becomes, woman") as Borde and Malovany-Chevallier do. For some, at stake in the inclusion/exclusion of the indefinite article is whether we read Beauvoir as a social constructivist or an existential phenomenologist.

Karen Offen's "Before Beauvoir, Before Butler: 'Gender' in France and the Anglo American World" reads Beauvoir as a social constructivist and explains, "by setting this sentence, and Beauvoir's work more broadly, in the context of French historical understandings of

THE COLONIALITY OF GENDER AND THE OTHER OTHERS   287

'gender,' I would hope to demonstrate that the sentence *should be* read in terms of social construction."[78] Likewise, Anna Bogić's "Becoming Woman: Simone de Beauvoir and Drugi pol in Socialist Yugoslavia" examines social-constructivist readings of Beauvoir beyond the United States and France, asserting, "The notion that women's roles and their 'essence' are always already socially constructed and manufactured has shown itself to be a powerful statement capable of sparking a desire for deep change in societies far removed from Beauvoir's France of the 1940s."[79] But what are the implications of these social-constructivist interpretations of Beauvoir for Oyewùmí's above claims about sex and gender assumptions in Western feminism?

Oyewùmí contends that social-constructivist claims about the sex/gender distinction do not really matter insofar as sex and gender remain deeply interconnected. On the one hand, she explains, "The idea that gender is socially constructed—that differences between males and females are to be located in social practices, not in biological facts—was one important insight that emerged early in second-wave feminist scholarship."[80] On the other hand, she notes, "This in turn led to the opposition between social constructionism and biological determinism, as if they were mutually exclusive," but, on the contrary, they are "two sides of the same coin, since both ideas continue to reinforce each other."[81] Oyewùmí argues, "Ultimately, the most important point is not that gender is socially constructed but the extent to which biology itself is socially constructed and therefore inseparable from the social" (a point with which I think Beauvoir would actually agree).[82] Oyewùmí offers the following if/then arguments:

> If gender is socially constructed, then gender cannot behave in the same way across time and space. If gender is a social construction, then we must examine the various cultural/architectural sites where it was constructed, and we must acknowledge that variously located actors (aggregates, groups, interested parties) were part of the construction. We must further acknowledge that if gender is a social construction, then there was a specific time (in different cultural/architectural sites) when it was "constructed" and therefore a time before which it was not. *Thus, gender, being a social construction, is also a historical and cultural phenomenon.* Consequently, it is logical

288   BEAUVOIR AND BELLE

to assume that in some societies, gender construction need not have existed at all.[83]

Oyewùmí revisits social construction later and argues, "Because gender is preeminently a cultural construct, it cannot be theorized in a cultural vacuum, as many scholars tend to do ... The frame of reference of a culture has to be identified and described on its own terms before one can make the sort of gratuitous claims that are being made about patriarchy and other social ills."[84] For Oyewùmí, Western feminism is informed by Western concerns and questions, and consequently, "feminism remains enframed by the tunnel vision and the bio-logic of other Western discourses."[85] Again, she is especially interested in how this manifests in "the Yorùbá case study," but there are implications for *The Second Sex*.

Some may argue that Beauvoir escapes the binary of social construction versus biological determinism. Not only does Beauvoir herself underscore the limits of biology (as was pointed out earlier in this chapter), but even if social constructivism is off the table, she offers the alternative of existential phenomenology. In the aforementioned edited collection "*On ne naît pas femme: on le devient . . .*": *The Life of a Sentence*, there are several essays emphasizing Beauvoir's existentialism and phenomenology. These include the Margaret Simons' "The Silencing of Simone de Beauvoir: Guess What's Missing from *The Second Sex*" and two chapters by Toril Moi, "While We Wait: The English Translation of *The Second Sex*" and "The Adulteress Wife." Both Simons and Moi cite omissions and mistranslations of philosophical concepts in the Parshley English translation that have contributed to readers not fully appreciating Beauvoir's existential phenomenology.[86] Megan M. Burke's "Becoming A Woman: Reading Beauvoir's Response to the Woman Question" also supports phenomenological readings and resists social-constructivist readings of *The Second Sex*—including claims that it makes the case for a sex/gender distinction. Burke asserts, "I think the exclusion of the indefinite article, the *a*, in 'the famous sentence' fails to read Beauvoir as giving a phenomenological account of feminine existence . . . [W]e come to read Beauvoir as a social constructionist. This not only makes it difficult for readers to grasp Beauvoir's account of feminine existence as a phenomenological

THE COLONIALITY OF GENDER AND THE OTHER OTHERS 289

one, but it also conceals the fruitfulness of her phenomenological approach."[87] And in "The Phenomenal Body Is Not Born; It Comes to Be a Body-Subject," Carmen López Sáenz reads the text phenomenologically and states, "It is the contention of this contribution that if we study the work of Beauvoir within the phenomenological framework of the lived body, we will understand that she goes much further that the mere distinction between given natural sex and socially constructed gender."[88]

Exploring these social-constructivist versus existential-phenomenologist debates in German translations of *The Second Sex*, Anna-Lisa Baumeister (in "French Women Become, German Women Are Made?: Simone de Beauvoir, Alice Schwarzer, Translation and Quotation") problematizes Alice Schwarzer's translation because it emphasizes a social-constructivist rather than a phenomenological account of woman. In "Retranslating *The Second Sex* into Finnish: Choices, Practices, and Ideas," Erika Ruonakoski reads the text phenomenologically, noting, "We were certainly heavily influenced by Heinämaa's interpretation of *The Second Sex*, especially in the following issues: that the phenomenological notion of the lived body was one of Beauvoir's most crucial starting points, and that explaining Beauvoir's conception of embodiment in terms of the sex-gender distinction does not do it justice (e.g., Heinämaa 1996: 1997)."[89] Bonnie Mann (in "Beauvoir Against Objectivism: The Operation of the Norm in Beauvoir and Butler") embraces the tensions and ambiguities of the social-constructionist readings alongside phenomenological readings and poststructuralist perspectives.[90] And in "The Floating 'A,' " Debra Bergoffen also offers ambiguity as an alternative to the social constructivism versus existential phenomenology binary. She explains, "Posing the translation question as an either/or choice . . . unreflectively (re) enforces the binary habits of thought that Beauvoir found questionable . . . we need to let the 'a' float between these English translations such that in speaking to, rather than against each other they are read as marking the phenomenological ambiguity and political undecidability of (a) woman—the subject of *The Second Sex* and of this particular sentence."[91]

Beauvoir is explicitly committed to offering an existential account of woman that goes beyond the limits of biology, psychoanalysis, and

290 BEAUVOIR AND BELLE

historical materialism. Nonetheless, her representation (or the lack thereof) of other Others remains problematic for reasons already articulated earlier by Markowitz and Al-Saji. Beauvoir's grand historical narratives present the non-West (from the East, to India, to Asia, to Africa, to Muslims, to Arabs—frequently presented as overlapping and undifferentiated from one another) as being stuck in a perpetual primitive past. On this point, Oyewùmí is also critical of what she calls the Western hegemony that assumes the superiority of Europe over Africa (at worst) or that seeks to draw equivalences between Europe and Africa (at best). Looking specifically at the example of philosophy's perceptions of Africa, she observes there are descriptions of "African thought as prephilosophic and prescientific" along with claims that "Africa was too early or too late in doing philosophy."[92] Oyewùmí explains why these attitudes are problematic, "Such thinking suggests that Africa is the West waiting to happen or that Africa is like the West, albeit a preformed or deformed West."[93] Again, we can see similarities between her critiques here and those discussed earlier by Markowitz and Al-Saji.

Conclusion

In the first three sections of this chapter, I considered some of Beauvoir's critiques of the limits of biology, psychoanalysis, and historical materialism insofar as they do not offer adequate accounts of how woman came to be situated as Other, as well as her push for an existentialist analysis. I also examined some of Beauvoir's problematic grand historical narratives that placed groups like Indians, Asians, Muslims, and Arabs, at times undifferentiated, but also presented as stuck in a perpetual primitive past, even in the present moment. I presented strong critiques of these narratives from the perspective of orientalism, the colonial gaze and colonial dissonance, and the imperceptabilty of Latinas, while noting the absence of the role of colonialism in the construction of gender, gender oppression, and the Othering of "woman" in Beauvoir's analysis. In the final two sections of the chapter, I complicated the narrative that emerges from Beauvoir's account by considering the counter-narratives offered by Lugones' notion of the

THE COLONIALITY OF GENDER AND THE OTHER OTHERS 291

coloniality of gender and the import of decolonial feminism, as well as Oyewùmí's examination of the invention of women, the imposition of Western gender categories, and Western feminist assumptions about sex difference.

If we want to read Beauvoir generously, we can consider the encyclopedic scope of *The Second Sex* and the rapid pace at which it was written. Of course, no one expects her to be omniscient. Still, offering a generous reading alongside a responsible reading, we cannot ignore what comes off as carelessness in the blurring and collapsing of different peoples from different places and different times as undifferentiated and interchangeable. Rather than continue to ignore these problematics in *The Second Sex*, or slip into knee-jerk defenses of Beauvoir, I would encourage readers take seriously these shortcomings and take the time to really engage and learn from (not just cite and dismiss) existing counter-arguments that I have been intentional about highlighting. There is plenty of room for moving beyond repetitive defensive apologetics to developing and expanding more accurate counter-narratives. For example, we could go deeper on the insightful critiques offered by Markowitz (on Beauvoir's orientalism), Al-Saji (on Beauvoir's colonial gaze and colonial dissonance, especially toward Muslim and Arab women), Berruz (on the imperceptibility of Latinas), Lugones (on the coloniality of gender), and Oyewùmí (on Western constructions of sex/gender and Western attitudes of superiority toward Africa). We could examine more closely how Beauvoir is using the term "Oriental" and her resulting "orientalism"—read through French understandings of the "Orient" as well as through Edward Said's *Orientalism* (1978).

We could also further investigate various stereotypes of Indians, Asians, Africans, Muslims, and so on in *The Second Sex*, to see if there is an implicit taxonomy. Is there an equivocation as well a hierarchy of stereotypes happening simultaneously? Furthermore, we could ask, where is the agency and futurity that is open to white Western woman but seems to be somehow closed off to the other Others presented in a perpetual past? We could take seriously the postcolonial and decolonial perspective and projects, the dynamic relationships between and coalitions among the other Others that exceed Beauvoir's text and imagination (as well as those of many of her defensive readers).

292 BEAUVOIR AND BELLE

Returning to points I raised in all of the previous chapters of this text, there have been Black feminist, Women of Color feminist, and transnational feminist projects, coalitions, alliances, and solidarities that predate the publication of *The Second Sex* and that have evolved and persisted long after.[94]

Notes

1. This analysis is frequently presented analogically or through comparative and competing frameworks of oppression insofar as the situation of "woman" as Other is analogized with or compared with the ways in which other groups (e.g., "the Black," "the Jew," "the proletariat") are situated as the Other. (See Chapter 5 in this text.)
2. Note, in the footnote to this quote Beauvoir cites E. Levinas' essay *Le temps et l'autre* and says that he deliberately adopts the man's point of view and says that woman is a mystery.
3. It is worth noting Beauvoir's attention to Chinese thought as well as India and Rome here. Marcel Granet was a French sociologist and author of *Fêtes et chansons anciennes de la Chine* (1919), *Les religions des chinois* (1922), *Danses et légendes de la Chine ancienne* (1926), *La civilisation chinoise* (1929), *Le pensee Chinois* (1934), and *La féodalité Chinois* (1952). Georges Edmond Raol Dumézil was a French religious-studies scholar. For more on Dumézil, see *The New Comparative Mythology: An Anthropological Assessment of the Theories of Georges Dumézil* (Berkeley: University of Caifornia Press,1982).
4. Recall from Chapter 5 in this text I noted that Beauvoir insists that white women's oppression is fundamentally different from other oppressions experienced by men because women have no reciprocity, there is not a historical event to account for their oppression, and women are complicit with rather than resistant to their oppression. I have also previously noted that the subjugation of non-white women is obscured in this analysis that does not account for their experiences of what Beauvoir calls antifeminism, nor does it account for salient aspects of anti-Black racism, antisemitism, and/ or classism that women within these groups experience simultaneously.
5. Note that in Chapter 5 I offered an in-depth analysis of the ways in which she presents women, "foreigners," Black people, Jewish people, and proletarians *comparatively* as Others. I also noted that she presents various systems of oppression as similar but separate—identifying similarities in

THE COLONIALITY OF GENDER AND THE OTHER OTHERS 293

the motives and strategies of oppression and then proceeding in a way that suggests these oppressions are generally separate and/or separable. But this is not the case for Black women, Jewish women, colonized women, and/or proletarian women (especially proletarian Women of Color) within the groups to whom Beauvoir compares the situation of the white bourgeois "woman"—another reminder (as noted in Chapter 5 of this text) that Beauvoir specifically names racist Americans and not French racists. This description does not consider anti-Black racism and colonialism as interconnected forms of alterity and systems of oppression.

6. We could also think about this in terms of the *third sex* in *The Second Sex*. I am inspired in part here by Kyoo Lee's references to the *second* and the *third* in her essays to be taken up in more detail in this chapter. I am also thinking "the third sex" in the sense of exceeding what Beauvoir is describing as "the second sex" as well as in the sense of the political notion of Third World feminism by Black women and other Women of Color. In terms of Beauvoir's readers, I have in mind Beauvoir scholars that have chosen to be silent on these issues at best or have attempted to defend Beauvoir on these issues at worst.

7. For more on Beauvoir as a white *"colon"* see Nathalie Nya, *Simone de Beauvoir and the Colonial Experience: Freedom, Violence, and Identity* (New York: Lexington Books, 2019).

8. As she states, "in purely biological terms, it would not be possible to posit the primacy of one sex concerning the role it plays in perpetuating the species" and adds, "biological data take on those values the existent confers on them" (TSS 47).

9. Beauvoir continues, "The question is how, in her, nature has been taken on in the course of history; the question is what humanity has made of the human female" (TSS 48).

10. It seems Beauvoir is drawing in part from *Indonesia: The Paga Tribes of Borneo*, by Charles Hose and William McDougall (1915). She returns to India, women, and the land later in the text when she states, "An Indian prophet advised his disciples not to dig up the earth . . . In central India the Baidya also thought that it was a sin to 'rip the breast of their earth mother with a plow'" (TSS 164).

11. Here she also notes, "He [Solon] bought Asian slaves and shut them up in *dicterions* located in Athens . . . each girl received wages, and net profit went to the state" (TSS 97).

12. On the topic of menstruation and philosophy, including Beauvoir's analysis of puberty in *The Second Sex*, see Kyoo Lee, "Just Throw Like a Bleeding Philosopher: Menstrual Pauses and Poses, Betwixt

294 BEAUVOIR AND BELLE

Hypatia and Bhubaneswari, Half Visible, Almost Illegible," in *Feminist Phenomenology Futures*, ed. Helen A. Fielding and Dorothea E. Olkowski (Bloomington: Indiana University Press, 2017), 21–46. In this essay, Lee also calls attention to the suicide of Bhubaneswari, a teenager who hanged herself while menstruating (evidence that she was not pregnant at the time) and Chakravoty Spivak's critical reading of this case and its gendered and imperialist implications.

13. In an earlier discussion of abortion, Beauvoir notes, "Generally, in Oriental and Greco-Roman civilization, abortion was allowed by law" (TSS 137).

14. Consistent in pointing out the incongruities about the morality of death/killing, she adds, "If this is morality, then what kind of morality is it? It must be said that men who most respect embryonic life are the same ones who do not hesitate to send adults to death in war" (TSS 525).

15. It is worth noting that her husband is referred to as her master here. Beauvoir also adds a footnote here referring back to the footnote on TSS 177 about Hottentots and African women being fed.

16. Beauvoir adds, "A Muslim is all the more respected if he possesses a large number of flourishing wives" (TSS 193).

17. Sally Markowitz, "Oriental Dreams: Orientalism and History in *The Second Sex*," *Signs: Journal of Women in Culture and Society* 34, no. 2 (2009): 271–294), 272. (Hereafter Markowitz 2009.)

18. Markowitz 2009, 272–273.

19. Markowitz 2009, 276. She continues, "Consider that while Hegel at least feels the need to give some sort of explanation for European superiority, Beauvoir simply notes that in the East the situation of woman has not evolved because Eastern man has not evolved" (278). In *Simone de Beauvoir and the Politics of Ambiguity* (Oxford: Oxford University Press, 2012), Sonia Kruks defends Beauvoir, stating, "Certainly, to the modern reader these passages sit uncomfortably in Beauvoir's text . . . However, I think that Markowitz badly overstates her case when she attributes Hegel's Orientalism to Beauvoir." (49). Kruks continues her defense of Beauvoir by claiming she was limited to the materials available to her at the time (50). Of course colonialism was being actively confronted and resisted by the colonized before, during, and long after the writing of *The Second Sex* (as mentioned in the Introduction to my text), which renders this defense dubious. We could also add the more recent text by Meryl Altman, *Beauvoir in Time* (Leiden: Brill Rodopi, 2020) to the list of Beauvoir's defensive readers.

20. Markowitz 2009, 273. Along similar lines that I have argued elsewhere, Markowitz states, "I suspect that there may be a subtle tension between

THE COLONIALITY OF GENDER AND THE OTHER OTHERS   295

reading Beauvoir from a postcolonial perspective and from a perspective internal to philosophy and aimed at securing for her work, and for the category of sexual difference generally, a central place in philosophy" (Markowitz 2009, 273).

21. Markowitz 2009, 290.

22. Markowitz 2009, 291.

23. Alia Al-Saji, "Material Life: Bergsonian Tendencies in Simone de Beauvoir's Philosophy," in *Differences: Rereading Beauvoir and Irigaray*, ed. Emily Anne Parker and Anne van Leeuwen (New York: Oxford University Press, 2017), 43–44. (Hereafter Al-Saji 2017.)

24. Al-Saji 2017, 45.

25. Al-Saji 2017, 46.

26. Al-Saji 2017, 46.

27. Al-Saji 2017, 45. She also explains, "Finally, this shows how life can itself become a trope to racialize *other* women" (Al-Saji 2017,46). And she adds, "At first view, the frameworks of existence and life work by proxy to define modern, Western civilization in opposition to its colonized cultural others (in need of civilizing and saving)" (Al-Saji 2017, 46).

28. Al-Saji 2017, 46–47. This is similar to Sabine Broeck's triangular framing of subject, object, and abject—in which white Man figures as *Subject*, white Woman figures as *Object*, and Black Slave, a seemingly gender-neutral and invisible third position, figures as *Abject*. See Broeck, "Re-reading de Beauvoir 'after Race': *Woman-as-Slave* Revisited," *International Journal of Francophone Studies* 14, nos. 1–2 (2011): 167–184. This framework by Broeck is taken up in more detail in Chapter 6 of this text.

29. Al-Saji 2017, 46. Al-Saji is referencing a 1974 interview with Beauvoir, Caroline Moorehead, "A Talk with Simone de Beauvoir," *New York Times*, June 2, 1974.

30. Al-Saji 2017, 47.

31. Reflecting on her own identity and/in relationship to philosophy in "Hypatia's Gaze," Lee states, "The fact that I, a woman philosopher 'of colo(u)r,' find Hypatia & Associates so colourfully relatable and mobilisable this allegorical way, is not irrelevant to the fact that philoSOPHY in its trans-radical contemporaneity, is such a conceptual storehouse for all who can think and think none the less" (74). See Kyoo Lee, "Hypatia's Gaze," in *Philosophy by Women: 22 Philosophers Reflect on Philosophy and Its Value*, ed. Elly Vintiadis (New York: Routledge, 2020).

32. Kyoo Lee, "Should My Bum Look Bigger in This?—Re-dressing the Beauvoirian Femme," *Women's Studies Quarterly* 41, nos. 1/2: Fashion (Spring/Summer 2012): 184–193. (Hereafter Lee 2012.) Lee reflects on the

296 BEAUVOIR AND BELLE

nude photographs of Beauvoir that appeared on the cover of the French magazine *Le Nouvel Observateur* on her hundredth birthday in 2008. She notes: "Now I am looking somewhere in between, with Beauvoir: the pages filled with the philosopher's brilliant reflection on bourgeois women's sartorial life and the rather 'obscene' photo that writes the philosopher into the very toiletry space she sought to question herself out of" (Lee 2012, 187–188).

33. Lee prefers the Borde and Malovany-Chevallier translation, without the indefinite article (Lee 2012, 185). She states, "central to the convoluted logic of gender configuration and identification that Beauvoir captured with such deceptive simplicity is this bonded slippage, the elliptical tension between 'a woman,' a countable noun, on the one hand, 'woman/female/feminine [femme]' with no article, on the other hand, more of traditionally or conventionally uncountable 'stuff' such as, say, cheese" (Lee 2012, 186).

34. Lee 2012, 186.

35. Lee 2012, 188.

36. Kyoo Lee, "Second Languaging *The Second Sex*, Its Conceptual Genius: A Translingual Contemporization of 'On ne naît pas femme: on le devient,'" in *A Companion to Simone de Beauvoir*, ed. Laura Hengehold and Nancy Bauer (Wiley and Sone, 2017), 500–513), 507. (Hereafter Lee 2017.) She concludes, "What keeps me going, coming back, what has been engaging me so far is this second act that *The Second Sex* performs almost perpetually across all kinds of binaries and boundaries, this mid-way doubleness of *femme* at work, this 'midpoint' midwifery intervention of feminist acts—the kind that could have saved the life of Naber today, Aug 6, 2016, 'a transgender inmate,' born Jason Lee Naber 'fought to be called Stacy . . . found dead in a men's prison at Dade Correctional Institution in Florida City (Wang 2016)" (Lee 2017, 512). Also note Lee's reference to the notion of double consciousness made famous by W. E. B. DuBois.

37. Kyoo Lee, "Why Asian Female Stereotypes Matter to All: Beyond Black and White, East and West," "Critical Philosophy of Race Beyond the Black/White Binary," special issue, *Critical Philosophy of Race* 1, no. 1 (2013): 86–103), 87. (Hereafter Lee 2013.) She elaborates, "A feeling of be(com)ing a problem, of auto-implication, arises when one feels arrested—objectified, framed, and staged—by forces and conditions that one also objectively recognizes as problematic" (Lee 2013, 87–88).

38. Lee 2013, 88. (Citing Beauvoir, TSS 2009, 3.)

39. Lee 2013, 90. (Lowercase of the second sex in the quote is original.) "What I am presenting is not, however, as systematic study . . . [rather this is] a

THE COLONIALITY OF GENDER AND THE OTHER OTHERS 297

snapshot of how I would—or one could—set out to explore the social ontology of the 'Asian woman,' a figure in the background" (Lee 2013, 90).

40. Lee 2013, 90.
41. Lee 2013, 91.
42. Lee 2013, 93 (with citations of Jessica Hagedorn and Jefferey Paul Chan). ·
43. Lee 2013, 100.
44. Lee 2013, 100–101.
45. Lee explains, "My suggestion, not so much new as more networked as it were, is then we approach Suzie Wong, this third woman, from at least a three dimensional intersection of feminism and critical race theory— the idea being that this 'third,' the post-Beauvoirian second, also beyond the black/white binary as well as male/female, could function as a kind of formal metonym for another dimension yet to be discovered from within and alongside any gendered, raced, and class-bound thoughts" (Lee 2013, 101).
46. Stephanie Rivera Berruz, "At the Crossroads: Latina Identity and Simone de Beauvoir's *The Second Sex*," *Hypatia* 31, no. 2 (2016): 319–333. (Hereafter Berruz 2016.) Berruz explains, "Beauvoir makes use of a race/gender analogy that necessarily compares the plight of the American black (male) slave to the 'typical' female 'other.' The comparison is intended to illuminate the alterity inherent in the situation of woman. The result of this analogy is the mapping of the category *woman* onto the position of the slave, which results in the imperceptibility of the intersection between racial and gendered embodiment and oppression" (Berruz 2016, 320, emphasis original). Berruz comes back to the issues of imperceptibility later, stating, "Thinking about Latina identity through the framework of *The Second Sex* generates conditions of imperceptibility because the competing discursive frames that separate the categories of race and gender are touchtone experiential categories for the identity of the Latina" (Berruz 2016, 329).
47. She explains, "Insofar as Beauvoir's frameworks rests on the problematic comparison between racial and gendered oppression, and sets up a privileging of a gender axis of identity, it does not lend itself to accurately portraying Latina identity (or any nontypical identity) and her oppression" (Berruz 2016, 329).
48. Berruz 2016, 329.
49. Berruz 2016, 330.
50. Berruz 2016, 330.
51. Berruz 2016, 320 and 323.

298 BEAUVOIR AND BELLE

52. Ortega's article was published before Berruz's article, but I think Ortega would agree with Berruz's critiques here.
53. Mariana Ortega, "Phenomenological Encuentros: Existential Phenomenology and Latin American & U.S. Latina Feminism," *Radical Philosophy Review* 9, no. 1 (2006): 45–64. (Hereafter Ortega 2006.)
54. Ortega 2006, 45.
55. Ortega 2006, 51.
56. Ortega 2006, 51.
57. Ortega 2006, 52.
58. Ortega 2006, 53.
59. María Lugones, "Heterosexism and the Colonial/Modern Gender System," *Hypatia* 22, no. 1 (Winter 2007): 186–209), 186. (Hereafter Lugones 2007.)
60. Lugones, 2007, 187.
61. Lugones, 2007, 187.
62. Lugones, 2007, 203.
63. Lugones, 2007, 187. I insert *white* here in brackets, noting Lugones' point: "I am cautious when calling it 'white' feminist theory and practice. One can suspect a redundancy involved in the claim" (Lugones, 2007,187). In addition to her critiques of feminist theory, Lugones is also critical of the indifference, complicity, and collaboration of white men and Men of Color in the oppression of Women of Color. She states, "I am also interested in investigating the intersection of race, class, gender and sexuality in a way that enables me to understand the indifference that men, but, more important to our struggles, men who have been racialized as inferior, exhibit to the systematic violences inflicted upon women of color" (Lugones 2007, 188). Lugones asserts, "Feminists of color have made clear what is revealed in terms of violent domination and exploitation once the epistemological perspective focuses on the intersection of these categories. But that has not seemed sufficient to arouse in those men who have themselves been targets of violent domination and exploitation any recognition of their complicity or collaboration with the violent oppression of women of color" (Lugones 2007, 188).
64. Lugones 2007, 193. Lugones finds Quijano's account of gender to be overly narrow and biologized "because it presupposes sexual dimorphism, heterosexuality, patriarchal distribution of power, and so on" (Lugones, 2007, 193). She turns to Oyèrónké Oyewúmí, *The Invention of Women: Making an African Sense of Western Gender Discourses* (Minneapolis: University of Minnesota Press, 1997) and Paula Gunn Allen, *The Sacred Hoop: Recovering the Feminine in American Indian Traditions* (Boston: Beacon Press, 1986) to expand on Quijano's conception of gender.

THE COLONIALITY OF GENDER AND THE OTHER OTHERS 299

65. "Towards a Decolonial Feminism," *Hypatia* 25, no. 4 (Fall 2010): 742–759), 742. (Hereafter Lugones 2010.) She explains, "Contemporary women of color and third-world women's critique of feminist universalism centers the claim that the intersection of race, class, sexuality, and gender exceeds the categories of modernity" (Lugones 2010, 742).

66. Lugones 2010, 742.

67. Lugones 2010, 746.

68. Lugones 2010, 745.

69. Lugones 2010, 746.

70. Lugones 2010, 753.

71. Oyérónké Oyewùmí, *The Invention of Women: Making An African Sense of Western Gender Discourses* (Minneapolis: University of Minnesota, 1997), ix. (Hereafter Oyewùmí 1997.)

72. Oyewùmí 1997, ix.

73. Oyewùmí 1997, ix. She notes that these gender discourses were developed through the slave trade and colonialism—which she describes as "logically as one process unfolding over many centuries, not only formal colonization from 1862–1960" (xi).

74. Oyewùmí 1997, xi.

75. Oyewùmí 1997, 28–29.

76. Oyewùmí 1997, 31. But, "gender was not an organizing principle in Yorùbá society prior to colonization by the West . . . Rather, the primary principle of social organization was seniority, defined by relative age" (Oyewùmí 1997, 31). She reiterates, "Seniority is the primary social categorization that is immediately apparent in Yorùbá language. Seniority is the social ranking of persons based on their chronological ages . . . age relativity is the pivotal principle of social organization . . . irrespective of anatomic sex" (Oyewùmí 1997, 40). "Kinship terms are also encoded by age relativity" (Oyewùmí 1997, 40). And the seniority principle "is the cornerstone of social intercourse," not just as a matter of privilege in everyday life. It is also about responsibility (Oyewùmí 1997, 41).

77. Oyewùmí 1997, xi–xii.

78. Karen Offen, "Before Beauvoir, Before Butler: 'Gender' in France and the Anglo American World," in *"On ne naît pas femme: on le devient . . .": The Life of a Sentence*, ed. Bonnie Mann and Martina Ferrari (Oxford: Oxford University Press, 2017), 13 (italics original).

79. Anna Bogić's "Becoming Woman: Simone de Beauvoir and Drugi pol in Socialist Yugoslavia," in *"On ne naît pas femme: on le devient . . . ": The Life of a Sentence*, ed. Bonnie Mann and Martina Ferrari (Oxford: Oxford University Press, 2017), 327.

300 BEAUVOIR AND BELLE

80. Oyewùmí 1997, 8.
81. Oyewùmí 1997, 8.
82. Oyewùmí 1997, 9.
83. Oyewùmí 1997, 10. (Emphasis added.)
84. Oyewùmí 1997, 21. She notes later, "Thus, despite the relentless feminist assault on mainstream essentialism, feminist constructionism contains within it the very problem it seeks to address" (Oyewùmí 1997, 35).
85. Oyewùmí 1997, 13. Here she has in mind the emphasis on the visual, the gaze, the body/body-reasoning, the physical world (Oyewùmí 1997, 14).
86. For example, Moi underscores how English translations contribute to mis-understanding about existentialist vocabulary in TSS, but she also notes that TSS provides the " . . . insight that women are not born but made, that every society has constructed a vast material, cultural, and ideolog-ical apparatus dedicated to the fabrication of femininity"—an insight that contributes to "the foundation of modern feminism" (*The Life of a Sentence*, 105).
87. Megan M. Burke, "Becoming A Woman: Reading Beauvoir's Response to the Woman Question," in *"On ne naît pas femme: on le devient . . ."*: *The Life of a Sentence*, ed. Bonnie Mann and Martina Ferrari (Oxford: Oxford University Press, 2017), 161.
88. Carmen López Sáenz, "The Phenomenal Body Is Not Born; It Comes to Be a Body-Subject," in *"On ne naît pas femme: on le devient . . ."*: *The Life of a Sentence*, ed. Bonnie Mann and Martina Ferrari (Oxford: Oxford University Press, 2017), 175.
89. In *"On ne naît pas femme: on le devient . . ."*: *The Life of a Sentence*, ed. Bonnie Mann and Martina Ferrari (Oxford: Oxford University Press, 2017), 338. It is also worth noting that Ruonakoski describes language in the text as outdated and offensive. For example, she states, "we did not modify Beauvoir's outdated concepts such as 'hermaphridite' (hermaphro-dite) . . . or 'négresses' (negro women) to fit the ideals of political correct-ness of our days." More importantly, Ruonakoski adds, "In point in fact, making some modernizing word choices would not have been enough to make the translation unoffending" (346). To give another example of offensive passages, she states, "Among other things, Beauvoir does not hesitate to call the Muslim woman 'a kind of slave' (2010, 92; *une sorte d'eslave*, 2008b, 141)" (346). Critiquing Beauvoir's overgeneralizations, Ruonakoski is clear, "even if she did not *intend* to be arrogant, she certainly made sweeping—and from today's perspective deeply problematic—generalizations about numerous ethnic groups" (346, italics original).

THE COLONIALITY OF GENDER AND THE OTHER OTHERS 301

90. Bonnie Mann, "Beauvoir against Objectivism: The Operation of the Norm in Beauvoir and Butler," in *"On ne naît pas femme: on le devient . . .": The Life of a Sentence*, ed. Bonnie Mann and Martina Ferrari (Oxford: Oxford University Press, 2017), 40–41 and 44.

91. Debra Bergoffen, "The Floating 'A,'" in *"On ne naît pas femme: on le devient . . .": The Life of a Sentence*, ed. Bonnie Mann and Martina Ferrari (Oxford: Oxford University Press, 2017), 143.

92. Oyewùmí 1997, 21.

93. She offers this caveat: "There is nothing wrong with Africans affirming their humanity . . . The problem is that many African writers have assumed Western manifestation of the human condition to be the human condition itself" (Oyewùmí1997, 21).

94. I would like to acknowledge and thank Kyoo Lee and Alia Al-Saji for reading an earlier version of this chapter and offering helpful feedback, including raising some of these important questions.

Conclusion

Simone de Beauvoir: "I think *The Second Sex* will seem like an old, dated book, after a while. But nonetheless . . . a book which will have made its contribution"

My conclusion begins with Simone de Beauvoir's reflections on *The Second Sex* in her own words.[1] The first section, "Reflections on *The Second Sex* in *Force of Circumstance* (1963)," explores her commentary on her text from one of her memoirs. The second section, "Reflections on *The Second Sex* in Interviews (1974–1986)," focuses on the several interviews over a twelve-year period, including an interview with Caroline Moorehead ("A Talk with Simone de Beauvoir," 1974), one with John Gerassi ("Simone de Beauvoir: *The Second Sex* Twenty-Five Years Later," 1976), one with Margaret A. Simons and Jessica Benjamin ("Simone de Beauvoir: An Interview," 1979), and one with Hélène V. Wenzel ("Interview with Simone de Beauvoir," 1986).[2] The third section, "Audre Lorde's Open Letter: Confronting White Feminist Racism," I return to Audre Lorde, specifically her "Open Letter to Mary Daly" and its implications for Beauvoir and *The Second Sex*. In the final section, "Coalitional Politics: Toward a Praxis of Intersectional Philosophy," I revisit identity politics and intersectionality as coalitional practices, come back to Maria Lugones on decolonial feminisms and coalition, and conclude with Mariana Ortega's call for coalitional politics and a praxis of intersectional philosophy.

Reflections on *The Second Sex* in *Force of Circumstance* (1963)

In one of her memoirs, *Force of Circumstance* (1963), Beauvoir describes her conceptualization of the massive project of *The Second*

Beauvoir and Belle. Kathryn Sophia Belle, Oxford University Press. © Oxford University Press 2024.
DOI: 10.1093/oso/9780197660195.003.0010

CONCLUSION 303

Sex in this way: "Wanting to talk about myself, I became aware that to do so I should first have to describe the condition of woman in general; first I considered the myths the men have forged about her through all their cosmologies, religions, superstitions, ideologies and literature" (FOC 185). She continues, "I tried to establish some order in the picture which at first appeared to me completely incoherent; in every case, man put himself forward as the Subject and considered the woman as an object, as the Other" (FOC 185). She also elaborates on her "habit of efficient working methods"—from sorting, to distilling, to making an inventory of texts in French and English, to her reliance on personal relationships and memory—which provided "an abundance of material" (FOC 186). Beauvoir often refers to *The Second Sex* as her "essay on Woman" (FOC 143) or her "study of the feminine condition" (FOC 143 and 162), though she eventually settled on the present title with Sartre and Bost (FOC 168). She also notes that she read Lévi-Strauss as she was writing *The Second Sex*. And although he was critical of her "for certain inaccuracies in the sections on primitive societies," when she read his thesis (*Structures de la Parenté*), she says, "it confirmed my notion of woman as *other*; it showed how the male remains the essential being, even within the matrilineal societies generally termed matriarchal" (FOC 169).

Beauvoir also reflects on how the book was received when it was first published and how it impacted people's perceptions of her. Some readers misunderstood the book and took her to be denying differences between men and women. To this she responds, "On the contrary, writing this book made me even more aware of those things that separate them [men and women]; what I contended was that these *dissimilarities are of a cultural and not of a natural order* ... to recount systematically, from childhood to old age, how they were created; I examined the possibilities this world offers women, those it denies them, their limits, their good and bad luck, their evasions and their achievements" (FOC 186, emphasis added). She says Volume 1 was "well received" and Volume 2 "shocked people" (FOC 186). Interestingly, Beauvoir "was taken aback by the fuss it provoked" but in the end notes that both volumes sold well (FOC 186).

304 BEAUVOIR AND BELLE

Reflecting on those who described Beauvoir as courageous for writing the book, she replies, "In any case, I had written this book just the way I wanted to write it, but there had been no thought of heroism in my mind at any time" (FOC 186). She also recalls her accusers, defenders, and the public confrontations she experienced, the violence of the latter often leaving her feeling "perplexed" (FOC 187). Along similar lines, Beauvoir comments on the mean vilification of women by "vulnerable and spiteful men" as well as assumptions by her male critics that she was somehow humiliated (FOC 187–188). On the issue of humiliation, she explains, "This theme of my humiliation was taken up by a considerable number of critics who were so naïvely imbued with their own masculine superiority that they could not even imagine that my condition had never been a burden to me" (FOC 188). At the other end of the spectrum, critics accused Beauvoir of misogyny: "Subtler readers concluded that I was a misogynist and that, while pretending to take up the cudgels of women, I was damning them" (FOC 189). She insists "this is untrue" and adds, "I have given too many women too much affection and esteem to betray them now by considering myself as an 'honorary male'; nor have I ever been wounded by their stares" (FOC 189). Beauvoir continues to itemize more critiques and defenses of *The Second Sex*, a text that has been "misread and misunderstood" and that "troubled people's minds" (FOC 191).

In addition to addressing critiques and defenses, along with specific arguments presented in *The Second Sex*, Beauvoir also takes time to reflect on the positive impact she perceives her book has had on women based on testimonials she received from readers. She surmises: "These women have found help in my work in their fight against images of themselves which revolted them, against myths by which they felt themselves crushed; they came to realize that their difficulties reflected not a disgrace particular to them, but a general condition. This discovery helped them to avoid the mistake of self-contempt, and many of them found in the book the strength to fight against that condition" (FOC 192). Beauvoir concludes: "When all is said and done, it is possibly the book that had brought me the greatest satisfaction of all those I have written . . . If I am asked what I think of it today, I have no hesitation in replying: I'm all for it" (FOC 191).

CONCLUSION 305

Reflections on *The Second Sex* in Interviews (1974–1986)

In a *New York Times* interview with Caroline Moorehead, "A Talk with Simone de Beauvoir" (1974) Beauvoir is invited to reflect on the status of women since the publication of *The Second Sex*.[3] Two things that stand out in her reflections are her continued comparisons between (white) woman's situation with slavery and her continued overgeneralizations about Muslim countries twenty-five years after *The Second Sex* is published. For example, Beauvoir recounts her analysis of marriage as obscene in the text and notes that today the social system should not be based on marriage—even though she is not sure what would be an appropriate alternative to marriage. She says, "It's hard to say what should be put in its place, but the fact that one criticizes it doesn't mean that one has to have something to replace it."[4] To support her point, Beauvoir makes an analogy with American slavery: "After all, the American slaves didn't ask themselves what was going to happen to the American economy when they won their freedom."[5]

Later in the interview Moorehead notes that Beauvoir was "outspoken on the War in Algeria," but then became "disillusioned by the French after Algeria," and "gave up her revolutionary hopes for the West and turned to the Third World"—which also disappointed her. Beauvoir responds with this commentary about Algeria:

> I don't think it [socialism] has worked at all in Algeria. It is state socialism, but that's nothing to do with real socialism. And then the thing that really revolts me in Algeria, *as in all Moslem countries,* is the condition of women. I can't accept the way they oppress their women; veil them, impose forced marriages on them. Frantz Fanon thought they would become emancipated after the Algerian war. On the contrary, they have been crushed.[6]

In some ways the earlier comment on American slavery has implications for the later comment about postwar Algeria. What does it mean to fight so hard for freedom and emancipation from slavery and from colonialism, only to be confronted by new systems of

306   BEAUVOIR AND BELLE

oppression, from post-reconstruction Jim Crow in the United States to neo-colonialism in Algeria and other former colonies who fought for independence from colonizing nations? But also troubling here is Beauvoir's continued description of "all Moslem countries" as oppressive toward "their women." On this point Alia Al-Saji notes that Beauvoir's, "subsequent blanket statements about the oppression of women 'in all Muslim countries' make it seem that her internalization of the colonial, racializing discourse on Muslim worlds remains unquestioned."[7] Furthermore, Beauvoir's reference to veils is followed by a reference to Fanon without regard for the ways that he disrupts assumptions and stereotypes about the veil in his essay "Algeria Unveiled" (1959). Again Beauvoir makes sweeping claims and overgeneralizations here without much nuance.[8]

Two years later, in an interview with John Gerassi ("Simone de Beauvoir: *The Second Sex* Twenty-Five Years Later," 1976), when asked if she would write "another book on women, a sort of a follow-up on *The Second Sex*," Beauvoir replies, "No." Then she explains why not: "In the first place, such a work would have to be a collective effort. And then it should be rooted in practice rather than in theory. *The Second Sex* went the other way. Now that's no longer valid . . . What is really needed is that a whole group of women, from all sorts of countries, assemble their lived experiences, and that we derive from such experiences the patterns facing women everywhere. What's more, such information should be amassed from all classes."[9] At first glance this reads as incredible self-awareness and great insight. Unfortunately, Beauvoir goes on to undermine this insight in multiple ways. I will bring attention to four specific examples: (1) class differences in political consciousness about liberation among white women in France, (2) the use of analogy in taking up gender separatism (which she analogizes with racial separatism), (3) racial differences between white women and Black women in America concerning their political consciousness (or assumed lack thereof) about liberation, and finally, (4) the framing of racism in individual rather than institutional terms.

Let us begin with class differences in political consciousness about liberation among white women in France. According to Beauvoir, the bourgeois intellectual women are fighting for liberation in France, but they are confronted by "workers' wives and even female workers

CONCLUSION 307

[who] remain firmly attached to society's middle-class value system."[10] Beauvoir asserts, "To raise the consciousness of women workers is a very slow process needing a great deal of tact."[11] She suggests here that bourgeois intellectual women have a greater feminist consciousness than working-class women (an interesting reversal of her analysis of the complicity of white bourgeois women presented in *The Second Sex*).

Next, we have Beauvoir's commentary on gender separatism, which she analogizes with racial separatism. Beauvoir compares the politics of white women who choose to become lesbians in France to the racial politics of the Black Power movement in the United States. She states, "There are other women who have become lesbian out of a sort of political commitment; that is, they feel that it is a political act to be lesbian, *the equivalent somewhat within the sex struggle of the black power advocates within the racial struggle*."[12] Here Beauvoir is drawing an analogy between white women's political lesbianism and gender separatism on the one hand and the racial separatism of the Black Power movement on the other. She also states, "We have to investigate why they're separatists. I can't speak for America, but here in France there are many groups, consciousness groups, which do exclude men because they find it very important to rediscover their identity as women, to understand themselves as women. They can only do this by speaking amongst themselves."[13] This is yet another problematic analogy. In this case, Beauvoir once again compares white women to Black men while ignoring Black women both as lesbians and as active participants in the Black Power movement.

Despite her claim that she "can't speak for America," Beauvoir goes on to problematically compare the feminist consciousness of white American women to the feminist consciousness of Black American women, assuming the former are more informed than the latter. Beauvoir arrogantly asserts, "It is the same in America, where black women refused to listen to the women's liberation movement proselytizers because they were white. Such black women remained supportive of their black husbands despite the exploitation, simply because the persons trying to make them aware of the exploitation were white."[14] Thus, in one of the few instances in which Beauvoir actually names and acknowledges the existence of Black women (having just ignored them as lesbians and as participants in the Black Power

308 BEAUVOIR AND BELLE

movement), she summarily dismisses them. Beauvoir assumes they are somehow ignorant of their own oppression and suggests that they ought to allow presumably more informed white women liberators to raise their consciousness concerning their situation. This claim undermines the insight she previously offered about the necessity of different women articulating their own experiences of oppression. It also ignores centuries of Black women's activism in the United States, arguably going back to Lucy Terry (Prince), the first Black woman to argue a case before a US Supreme Court Justice in the 1790s, and including Maria Stewart's 1831 speech "Religion and the Pure Principles of Morality: The Sure Foundation on Which We Must Build" that critiques sexism and racism, and the continuation of Black feminist critique that persisted unabated into the 1970s when this interview was published, and still continues until today.

Two other points I will touch on in this interview with Gerassi pertain to another use of analogy as well as Beauvoir's framing of oppression in individual rather than institutional terms. We see yet another analogy between racism and sexism when she compares the racist Southerner to the sexist man. The racist Southerner has been racist all his life—and even though "now he never says 'nigger'" and his behaviors, habits, and actions are no longer racist—the fact remains that he is still racist.[15] Beauvoir asks rhetorically, "Do you think the blacks give a damn that he is just as racist now as before 'in his soul'?"[16] She clarifies her point—namely, that she does not care if a sexist man is no longer sexist "in his soul" as long as his habits and actions are nonsexist. She tells Gerassi, "So play at being nonsexist, and keep playing. Think of it as a game. In your private thoughts, go ahead and think of yourself as superior to women."[17] Here Beauvoir emphasizes individual actions and habits over thoughts and feelings. I am not so much interested in the false dichotomy presented here. For me, Beauvoir's emphasis on an individual approach (whether focused on action and habits or thoughts and feelings) does not address racism and sexism as institutional and structural systems of oppression. The question is not whether a racist is racist *in his soul or mind*, but rather, how anti-Black racism directly impacts Black lives and other lives. For example, can racist people shoot and kill unarmed Black men, women,

CONCLUSION 309

and children with little or no consequences (as is still happening two decades into the twenty-first century in the United States)? Not to mention the persistence and ongoing relevance of structural and institutional issues outlined by Claudia Jones back in 1949: racism, fascism, imperialism, capitalism, poverty, sexism, health issues, sexual assault, voting rights, lynching, and police brutality.

In their introduction to "Simone de Beauvoir: An Interview" (1979), Margaret A. Simons and Jessica Benjamin warn about "our tendency to idealize women such as Simone de Beauvoir."[18] Rather than idealize, "What is called for is an accurate understanding of both her life . . . and of her work, which has thus far certainly not received the critical analysis that it warrants—even from feminist philosophers."[19] In articulating the importance and impact of *The Second Sex*, they end up reinforcing the grand historical narrative it offers about woman, "*The Second Sex* also helped lay the theoretical foundation for radical feminist theory . . . She saw aspects of women's lives as distorted by a *patriarchal ideology common to all cultures throughout history*, and permeating our laws, religions, and literature."[20] They also note issues of difference in her analysis: "But she was also aware of the situations that divide women. Her comparative analysis of racism and sexism is more cognizant of their dissimilarities than are many of the theories of contemporary, white feminist theorists."[21] And, to their credit, they acknowledge some critiques of the text along similar lines: "De Beauvoir's analysis of woman's oppression in *The Second Sex* is open to many criticisms . . . for its ethnocentrism . . . her tendency to generalize from the experience of European bourgeois women, with a resulting emphasis on woman's historic ineffectiveness."[22] Although Simons and Benjamin lead the interview with questions about influences on Beauvoir, Beauvoir herself insists, "I wrote *The Second Sex* from my own experience; from my own reflections; not so much from another's influence."[23]

In this 1979 interview, Simons references the discussion of motherhood in Beauvoir's 1976 interview with Gerassi. We see that Beauvoir maintains her slave/woman analogy (here presented as slave/mother analogy) in her response to Simons' inquiry about motherhood. Beauvoir repeatedly reinforces a slave/mother analogy in this extended quote:

310   BEAUVOIR AND BELLE

> I think that by changing the concept of motherhood . . . society will change completely. Because it is through this idea of feminine vocation that women are enslaved to the home, that they are enslaved to their husbands, that they are enslaved to man, to housekeeping, etc. . . . maternity is a trap for women because it enslaves them to man, to the home . . . Therefore, if the world were made in a different way, if woman did not become a slave as soon as she became mother . . . then, what would be the need of eliminating motherhood? But as motherhood is today, maternity-slavery, as some feminists call it, does indeed turn today's women into slaves.[24]

This slave/woman analogy, or more specifically slave/mother analogy, is no less problematic in 1979 than it was thirty years earlier in 1949.

Beauvoir also continues to emphasize individual oppression rather than institutional oppression in the interview with Simons and Benjamin, as she did earlier in the Gerassi interview. In a discussion about men's hatred of women, Beauvoir notes, "There are many other reasons for men's hatred of women . . . In my opinion, it is above all an individual matter."[25] But she takes a very different position on gender separatism in the interview with Simons and Benjamin than she did in the interview with Gerassi. Simons says to Beauvoir, "There is a big movement in American feminism which I think is a parallel to the movement in French feminism . . . It is a foundation for separatism, and it is very much opposed to the position of *The Second Sex*."[26] Beauvoir replies, "Well, I am against this opposition to *The Second Sex* . . . In France also, some women have taken this stance . . . As for myself, I am absolutely against all this since it means falling once more into the masculine trap of wishing to close ourselves in our differences. I do not believe we should deny these differences; neither do I believe that we should despise or ignore them."[27] It is possible that Beauvoir is being more nuanced here on what constitutes gender separatism—agreeing with gender separatism for the purpose of consciousness-raising groups, but rejecting a gender separatism rooted in biological essentialism (or biological difference framed as essential difference, as Simons puts it). Beauvoir states, "it comes down to playing a man's game to say that the woman is essentially different from the man. There

CONCLUSION 311

exists a biological difference, but this difference is not the foundation for the sociological difference."[28]

Finally, there is the question of gender oppression in relationship to other oppressions. Simons asks, "Do you think that women, because of our situation of oppression, share experiences with other people who are oppressed? Instead of seeing feminism as being isolated from other movements, do you see unity because, perhaps, of this shared situation of oppression?"[29] Beauvoir replies with an unequivocal, "No."[30] So while Beauvoir often compares white woman's oppression to other forms of oppression (e.g., with slavery and racism) in *The Second Sex* and in these interviews, she sees no shared situation of oppression between women and other groups and no possibilities for unity built upon shared experiences of oppression. Benjamin follows up, "This is a problem you talk about in *The Second Sex*, that woman's oppression is very peculiar because no one else is tied to their oppression in that way."[31] To which Beauvoir says, "Yes, exactly."[32] This analogical and comparative approach to gender oppression and other forms of oppression, without regard for how they are interlocking and intersecting, were also reflected in Beauvoir's earlier assumptions in the Gerassi interview about the bourgeois intellectual women in France knowing more about feminism than the working-class women (workers' wives and women workers), as well as the claim that white women in America know more about feminism than Black women, despite her earlier casual comparison between white women lesbians' gender separatism with the racial separatism of the Black Power movement.

The last interview I take up is Hélène V. Wenzel's "Interview with Simone de Beauvoir" (1986), specifically the point at which Black women and other Women of Color suddenly become visible in this exchange. Wenzel clearly and succinctly poses a question about critiques of feminism on issues of difference as she sees them being taken up in the United States:

In the States over the last decade, there has been a large increase in the numbers of voices raised, and the writings emerging, from women of color. Both individually and collectively, these loud,

312   BEAUVOIR AND BELLE

clear, and multiethnic voices have sought to remind us—white, predominantly university women who too often think we speak for all women and who define feminism in our writings—that the women's fight is much more complex than either we, Betty Friedan or *Ms* magazine seem to think it is, and write about it. Is there a similar situation in France, have other voices, other writings begun to manifest themselves?[33]

Beauvoir replies by saying that there are not examples of this in France, except for the attention being given to "the problem of excision (clitoridectomy), which is a particularly African problem . . . And there is presently much talk about this problem."[34] To her credit, Wenzel attempts to nuance this issue, noting, "in the States, some women have begun to write and speak out against these manifestos decrying excision" and adds, "There are Black women, and African women who have begun to say that for Western women to look at African women's problems." At this point Beauvoir interrupts Wenzel and asserts, "It has nothing to do with Western women . . . I've heard that. But there are nevertheless African women who say that this problem belongs as much to Western women as to others, because it's a question of human rights."[35] Beauvoir then adds, "and there is a kind of racism, on the contrary, in not wanting to look at these sorts of conditions . . . Because that means deep down one doesn't care about what happens to little black girls . . . And it's much more feminist, logical and universal, and not racist, to be involved in these sorts of questions"[36]

I find it striking that when asked about decentering white university women in feminism and being open to hear the voices of Women of Color, this is the issue that Beauvoir names. Returning to Al-Saji's analysis of the colonial gaze, Beauvoir can point to the veil as a tool of oppression against Muslim women, or what she calls excision as a tool of oppression for African women, but she does not reflect critically on her own assumptions about the lack of agency and consciousness among Muslim women and African women. These assumptions and arguments—evident not only in *The Second Sex* but also in these interviews conducted decades later—bring to mind Audre Lorde's critiques of white feminist racism in general and of Mary Daly in

CONCLUSION 313

particular. With this in mind, in the next section I turn my attention to Lorde.

Audre Lorde's Open Letter: Confronting White Feminist Racism

In *Warrior Poet: A Biography of Audre Lorde*, Alexis De Veaux contextualizes the significance of Lorde's presence at *The Second Sex Conference* in 1979, her now-renowned "The Master's Tools Will Never Dismantle the Master's House," and the debate with and letter to Mary Daly. Noting that Adrienne Rich helped to arrange a meeting between Lorde and Daly at the 1979 conference, De Veaux explains, "Daly's presence at the conference's Friday afternoon panel on 'Developing Feminist Theory' situated her within contending and shifting truths confronting white feminist academics: success, promotion, acceptability within academe depended largely upon white male approval."[37] De Veaux also contextualizes this in terms of the shifts happening in academic networks, "While struggling within an 'ole boys network' from which they wrested a degree of power, the white feminist academics were the main distributors and consumers of that power, as the managers of women's studies programs and, later, departments; constituting, in ensuing decades, an 'ole girls network' and becoming, in effect, 'the new boys.'"[38] Of course, Lorde also gives examples of white women as gatekeepers, not only for academic conferences, but also for art exhibitions, feminist publications, and reading lists.[39]

According to De Veaux, Daly was both a target and a symbol of Lorde's anger with white feminist racism: "Daly's work was that catalyst which made it possible for Lorde to challenge the imperialist nature of white feminist thought as it was embedded in Western cultural and historical frameworks, and as it presumed to speak for a global sisterhood."[40] Lorde's "Master's Tools" speech coupled with this "Open Letter" called for feminist communities to be attentive to the power of difference and interdependence. De Veaux explains Lorde's impact in this way: "In the long run, Lorde's 'open letter' served notice to the feminist community that the fixation on gender oppression, as reality and

314 BEAUVOIR AND BELLE

theory, obscured and skewed knowledge by women whose identities were informed by cultural and historic contexts beyond those of the West."[41] She adds, "That fixation also derailed opportunities for true *solidarity* between differing women and denied the movement the potential to be revolutionary rather than reformist."[42]

Written on May 6, 1979, "An Open Letter to Mary Daly" was published four months later in September 1979 (the same month of the "*The Second Sex*—Thirty Years Later: A Commemorative Conference on Feminist Theory," where Lorde would present her "Master's Tools" speech). In many ways Lorde's "Master's Tools" (taken up in Chapter 4 of this book) and "Open Letter" (taken up here in the conclusion) are interconnected critical commentaries. I will focus on the "Open Letter" and its implications not only for Daly's *Gyn/Ecology: The Metaethics of Radical Feminism* (1978), but also for Beauvoir's *The Second Sex*, and for white feminism more generally. In her letter, Lorde takes up what will later be described by Kristie Dotson as the epistemic violence toward and epistemic silencing of Black women.[43] Lorde identifies at least two ways in which this happens. At one and of the spectrum there is the exclusion of positive representations of Black women, and at the other end of the spectrum there is the selective misrepresentation and misappropriation of Black women's work and words.

Lorde begins her letter with the long standing problem of white women's epistemic violence toward and silencing of Black women's work and words. She laments, "The history of white women who are unable to hear Black women's words, or to maintain dialogue with us, is long and discouraging."[44] Continuing with the language of difference that she also used in "The Master's Tools," Lorde invites Daly "to a joint clarification of some of the differences which lie between us as a Black and a white woman."[45] Lorde observes that in *Gyn/Ecology: The Metaethics of Radical Feminism* (1978), Daly uses white figures to offer positive frameworks for white women, but does not consider positive images of women that are not white. Reflecting specifically on Daly's exclusions of positive representations of Black figures, Lorde notes, "So I wondered, why doesn't Mary deal with Afrekete as an example? Why are her goddess images only white, western, European, judeo-christian? Where was Afrekete, Yemanje, Oyo, and Mawulisa? Where were the warrior goddesses of the Vodun, the Dahomeian Amazons

CONCLUSION 315

and the warrior-women of Dan?"[46] Again, for Lorde, this is not a matter of token representation, but rather a missed opportunity for connecting and celebrating the strengths of our differences. She explains, "What you excluded from *Gyn/Ecology* dismissed my heritage and the heritage of all other noneuropean women, and denied the real connections that exist between all of us."[47] Anticipating Daly defending herself on the basis of a lack of materials available to her (a defense that is also used for Beauvoir), Lorde asserts, "But simply because so little material on non-white female power and symbol exist in the white women's words from a radical feminist perspective, to exclude this aspect of connection from even comment in your work is to deny the fountain of noneuropean female strength and power that nurtures each one of our visions."[48] For Lorde, this is not about the circumstances of limited source materials: rather it is a political choice.[49]

In addition to the above exclusions, Lorde also critiques the misrepresentations of noneuropean women and misappropriations of Black women (including Lorde) in Daly's text. She states, "Then I came to the first three chapters of your Second Passage, and it was obvious that you were dealing with noneuropean women, but only as victims and preyers-upon each other."[50] So when Women of Color do appear in the text, they are not represented as empowered but rather as victims, despite the fact that there are several examples of non-white figures who are positive and empowered women. Lorde notes that Daly's quotations from Black women are limited to an introduction to a chapter on African genital mutilation. She discloses, "For my part, I felt that you had in fact misused my words, utilized them only to testify against myself as a woman of Color."[51] The she asks, "Mary, do you ever really read the work of Black women? Did you ever read my words, or did you merely finger through them for quotations which you thought might valuably support an already conceived idea concerning some old and distorted connection between us? This is not a rhetorical question."[52] We can apply Lorde's critiques of Daly to Beauvoir's (mis-)representations of other Others as outlined in Chapter 8 of this text and to the ways that Beauvoir takes up "clitoridectomy" as a "particularly African problem"—her only commentary on African women in the 1986 interview with Wenzel. We could also ask, not rhetorically, did Beauvoir ever read the work of Black women?

316 BEAUVOIR AND BELLE

Lorde then expands her scope from how her own words were extracted and exploited to the broader misappropriations of the words of Women of Color by white women: "To me, this feels like another instance of the knowledge, crone-ology and work of women of Color being ghettoized by a white woman dealing only out of a patriarchal western European frame of reference."[53] Lorde invites Daly into more critical awareness and consciousness: "Mary, I ask that you be aware of how this serves the destructive forces of racism and separation between women—the assumption that the herstory and myth of white women is the legitimate sole herstory and myth of all women to call upon for power and background, and that non-white women and our herstories are noteworthy only as decorations, or examples of female victimization."[54] Lorde continues, "I ask that you be aware of the effect that this dismissal has upon the community of Black women and other women of Color, and how it devalues your own words."[55]

To be sure, these problematic practices identified by Lorde, namely the exclusions of positive representations of Women of Color on the one hand, and the selective misrepresentation and misappropriation of the work and words of Women of Color on the other hand, are not mutually exclusive, but rather co-constitutive. Lorde asserts:

> The oppression of women knows no ethnic nor racial boundaries, true, but that does not mean it is identical within those differences. Nor do the reservoirs of our ancient power know these boundaries. To deal with one without even alluding to the other is to distort our commonality as well as our difference. *For then beyond sisterhood is still racism.*[56]

Lorde is showing that while women may experience oppression across ethnic and racial lines, women's oppression is not the same as racial and ethnic oppression. (And, of course, Women of Color experience these multiple oppressions simultaneously.) But Lorde is also pointing to the problem of Daly presenting positive representations of European women and then presenting negative representations of Women of Color without considering the fact that Women of Color also have agency and reservoirs of ancient power. Lorde is calling out

CONCLUSION 317

white feminist racism. Again, these critiques are applicable to Beauvoir and *The Second Sex*.

By this point, after her many efforts at consciousness raising and co-alition building with white feminists, Lorde had grown weary from her experiences of their epistemic violence and epistemic silencing. She explains, "I had decided never again to speak to white women about racism. I felt it was wasted energy because of destructive guilt and de-fensiveness, and because whatever I had to say might better be said by white women to one another at far less emotional cost to the speaker, and probably with a better hearing."[57] Thus, Lorde calls on white women to have difficult dialogues and complex communication with one another on these matters, rather than subjecting themselves and other Women of Color to constant misrecognition and vilification re-ceived from white women.[58] For all of these reasons, I have no patience for white feminist defenses of and apologetics for the problematics of *The Second Sex* that are thoroughly outlined in this project.

Coalitional Politics: Toward a Praxis of Intersectional Philosophy

Beauvoir's *The Second Sex* has been touted by some as a source for the positive possibilities for coalitions. I have no vested interest in denying these possibilities. Anything is possible. Figures and texts can be repurposed for more radical means and ends than they them-selves articulated. What is problematic is not the claim that *The Second Sex* has resources for the positive possibilities of coalition, but rather the framing of coalition as a corrective to identity politics and to intersectionality.[59] First of all, such framing ignores the challenges to coalitions that Beauvoir herself raises in remarks about the limits of solidarity. Recall that Beauvoir articulates plainly in the introduc-tion to *The Second Sex* why race and class coalitions would falter if attempted with white bourgeois women: "As bourgeois women, they are in solidarity with bourgeois men and not with women proletarians; as *white* women, they are in solidarity with *white* men and not with *black* women" (TSS 8, emphasis added). There are also her own con-descending attitudes toward Black women and other Women of Color

318 BEAUVOIR AND BELLE

(the other Others) in *The Second Sex* with similar sentiments plainly reiterated in the aforementioned interviews. We must take seriously the very negative lived experiences that Black feminists and other Women of Color feminists have had with white women that have impeded building coalitions with white women in particular. But even if we were to bracket all of that (and I do not think we should), there are also several other problems with such framing. It assumes a false dichotomy between coalition and identity politics as well as between coalition and intersectionality, and by defaulting to Beauvoir as if she is the only or ultimate source of coalitional thinking, it ignores not only the scholarship on coalition by Black women and other Women of Color but also their coalitional activism.

Recall that the term "identity politics" dates back to "The Combahee River Collective: A Black Feminist Statement" (April 1977) by Barbara Smith, Beverley Smith, and Demita Frazier.[60] They state, "We realize that the only people who care enough about us to work consistently for our liberation are us . . . This focusing upon our own oppression is embodied in the concept of *identity politics*."[61] Also recall Barbara Smith's explanation of what identity politics is *not*: "We didn't mean that if you're not the same as us, you're nothing" and furthermore, "We were not saying that we didn't care about anybody who was not exactly like us."[62] Keeanga-Yamahtta Taylor offers the following observations about their concept of identity politics: "The women of the CRC did not define 'identity politics' as exclusionary, whereby only those experiencing a particular oppression could fight against it. Nor did they envision identity politics as a tool to claim the mantle of the 'most oppressed.' "[63] She goes on to frame CRC's notion of identity politics in terms of solidarity and coalition:

> To that end, the CRC Statement was clear in its calls for solidarity as the only way for Black women to win their struggles. Solidarity did not mean subsuming your struggles to helps someone else; it was intended to strengthen the political commitments from other groups by getting them to recognize how the different struggles were related to each other and connected under capitalism . . . The CRC referred to this kind of approach to activism as coalition building, and they saw it as key to winning their struggles.[64]

CONCLUSION 319

Barbara Smith confirms and elaborates on this connection among coalition, solidarity, identity politics, and activism. She states, "I mean, we actually worked in coalitions," and "we absolutely believed in coalition building and solidarity."[65] Smith adds, "The only way that we can win—and before winning, the only way we can survive is by working with each other, and not seeing each other as enemies."[66] Thus, to frame coalition as a corrective to identity politics is to misrepresent both concepts. Rather than understanding one concept as a corrective to the other, I will note that successful efforts at coalition are actually facilitated by the CRC frameworks of identity politics (as well as their concept of interlocking systems of oppression).

Also recall the term intersectionality coined by Kimberlé Crenshaw in "Demarginalizing the Intersection of Race and Sex: A Black Feminist Critique of Antidiscrimination Doctrine, Feminist Theory and Antiracist Politics" (1989) and elaborated in "Mapping the Margins: Intersectionality, Identity Politics, and Violence Against Women of Color" (1991). She constructed a framework that brings visibility to Black women's experiences that are rendered invisible by previous frameworks that ignore them. Going beyond Black women to also include other Women of Color, she asserts, "Because women of color experience racism in ways not always the same as those experienced by men of color and sexism in ways that are not always parallel to experiences of white women, antiracism and feminism are limited, even on their own terms."[67] But Crenshaw also explicitly takes up identity groups as coalitions. She asks us to, "first recognize that the organized identity groups in which we find ourselves in are in fact *coalitions, or at least potential coalitions waiting to be formed*."[68] Crenshaw continues, "intersectionality provides a basis for reconceptualizing race as a coalition between men and women of color" and adds that "Intersectionality may provide the means of dealing with other marginalizations as well. For example, race can also be a *coalition* of straight and gay people of color, and thus serve as a basis for critique of churches and other cultural institutions that reproduce heterosexism."[69] She concludes: "Recognizing that *identity politics takes place at the site where categories intersect* thus seems more fruitful than challenging the possibility of talking about categories at all. Through an awareness of intersectionality, we can better acknowledge and ground

320 BEAUVOIR AND BELLE

the differences among us and negotiate the means by which these differences will find expression in constructing group politics."[70] Thus, to frame coalition as a corrective to intersectionality is to misrepresent both concepts. Rather than understanding one concept as a corrective to the other, I will note that successful efforts at coalition are actually facilitated by intersectionality, including intersectional critiques of white feminism.[71]

Finally, let us consider three examples of coalitional frameworks as presented by Bernice Johnson Reagon, Maria Lugones, and Mariana Ortega—rather than making white feminism in general and Beauvoir's *The Second Sex* in particular the default sources for conceptualizing coalition. Beginning with Bernice Johnson Reagon's "Coalition Politics: Turning the Century," this essay was first presented and recorded at the West Coast Music Festival in 1981 before being circulated as an audio cassette and then being published in Barbara Smith's *Homegirls: A Black Feminist Anthology* in 1983.[72] Smith explains, "I always tell people, the reason 'Coalition Politics: Turning the Century' is the last piece in the book is because that's what I wanted people to leave the book with: the idea of working together across differences."[73] Reagon opens by noting that she is in this space (a predominantly white women's music festival) with other Women of Color who find it hard to be and breathe in that space. She states, "I feel as if I am going to keel over any minute and die. That is often what I feels like if you are really doing coalitional work. Most of the time you feel threatened to the core and if you don't, you're not really doing no coalescing."[74]

Thus, Reagon is clear that coalition is not about comfort, "You don't go into coalition because you like it. The only reason you would consider trying to team up with somebody who could be trying to kill you, is because that's the only way you can figure out how to stay alive."[75] It is about survival. Coalition does not feel good, and it does not happen in safe and protected spaces—at home, in a womb (soft and without a covering), or in what she calls the "barred room" (i.e., a room that keeps others out so you can stay safe and comfortable inside). Rather, "Coalition work has to be done in the streets. And it is some of the most dangerous work you can do."[76] Furthermore, coalition is about giving, and it is insatiable. She warns, "Coalition *can* kill; however it is not by nature fatal."[77] With this in mind, she also emphasizes the importance

CONCLUSION 321

of pulling back and taking care, cautioning against becoming martyrs to coalition and/or becoming suicidal in the face of all the challenges. Reagon also warns to watch for the polarities of going too narrow at one extreme or too broad at the other with coalition. On the one hand she states, "Watch these mono-issue people. They ain't gonna do you no good . . . Watch these groups that can only deal with one thing at a time."[78] She adds, "On the other hand, learn about space within coalition. You can't have everybody sitting up there talking about everything that concerns you at the same time or you won't get no place."[79] Temporally, coalition is about past, present, and future, and it must be intergenerational. Coalitions build on past movements and are attentive to the present moment, while also projecting out into the future, "It might be wise as you deal with coalition efforts to think about the possibilities of going for fifty years."[80] Reagon elaborates, "And what I am talking about is being very concerned with the world you live in, and be able to do the kind of analysis that says that what you believe in is worthwhile for human beings in general, and in the future, and do everything you can to throw yourself into the next century."[81]

It is worth considering some background and context for Reagon's remarks. Barbara Gagliardi offers some context in "West Coast Women's Music Festival" (1981). Gagliardi is a self-identified white woman reflecting on how white feminist anti-racist ideals often fall short, citing this gathering as one example. Unlike Jessica Benjamin's condescending and defensive response to Audre Lorde's commentary at the 1979 Beauvoir conference, Gagliardi sits with the realities of this predominantly white-woman space and how white women exploited and appropriated, then rejected, Women of Color in that space. She offers examples of the exploitation of the energies of Third World women and white women's token commitments to real Third World struggles.

Gagliardi names the mockery of the "Solidarity Day" at the festival, supposedly demonstrating solidarity with Latin America, but staged (on a side stage and not the main stage) against the backdrop of white women drinking and playing during speeches meant to raise awareness about Nicaragua, Chile, El Salvador, and Argentina. Ironically, these speeches were delivered mostly by white women, "to protect the emotional security of white women."[82] And while the white women at

322   BEAUVOIR AND BELLE

the festival had little interest in hearing about Latin America in these side-stage speeches, Gagliardi notes that these same white women were happy to consume their culture in the form of their musical performances:

> Listen to the reality of the struggle and death in Latin America? No, but when it came to the music, white women were there . . . White women so willing to rip off the music, the fun, the rich cultural tradition of the Third World, to imitate in their movements their imagined portrayal of African dancing, and so unable, or unwilling, to see their lack of commitment to Third World Struggle, to deaths that were occurring while they danced.[83]

She observes the following pattern, "Third World women give, white women benefit, and walk away 'legitimizing' their experience, because it is supposedly 'anti-racist.' "[84] When a group of Latinas and supporters wrote and wanted to read a statement naming the racism and classism at the conference, they were refused: "When they attempted to gain access to the main stage that night, they were met with increased security and a refusal to have their statement read. One Latina was escorted from the land."[85] Meetings were held, and more statements were written (by white women, Jewish women, and Women of Color), this time they were given access to the stage to read new statements. They were met with defensiveness and anger, "charging us with invalidating the work that had been done, and with trying to destroy the festival."[86] Leaving the concert area, these women regrouped, discussing their shared experiences of pain and sense of invalidation, "We supported each other and reaffirmed our solidarity as Third World, Jewish and white women."[87] As Reagon noted at this very festival, coalition is not comfortable, it is not home. It is hard. But it is necessary.

In "On Complex Communication" (2006), Maria Lugones also calls for coalition, even while noting the challenge of coalition. Lugones examines liminality, communicative openings, and the necessity of complex communication to create coalitional spaces. She describes narrow understandings of the situation of the oppressed and the logic of narrow identity in this way: "From within this narrow understanding one does not seek deep coalitions among people who are differently

CONCLUSION 323

oppressed at the many intersections of gender, race, class, and sexuality."[88] And she asserts that coalition is "exceedingly difficult on two counts: it requires recognition of the intersectionality of oppressions as real and important for struggle and it requires a movement outward toward other affiliative groups recognized as resistant."[89]

Lugones revisits and clarifies her analysis of Women of Color coalitions and decolonial feminism in "Methodological Notes toward a Decolonial Feminism" (2011).[90] Noting how coalitional feminisms of Women of Color have transformed the meaning of gender, Lugones turns to Sojourner Truth, describing the question "Ain't I a woman?" as constituting "an existential, material, and social response to the idea of universal 'woman.'"[91] She reiterates her earlier claim that, "'colonized woman' is an empty category. No women are colonized. No colonized females are women. Thus, the colonial answer to Sojourner Truth is clearly—*No*."[92] But here she prefaces the claim with the nuance that the emptiness of this category, the no, is the "semantic consequence of the coloniality of gender."[93] Lugones underscores her own emphasis on the characteristic contributions of Women of Color feminisms (e.g., multiplicity, coalitional infrapolitics, intersectionality, double or multiple perception, love, and social erotics) and insists that she is not departing from Women of Color feminisms.[94] Nevertheless, she pushes Women of Color feminisms on the issue of colonization, claiming more specifically, "it has not been clear how colonization has affected the meaning of 'woman.'"[95] She names several characteristics of Women of Color feminisms that have been unclear on the coloniality of gender, while making the case for her move toward a decolonial feminism.[96]

Mariana Ortega's *In-Between: Latina Feminist Phenomenology, Multiplicity, and the Self* (2016) offers an account of the multiplicitous self that is informed by intersectionality, Women of Color (including Black feminists and Latina feminist phenomenologies), and an explicitly ontological and existential analysis. Ortega goes on to offer possibilities for "Coalitional Politics" and to propose that we engage in what she calls "Praxis of Intersectional Philosophy." Understanding the multiplicitous self provides context for both possibilities. She states, "I propose that we understand the multiplicitous self as capable of having a coalitional politics that is attuned to multiplicity, difference,

324 BEAUVOIR AND BELLE

and the intersectional or intermeshed aspect between race, class, sexuality, gender, ability, nationality, and other categories."[97] For Ortega, coalitional politics has three key elements: (1) "an understanding that coalitional politics is both a matter of being/belonging as well as becoming, which includes location, being-with, and becoming-with that lead to transformation"; (2) "an attunement to the intersectional or intermeshed aspect of our identities or an understanding that the experience of multiplicitous selfhood is informed by the intersection of various axes of power"; and (3) "a recognition not only of shared oppression but resistant agency, which is dependent on what Lugones theorizes as 'complex communication' that can lead to 'deep coalition.'"[98]

To engage in the "Praxis of Intersectional Philosophy" for Ortega is "to practice philosophy in a way that is mindful of [1] both how philosophical texts, traditional or contemporary, can be read in light of concerns related to race, class, gender, sexual orientation, physical ability, nationality, and so forth, and [2] the way these are intermeshed or inform one another and [3] in light of how philosophical texts intersect with texts from other disciplines."[99] She elaborates, "Practicing intersectional philosophy would thus require us to [4] read philosophical texts not merely to dissect them for the sake of knowing what Kant, Hegel, Arendt, Beauvoir, Fanon, and others said, but [also, 5] with both the diagnostic and constructionist projects in mind, [and 6] with an attunement to how these texts can be connected to our current social world and [7] how they can help us create new possibilities within our discipline and [8] in the worlds in which we dwell."[100] Thus, Ortega offers another vantage point from which to see and a different entry point for participation in what Lugones calls complex communication that can lead to deep coalition. Ortega makes the following call: "Let us then keep practices of *mestizaje* and intersectionality as we engage in philosophical work. Intersectionality may be helpful not only in the way we approach philosophical texts but also in how we view ourselves as philosophers."[101] It has been my intention in my Black feminist critique of Simone de Beauvoir's *The Second Sex*, coupled with attentiveness to critical and generative engagements with this figure and text by Black women and other Women of Color, to practice being attuned to and responding to this clarion call.

CONCLUSION   325

Notes

1. Alice Jardine, "An Interview with Simone de Beauvoir," *Signs* 5, no. 2 (Winter 1979): 224–236, 236.

2. Caroline Moorehead, "A Talk with Simone de Beauvoir," *New York Times*, June 2, 1974. John Gerassi, "Simone de Beauvoir: The Second Sex 25 Years Later," *Society* 13 (January–February 1976). Margaret A. Simons and Jessica Benjamin, "Simone de Beauvoir: An Interview," *Feminist Studies* 5, no. 2 (Summer 1979): 330–345. Hélène V Wenzel, "Interview with Simone de Beauvoir," *Yale French Studies*, no. 72, *Simone de Beauvoir: Witness to a Century* (1986): 5–32.

3. Caroline Moorehead, "A Talk with Simone de Beauvoir," *New York Times*, June 2, 1974. (Hereafter Moorehead 1974.)

4. Moorehead 1974, 22.

5. Moorehead 1974, 22.

6. Moorehead 1974. (Emphasis added.)

7. Alia Al-Saji, "Material Life: Bergsonian Tendencies in Simone de Beauvoir's Philosophy," in *Differences: Rereading Beauvoir and Irigary*, ed. Emily Anne Parker and Anne can Leeuwen (New York: Oxford University Press, 2017), 46.

8. These claims are followed by Beauvoir's more positive impressions of China. Ironically, given her previous statement, she notes, "I know it is easy to construct myths about countries that are very far away, but in China they do seem to be making an effort toward real equality" (Moorehead 1974).

9. John Gerassi, "Simone de Beauvoir: The Second Sex Twenty-Five Years Later," *Society* 13 (January–February 1976): 84. (Hereafter Gerassi 1976.)

10. Gerassi 1976, 84.

11. Gerassi 1976, 84.

12. Gerassi 1976, 82. (Emphasis added.)

13. Gerassi 1976, 82

14. Gerassi 1976, 84.

15. Gerassi 1976, 82.

16. Gerassi 1976, 82.

17. Gerassi 1976, 82.

18. Margaret A. Simons and Jessica Benjamin, "Simone de Beauvoir: An Interview," *Feminist Studies* 5, no. 2 (Summer 1979): 330–345. (Hereafter Simons and Benjamin 1979.) It is also worth noting that this interview is published in summer 1979, before the September 1979 conference organized by Benjamin to commemorate the thirtieth anniversary of

326   BEAUVOIR AND BELLE

the publication of *The Second Sex* where Lorde delivers her commentary, "The Master's Tools Will Never Dismantle the Master's House." The questions posed in the interview show that Benjamin was in fact aware of these critiques of white feminism ahead of the conference and Lorde's commentary—contra her claims in her 2000 letter to Olson. (See Chapter 4 in this text for more details.) Simons and Benjamin 1979, 331.

19. Simons and Benjamin 1979, 331.
20. Simons and Benjamin 1979, 335. (Emphasis added.) This brings us back to several critiques of this approach by Beauvoir that are taken up in Chapter 8 of this text.
21. Simons and Benjamin 1979, 335–336.
22. Simons and Benjamin 1979, 336. It is interesting that Benjamin could name this here (before the conference she organized in 1979 to celebrate the thirtieth anniversary of the publication of *The Second Sex*), but this insight seems to be lost in Benjamin's remarks against Lorde in her "Reply to Olson" (2000), all taken up in Chapter 4 of this book. In contrast, Simons is able to take seriously these critiques and engages them without excuses and apologetics in later publications like *Beauvoir and The Second Sex: Feminism, Race, and the Origins of Existentialism* (1999) and "Beauvoir and the Problem of Racism" (2001).
23. Simons and Benjamin 1979, 337.
24. Simons and Benjamin 1979, 340–341.
25. Simons and Benjamin 1979, 340.
26. Simons and Benjamin 1979, 342.
27. Simons and Benjamin 1979, 342.
28. Simons and Benjamin 1979, 343.
29. Simons and Benjamin 1979, 343.
30. Simons and Benjamin 1979, 343.
31. Simons and Benjamin 1979, 343–344.
32. Simons and Benjamin 1979, 344.
33. Hélène V. Wenzel, "Interview with Simone de Beauvoir." *Yale French Studies*, no. 72, *Simone de Beauvoir: Witness to a Century* (1986): 5–32, 15. (Hereafter Wenzel 1986.)
34. Wenzel 1986, 15.
35. Wenzel 1986, 15.
36. Wenzel 1986, 15.
37. Alexis De Veaux, *Warrior Poet: A Biography of Audre Lorde* (New York: W.W. Norton & Company, 2004), 247. (Hereafter De Veaux 2004.)
38. De Veaux 2004, 247.

CONCLUSION   327

39. Audre Lorde, "The Master's Tools Will Never Dismantle the Master's House," in *Sister Outsider: Essays and Speeches by Audre Lorde* (Freedom, CA: The Crossing Press, 1984), 113.

40. De Veaux 2004, 253.

41. De Veaux 2004, 253.

42. De Veaux 2004, 253. (Emphasis added.)

43. Kristie Dotson takes up this phenomenon in "Tracking Epistemic Violence, Tracking Practices of Silencing," *Hypatia* 26, no. 2 (Spring 2011): 236–257.

44. Lorde, "Open Letter," in *Sister Outsider: Essays and Speeches by Audre Lorde* (Freedom, CA: The Crossing Press, 1984), 66. (Hereafter Lorde, 1984c.)

45. Lorde 1984c, 67.

46. Lorde 1984c, 67. Lorde would take up some of these figure in her poetry collection published the previous year, *The Black Unicorn* (New York: Norton and Company, 1978).

47. Lorde 1984c, 68.

48. Lorde 1984c, 68.

49. "It is to make a point by choice" (Lorde 1984c, 68).

50. Lorde 1984c, 67. She adds, " I began to feel my history and my mythic background distorted by the absence of any of my foremothers in power" (Lorde 1984c, 68).

51. Lorde 1984c, 68.

52. Lorde 1984c, 68.

53. Lorde 1984c, 68.

54. Lorde 1984c, 69.

55. Lorde 1984c, 69.

56. Lorde 1984c, 70. (Emphasis added.)

57. Lorde 1984c, 70–71.

58. Jessica Benjamin's "Letter to Lester Olson" (2000) discussed in Chapter 4 of this text offers one example.

59. For example, see Elaine Stavro, "Rethinking Identity and Coalitional Politics, Insights from Simone de Beauvoir," *Canadian Journal of Political Science/ Revue canadienne de science politique* 40, no. 2 (June 2007): 439–463, and Emma McNicol, "Coalition as a Counterpoint to the Intersectional Critique of *The Second Sex*," *Sartre Studies International* 27, no. 2 (2021): 101–108.

60. Keeanga-Yamahtta Taylor, ed., *How We Get Free: Black Feminism and the Combahee River Collective* (Chicago: Haymarket Books, 2017). (Hereafter Taylor 2017.)

328 BEAUVOIR AND BELLE

61. Taylor 2017, 18–19. (Emphasis added.) There is a more detailed discussion of this in Chapter 4.

62. Taylor 2017, 61.

63. She adds, "They saw it as an analysis that would validate Black women's experiences while simultaneously creating an opportunity for them to become politically active to fight for the issues most important to them" (Taylor 2017, 11). See also Keeanga-Yamahtta Taylor's "Introduction" (Taylor 2017, 8–9).

64. Taylor 2017, 11.

65. Taylor, 2017, 62 and 63.

66. Taylor 2017, 64.

67. Kimberlé Crenshaw, "Mapping the Margins: Intersectionality, Identity Politics, and Violence against Women of Color," *Stanford Law Review* 43, no. 6 (July 1991): 1241–1299, 1252. (Hereafter Crenshaw 1991.)

68. Crenshaw 1991, 1299. (Emphasis added.)

69. Crenshaw 1991, 1299. (Emphasis added.)

70. Crenshaw 1991, 1299. (Emphasis added.)

71. For an extended analysis of intersectionality and coalitions in Crenshaw, see Anna Carastathis, "Identity Categories as Potential Coalitions," *Signs* 38, no. 4, *Intersectionality: Theorizing Power, Empowering Theory* (Summer 2013): 941–965. It is also worth noting that some have presented Beauvoir as offering an intersectional analysis in *The Second Sex* by pointing to places where she differentiates between white women bourgeoisie and white women proletariat (e.g., Meryl Altman, *Beauvoir in Time*). What is missed in these efforts to frame Beauvoir as intersectional is the fact that she is often centering white bourgeois women and men and/or white proletariat women and men in her comparison of (white) "woman's" oppression to other systems of oppression. To present white proletariat women as an example of Beauvoir's "intersectional" analysis continues to center whiteness while ignoring the differential experiences of people who are not white, specifically but not exclusively Black women of various classes. This is a misappropriation of the term Crenshaw coined and the corresponding theoretical framework that she constructed to bring visibility to the experiences of Black women and other Women of Color (i.e., those who are often ignored in these analogical approaches in *The Second Sex*).

72. For more on the 1981 West Coast Music Festival see: Barbara Gagliardi, "West Coast Women's Music Festival," *Big Mama Rag* (November 1981): 3, 22. (Hereafter Gagliardi 1981.) See also: Kristen Hogan, *The Feminist*

CONCLUSION 329

Bookstore Movement: Lesbian Antiracism and Feminist Accountability (Durham, NC: Duke University Press, 2016), https://revolution.berkeley.edu/west-coast-womens-festival/ and https://www.queermusicheritage.com/wmf-westcoast.html.

73. Taylor 2017, 64.
74. Bernice Johnson Reagon, "Coalition Politics: Turning the Century," *Feministische Studien* 33, no. 1 (2015): 115–123, 115. (Hereafter Reagon 2015.)
75. Reagon 2015, 115.
76. Reagon 2015, 117.
77. Reagon 2015, 118.
78. Reagon 2015, 120.
79. Reagon 2015, 120.
80. Reagon 2015, 118.
81. Reagon 2015, 121.
82. Gagliardi 1981, 22.
83. Gagliardi 1981, 22.
84. Gagliardi 1981, 22.
85. Gagliardi 1981, 22.
86. Gagliardi 1981, 22.
87. Gagliardi 1981, 22.
88. María Lugones, "On Complex Communication," *Hypatia* 21, no. 3 (Summer 2006): 75–85), 75. (Hereafter Lugones 2006.)
89. Lugones 2006, 76.
90. María Lugones, "Methodological Notes toward a Decolonial Feminism," in *Decolonizing Epistemologies: Latina/o Theology and Philosophy*, ed. Ada Mara Isasi-Daz and Eduardo Mendieta (Fordham University Press, 2011), 68–69). (Hereafter Lugones 2011.) I would like to thank Emma Velez for bringing my attention to this essay by Lugones. See also Emma Velez, "Decolonial Feminism at the Intersection: A Critical Reflection on the Relationship Between Decolonial Feminism and Intersectionality," *Journal of Speculative Philosophy* 33, no. 3 (2019): 390–406).
91. Lugones 2011, 75.
92. Lugones 2011, 75. (Emphasis original.)
93. Lugones 2011, 75.
94. Lugones 2011, 71, 72.
95. Lugones 2011, 72.
96. Lugones 2011, 72.

330 BEAUVOIR AND BELLE

97. Mariana Ortega, *In-Between: Latina Feminist Phenomenology, Multiplicity, and the Self* (New York: SUNY Press, 2016), 162. (Emphasis original.) (Hereafter Ortega 2016.)
98. Ortega 2016, 163.
99. Ortega 2016, 218.
100. Ortega 2016, 219.
101. Ortega 2016, 219.

Bibliography

Norma Alarcón. "The Theoretical Subject(s) of *This Bridge Called My Back* and Anglo-American Feminism." In *The Postmodern Turn: New Perspectives on Social Theory*, edited by Steven Seidman, 140–152. Cambridge University Press, 1994.

Allen, Paula Gunn. *The Sacred Hoop: Recovering the Feminine in American Indian Traditions*. Boston: Beacon Press, 1986.

Al-Saji, Alia. "Material Life: Bergsonian Tendencies in Simone de Beauvoir's Philosophy." In *Differences: Rereading Beauvoir and Irigary*, edited by Emily Anne Parker and Anne can Leeuwen, 21–53. New York: Oxford University Press, 2018.

Altman, Mary. *Beauvoir in Time*. Leiden: Brill Rodopi, 2020.

Amadiume, Ifi. *Male Daughters, Female Husbands: Gender and Sex in an African Society*. London: Zed Books, 1987.

Amadiume, Ifi. *Reinventing Africa: Matriarchy, Religion and Culture*. London: Zed Books, 1997.

Baker, Ella, and Marvel Cooke. "The Bronx Slave Market." *The Crisis: A Record of the Darker Races* (November 1935), 330–332.

Bambara, Toni Cade, ed. *The Black Woman: An Anthology*. New York: Washington Square Press, 1970.

Barrier Williams, Fannie. "A Northern Negro's Autobiography." *The Independent* 57, no. 2902 (July 14, 1904).

Bauer, Nancy. *Simone de Beauvoir, Philosophy, and Feminism*. New York: Columbia University Press, 2001.

Bauer, Nancy, and Hengehold, Laura, eds. *Blackwell Companion to Beauvoir*. Hoboken, NJ: Wiley-Blackwell, 2017.

Beauvoir, Simone de. *The Ethics of Ambiguity*. New York: Kensington Publishing Group, 1948.

Beauvoir, Simone de. *L'Amérique au jour le jour*. Paris: Editions Gallimard, 1954. *America Day By Day*. Translated by Carole Cosman. Berkeley: University of California Press, 1999.

Beauvoir, Simone de. *Le Deuxième Sexe*, Volumes 1 (*Les faits et les mythes*) and 2 (*L'experience vécue*). Paris: Gallimard, 1949. *The Second Sex*. Translated by Constance Borde and Sheila Chevallier. New York: Knopf, 2010.

332 BIBLIOGRAPHY

Beauvoir, Simone de. *Lettres à Sartre*. Edited by Sylvie Le Bon de Beauvoir. Paris: Gallimard, 1990. *Letters to Sartre*. Translated by Quintin Hoare. New York: Vintage Books, 1991.

Beauvoir, Simone de. *Simone de Beauvoir: Diary of a Philosophy Student*. Volume 1, *1926–1927*. Edited by Barbara Klaw, Sylvie Le Bon Beauvoir, Margaret Simons, and Marybeth Timmerman. Urbana: University of Illinois Press, 2006.

Beauvoir, Simone de. *Simone de Beauvoir: Feminist Writings*. Edited by Margaret Simons and Marybeth Timmerman. Urbana: University of Illinois Press, 2015.

Beauvoir, Simone de. *Simone de Beauvoir: Philosophical Writings*. Edited by Margaret Simons and Marybeth Timmerman. Chicago: University of Illinois Press, 2004.

Beauvoir, Simone de. *Simone de Beauvoir: Political Writings*. Edited by Margaret Simons and Marybeth Timmerman. Urbana: University of Illinois Press, 2012.

Beauvoir, Simone de. *Simone de Beauvoir: "The Useless Mother" and Other Literary Writings*. Edited by Margaret Simons and Marybeth Timmerman. 2013.

Beauvoir, Simone de. *Simone de Beauvoir: Wartime Diary*. Edited by Margaret Simons. Urbana: University of Illinois Press, 2008.

Beauvoir, Simone de. *Simone de Beauvoir: Diary of a Philosophy Student*. Volume 2, *1928–1929*. Edited by Barbara Klaw, Sylvie Le Bon Beauvoir, Margaret Simons, and Marybeth Timmerman. Urbana: University of Illinois Press,2019.

Beauvoir, Simone de. *A Transatlantic Love Affair: Letters to Nelson Algren*. Edited by Sylvie Le Bon-de Beauvoir. Translated by Ellen Gordon Reeves. New York: New Press, 1998.

Bell, Roseann P., Parker, Bettye J., and Guy Sheftall, Beverly, eds. *Sturdy Black Bridges: Visions of Black Women in Literature*. New York: Anchor Books, 1979.

Bell, Vikki. "Owned Suffering: Thinking the Feminist Imagination with Simone de Beauvoir and Richard Wright." In *Transformations* edited by Sarah Ahmed, Jane Kilby, Celia Lury, Maureen McNeil, and Beverley Skeggs, 61–76. London: Routledge, 2000.

Belle, Kathryn Sophia. (formerly Gines, Kathryn T.). "Black Feminism and Intersectional Analyses: A Defense of Intersectionality." *Philosophy Today* 55, SPEP Supplement (2011): 275–284.

Belle, Kathryn Sophia (formerly Gines, Kathryn T.). "Black Feminist Reflections on Charles Mills's 'Intersecting Contracts.'" In "Charles Mills." Special issue, *Critical Philosophy of Race* 5, no. 1 (Spring 2017): 19–28.

BIBLIOGRAPHY 333

Belle, Kathryn Sophia (formerly Gines, Kathryn T.). "Comparative and Competing Frameworks of Oppression in Simone de Beauvoir's *The Second Sex*." *Graduate Faculty Philosophy Journal* 35, nos. 1–2 (2014): 251–273.

Belle, Kathryn Sophia (formerly Gines, Kathryn T.). "A Critique of Postracialism: Conserving Race and Complicating Blackness Beyond the Black-White Binary." *Du Bois Review* 11, no. 1 (Spring 2014): 75–86.

Belle, Kathryn Sophia (formerly Gines, Kathryn T.). "Interlocking, Intersecting, and Intermeshing: Critical Engagements with Black and Latina Feminist Paradigms of Identity and Oppression." *Critical Philosophy of Race* 8, nos. 1–2 (2020): 165–198.

Belle, Kathryn Sophia (formerly Gines, Kathryn T.). "Queen Bees and Big Pimps: Sex and Sexuality in Contemporary Hip-Hop." In *Hip Hop and Philosophy: Rhyme 2 Reason*, edited by Tommie Shelby and Derrick Darby, 92–104. A Series in Pop Culture and Philosophy 16. Chicago: Open Court, 2005.

Belle, Kathryn Sophia. (formerly Gines, Kathryn T.). "Race Women, Race Men and Early Expressions of Proto-Intersectionality, 1830s–1930s." In *Why Race and Gender Still Matter: An Intersectional Approach*, edited by Namita Goswami, Maeve M. O'Donovan and Lisa Yount, 13–25. Brookfield, VT: Pickering and Chatto Publishers Limited, 2014.

Belle, Kathryn Sophia (formerly Gines, Kathryn T.). "Reflections on the Legacy and Future of Continental Philosophy With Regard to Critical Philosophy of Race." *The Southern Journal of Philosophy* 50, no. 2 (June 2012): 329–344.

Belle, Kathryn Sophia (formerly Gines, Kathryn T.). Review of *"On ne naît pas femme: on le devient . . .": The Life of a Sentence*, edited by Bonnie Mann and Martina Ferrari. *Notre Dame Philosophical Review*, June 28, 2018. https://ndpr.nd.edu/news/on-ne-nait-pas-femme-on-le-deviant-the-life-of-a-sentence/.

Belle, Kathryn Sophia (formerly Gines, Kathryn T.). "Sartre and Fanon Fifty Years Later: To Retain or Reject the Concept of Race." *Sartre Studies International* 9, no. 2 (2003): 55–67.

Belle, Kathryn Sophia. (formerly Gines, Kathryn T.). "Sartre, Beauvoir, and the Race/Gender Analogy: A Case for Black Feminist Philosophy." In *Convergences: Black Feminism and Continental Philosophy*, 35–51. Albany: State University of New York Press, 2010.

Belle, Kathryn Sophia (formerly Gines, Kathryn T.). "Simone de Beauvoir and the Race/Gender Analogy Revisited." In *Blackwell Companion to Beauvoir*, edited by Nancy Bauer and Laura Hengehold. 2017.)

Belle, Kathryn Sophia (formerly Gines, Kathryn T.). "Book Review: *Anna Julia Cooper, Visionary Black Feminist: A Critical Introduction*. By Vivian M. May (New York: Routledge, 2007); *Black Women's Intellectual Traditions: Speaking Their Minds*. By Kristin Waters and Carol B. Conaway (eds.) (Burlington: University of Vermont Press, 2007); *Black Women in the Ivory Tower, 1850–1954: An Intellectual History*. By Stephanie

334 BIBLIOGRAPHY

Y. Evans (Gainesville: University Press of Florida, 2007.); and *Daughter of the Revolution: The Major Nonfiction Works of Pauline E. Hopkins*. By Ira Dworkin (ed.) (New Brunswick: Rutgers University Press, 2007); *SIGNS* 34, no. 2 (Winter 2009): 451–459.

Belle, Kathryn Sophia (formerly Gines, Kathryn T.), and Ronald R. Sundstrom. "Philosophia Africana." In "Anna Julia Cooper." Special issue, *Analysis of Philosophy and Issues in African and the Black Diaspora* 12, no. 1 (March 2009).

Benhabib, Seyla, Butler, Judith, Cornell, Drucilla, and Fraser, Nancy, eds. *Feminist Contentions: Philosophical Exchange*. New York: Routledge, 1994.

Benjamin, Jessica. *The Bonds of Love: Psychoanalysis, Feminism, and the Problem of Domination*. New York: Pantheon Books, 1988.

Benjamin, Jessica. "Letter to Lester Olson." *Philosophy and Rhetoric* 33, no. 3: *On Feminizing the Philosophy of Rhetoric* (2000): 286–290.

Berruz, Stephanie Rivera. "At the Crossroads: Latina Identity and Simone de Beauvoir's *The Second Sex*." *Hypatia* 31, no. 2 (2016): 319–333.

Berruz, Stephanie Rivera. "Review: Kathryn T. Gines—Sartre, Beauvoir, and the Race/Gender Analogy: A Case for Black Feminist Philosophy." *Sapere Aude, Belo Horizonte* 3, no. 6 (2012): 504–507.

Blair, Deidre. *Simone de Beauvoir: A Biography*. New York: Summit Books, 1990.

Boyce Davies, Carole. *Claudia Jones: Beyond Containment*. Banbury, UK: Ayebia Clark Publishing Limited, 2011)

Boyce Davies, Carole. *Left of Karl Marx The Political Life of Black Communist Claudia Jones*. Durham, NC: Duke University Press, 2008.

Bridenbaugh, Carl. "The Earliest Published Poem of Phillis Wheatley." *New England Quarterly* 42 (1969): 583–584

Broeck, Sabine. "Re-reading de Beauvoir 'After Race': *Woman-as-Slave* Revisited." *International Journal of Francophone Studies* 14, nos. 1 and 2 (2011): 167–184.

Broeck, Sabine. *Gender and the Abjection of Blackness*. New York: SUNY Press, 2018.

Brown, Elaine. *A Taste of Power: A Black Woman's Story*. New York: HarperCollins, 1993.

Butler, Judith. *Gender Trouble: Feminism and the Subversion of Identity*. New York: Routledge, 1990.

Chen, Shirley. "'To work, write, sing and fight for women's liberation': Proto-Feminist Currents in the American Left, 1946–1961." MA thesis, University of Michigan, 2011.

Césaire, Suzanne. "1943: Le Surréalisme et nous." *Tropiques* 8–9 (October 1943): 14–18.

Césaire, Suzanne. "Alain et esthètique." *Tropiques* 2 (July 1941): 53–61.

Césaire, Suzanne. "André Breton, poet." *Tropiques* 4 (January 1942): 31–37.

BIBLIOGRAPHY 335

Césaire, Suzanne. "Le Grand camouflage." *Tropiques* 13–14 (September 1945): 267–273.

Césaire, Suzanne. "Léo Frobenius et le problém des civilisations." *Topiques* 1 (April 1941): 27–36.

Césaire, Suzanne. "Malaise d'une civilization." *Tropiques* 5 (April 1942): 43–49.

Césaire, Suzanne. "Misère d'une poésie: John Antoine-Nau." *Tropiques* 4 (January 1942): 48–50.

Church Terrell, Mary. "Lynching from a Negro's Point of View." *North American Review* 178. no. 572 (June 1904): 853–868.

Colbert, Soyica Diggs. "Practices of Freedom: Lorraine Hansberry, Freedom Writer." *Callaloo* 40, no. 2 (Spring 2017): 157–173.

Colbert, Soyica Diggs. *Radical Vision: A Biography of Lorraine Hansberry*. New Haven, CT: Yale University Press, 2021.

Conaway, Carole B., and Waters, Kristin. *Black Women's Intellectual Traditions: Speaking Their Minds*. Burlington: University of Vermont Press, 2007.

Cooper, Anna Julia. *A Voice from the South by a Black Woman from the South*. Xenia, OH: Aldine Printing House, 1892.

Cooper, Anna Julia. *The Voice of Anna Julia Cooper: Including A Voice from the South and Other Important Essays, Papers, and Letters*, edited by Charles Lemert and Esme Bhan. New York: Rowman and Littlefield, 1998.

Cooper, Brittany. *Beyond Respectability: The Intellectual Thought of Race Women*. Urbana: University of Illinois Press, 2017.

Cooper, Esther. "The Negro Woman Domestic Worker in Relation to Trade Unionism." MA Thesis, Fisk University, 1940.

Crenshaw, Kimberlé. "Demarginalizing the Intersection of Race and Sex: A Black Feminist Critique of Antidiscrimination Doctrine, Feminist Theory and Antiracist Politics." *University of Chicago Legal Forum* 139, no. 1 (1989): article 1, 139–167.

Crenshaw, Kimberlé. "Mapping the Margins: Intersectionality, Identity Politics, and Violence against Women of Color." *Stanford Law Review* 43, no. 6 (July 1991): 1241–1299.

Crenshaw, Kimberlé. "The Obama Phenomenon." The Future of Minority Studies Colloquium, Cornell University.

Curtius, Anny Dominqiue. *Suzanne Césaire: Archéologie littéraire et artistique d'une mémoire empêchée*. Paris: Karthala, 2020.

Davis, Angela. "Reflections on the Black Woman's Role in the Community of Slaves." *The Black Scholar* 3, no. 4 (1971): 2–15.

Davis, Angela. "Rape, Racism, and the Capitalist Setting." *The Black Scholar* 9, no. 7, *Blacks and The Sexual Revolution* (April 1978): 24–30.

Davis, Angela. *Women, Race, and Class*. New York: Random House 1981.

Deutscher, Penelope. *The Philosophy of Simone de Beauvoir: Ambiguity, Conversion, Resistance*. Cambridge: Cambridge University Press, 2008.

336 BIBLIOGRAPHY

Deutscher, Penelope. "Beauvoir's Old Age." In *The Cambridge Companion to Simone de Beauvoir*, edited by Claudia Card, 286–304. Cambridge: Cambridge University Press, 2003.

De Veaux, Alexis. *Warrior Poet: A Biography of Audre Lorde*. New York: W.W. Norton & Company, 2004.

Dollard, John. *Caste and Class*. Madison: University of Wisconsin Press, 1988.

Eisenstien, Zillah. *Capitalist Patriarchy and the Case for Socialist Feminism*. New York: Monthly Review Press, 1978.

Evans, Stephanie Y. "The Black Women's Studies Booklist." https://bwstbookl ist.net.

Fanon, Frantz. *Black Skin, White Masks*. Translated by Charles Lam Markmann. New York: Grove Press, 1967.

Fanon, Frantz. "L'éxperience vécue du Noir." *Esprit* 19, no.179 (May 1951): 659–679. "The Lived Experience of the Black." Translated by Valentine Moulard. In *Race*, edited by Robert Bernasconi. Boston: Blackwell Publishers, 2001.

Fanon, Frantz. *The Wretched of the Earth*. New York: Grove Press, 1963.

Ferguson, Kathy E. *The Man Question: Visions of Subjectivity in Feminist Theory*. Berkley: University of California Press, 1993.

Finot, Louis-Jean. "Egalité des races." *La revue du monde noir* 1 (1931): 5–11.

Flexner, Eleanor, and Fitzpatrick, Ellen. *Century of Struggle: The Woman's Rights Movement in the United States/* Cambridge, MA: Harvard University Press, 1959.

Freedman, Estelle. *The Essential Feminist Reader*. New York: Random House, 2007.

Fullbrook, Kate and Edward. *Simone de Beauvoir and Jean-Paul Sartre: The Remaking of a Twentieth Century Legend*. New York: Basic Books A Division of Harper Collins Publishers, 1994.

Fusco, Coco. *English Is Broken Here: Notes on Cultural Fusion in the Americas*. New York: New Press, 1990.

Gates, Henry Louis Jr. "Foreword to the Schomburg Supplement." In *The Pen Is Ours: A Listing of Writings by and about African American Women before 1910 With Secondary Bibliography to the Present*. Compiled by Jean Fagan Yellin and Cynthia D. Bond. New York: Oxford University Press, 1991.

Gerassi, John. "Simone de Beauvoir: *The Second Sex* Twenty-Five Years Later." *Society* 13 (January–February 1976): 79–85.

Giddings, Paula. *When and Where I Enter: The Impact of Black Women on Race*. New York: W. Morrow, 1984.

Gilley, Jennifer. "Ghost in the Machine: Kitchen Table Press and the Third Wave Anthology that Vanished." *Frontiers: A Journal of Women's Studies* 38, no. 3 (2019): 141–163.

Glass, Kathy. "Calling All Sisters: Continental Philosophy and Black Feminist Thinkers." In *Convergences: Black Feminism and Continental Philosophy*, edited by Maria del Guadalupe Davidson, Kathryn Sophia Belle (formerly

BIBLIOGRAPHY 337

Kathryn T. Gines), and Donna Dale Marcano, 225–239. New York: SUNY Press, 2010.

Gobineau, Arthur de. "L'Inegalité des races humaines." Paris: Librarie De Firmin Didot Freres, 1853–1855.

Gordon, Ann D., and Collier-Thomas, Bettye, eds. *African American Women and the Vote, 1837–1965.* Amherst: University of Massachusetts Press, 1997.

Gordon, Lewis. *Bad Faith and Anti-Black Racism.* Humanity Books, 1995.

Gordon, Lewis. *Existence in Black: An Anthology of Black Existential Philosophy.* New York: Routledge, 1997a.

Gordon, Lewis. *Existentia Africana: Understanding Africana Existential Thought.* New York: Routledge, 2000.

Gordon, Lewis. *Fanon: A Critical Reader,* edited by L. Gordon, T. D. Sharpley-Whiting, and R. T. White. Oxford: Blackwell Publishers, 1996.

Gordon, Lewis. *Fanon and the Crisis of European Man.* New York: Routledge, 1995.

Gordon, Lewis. *Her Majesty's Other Children: Sketches of Racism from a Neocolonial Age.* Lanham, MD: Rowman & Littlefield, 1997b.

Gordon, Lewis. "Racism as a Form of Bad Faith." In "Newsletter on Philosophy and the Black Experience," edited by Jesse Taylor and Leonard Harris. *American Philosophical Association Newsletters* 99, no. 2 (April 2000): 139–141.

Gordon, Lewis. "A Short History of the 'Critical' in Critical Race Theory." In "Newsletter on Philosophy and the Black Experience," edited by Richard Nunan and Jesse Taylor. *American Philosophical Association Newsletters* 99, no. 2 (April 2000): 151–154.

Grant, Jaime. "Building Community-Based Coalitions from Academe: The Union Institution and the Kitchen Table: Women of Color Press Transition Coalition." *Signs* 21, no. 4, *Feminist Theory and Practice* (Summer 1996): 1024–1033.

Grillo, Trina, and Wildman, Stephanie. "Obscuring the Importance of Race: The Implication of Making Comparisons between Sexism and Racism (or Other Isms)." *Duke Law Journal* 1991, no. 2 (April 1991): 397–412.

Gumbs, Alexis Pauline. "1764–1769: Phillis Wheatley." In *Four Hundred Souls: A Community History of African America, 1619–2019,* edited by Ibram X. Kendi and Keisha N. Blain, 130–134. New York: One World, 2021.

Guy-Sheftall, Beverly. "1909–1914: The Black Public Intellectual." In *Four Hundred Souls: A Community History of African America, 1619–2019,* edited by Ibram X. Kendi and Keisha N. Blain, 274–277. New York: One World, 2021.

Guy-Sheftall, Beverly. *Traps: African American Men on Gender and Sexuality,* edited by Beverly Guy-Sheftall and Rudolph Byrd. Bloomington: Indiana University Press, 2001.

Guy-Sheftall, Beverly. *Words of Fire: An Anthology of African American Feminist Thought.* New York: The New Press, 1995.

338 BIBLIOGRAPHY

Hansberry, Loraine. "Simone de Beauvoir and *The Second Sex*: An American Commentary." In *Words of Fire: An Anthology of African American Feminist Thought*, edited by Beverly Guy Sheftall, 128–142. New York: The New Press, 1995.

Hill Collins, Patricia. *Black Feminist Thought: Knowledge, Consciousness, and the Politics of Empowerment*. Boston: Unwin Hyman, 1990.

Hill Collins, Patricia. "Simone de Beauvoir, Woman's Oppression and Existential Freedom." In *Blackwell Companion to Beauvoir*, edited by Nancy Bauer and Laura Hengehold, 325–338. Hoboken, NJ: Wiley-Blackwell, 2017.

Hodin, Mark. "Lorraine Hansberry's Absurdity: *The Sign in Sidney Brustein's Window*." *Contemporary Literature* 50, no. 4 (Winter 2009): 742–774.

Holland, Sharon Patricia. *The Erotic Life of Racism*. Durham, NC: Duke University Press, 2012.

hooks, bell. *Ain't I a Woman: Black Women and Feminism*. Boston: South End Press, 1981.

hooks, bell. "True Philosophers: Beauvoir and bell." In *Simone de Beauvoir in Western Thought: Plato to Butler*, edited by Shannon M. Mussett and William S. Wilkerson, 212. Albany, NY: SUNY Press, 2012.

Higashida, Cheryl. *Black Internationalist Feminism: Women Writers of the Black Left. 1945–1995*. Urbana: University of Illinois Press, 2013.

Higashida, Cheryl. "To Be(come) Young, Gay, and Black: Lorraine Hansberry's Existentialist Routes to Anticolonialism." *American Quarterly* 60. no. 4 (December 2008): 899–924.

Horne, Alistair. *A Savage War of Peace: 1954–1962*. New York: New York Review Books, 2006.

Hull, Gloria T., Bell Scott, Patrica, and Smith, Barbara, eds. *All of the Women Are White, All of the Blacks Are Men, But Some of Us Are Brave: Black Women's Studies*. New York: The Feminist Press, 1982.

James, Susan. "Complicity and Slavery in The Second Sex." In *The Cambridge Companion to Simone de Beauvoir*, edited by Claudia Card, 149–167. Cambridge: Cambridge University Press, 2006.

James, V. Denise. "Denise James on Political Illusions." In *Unmuted: Conversations on Prejudice, Oppression, and Social Justice*, edited by Myisha Cherry, 11–23. New York: Oxford University Press, 2019.

Jardine, Alice. "An Interview with Simone de Beauvoir." *Signs* 5, no. 2 (Winter 1979): 224–236.

Jeffery, Julie Roy. *The Great Silent Army of Abolition: Ordinary Women in the Antislavery Movement*. Chapel Hill: University of North Carolina Press, 1998.

Jones, Claudia. "An End to the Neglect of the Problems of Negro Women!" *Political Affairs: A Magazine Devoted to the Theory and Practice of Marxism-Leninism* 28, no. 6 (June 1949): 3–19.

BIBLIOGRAPHY   339

Jones, Claudia. "For New Approaches to Our Work Among Women." *Political Affairs: A Magazine Devoted to the Theory and Practice of Marxism-Leninism* 27 (August 1948): 738–743.

Jones, Martha S. *Vanguard: How Black Women Broke Barriers, Won the Vote, and Insisted on Equality for All.* New York: Basic Books, 2020.

King, Deborah. "Multiple Jeopardy, Multiple Consciousness: The Context of a Black Feminist Ideology." *Signs* 14, no. 1 (1988): 42–72.

Kruks, Sonia. *Simone de Beauvoir and the Politics of Ambiguity.* Oxford: Oxford University Press, 2012.

Lawson, Elizabeth. "Woman: Second Sex." *Worker*, October 24, 1954, 12.

Leboeuf, Celine "'One is not born, but rather becomes, a woman': The Sex-Gender Distinction and Simone de Beauvoir's Account of Woman: *The Second Sex.*" In *Feminist Movements: Reading Feminist Texts*, edited by Katherine Smits and Susan Bruce, 138–145. Bloomsbury Academic, 2016.

Lee, Kyoo. "Hypatia's Gaze." In *Philosophy by Women: 22 Philosophers Reflect on Philosophy and Its Value*, edited by Elly Vintiadis, 67–75. New York: Routledge, 2020.

Lee, Kyoo. "Just Throw Like a Bleeding Philosopher: Menstrual Pauses and Poses, Betwixt Hypatia and Bhubaneswari, Half Visible, Almost Illegible." In *Feminist Phenomenology Futures*, edited by Helen A Fielding and Dorothea E. Olkowski, 21–46. Bloomington: Indiana University Press, 2017.

Lee, Kyoo. "Second Languaging *The Second Sex*, Its Conceptual Genius: A Translingual Contemporization of 'On ne naît pas femme: on le devient.'" In *A Companion to Simone de Beauvoir*, edited by Laura Hengehold and Nancy Bauer, 500–513. Hoboken, NJ: Wiley and Sons, 2017.

Lee, Kyoo. "Should My Bum Look Bigger in This?—Re-dressing the Beauvoirian Femme." *Women's Studies Quarterly* 41, nos. 1/2 (Spring/Summer 2012): 184–193.

Lee, Kyoo. "Why Asian Female Stereotypes Matter to All: Beyond Black and White, East and West." *Critical Philosophy of Race* 1, no. 1 (2013): 86–103.

Lerner, Gerda. *Black Women in White America: A Documentary History.* New York: New York Vintage Books, 1972, 1992.

Lorde, Audre. "Age, Race, Class and Sex: Black Women Redefining Difference." In *Sister Outsider: Essays and Speeches by Audre Lorde*, 114–123. Freedom: The Crossing Press, 1984.

Lorde, Audre. "The Master's Tools Will Never Dismantle the Master's House." In *Sister Outsider: Essays and Speeches by Audre Lorde*, 110–114. Freedom, CA: The Crossing Press, 1984.

Lorde, Audre. "An Open Letter to Mary Daly." In *Sister Outsider: Essays and Speeches by Audre Lorde*, 66–71. Freedom, CA: The Crossing Press, 1984.

Lugones, Maria. "Heterosexism and the Colonial/Modern Gender System." *Hypatia* 22, no. 1 (Winter 2007): 186–209.

Lugones, Maria. "Towards a Decolonial Feminism." *Hypatia* 25, no. 4 (Fall 2010): 742–759.

340 BIBLIOGRAPHY

Mann, Bonnie, and Ferrari, Martina, eds. *"On ne naît pas femme: on le devient...": The Life of a Sentence*. Oxford: Oxford University Press, 2017

Marcano, Donna Dale. "Talking Back: bell hooks, Feminism and Philosophy." In *Critical Perspectives on bell hooks*, edited by Maria del Guadalupe Davidson and George Yancy, 111–120. New York: Routledge, 2009.

Markowitz, Sally. "Oriental Dreams: Orientalism and History in *The Second Sex*." *Signs: Journal of Women in Culture and Society* 34, no. 2 (2009): 271–294.

Martin, Charles H. "Race, Gender, and Southern Justice: The Rosa Lee Ingram Case." *The American Journal of Legal History* 29, no. 3 (July 1985): 251–268.

Mason, Julian. "'Ocean; A New Poem by Phillis Wheatly." *Early American Literature* 34, no. 1 (1999): 78–83.

Mason, Qresent Mali. "An Ethical Disposition toward the Erotic: The Early Autobiographical Writings of Simone de Beauvoir and Black Feminist Philosophy." PhD dissertation, Temple University, 2014.

Massa, Ann. "Black Women in the 'White City.'" *Journal of American Studies* 8 (1974): 319–337.

May, Vivian M. *Anna Julia Cooper, Visionary Black Feminist: A Critical Introduction*. New York: Routledge, 2007.

McDuffie, Erik. "'No Small Amount of Change Could Do': Esther Cooper Jackson and the Making of a Black Left Feminist." In *Want to Start a Revolution?: Radical Women in the Black Freedom Struggle*, edited by Dayo F. Gore, Jeanne Theoharris, and Komazi Woodward, 25–46. New York: New York University Press, 2009.

McDuffie, Erik. *Sojourning for Freedom: Black Women, American Communism, and the Making of Black Left Feminism*. Durham, NC: Duke University Press, 2011.

McGill, Lisa. "Sister Outsider: African God(desse)s, Black Feminist Politics, and Audre Lorde's Liberation." In *Constructing Black Selves: Caribbean American Narratives and the Second Generation*, 117–160. New York: NYU Press, 2005.

Millard, Betty, "Woman Against Myth." New York: International Publishers, 1948.

Mills, Charles. "Intersecting Contracts." In *Contract and Domination* by Charles Mills and Carole Pateman, 165–199. Cambridge: Polity Press, 2007.

Moi, Toril. *Simone de Beauvoir: The Making of an Intellectual Woman*. Oxford: Oxford University Press, 2008.

Moody-Turner, Shirley. *The Portable Anna Julia Cooper*. New York: Pengin Books, 2022.

Moorehead, Caroline. "A Talk with Simone de Beauvoir." *New York Times*, June 2, 1974, 16–34.

Morrison, Toni. "A Humanist View." Speech from Portland State University's Public Speakers Collection: "Black Studies Center public dialogue Pt. 2," May 30, 1975.

BIBLIOGRAPHY 341

Morrison, Toni. *The Origin of Others*. Cambridge, MA: Harvard University Press, 2017.

Myrdal, Alva. "A Parallel to the Negro Problem." Appendix 5 in *An American Dilemma: The Negro Problem and Modern Democracy*, edited by Gunnar Myrdal, Volume 2, 1073–1078. New York: Harper, 1944.

Myrdal, Gunnar. *An American Dilemma: The Negro Problem and Modern Democracy*. New York: Harper, 1944.

Nya, Nathalie. *Simone de Beauvoir and the Colonial Experience: Freedom, Violence, and Identity*. Lanham, MD: Lexington Books, 2019.

O'Brien, Mary. *The Politics of Reproduction*. London: Routledge, 1983.

Ogunyemi, Chikwenye. "Womanism: The Dynamics of the Contemporary Black Female Novel in English." *Signs* 11, no. 1 (Autumn 1985): 63–80.

Olson, Lester C. "The Personal, the Political, and Others: Audre Lorde Denouncing 'The Second Sex Conference.'" *Philosophy and Rhetoric* 33, no. 3, *On Feminizing the Philosophy of Rhetoric* (2000): 259–285.

Ortega, Mariana. "Phenomenological Encuentros: Existential Phenomenology and Latin American & U.S. Latina Feminism." *Radical Philosophy Review* 9, no. 1 (2006): 45–64.

Oyěwùmí, Oyèrónké. "Family Bonds/Conceptual Binds: African Notes on Feminist Epistemologies." *Signs* 25, no. 4, *Feminisms at a Millennium* (Summer 2000): 1093–1098

Oyěwùm í, Oyèrónké. *The Invention of Women: Making an African Sense of Western Gender Discourses*. Minneapolis: University of Minnesota Press, 1997.

Paddon, Anna R., and Turner, Sally. "African Americans and the World's Columbian Exposition." *Illinois Historical Journal* 88, no. 1 (Spring 1995): 19–36.

Painter, Nell Irvin. "Introduction." In *Narrative of Sojourner Truth*, vii–xx. New York: Penguin Classics, 1998.

Painter, Nell Irvin. *Sojourner Truth: A Life, A Symbol*. London: W. W. Norton and Company, 1997.

Painter, Nell Irvin. "Sojourner Truth in Life and Memory: Writing the Biography of and American Exotic." *Gender and History* 2 (1990): 3–19.

Perina, Mickaella. "Encountering the Other: Aesthetics, Race and Relationality." *Contemporary Aesthetics* 2 (2009): 1.

Perry, Imani. *Looking for Lorraine: The Radiant and Radical Life of Lorraine Hansberry*. Boston: Beacon Press, 2018.

Pohlhaus, Jr., Gaile. "Understanding Across Difference and Analogical Reasoning in Simpson's Unfinished Project." *Journal for Peace and Justice Studies* 19, no. 1 (2009): 37–49.

Relyea, Sarah. *Outsider Citizens: The Remaking of Postwar Identity in Wright, Beauvoir, and Baldwin*. New York: Routledge, 2006.

Richardson, Marilyn. *Maria W. Stewart, America's First Black Political Writer: Essays and Speeches*. Bloomington: Indiana University Press, 1987.

342 BIBLIOGRAPHY

Sartre, Jean-Paul. *Anti-Semite and Jew*. Translated by George J. Becker. New York: Schocken Books, 1948.

Sartre, Jean-Paul. *Being and Nothingness*. Translated by Hazel E. Barnes. New York: Washington Square Press, 1956.

Sartre, Jean-Paul. *Carnets de la drôle de guerre*. Paris: Gallimard, 1983. *War Diaries: Notebooks from a Phony War 1939–40*. Translated by Quintin Hoare. London: Verso, 1984.

Sartre, Jean-Paul. *Critique of Dialectical Reason*. Translated by Alan Sheridan Smith. New York: Verso, 1976.

Sartre, Jean-Paul. *Notebooks for an Ethics*. Chicago: University of Chicago Press, 1992.

Sartre, Jean-Paul. "Orphée Noir." In *Anthologie de la nouvelle poésie nègre et malgache de langue française*. Paris: Presses Universitaires de France, 1948. Reprinted with minor revisions as "Black Orpheus," translated by John MacCombie, in *Race*, edited by Robert Bernasconi, vii–xx. Boston: Blackwell Publishers, 2001.

Scarth, Fredrika. *The Other Within: Ethic, Politics, and the Body in Simone de Beauvoir*. New York: Rowman and Littlefield Publishers, Inc., 2004.

Sharpley-Whiting, T. Denean . *Beyond Negritude: Essays from Women in the City*. Albany, NY: SUNY Press, 2009.

Sharpley-Whiting, T. Denean. *Negritude Women*. Minneapolis: University of Minnesota Press, 2002.

Sharpley-Whiting, T. Denean. "Tropiques and Suzanne Césaire: The Expanse of Negritude and Surrealism." In *Race and Racism in Continental Philosophy*, edited by Robert Bernasconi; co-edited by Symbol Cook, 115–128. Bloomington: Indiana University Press, 2003.

Shockley, Ann Allen. *Afro-American Women Writers 1746–1933: An Anthology and Critical Guide*. Boston: G.K. Hall & Co, 1988.

Simmons, Margaret. "Beauvoir and the Problem of Racism." In *Philosophers on Race: Critical Essays*, edited by Julie K. Ward and Tommy L. Lott, 260–284. Malden, MA: Blackwell Publishers Ltd., 2001.

Simmons, Margaret. *Beauvoir and the Second Sex: Feminism, Race, and the Origins of Existentialism*. Lanham, MD: Rowman and Littlefield, 1999.

Simmons, Margaret. *Feminist Interpretations of Simone de Beauvoir*. University Park: Pennsylvania State University Press, 1995.

Simmons, Margaret. "Introduction." In *Simone de Beauvoir: Philosophical Writings*, edited by Margaret Simons and Marybeth Timmerman, 1–12. Chicago: University of Illinois Press, 2004.

Simmons, Margaret. *The Philosophy of Simone de Beauvoir: Critical Essays*. Bloomington: Indiana University Press, 2006.

Simmons, Margaret, and Jessica Benjamin. "Simone de Beauvoir: An Interview." *Feminist Studies* 5, no. 2 (Summer 1979): 330–345.

Simpson, Lorenzo Charles. *The Unfinished Project: Toward a Post-Metaphysical Humanism*. New York: Routledge, 2001.

BIBLIOGRAPHY 343

Smith, Barbara, Beverly Smith, and Demita Frazier. "Combahee River Collective: A Black Feminist Statement." 1977.

Smith, Barbara. "A Press of Our Own, Kitchen Table: Women of Color Press." *Frontiers: A Journal of Women's Studies* 10, no. 3, *Women and Words* (1989): 11-13.

Smith, Valerie. "Black Feminist Theory and the Representation of the 'Other.'" In *The Woman that I Am: Literature and Culture of Contemporary Women of Color*, edited by D. Soyini Madison, 671-687. New York: Routledge, 1998.

Spelman, Elizabeth. *Inessential Woman: Problems of Exclusion in Feminist Thought*. Boston: Beacon Press, 1988.

Spillers, Hortense. "Mama's Bay, Papa's Maybe: An American Grammar Book." *Diacritics* 17, no. 2, *Culture and Countermemory: The "American" Connection* (Summer 1987): 64-81.

Spillers, Hortense, Hartman, Saidiya, Griffin, Farah Jasmine, Eversley, Shelly, and Morgan, Jennifer L. "Whatcha Gonna Do?—Revisiting 'Mama's Bay, Papa's Maybe: An American Grammar Book.'" *Women's Studies Quarterly* 35, nos. 1/2, *Social Science Premium Collection* (Spring 2007): 299-309.

Starobin, Joseph Robert. *American Communism in Crisis: 1943-1957*. Berkley: University of California Press, 1972.

Taylor, Keeanga-Yamahtta. *How We Get Free: Black Feminism and the Combahee River Collective*. Chicago: Haymarket Books, 2017.

Terborg-Penn, Rosalyn. *African American Women and the Struggle for the Vote, 1850-1920*. Bloomington: Indiana University Press, 1998.

Terborg-Penn, Rosalyn. "Discrimination Against Afro-American Women in the Women's Movement, 1830-1920." In *The Afro-American Woman: Struggles and Images*, edited by Sharon Harley and Rosalyn Terborg-Penn, 17-27. Baltimore, MD: Black Classic Press, 1997.

Tetrault, Lisa. *The Myth of Seneca Falls: Memory and the Women's Suffrage Movement, 1848-1898*. Chapel Hill: University of North Carolina Press, 2014.

Thompson-Spires, Nafissa. "1744-1749: Lucy Terry Prince." In *Four Hundred Souls: A Community History of African America, 1619-2019*, edited by Ibram X. Kendi and Keisha N. Blain, 115-118. New York: One World, 2021.

Valens, Keja L. "Lost Idyll: Mayotte Capécia's Je suis martiniquaise." In *Desire Between Women in Caribbean Literature*, 45-64. New York: Palgrave Macmillan, 2013.

Washington, Mary Helen. "Alice Childress, Lorraine Hansberry, and Claudia Jones: Black Women With the Popular Front." In *Left of the Color Line; Race, Radicalism, and Twentieth Century Literature of the United States*, edited by Bill Mullen James Smethurst, 183-204. Chapel Hill: University of North Carolina Press, 2003.

Waters, Kristin. *Maria Stewart and the Roots of Black Political Thought*. Jackson: University of Mississippi Press, 2022.

344 BIBLIOGRAPHY

Weigand, Kate. *Red Feminism: American Communism and the Making of Women's Liberation*. Baltimore: Johns Hopkins University Press, 2001.

Wells, Ida B. *Crusade for Justice: The Autobiography of Ida B. Wells*. Edited by Alfreda M. Barnett Duster. Chicago: University of Chicago Press, 1970.

Wenzel, Hélène V. "Interview with Simone de Beauvoir." *Yale French Studies*, no. 72, *Simone de Beauvoir: Witness to a Century* (1986): 5–32.

Wilkerson, Margaret B. "Lorraine Hansberry (1930–1965)." In *Words of Fire: An Anthology of African American Feminist Thought*. New York: The New Press, 1995.

Wilkerson, Margaret B. "The Sighted Eyes and Feeling Heart of Lorraine Hansberry." *African American Review* 50, no. 4 (Winter 2017): 698–703.

Wright, Richard. *Black Boy*.

Yee, Shirley J. *Black Women Abolitionists: A Study in Activism, 1825–1860*. Knoxville: University of Tennessee Press, 1992.

Index

For the benefit of digital users, indexed terms that span two pages (e.g., 52–53) may, on occasion, appear on only one of those pages.

abolitionist movement
    anti-Indigenous sentiments, 234–35, 242, 250–51
    anti-slavery, 236–40, 242–43
    Beauvoir's approach to, 24
    suffrage and, 232–40
activism
    anti-lynching, 47–48, 49, 246
    anti-segregation, 47–48
    by Black women, 18, 307–8
Africa, 271–72, 278–79, 284–90
African American Communists, 90
Ahmed, Sara, 11–12
Ain't I a Woman: Black Women and Feminism (hooks), 219–20
Alarcón, Norma, 19–20, 216–17
Alexander, Sadie Tanner Mossell, 52
Algeria, 305–6
Algren, Nelson, 176–77
Alpha Suffrage Club, 246
Al-Saji, Alia, 20–21, 24–25, 275–77
alterity, 172–73, 286
Altman, Meryl, 11–12
America Day By Day (Beauvoir), 18
American Anti-Slavery Society, 236
American Communist Party (CPUSA), 74–75
American Equal Rights Association (AERA), 245–46
American Federation of Labor, 54
analogy/analogies. *See also* Beauvoir, Simone de, analogical approach; race/gender analogy; slave/woman analogy
    false analogies, 191–92, 193

marriage-as-prostitution, 153–54
proper analogies, 191–92
slave/mother, 309–10
Angelou, Maya, 1–2
Anthony, Susan B., 236–37, 246–47
Anthony Amendment, 249
antifeminism, 165, 168, 181, 184
anti-imperialism, 75, 138
anti-Indigenous sentiments, 234–35, 242, 250–51
anti-intellectualism, 116–17
anti-lynching activism, 47–48, 49, 246
antiracism, 41, 57–62, 168, 206, 214, 238–40, 319–20, 321–22
anti-segregation activism, 47–48
antisemitism, 93, 165, 185–86, 265
antisexism, 58–59
anti-slavery, 236–40, 242–43
Arabs, 266–67, 271–73, 275–76, 289–91
Asian, 266–67, 270–71, 274–81, 285–86, 289–91
Asian woman-ness, 278–79

bad faith, 7–8, 16–17, 117–18, 120, 122–23
Baker, Ella, 53–55
Barnett, Ida B. Wells, 234
Bauer, Nancy, 8–10, 113–14, 213–14
Baumeister, Anna-Lisa, 289
Beale, Francis, 57–58
Beauvoir, Simone de. See also *The Second Sex*
    abolition and suffrage movements, 233–35, 250–52
    Altman, Meryl on, 11–12

346 INDEX

Beauvoir, Simone de (*cont.*)
  Bauer, Nancy on, 8–10
  historical materialism, 119–21
  hooks, bell on, 1–6, 20–21
  Moi, Toril on, 9–11
  as philosopher, 6–12
  Sartre, Jean-Paul and, 6–8, 112–
    13, 169–70
Beauvoir, Simone de, analogical approach
  antifeminism, 165, 168, 181, 184
  critiques of, 184–90
  false analogies and, 191–92, 193
  to identity, 23–24
  introduction to, 165–67
  oppression, 165–66, 178–84
  potential and pitfalls of, 190–94
  proper analogies, 191–92
  race/gender analogy, 166–78
Beauvoir and The Second Sex:
  Feminism, Race, and the Origins of
  Existentialism (Simons), 7–8
Beauvoir in Time (Altman), 11–12
Beauvoir's slave/woman analogy. *See*
  slave/woman analogy
Benjamin, Jessica, 23, 144–53, 309, 321
Bergoffen, Debra, 289
Berruz, Stephanie Rivera, 20–21, 24–25,
  188, 279–80
biological determinism, 287, 288–89
black femaleness, 14
Black feminism
  abolition and suffrage
    movements, 250–52
  background on, 13–16
  Benjamin, Jessica and, 144–45
  in eighteenth century, 41–43
  introduction to, 1–6, 39–41
  in 1940s America, 16–18
  in nineteenth century, 44–48
  overview of, 21–26, 63
  superexploitation of Black women,
    80–81, 88–89
  in twentieth century, first half, 48–56
  in twentieth century, second
    half, 56–62
black feminist thought, vii–viii, ix–x, 16–
  18, 23, 59–60, 139, 149–50, 188
Black internationalist feminism, 74–76

Black left feminism, 74–76
Black lesbian feminist, 139–41, 142–44,
  145–46, 152–53
Black liberation, 74–75, 83–84, 237–38,
  244, 248
Black men raping white women
  myth, 49–50
Black Power movement, 307–9
Black/white binary, 24–25, 278–80
Black womanism, 179–80
Black women activism, 18, 307–8
Black Women's Club Movement, 87–88
Bogić, Anna, 286–87
Boupacha, Djamila, 276–77
Broeck, Sabine, 184–85, 214–16, 224–25
Bronx Slave Market, 53–55
Butler, Octavia, 40–41

Capécia, Mayotte, 15
capitalism, 2–3, 22, 57–59, 75–76, 83, 148,
  282–84, 308–9, 318
Carter, Emma Lean, 86
Carter, William Tim, 86
Cary, Mary Ann Shadd, 249
Center for Disease Control (CDC), 79–80
Césaire, Suzanne, 14, 15
Chen, Shirley, 96–97
Civil Rights Congress, 87
civil rights movement, 56–57, 90, 235–36
class differences, 5, 183–84, 238, 306–7
classism, 44–45, 165
class oppression, 22, 44–45, 51, 52–53,
  58–59, 75–76, 89, 91–92, 149, 165,
  181, 188–90, 240–41
Claudia Jones: Beyond Containment
  (Davies), 75
coalitional politics, 25–26, 302, 317–24
Colbert, Soyica Diggs, 119–21
colonialism
  Beauvoir, Simone de on, 20–21, 165
  coloniality of gender and, 274–81
  Hansberry, Lorraine on, 120, 126–27
  Moi, Toril on, 11
  Negritude movement and, 14–16
  neocolonialism, 305–6
  Sartre, Jean-Paul and, 15–16
coloniality of gender
  colonialism and, 274–81

INDEX   347

decolonial feminism, 281–84
historical materialism and, 268–69
historical narratives on, 269–74
Latina feminism, 266–67, 280–81
Lugones, María on, 267–68, 281–84
orientalism, 25–26, 266–67, 274–81, 290–91
others/othering, 263–68, 274–81
Western gender discourses, 284–90
colonized woman, 165, 194, 283, 323
Colored Women's League, 46
Communist Party USA, 54, 55–56, 77, 88–94
complex communication, 317, 322–24
complicity, 22–23, 121–24
Congress of American Women, 94
Cook, Joyce Mitchell, 1
Cooke, Marvel, 53–55
Cooper, Anna Julia, 11–12, 46–47, 91–92
Cooper (Jackson), Esther, 54–55
CRC statement, 58–59
Crenshaw, Kimberlé
  demarginalizing, 41, 60–62, 319–20
  intersectionality and, 319–20
  white feminism, 220

Daly, Mary, 314–15
Davies, Carol Boyce, 75, 95
Davis, Angela
  abolition and suffrage movements, 234, 236, 239–47, 248
  Communist Party and, 90–91
  slave/woman analogy, 218–19, 221–23
  decolonial feminism, 24–26, 267–68, 281–84, 290–91, 302, 323
demarginalizations, 41, 60, 62, 319–20
Deutscher, Penelope, 177, 184–85, 186
De Veaux, Alexis, 145–46, 152, 153–55, 313–14
domestic duties, 24, 53–55, 80–82, 179–80, 206
Dotson, Kristie, 314
double consciousness, 172, 173, 277–78
Douglass, Frederick, 239–40, 245, 246–47
Douglass, Rosetta, 239–40
Du Bois, W. E. B., 173–74

economic exploitation, 48–49, 56–57, 81–82

"An End to the Neglect of the Problems of the Negro Woman!" (Jones), 55–56, 74–75, 76
Engels, Friedrich, 119
epistemic silencing, 314, 317
epistemic violence, 12, 314–15, 317
Equal Suffrage Association, 246–47
erotic, 20–21, 142, 189–90, 323
The Essential Feminist Reader (Freedman), 137–38
essentialism, 14, 80–81, 148–49, 280–81, 286, 310–11
ethnocentrism, 186, 190–92, 216–17, 309
excision (clitoridectomy), 312–13
existentialism
  Beauvoir, Simone de on, 110, 118–21, 280, 286
  feminist engagements with, 20–21
  Hansberry, Lorraine on, 22–23, 119–21
  Sartre, Jean-Paul and, 7–8

false analogies, 191–92, 193
fascism, 55–56, 93
female identity, 2–3, 20–21
Femenías, María Luisa, 280
femininity stereotype, 57–58
feminism. *See also* Black feminism; white feminism
  antifeminism, 165, 168, 181, 184
  decolonial feminism, 24–26, 267–68, 281–84, 290–91, 302, 323
  existentialism and, 20–21
  French feminist perspective, 9–10, 310–11
  intersectionality and, 319–20
  Latina feminism, 20–21, 23–24, 166–67, 186, 266–67, 280–81, 323–24
  material feminism, 10, 276–77
  Ortega, Mariana, 280–81
  proto-feminism, 144–45, 167–68
  racist feminism, 141
  sexism and, 7–8
feminist consciousness, 138, 251, 306–8
fetish, 218
Flexner, Eleanor, 235–36
Force of Circumstance (Beauvoir), 302–4
Freedman, Estelle B., 137–38
free woman myth, 124–26

348 INDEX

French feminist perspective, 9–
   10, 310–11
Fullbrook, Edward, 6–7
Fullbrook, Kate, 6–7

Gagliardi, Barbara, 321–22
Garrison, William Lloyd, 239–40
Gates, Henry Louis, Jr., 43
gender, coloniality of. *See* coloniality
   of gender
gendered identity, 92, 144–45, 221
gender oppression
   Beauvoir, Simone de on, 166–68, 172–
     73, 187–88, 189–90, 311
   Jones, Claudia on, 22
   others/othering/otherness, 263–68
   Stewart, Maria W. on, 44–45
   Wells, Ida B. on, 47–48
   Western gender discourses, 284–90
gender politics, 12–13, 19–20, 92
gender separatism, 306–7, 310–11
gender subordination, 170–71, 181
Gerassi, John, 25–26, 306, 308–9, 310–11
ghetto existence, 82–83, 316
Giddings, Paula, 234, 236, 247–
   48, 249–50
Glass, Kathy, 20–21, 188–89, 223–25
Gordon, Lewis, 119–20
Gouges, Olympe de, 167–68
Grillo, Trina, 192–94
Grimke, Angelina, 223, 237
Grimke, Sarah, 223, 237
Guy-Sheftall, Beverly, 44, 45–46, 56–
   57, 247

Hansberry, Lorraine
   biological imperative, 111–14
   colonialism and, 120, 126–27
   complicity and resistance, 121–24
   existentialism and historical
     materialism, 119–21
   introduction to, 11–12, 19–20, 108–11
   Marxism and, 22–23, 126–27
   negative readings of, 115–17
   Negro *vs.* woman question, 22–
     23, 126–27
   oppression and, 121–24
   positive readings of, 114–15

sexuality and, 120–21, 126–27
theoretical rigor of, 117–19
woman's experiences and, 124–26
Harlem Renaissance, 51
Heidegger, Martin, 280
heterosexism, 44, 58–59, 282–84, 319–20
Hierro, Graciela, 280
Higashida, Cheryl, 119–21
Hill Collins, Patricia, 20–21, 51, 187–88,
   220–21, 224–25
historical materialism, 22–23, 119–21
Holland, Sharon Patricia, 20–21
holocausts, 179–80, 194–95
homosexuality, 113
hooks, bell
   abolition and suffrage movements, 234
   anti-slavery, 236–40
   on Beauvoir, Simone de as philosopher,
     1–6, 20–21
   self-naming, 1–2
   slave/woman analogy, 223
   on Stanton, Elizabeth Cady, 244
   as true philosopher, 1, 2–3, 5–6
   woman-as-slave metaphor, 219–20
Horner, Elizabeth, 87
Horner, William, 87
hostile men, 110, 115–17

identity
   Beauvoir, Simone de on, 23–24, 165
   female identity, 2–3, 20–21
   gendered identity, 92, 144–45, 221
   Latina identity, 188
   sexual identity, 44, 145–46
identity politics
   Altman, Meryl on, 12
   Benjamin, Jessica and, 146–48
   Lorde, Audre on, 139
   misappropriation of, 23
   oppression and, 148, 318
   solidarity and coalition frame, 318–19
ignorant women, 110, 115–17
imperialism, 75–76, 77–78, 83, 145–46,
   147, 148, 185–86, 218, 244, 308–
   9, 313–14
Indians, 266–67, 269–73, 285–86, 290–91
Indian tribes. *See* non-specified
   "primitives"

INDEX 349

Ingram, Rosa Lee, 85–86
Inman, Mary, 90
intelligent women, 115–16
interdependency, 138, 139–44,
    150, 313–14
interlocking systems of oppression, 44,
    58–60, 63, 75–76, 83
International Ladies Garment Workers
    Union, 57–58
intersectionality, 25–26, 60–62, 83,
    302, 317–24
interviews, *The Second Sex* in, 302, 305–
    13, 315, 317–18

Jane Crow, 56–57
Je suis Martiniquaise (Capécia), 15
Jim Crow, 56–57, 82–83, 168–69, 305–6
Jones, Claudia
    abolition and suffrage movements, 234
    domestic labor market, 80–82
    introduction to, 22, 74–77
    Negro *vs.* woman question
    on slavery, 77–80
    triple-oppression analysis, 75–77, 82–
        88, 91–92, 93–95
    white and male chauvinism, 77, 88–94
    on working-class, 55–56
Jones, Dora, 84–85

Kelly, Abby, 235–36
Kincaid, Jamaica, 19–20
King, Deborah, 186–87, 234, 235–36

Lacasade, Suzanne, 14
Latina feminism, 20–21, 23–24, 166–67,
    186, 266–67, 280–81, 323–24
Latina identity, 188, 279–81
Lawson, Elizabeth, 19–20, 96–97
Leboef, Céline, 20–21
Le deuxième sexe (Beauvoir). See *The
    Second Sex*
Lee, Kyoo, 20–21, 24–25, 277–79
*Left of Karl Marx: The Political Life of
    Black Communist Claudia Jones*
    (Davies), 75
legalized rape of Black women, 78–79,
    211, 221
Les Temps Modernes, 11

*Looking for Lorraine: The Radiant and
    Radical Life of Lorraine Hansberry*
    (Perry), 108–9
Lorde, Audre
    Benjamin, Jessica and, 144–53
    on difference of race, sexuality, class,
        and age, 139–40
    introduction to, 19–20, 23, 137–39
    Master's Tools and, 153–56
    sexuality and, 138, 139–40, 149, 152, 155
    white feminist racism, 141, 313–17
Lugones, María
    coalitional frameworks, 320, 322–23
    colonialism, 267–68, 281–84
    decolonial feminism, 24–26, 267–68,
        281–84, 290–91, 302, 323
    sexuality and, 282–83, 322–23
lynching
    anti-lynching activism, 47–48, 49, 246
    Jones, Claudia on, 85–86
    in twentieth century, first half, 48–49
    Wells, Ida B. on, 47–48

male chauvinism, 77, 88–94
Mallard, Amy, 85, 86
Mallard, Robert, 86
mammy stereotype, 77–78, 79
manhood stereotype, 57–58
marginalizations, 7–8, 12, 15, 60–61, 75–
    76, 193, 234–35, 251–52, 319–20
Markowitz, Sally, 24–25, 275
marriage-as-prostitution analogy, 153–54
marriage *vs.* working class
    women, 183–84
Marxism, 22–23, 126–27, 176, 280–81
master-slave dialectic, 24, 206–7,
    209, 211–14
master's tools, 142–44, 145–46, 151–52
"The Masters Tools Will Never Dismantle
    the Master's House" (Lorde), 19–20,
    137, 138–40, 153–56
material feminism, 10, 276–77
maternal death rates, 75–76, 79–80
matrilineal legacy, 1–2, 21–22, 40–41,
    63, 302–3
May, Vivian, 111–12
McDougald (Ayer), (Gertrude) Elise
    Johnson, 51–52

350 INDEX

McDuffie, Erik S., 74–75, 85–86, 91–92
Men of Color, 62, 148–49, 167–
68, 319–20
Meyer, Agnes E., 123
militant agency, 22, 55–57, 75–78, 82–
88, 241–42
Millard, Betty, 90, 92–95
minimum-wage laws, 48–49
miscegenation, 16–18
misogyny, 12–13, 223, 304
Moi, Toril, 9–11, 113–14
Moorehead, Caroline, 305
Morrison, Toni, 1–2, 151–52
motherhood, 77–80, 309–10
Mott, Lucretia, 233
Murray, Pauli, 1–2, 56–57
Muslim women, 273–74, 275–76
mutual understanding, 190–93
Myrdal, Alva
abolition and suffrage movements, 232–
33, 234–35, 236–37, 242–43, 250–52
oppression and, 24, 169–74
woman-as-slave metaphor, 207–9
Myrdal, Gunnar, 176–77
*The Myth of Seneca Falls: Memory and the
Women's Suffrage Movement, 1848–
1898* (Tetrault), 240

Nardal sisters (Paulette, Jane, and
Andrée), 14–15
National Association for the
Advancement of Colored People
(NAACP), 48–49, 87
National Association of Colored Women, 49
National Colored Labor Union (NCLU), 249
national liberation movements, 74–75
National Negro Congress, 54
Negritude movement, 14–16
Negritude Women (Sharpley-Whiting), 14
Negro *vs.* woman question, 22–
23, 126–27
neocolonialism, 305–6
new world experiences, 57–58, 125
non-specified "primitives," 269–74
Nya, Nathalie, 20–21

objectification, 3, 10, 122–23
Offen, Karen, 286–87

Ogunyemi, Chikwenye, 19–20, 179–80
Olson, Lester, 144–53
One/Other dynamic. *See* others/othering/
otherness
oppositional difference, 187–88
oppression. *See also* gender oppression;
race/gender analogy; racial
oppression
Alexander, Sadie Tanner Mossell on, 52
Beal, Francis on, 57–58
Beauvoir, Simone de on, 3, 23–24, 165–
66, 178–84
Black/white binary and, 24–25, 278–80
by bourgeois women, 180–81, 183–84
class oppression, 22, 44–45, 51, 52–53,
58–59, 75–76, 89, 91–92, 149, 165,
181, 188–90, 240–41
CRC statement on, 58–59
excision (clitoridectomy) as, 312–13
Hansberry, Lorraine on, 121–24
interlocking systems of, 44, 58–60, 63,
75–76, 83
McDougald (Ayer), (Gertrude) Elise
Johnson on, 51–52
Myrdal, Alva on, 24, 169–74, 177–78
sex oppression, 3, 59–60, 168, 177–78
triple oppression, 22, 44–45, 52–53, 56,
60, 75–77, 82–88, 91–92, 93–95
orientalism, 25–26, 266–67, 274–
81, 290–91
Ortega, Mariana, 20–21, 280–82,
320, 323–24
others/othering/otherness of Beauvoir
colonialism and, 267–68, 274–
84, 290–91
gender oppression, 263–68
historical materialism, 268
introduction to, 3, 166–67, 184, 263–68
of non-specified "primitives," 269–74
orientalism and, 25–26, 266–67, 274–
81, 290–91
psychoanalysis of, 24–25, 96–97, 263,
266–67, 268–69, 280–81, 289–91
Western gender discourses, 284–90
Oyĕwùmí, Oyèrónké, 20–21, 24–25, 267–
68, 284–90

Pan African Congress, 46

INDEX 351

patriarchy/patriarchal ideology
  of Black Church, 92
  hooks, bell on, 2–3
  Moi, Toril on, 9
  naming, 1–2
  socialization of women, 140
Perry, Imani, 108–9
Philadelphia Female Anti-Slavery
  Society, 236
Pohlhaus, Gaile, Jr., 166–67, 192–93, 220
police brutality, 22, 75–76, 77–78, 81
political consciousness, 83, 234–40,
  250, 306–7
political intersectionality, 62
pregnancy related mortality ratio
  (PRMR), 79–80
prison industrial complex, 16–17
private household workers, 56–57
proper analogies, 191–92
proto-feminism, 144–45, 167–68
psychoanalysis of othering, 24–25,
  96–97, 263, 266–67, 268–69, 280–
  81, 289–91

Quijano, Anibal, 282

race/gender analogy
  Beauvoir, Simone de on, 23–24, 166–
  78, 185–86
  Hill Collins, Patricia on, 187–88
  Spelman, Elizabeth on, 185–86
racial discrimination, 16, 168–69, 193
racialized slavery, 24, 206–9
racial oppression. See also oppression
  Beauvoir, Simone de on, 167–
  68, 177–78
  Jones, Claudia on, 22, 77, 88–94
  Wells, Ida B. on, 47–48
racial separatism, 306–7, 311
racism
  antiracism, 41, 57–62, 238, 319–20
  Beauvoir, Simone de on, 165, 184–86
  Broeck, Sabine on, 184–85
  Davis, Angela on, 248
  intersectionality and, 319–20
  Moi, Toril on, 11
  racial discrimination, 16, 168–
  69, 193

sexual exploitation and, 15, 16–18, 48–
  49, 57–58, 180, 211, 219, 223
Stewart, Maria W. on, 44–45
structural racism, 144–45, 192
racist feminism, 141
radical leftist women, 2–3
Reagon, Bernice Johnson, 320–21
*Red Feminism: American Communism
  and the Making of Women's
  Liberation* (Weigand), 89–90
relational difference, 187–88
Relyea, Sarah, 176–77
Remond, Charles, 239–40
representational intersectionality, 62
reproductive function of women, 39–
  40, 210–11
resistance, 121–24
Rich, Adrienne, 141
Richardson, Marilyn, 44–45
Rogers, Nathaniel P., 239–40
Ruonakoski, Erika, 289

Sáenz, Carmen Lopez, 288–89
Said, Edward, 218
Sartre, Jean-Paul, 6–8, 15–16, 213–14
#SayHerName, 1
Schueller, Malini Johar, 218
Scott, Anne Firor, 238
The Second Sex (Beauvoir)
  background on, 12–16
  Beauvoir, Simone de on, 302–13
  Black feminism and, 16–18
  Black/white binary and, 24–25, 278–80
  coalitional politics of, 25–26,
  302, 317–24
  in interviews, 302, 305–13, 315, 317–18
  Jones, Claudia and, 95–98
  Moi, Toril on, 12–13
  sexual relations of animals, 221–22
  as white feminist text, 3–6
  white women's rights, 233
  Women of Color engagement
  with, 19–21
segregation, 47–48, 75–76, 168–70, 184
self-adornment practices, 117–19
self-naming, 1–2
Self/Other dynamic. See others/othering/
  otherness

352 INDEX

Seneca Falls Declaration, 241, 243
separate but equal doctrines, 168–69
sexism
  antisexism, 58–59
  Beauvoir, Simone de on, 165
  Davis, Angela on, 248
  racial discrimination and, 193
  Stewart, Maria W. on, 44–45
sex oppression, 3, 59–60, 168, 177–78
sexual difference, 10
sexual exploitation, 15, 16–18, 48–49,
  57–58, 180, 211, 219, 223
sexual identity, 44, 145–46
sexuality
  Beauvoir, Simone de on, x, 20–
  21, 108–9
  Benjamin, Jessica on, 139
  Berruz, Stephanie Rivera on, 188
  black feminist thought, ix–x
  Hansberry, Lorraine on, 120–
  21, 126–27
  Hill Collins, Patricia on, 224–25
  Lorde, Audre on, 138, 139–40, 149,
  152, 155
  Lugones, María on, 282–83, 322–23
  May, Vivian on, 111–12
  Ortega, Mariana on, 323–24
  Schueller, Malini Johar on, 218
  Women of Color feminists and, 23
sex workers, 153–54, 165–66, 178–
  79, 194–95
Shange, Ntozake, 40–41
Sharpley-Whiting, T. Denean, 14
Sheftall, Beverly Guy, 17–18, 108
Shockley, Ann Allen, 41–42
*Simone de Beauvoir: Philosophical
  Writings* (Simons), 8
*Simone de Beauvoir and Jean-Paul Sartre:
  The Remaking of a Twentieth-
  Century Legend* (Fullbrook,
  Fullbrook), 6–7
Simons, Margaret, 7–8, 113–14, 172,
  175–76, 309
Simpson, Lorenzo, 166–67, 190–93
slave/mother analogy, 309–10
slavery
  anti-Indigenous sentiments, 234–35,
  242, 250–51

anti-slavery, 236–40, 242–43
De Veaux, Alexis on, 154–55
eighteenth century, 41–43
Jones, Claudia on, 77–80
legalized rape of Black women, 78–79,
  211, 221
Millard, Betty on, 94
Muslim women and, 273–74, 275–76
racialized slavery, 24, 206–9
woman's reproductive function
  as, 210–11
slave/woman analogy
  Davis, Angela on, 218–19, 221–23
  exploitation of, 221–25
  interventions, 215–18
  introduction to, 24, 206–7
  master-slave dialectic, 24, 206–7,
  209, 211–14
  problematics, 218–21
  slave/mother analogy and, 309–10
  woman-as-slave metaphor, 139,
  184–85, 206, 207–11, 214–15, 219–
  21, 224–25
Smith, Barbara, 148–49, 319, 320
social constructionism, 176–77, 286–89
social equality, 10, 49–50, 238–39
Social Security benefits, 81–82
Spelman, Elizabeth, 184–86, 212
Spillers, Hortense, 39–40
Stanton, Elizabeth Cady, 236–37, 239–
  40, 244
Starobin, Joseph Robert, 89
Stewart, Maria W., 41, 44–45, 307–8
Stewart, Mary, 17–18
Stowe, Harriet Beecher, ` 233
structural intersectionality, 62
structural racism, 144–45, 192
suffrage
  abolitionist movement and, 232–40
  Beauvoir's approach to, 24
  Black feminism and, 250–52
  suppression of, 244–50
  universal suffrage, 45–46, 243, 251
superexploitation of Black women, 80–
  81, 88–89

Taylor, Keeanga-Yamahtta, 318
Terrell, Mary Church, 49–50

INDEX 353

Terry, Lucy, 41–42, 307–8
Tetrault, Lisa, 240
Third World women, 59–60, 139–40, 142, 143–44, 283, 321, 322
Thompson-Spires, Nafissa, 42
Trenton Six, 87
triple oppression, 22, 44–45, 52–53, 56, 60, 75–77, 82–88, 91–92, 93–95
true philosopher, 1, 2–3, 5–6
"True Philosophers: Beauvoir and bell" (hooks), 1, 2–3
true womanhood, 170–71, 238, 248
Truth, Sojourner, 1–2, 45–46, 243, 323

The Unfinished Project: Toward a Post-Metaphysical Humanism (Simpson), 190–91
universal suffrage, 45–46, 243, 251

A Voice from the South (Cooper), 46

Wallace, Michele, 144–45
Warrior Poet: A Biography of Audre Lorde (De Veaux), 313
Washington, Mary Helen, 144–45
Watkins, Gloria Jean. *See* hooks, bell
Weigand, Kate, 89–93
Wells, Ida B., 47–48, 246–47
Wenzel, Hélène V., 311–12
Western gender discourses, 284–90
Wheatley, Phillis, 41–43

white chauvinism, 77, 88–94
white epistemic isolation, 214
white feminism
Beauvoir, Simone de on, 3, 96–97, 113–14, 192
Benjamin, Jessica and, 147
Crenshaw, Kimberlé on, 220
literature on Beauvoir, 6–7
Lorde, Audre on, 141, 313–17
Ogunyemi, Chikwenye on, 179–80
Schueller, Malini Johar, 218
Wallace, Michele on, 144–45
white male theory, 150
white supremacy, 2–3, 77, 85, 88–94
Wildman, Stephanie, 192–94
Wilkerson, Margaret B., 108, 109
Williams, Fannie Barrier, 48–49
Wilson, Judith, 20–21
Wollstonecraft, Mary, 167–68
woman-as-slave metaphor, 139, 184–85, 206, 207–11, 214–15, 219–21, 224–25
woman's oppression, 22–23, 263–68, 311. *See also* oppression
Women, Race, and Class (Davis), 218–19
Women of Color, 3–5, 19–26
Words of Fire: An Anthology of African American Feminist Thought (Sheftall), 17–18, 108
Wright, Richard, 16, 174–77

The manufacturer's authorised representative in the EU for product safety is Oxford University Press España S.A. of El Parque Empresarial San Fernando de Henares, Avenida de Castilla, 2 – 28830 Madrid (www.oup.es/en or product.safety@oup.com). OUP España S.A. also acts as importer into Spain of products made by the manufacturer.

Printed in the USA/Agawam, MA
June 2, 2025

888375.001